WIFEDOM

ALSO BY ANNA FUNDER

Stasiland

All That I Am

The Girl with the Dogs

WIFEDOM

MRS ORWELL'S INVISIBLE LIFE

Anna Funder

HAMISH HAMILTON
an imprint of
PENGUIN BOOKS

HAMISH HAMILTON

UK | USA | Canada| Ireland | Australia
India | New Zealand | South Africa | China

Hamish Hamilton is part of the Penguin Random House group of companies
whose addresses can be found at global.penguinrandomhouse.com.

First published by Hamish Hamilton, 2023

Cover photography by Pictorial Press Ltd / Alamy Stock Photo
Cover adaptation by Adam Laszczuk © Penguin Random House Australia Pty Ltd
Text design by Adam Laszczuk © Penguin Random House Australia Pty Ltd
Typeset in Adobe Caslon Pro 11.5 / 16.5 pt by Midland Typesetters, Australia

Printed and bound in Australia by Griffin Press, an accredited
ISO AS/NZS 14001 Environmental Management Systems printer

A catalogue record for this
book is available from the
National Library of Australia

ISBN 978 0 14378 711 2

penguin.com.au

*We at Penguin Random House Australia acknowledge that Aboriginal and Torres Strait Islander
peoples are the Traditional Custodians and the first storytellers of the lands on which we live and work.
We honour Aboriginal and Torres Strait Islander peoples' continuous connection to Country, waters,
skies and communities. We celebrate Aboriginal and Torres Strait Islander stories, traditions
and living cultures; and we pay our respects to Elders past and present.*

For Craig

and for Imogen, Polly and Max

Love, . . . sexual or non-sexual, is hard work.

George Orwell

We all make up the people we love.

Phyllis Rose

[M]en and women read ... books in order to love life more.

Vivian Gornick

All
~~Some~~ Tobacco is pleasant
Some Tobacco is poison
∴ Some poison is pleasant

Eileen O'Shaughnessy's notebook from Oxford, *c.*1924.

In 2005 six letters from George Orwell's first wife, Eileen O'Shaughnessy, to her best friend, Norah Symes Myles, were discovered. They cover the period of her marriage to Orwell, from 1936 to 1945. Eileen's letters appear in this book in italics.

Contents

I   **WIFEDOM, A COUNTERFICTION**   *1*

II **INVISIBLE WARRIOR**   *95*

III **INVISIBLE WORKER**   *185*

IV **HAPPY ENDING**   *295*

V **AFTERLIFE**   *333*

   CODA   *393*

Notes   *403*

Image credits   *443*

Bibliography   *445*

Acknowledgements   *449*

I

WIFEDOM,
A COUNTERFICTION

Suffolk
November 1936

It has been six months since the wedding. She uncaps
the pen.

38 High Street
Southwold, Suffolk
a Tuesday

Now what?

She gets up and pokes the fire. Sits down again. The cat,
a silver thing that knows its own mind, jumps into her lap.
She lights a match, lets it burn out in the ashtray. Lights
another.

'Who are you writing to?' George asks from his
armchair, creasing the newspaper firmly so she knows he's
annoyed. Fair enough, she *has* been annoying.

'Norah.'

'Ah. The famous Norah.' This is a joke. He's never met
her. 'Is it so hard?' His eyes are blue, with laughter in them.

She smiles. 'Shouldn't be, should it?'

He gets up. 'I'll leave you to it.'

She's at a desk in the front room of her new in-laws'
house in sleepy Southwold. In the kitchen they are clearing
away the lunch dishes; she's done it each day since they got

here so is giving herself a reprieve. His mother and Avril, the younger sister, will be doing it. The older sister, Marjorie, has married and moved away, which is just as well because this place could barely fit another body.

She rolls a cigarette with the little contraption, licks it closed. It's hard to know how to even begin explaining what has happened to her since her wedding day. She and Norah rarely write 'Dear Norah' or 'Dear Eileen' on their letters – a habit of intimacy from college days, as if theirs were a single, uninterrupted conversation. She lights the roll-up, puffs twice and rests it in the ashtray. The cat pours itself off her lap.

I wrote the address quite a long time ago & have since played with three cats, made a cigarette (I make them now but not with the naked hand), poked the fire & driven Eric (i.e. George) nearly mad—all because I didn't really know what to say. I lost my habit of punctual correspondence during the first few weeks of marriage because we quarrelled so continuously & really bitterly that I thought I'd save time & just write one letter to everyone when the murder or separation had been accomplished.

Norah will laugh. But she'll read between the lines too.

She wedges the cigarette in the corner of her mouth. George is banging nails into something out the back – a risk for all involved. She might as well say it –

Eric had decided that he mustn't let his work be interrupted & complained bitterly when we'd been married a week that he'd only done two good days' work out of seven.

The window in front of her gives directly on to the high street. A woman in a yellow hat moves past barely ten feet away, holding the hand of a small boy. Both their noses are red-tipped with cold. This is a seaside town and she's hoping for snow; she's never seen snow on a beach.

*Then Eric's aunt came to stay & was so dreadful (she stayed
<u>two months</u>) that we stopped quarrelling & just repined. Then
she went away and all our troubles are over.*

She likes it here, she writes, *though nothing has surprised
me more, particularly since I saw the house which is very small
& furnished almost entirely with paintings of ancestors.*

The ancestors are all on the father's side, though
his mother, Ida, is much more interesting – funny, and
glamorous with her dangling Burmese silver earrings and
long cigarette holder. Ida has an air of freedom about her,
with her sparrow-like half-French charm, her Fabian
politics and suffragettism. She treats the father, a rigid old
dear with a stale carnation in his buttonhole, like another
piece of the inherited furniture. At dinner last night he
took out his false teeth and set them next to his plate, as
if to mute himself while he gummed his food. The only
words Ida spoke to him were 'Tapioca, your favourite,' as
pudding was served. Then she went on talking about 'those
brutes' (her word for men, apparently) coming to fix the
drains. Hilarious – though hopefully it won't come to that
in her own marriage.

She can hear them putting the dishes away now. It is
a relief not to be at the cottage, where all the work is hers.
She won't say this to Norah. Nor will she tell her that at
the cottage there's no sanitation, no heat or electricity.
Nor about the Disastrous Latrine Event. Let alone about
the sex, such as it is. There are thoughts you can – almost –
stop yourself thinking, until you realise that all the things
you're not telling your best friend are stopping you telling
her anything much. It is too extreme for words to have
wilfully fallen out of her class in this way, to be risking it
all – the Oxford education, the supposed 'gift' – for his work.

She certainly won't mention that he's going to Spain to fight. Next week. She encouraged him to go, but it's hard to explain it, being so barely, tenuously married. Maybe in the next letter. Instead, she'll tell her about her new family.

The Blairs are by origin Lowland Scottish & dull but one of them made a lot of money in slaves & his son Thomas who was inconceivably like a sheep married the daughter of the Duke of Westmoreland (of whose existence I never heard) & went so grand that he spent all the money & couldn't make more because slaves had gone out. So his son went into the army & came out of that into the church & married a girl of 15 who loathed him & had ten children of whom Eric's father, now 80, is the only survivor & they are all quite penniless but still on the shivering verge of gentility as George says.

They all call him Eric but to her he's George, the name he's chosen to write under. His two identities mean home life can turn into a comedy of errors at any minute. And they *are* funny – the mother deliberately and Avril without meaning to be. Also, they seem to be on her side against Eric/George.

In spite of all this the family on the whole is fun & I imagine quite unusual in their attitude to me because they all adore Eric & consider him quite impossible to live with— indeed on the wedding day Mrs Blair shook her head & said that I'd be a brave girl if I knew what I was in for, and Avril the sister said that obviously I didn't know what I was in for or I shouldn't be there. They haven't I think grasped that I am very much like Eric in temperament which is an asset once one has accepted the fact.

Avril's head in the door now, a long androgynous face, the mushroom cap of hair, same pale eyes as George. Will she come and walk on the pier with them?

'Now?' She doesn't put down her pen.

'Yes, now.'

She folds the letter to finish later, slips it under the ashtray as a paperweight. Then she thinks of one more thing to say, and slips it out again.

I thought I could come & see you & have twice decided when I could, but Eric always gets something if I'm going away if he has notice of the fact, & if he has no notice (when Eric my brother arrives & removes me as he has done twice) he gets something when I've gone so that I have to come home again.

The diseased lungs she knew about of course, but not how he'd use them. She hadn't expected that.

How did she get here?

Present, Tense

How did I get here?

At the end of summer 2017 I found myself at a moment of peak overload: organising separate new schools for my teenage daughters – uniforms, books, dozens of emails – orthodontics, euphonium hire, my son's holiday program (bring extra shirt for tie-dye!), ferrying a depressed French exchange student to see the sights, arranging for recalcitrant, condescending tradesmen to patch up my old house in three-hour windows of their choosing, sorting out a relative's hospital care, and hosting dear interstate family at a time of great sadness. All of this was taking me away from work deadlines ticking under every waking minute. I shopped for groceries, yet again, in the soul-sapping local mall. I wound the car, yet again, down the ramps from floor to floor, following EXIT signs I knew were empty promises: I could never, really, leave. When the greedy boom-gate machine inhaled my ticket, I knew: the mall had sucked out my privileged, perimenopausal soul. I had to get her back.

So instead of going home I pulled in around the corner at a second-hand bookshop, Sappho. The ice cream could melt in the boot; the meat could sweat in its toxic plastic. Sappho Books is a relic from my mother's liberation era, the 1970s. It is an unrenovated warren of a terrace house, with handmade signs sticking out from the shelves and a café with potted palms tucked in its wobbly, welcoming courtyard. To climb the creaky wooden stairs to non-fiction is to go back to a gentler, pre-digital era of shabby armchairs and serendipitous discovery. This place is a trove of works sifted from the mass of forgettable books published every decade and found to transcend their time. It is what you missed or never got to, it is what you don't even know you need. Sappho is the opposite of a mall: no one is trying to sell you anything. In fact, the tattooed woman at the till sighs ruefully when you buy one of their books, as if money couldn't, possibly, make up the loss. This place is entirely soul.

In that upstairs back room I found a first-edition, four-volume series of Orwell's *Collected Essays, Journalism and Letters* from 1968. I've always loved Orwell – his self-deprecating humour, his laser vision about how power works, and who it works on. I sank into an armchair. The pages, dark and fragile, smelt like the past. I opened to the essay 'Shooting an Elephant'. It begins:

> In Moulmein, in Lower Burma, I was hated by large numbers
> of people – the only time in my life that I have been important
> enough for this to happen to me. I was subdivisional police
> officer of the town . . .

That voice! I dropped the groceries at home, and took Orwell and the French exchange student to the Dawn Fraser Baths on the harbour. The exchange student would swim, maybe cheer up. I would sit in the shade of 140-year-old bleachers and read Orwell's making, piece by short piece, of his writing self.

Towards the end of the day I came to the famous essay 'Why I Write'. 'I knew,' Orwell says, 'that I had a facility with words and a power of facing unpleasant facts, and I felt that this created a sort of private world in which I could get my own back for my failure in everyday life.'

I looked over the sparkling water to Cockatoo Island and considered today's everyday failures – toxic plastic, soul-murder in a car park, the poor French exchange student doing lap after miserable lap. To say nothing of the work undone, piling up now in anxious, red-flagged messages in my inbox. I needed to face the 'unpleasant fact' that despite Craig and I imagining we divided the work of life and love equally, the world had conspired against our best intentions. I'd been doing the lion's share for so long we'd stopped noticing. For someone who notices things for a living, this seemed, to borrow our nine-year-old son's term, an 'epic fail'.

I looked back at the page.

'After the age of about thirty,' Orwell writes, most people 'abandon individual ambition – in many cases, indeed, they almost abandon the sense of being individuals at all – and live chiefly for others, or are simply smothered under drudgery.'

'Anna?' I looked up into the wet shadow of Benoît and handed over my credit card – to buy time, with ice cream.

'But there is also,' Orwell continues, 'the minority of gifted, wilful people who are determined to live their own lives to the end, and writers belong in this class.'

If I couldn't see my own fury clearly enough yet to excise it, I thought, at least I could give it company. And then:

My starting point is always a feeling of partisanship, a sense of injustice. When I sit down to write a book, I do not say to myself, 'I am going to produce a work of art.' I write it because there is some lie that I want to expose, some fact to which I want to draw attention . . .

I closed the book. I had a plan. If my three children – two teens and a tween – were going to emerge from childhood and see me for what I am, I would have to become visible to myself. I would look under the motherload of wifedom I had taken on, and see who was left. I would read Orwell on the tyrannies, the 'smelly little orthodoxies' of his time, and I would use him to liberate myself from mine.

As summer shifted into autumn I read the six major biographies of Orwell, published between the 1970s and 2003. They are by Peter Stansky and William Abrahams (1972 and 1979), Bernard Crick (1980), Michael Shelden (1991), Jeffrey Meyers (2001), D. J. Taylor (2003) and Gordon Bowker (also 2003). I've long loved Orwell's writing so it was a joy to learn about the man described as 'one of the greatest writers of the twentieth century', and 'a moral force, a light glinting in the darkness, a way through the murk'. I read of Orwell's childhood in the 1910s, his time at Eton, then in Burma as a young policeman. I read that he married Eileen O'Shaughnessy in 1936, fought the fascists in the Spanish Civil War, then lived in London under fascist bombardment there, writing his masterpiece, *Animal Farm*, and, later, the dystopian marvel *Nineteen Eighty-Four*.

Then, as winter set in, I came to this, which Orwell wrote during his final illness, after the marriage was over. He wrote it in his private literary notebook, in the third person, as if to distance himself from feelings that were hard to own.

> There were two great facts about women which . . . you could
> only learn by getting married, & which flatly contradicted the
> picture of themselves that women had managed to impose upon
> the world. One was their incorrigible dirtiness & untidiness.
> The other was their terrible, devouring sexuality . . . Within

any marriage or regular love affair, he suspected that it was
always the woman who was the sexually insistent partner.
In his experience women were quite insatiable, & never seemed
fatigued by no matter how much love-making . . . In any
marriage of more than a year or two's standing, intercourse
was thought of as a duty, a service owed by the man to the
woman. And he suspected that in every marriage the struggle
was always the same – the man trying to escape from sexual
intercourse, to do it only when he felt like it (or with other
women), the woman demanding it more & more, & more &
more consciously despising her husband for his lack of virility.

Orwell only ever lived with one wife. These comments refer to Eileen.

I scoured the biographies. Some of them include parts of this
extract. Could they help work out what was going on? One of them
follows it with this observation: 'Referring later to a notorious
Edwardian murderer, he wrote of "the sympathy everyone feels for
a man who murders his wife" – clearly Orwell in misogynist mood
(even if ironically so), a mood he normally made an effort to muffle
or suppress.' This was bewildering, and not much help. Another
biographer implies it's fictional, possibly 'passages for some other
novel or short story, of mildly sadistic sexual fantasy'. But then,
perhaps worried by Orwell's confessed 'lack of virility', he tries to
blame women for that, saying that these comments 'reflect upon a
type of woman who is sexually over-demanding'. Less than helpful.
A third biographer writes: 'Wives, [Orwell] suggested, use sex as a
means of controlling their husbands.' This is the misogynist trope of
a woman 'controlling' a man when what she is controlling is access
to her own body – so, no help at all, particularly when Orwell is
saying he does *not* want his wife's body. There seemed to be no way
for the biographers to deal with the anti-woman, anti-wife, anti-
sex rant other than by leaving it out, sympathising with the impulse,

trivialising it as a 'mood', denying it as 'fiction' or blaming the woman herself.

Orwell's thoughts are painful to read. Women disgust him; he disgusts himself. He's paranoid, feeling he's been tricked by a politico-sexual conspiracy of filthy women 'imposing' a false 'picture of themselves' on the world. He sees women – as wives – in terms of what they do for him, or 'demand' of him. Not enough cleaning; too much sex. How was it, then, for her? My first guess: too much cleaning and not enough, or not good enough, sex.

This is how I moved from the work to the life, and from the man to the wife.

House of Wax

It's mid-morning. I come in the back door from the studio for more coffee. My sixteen-year-old daughter is buttering toast in the kitchen.

'What are you working on?' she asks. It's a new, adult question for her.

'It's . . . the story of a wife. And of a marriage,' I say. 'Orwell's. It's hard,' I add. This is a new response from me too, adult to adult in its vulnerability.

'Why is it so hard?' she asks. I feel our roles changing; the tectonic plates of my family are shifting apart. I'm usually the sympathetic coach, the annoying encourager.

'Because,' I say, closing the fridge, 'it's hard to know how to think about an author you've long loved if you find out they were . . .'

'An arsehole?' She licks peanut butter off the knife.

'Maybe.' I make a lot of noise with the coffee grinder.

My daughter is growing up as the revelations of #MeToo erupt: 'arseholes' everywhere. It is an age of unspeakable truths – unspeakable because so common as to go without saying but, once spoken, unspeakably bad: of tearful women and livid men on the nightly news, the outing of serial sexual predators acting individually or sheltered by institutions, revelations of Weinstein and Epstein, rampant abuse in churches and schools, rape allegations in the White House and

Australia's Parliament House, and against the attorney-general, the highest lawman in the land. If, like me, you grew up feeling the vast unspoken thing – when the priest called you in, or the professor closed his door, or the law partner made you stay late – it's a liberation to see it, like the outing of ghouls. But I would do anything to spare her this glimpse of the rotten substrate of our world. This quick sad leap to 'arsehole'.

'It's hard to know how to think about it,' I say, 'when the whole world was set up to allow men to treat women badly, and still think of themselves as decent people.'

'Was?'

I take a deep breath. Part of mothering seems to be filtering the world so it's bearable, taking in toxins and pumping out oxygen like a tree.

'Things are changing. For instance with actors – where the sexual bullies and paedophiles and creeps are being pulled from our screens pronto, although we felt fine about enjoying their work before we knew what they'd done.'

'Like the pot-plant guy?'

A celebrity comedian who liked, as the world is now sadly aware, to masturbate in front of young women and, allegedly, into pot plants. The world is full of things we don't want to know.

'Yes. And Orwell worried about this, too. Not about himself, but about other writers who mistreated their wives. I'm struggling with all of this.'

'Because you still like his work.'

'Yes.'

'And because you're a wife.'

I laugh. 'Among other things.'

My daughter puts the knife down, takes a spoon from the drawer and plunges that into the peanut butter jar. 'Orwell must have known at some level that he was an arsehole,' she says, 'which was why he was interested in this question.' She looks at me squarely, a cautious smile playing about her shiny lips. 'Why are *you* interested in this, Mum?'

I laugh again, taken aback at the insight into Orwell, into me. 'Maybe I'm an arsehole?' I say. I've never said anything like this to her before.

She doesn't miss a beat. 'Isn't everybody?'

Back in the studio I sit in the bay window that contains my desk. Wasps are building a nest in the shutters. They seem to be on a break, narrow-waisted and hovering, though it's hard to tell work from life as they hang about their hexagons. I am part proud and part heartbroken, which may be the defining emotional condition of parenting young adults. We watch as those who were our children come to see the world – from which we have spent over a decade and a half vainly sheltering them – for what it is. Including, of course, us.

We need a new word for it: one to combine pride in their intellect, as it shatters the paltry protections we put up, frail as a house of wax, and anguish as they come out of childhood and into the human condition, tooth and claw – and arseholes – galore.

Southwold
Still at the In-Laws'

⌣→

They've had tea. Old Mr Blair is snoring in a wing chair. She slips behind the desk. The sun is fading outside, the buildings across the street glowing with the last of it. One is covered in ivy, and its glossy leaves jostle one another to catch the light.

There was no snow on the beach.

'Why would there be snow on the beach, Eileen?' Avril had said, as they walked out along the pier. Avril is someone who manages to include the word 'idiot' in most of her sentences without saying it. She works in a teashop she calls a 'fine establishment' as if it only accepted certain kinds of tea drinkers, possibly the kind who obey unspoken commands. Eileen suspects Avril is held together by rules and frightened of a lot of things.

But the sky today was huge and high and blue. From the end of the pier the beach a golden smile. She felt she could walk forever.

As she slides the half-written letter to Norah from under the ashtray, she hears Ida closing the oven door. At the cottage, where she and George have lived since the wedding, the oven is dodgy. She takes up her pen. *I couldn't make the oven cook anything & boiled eggs (on which Eric had lived almost exclusively) made me sick. Now I can make the oven cook a reasonable number of things & he is working very rapidly.*

So much for the domestic basics – or heroics. George had also been ill. *I forgot to mention that he had his 'bronchitis' for three weeks in July.* And then there were six weeks of rain *during the whole of which the kitchen was flooded & all the food went mouldy in a few hours.* She lights a cigarette, then adds, *It seems a long time ago but at the time seemed very permanent.*

Suddenly he's behind her. He moves her hair, kisses the nape of her neck. His eyes fall on the letter.

'"Bronchitis" needs inverted commas?' he whispers.

'Until you'll see a doctor it does,' she smiles.

'Well, I'm better now anyway.' He turns to face her, leaning against the desk. 'I thought I'd walk out for some cigarettes. You need anything?'

His eyes are ridiculously blue, his fingers long, with spatulate tips. The reality of him has an awkwardness, a sweetness. She can see, in a way neither of them will ever find the words for, that he looks at her from across a chasm, wanting closeness but unsure, if he sets out, if he'll fall in.

'No,' she says. 'Thank you, though.'

Behind him Avril bustles past in the corridor, an empty laundry basket in her arms.

'Actually, I will come,' she says. She folds the letter and slips it into her trouser pocket.

Mr Blair shifts his weight in the chair, sleeps on.

Black Box

A man stands on a stage dressed in a heavy black suit, chin ballooning over a white collar, wand in his right hand. Behind him is a black box, like an upright coffin with a door; in front of him a stool with his top hat on it. To one side of the box stands a woman in a black leotard, stockings and heels, smiling for no reason. He bows. Sweat shines on his broad forehead.

He has decided not to saw her in half today. He gestures for her to step into the box, closes the door behind her and walks over to the stool. He shrugs.

'Abracadabra?' he says, like a joke we're all in on as he fumbles in the top hat and pulls out – a handkerchief.

We laugh.

'*That's* not a trick!' he says. He sits on the stool and mops his brow. 'Lemme tell you something. The trick to life,' he says, 'is not to expect too much.'

The audience titters. A long pause. The audience titters more. He looks back at the box and sighs.

'A man's gotta do what a man's gotta do,' he says. He walks back to the box. 'Remember,' he says, reaching for the handle, 'don't expect too much.'

He opens the door – to nothing. The audience is delighted.

'Oh, no, what have I done?' he cries. He feels up and down inside the box with his hands, arms – there's nothing. He goes back to the stool, checks inside the top hat, but it's empty so he puts it on. He returns to the box, still open.

'I suppose that's it then. Better close up.' As he shuts the door the audience gasps.

Because there she is behind it, standing outside the box.

The wordless woman smiles, gesturing to him with an open palm.

She could be any one of us.

He bows. It's his trick. But the question is: Where has she been?

She hasn't really been in the biographies. Orwell's biographers are seven men looking at a man. Each of them is brilliant, and each tells a slightly different story – slanted now towards heroism and forgiveness, now towards 'dark recesses' of unnamed complexity. But all of them minimise the importance of the women in Orwell's life. In the end, the biographies started to seem like fictions of omission.

So, I went to their sources and found other facts and other people – those that had been left out. Eileen began to come to life. A colleague in a political office considered her 'a superior person' compared to everyone else there – a detail quoted by no biographer. She was '[d]iffident and unassuming in manner', another co-worker and friend said, but 'had a quiet integrity that I never saw shaken'. I discovered a woman who saw things and said things no one else did. Eileen loved Orwell 'deeply, but with a tender amusement'. She noted his *extraordinary political simplicity* – which seems to have worried one of the biographers, who rewrote her words to give him an 'extraordinary political sympathy' instead. And she objected to him being called 'Saint George' on the grounds of his wizened, Christlike face. It was merely due, she said, to him having one or two teeth missing.

Eileen made me laugh. I decided to go into the black box and get her out.

From the outside, it looked to anyone who bothered as though nothing was happening. A coffin-sized black box was rocking, small grunts escaped it, sometimes smoke, the occasional bark. It was dark in there. On grandiose days (there weren't many) I felt like Orpheus going down to hell to find Eurydice, especially when I met in the gloom the incarnation of my foes: a fierce, three-headed dog. The Cerberus blocking the way was called Omission-Triviality-Consent. The most shocking thing was, that this beast was my familiar too. If I could see it, I thought, I might be able to get past it, and find Eileen.

I did find her, but in scraps of facts, ripped up like a chew toy – a blue eye, the corner of a shoulder blade under a suit jacket. A young woman who'd won a scholarship to Oxford and published, in 1934, a dystopian poem called 'End of the Century, 1984'. Someone who twice organised co-workers to stand up to bullying bosses. Eileen was a wisp of a human but inhumanly strong; her nickname, for reasons no one remembers, was Pig.

After I took Eileen out of the box, I had a life in facts, a woman in pieces. I considered writing a novel – a counterfiction to the one in the biographies. But I continued to be fascinated by the sly ways she'd been hidden, and a novel couldn't show those.

And then I found the letters.

Six letters from Eileen to her best friend, Norah Symes Myles, were discovered in 2005, in Norah's nephew's effects, after the biographies were all written. The biographers didn't have the advantage of them.

I wondered what they would have done with them if they had. One eminent Orwell scholar has noted that they reveal 'a very affectionate nature'. That's true, but the reality is much, much more.

Norah lived from 1906 to 1994. Little is known about her, and there's no trace of her letters to Eileen. Norah was, apparently, one of the 'liveliest' girls at St Hugh's in Oxford. An early love of hers had died young. After graduation she married a doctor, Quartus St Leger Myles (known as 'Q'), and settled in Bristol. They had no children. Norah and Eileen were so close that Eileen named Norah in her will as the person she wanted, in the event of her early death, to look after her son.

The letters to Norah date from shortly after Eileen's wedding, through the Spanish Civil War, the couple's time in Morocco, and into wartime London during the Blitz. They are a revelation. It is as if, more than half a century after his death, a door to Orwell's private life has been opened, revealing the woman who lived behind it – and the man who wrote there – in a whole new light.

A novel was impossible now, because it would devour the letters as 'material' and privilege my voice over hers. And Eileen's voice is electrifying. I wanted to make her live, and at the same time to reveal the wicked magic trick that had erased her, and that still holds sway today. I thought of it as writing a fiction of inclusion.

And so I disappeared, for months and years, into Orwell scholar-ship. In the Orwell Archive at University College London I found Eileen's university notebooks and letters to Orwell, in her clear, round hand. I travelled through Catalonia with Richard Blair, the son she and Orwell adopted in 1944, to trace Orwell's time there during the Spanish Civil War. I ended up on the Isle of Jura, in Scotland, in the house where Orwell wrote his last work, *Nineteen Eighty-Four*, drinking whisky with the grandson of the woman who rented it to him.

As serendipity would have it, in 2020 Sylvia Topp published *Eileen: The Making of George Orwell*, which contained much material I hadn't

Norah Symes Myles

found, and was thrilled to read, though we interpret it differently, and so build differing portraits of Eileen.

Looking for Eileen involved the pleasure of reading Orwell on how power works. Finding her held the possibility of revealing how it works on women: how a woman can be buried first by domesticity and then by history.

But Orwell's work is precious to me. I didn't want to take it, or him, down in any way. I worried he might risk being 'cancelled' by the story I'm telling. Though she, of course, has been cancelled already – by patriarchy. I needed to find a way to hold them all – work, man and wife – in a constellation in my mind, each part keeping the other in place.

So, my home-made ground rules for a fiction that tries not to lie: Eileen will live writing the letters she did – six to her best friend, three to her husband and a few others. I know where she was when she wrote them. I know that the dishes were frozen in the sink, that she was bleeding, that he was in bed with another woman – and she knew it. In this story, the lines are hers. Sometimes I write a scene based on what happened. Mostly I supply only what a film director would, directing an actor on set – the wiping of spectacles, the ash on the carpet, a cat pouring itself off her lap.

Falling in Love
Hampstead, Spring 1935

When she meets Orwell Eileen is living in London with her mother, though she often stays with her brother, Laurence, and his wife, Gwen, in their grand house opposite Greenwich Park.

Laurence, sometimes referred to as 'Eric' (short for his second name, Frederick), is four years older than Eileen. Her only sibling, he is charismatic, handsome and driven, and she adores him. Laurence is a rising Harley Street lung and thoracic surgeon, and already a noted authority on tuberculosis. He has recently returned from training in Berlin with the renowned Professor Sauerbruch, who's been treating Hitler. Having seen the Nazi regime up close Laurence is now a passionate anti-fascist. Gwen is a doctor too, 'a slight woman with a quiet presence, gentle and very open-minded and a socialist'. She and Laurence had worked together in Sudan for seven years, marrying while they were there. Now, Gwen runs a thriving general practice from ground-floor rooms at their house, often caring for unmarried mothers and the poor of South East London.

Eileen likes it at Greenwich. It's a lively home, and comfortable. She's done a range of odd and interesting jobs in the nine years since graduating. She often edits and types her brother's scientific papers. In 1934 she enrolled in a Master of Arts in Psychology at University College London, where she met Lydia Jackson.

Laurence and Gwen's home at Greenwich.

Lydia is Russian, recently divorced from a Cambridge don and suffering, in her own words, 'an almost complete lack of self-confidence'. She has invited Eileen to a party in Hampstead.

On the way there Lydia skins her knee. Though her English is perfect it's her second language and she says things plainly. 'I arrived at that house in a far from festive mood,' she writes in her memoir. 'I had had a fall in the street and my knee was bleeding.'

Lydia's friend Rosalind Obermeyer is divorced too. Rosalind, a Jungian psychologist, is throwing this small party at the suggestion of her flatmate, a man called Eric who works in a bookshop and writes mornings and nights in his room. But in the end Rosalind invited most of the guests – other psychologists and university people. Eric hasn't been to university. He's invited only one friend, the editor of a magazine he is writing for, a gentle, left-wing aristocrat called Richard Rees.

When they get there, Lydia recalls, 'The room our hostess showed us into was sparsely furnished and poorly lit. Two tall men were standing, draped over an unlit fireplace; both looked to me, in Chekhov's immortal phrase, rather "moth-eaten". Their clothes were drab and their faces lined and unhealthy. I made no attempt to talk to either of them. But,' she adds, 'Eileen must have done so.'

Everyone drinks and talks and smokes. Possibly, there is music.

A *coup de foudre* is invisible, felt only by the people, or the person, it happens to. Later, others tried to remember the evening, knowing what had happened there that they hadn't seen. Kay Ekevall, a 'jolly, smiling, warmhearted' woman with a boy-bob, was sleeping with Orwell at the time, so she watched especially closely. Eileen, Kay said, was 'gay and lively and interesting, and much more on his level. She was older than me, she'd been to university, and she had an intellectual standing in her own right . . .' Rosalind, who went on to have an eminent career in psychotherapy, recalled 'Eric and Richard standing together in front of the fireplace, both of them tall, thin and ungainly, talking together, glancing at guests as they entered the room and going on with their conversation'.

Orwell warms up over the evening. At the end of it he insists on walking Eileen and Lydia to the bus stop. When he comes back he helps Rosalind collect glasses and ashtrays. And then, according to the earliest biographers, 'he turned to her – it is the only other detail of that far-off occasion that Mrs Obermeyer still vividly, exactly remembers – and said, "Eileen O'Shaughnessy is the girl I want to marry."'

It is so unusual for Orwell to say anything personal that this sticks in Rosalind's mind for thirty years.

The next day at university Eileen seeks Rosalind out to thank her – and to apologise: 'I was rather drunk, behaving my worst, very rowdy,' she laughs. Rosalind notices that Eileen has a copy of Orwell's first novel, *Burmese Days*, under her arm. Rosalind tells her she made a big impression on its author and promptly offers to host a supper for the two of them at the flat.

The dinner takes place the next week. Shortly after they've eaten, Rosalind makes herself scarce.

'Not very long after that party,' Lydia recalls, 'Eileen told me that she had met one of those men again and that he had proposed to her.'

'What! Already?' I exclaimed. 'What *did* he say?'

'He said he wasn't really eligible but . . .'

'And what did you reply?'

'Nothing . . . I just let him talk on.'

'But who is he?'

'Rosalie says he's a writer – George Orwell.'

'Never heard of him.'

'Neither have I.'

'I only half believed her then,' Lydia writes, 'but when I saw she was serious, I did not like it at all.'

Lydia can't stand it. 'What are you going to do about it?' she presses.

'I don't know . . .' Eileen replies. 'You see, I told myself that when I was thirty, I would accept the first man who asked me to marry him. Well . . . I shall be thirty next year . . .'

That playful tone is torturous for Lydia, who was not born to whimsy, or Anglo indirection. But it 'was typical of Eileen', Lydia says. 'I was never sure whether remarks of this kind were meant by her to be taken seriously, or as a joke. I preferred to take this one as a joke and laughed but I have wondered since whether she had acted on this decision when she accepted Orwell's proposal of marriage.'

Perhaps Lydia can't see that a man who can propose in the same breath as he declares his ineligibility for marriage may have met his match in a woman who just lets him talk on, and whose acceptance might, or might not, be part of a bet with herself.

Years later Lydia described Eileen and George's encounter at Rosalind's as a 'doom-laden meeting'. She had a long friendship with both of them, but she never really changed her mind.

Lydia Jackson

Lidiia Vitalevna Jiburtovich was born in St Petersburg in 1899. When she met Eileen she was, at thirty-five, six years older than her, and going by her married name, Lydia Jackson. Alone in London, she was at a low ebb, though that didn't stop her asking, as she admits, 'pointed' and 'naïve' questions in class. The first time she did it other students rolled their eyes, but Eileen had turned around to look at her, squinting in her short-sighted way. 'In the break she came up and spoke to me,' Lydia remembered. 'It was the beginning of our friendship.' Eileen invited Lydia for supper.

Lydia was so lonely that when Laurence collected them after class in his huge black car, she got a frisson of – something – as he took her hand and gave her 'a penetrating look straight in the eye'. Her attraction to him made her radically underestimate clever, committed Gwen as a 'mousy woman with thick ankles'.

Lydia had love to give that had nowhere to go. Once, before Orwell entered their lives, she slept over with Eileen at Laurence and Gwen's.

The two women shared a bedroom on the top floor: '. . . I was struck and strangely moved by Eileen's exceptional thinness when I saw her standing in her nightdress before a looking-glass and shivering with cold. I felt sorry for her and wondered what kind of man would lust after a body as ethereal as that.'

There are so many kinds of desire, possibly a spectrum beyond words. Some kind of yearning, opaque to Lydia, underlies her words here. She is 'strangely moved' to pity: who will love this woman? If there is no one, will she then be hers? But if there is someone, will he care for her as much as Lydia does?

After graduation Lydia became an esteemed psychologist, and a translator of Chekhov. She never married again. In the 1960s she wrote an essay about Eileen, and she wrote of her in her memoirs. In the 1980s she spoke about Eileen to Canadian radio interviewers. Eileen, Lydia said, 'opened a family home' to her and saved her. Lydia spent the rest of her life trying to save Eileen in return.

Who is he?

When Eileen meets Eric Blair, draped over that fireplace, he is thirty-two years old, 6 foot 2½ inches tall and thin as a folding ruler. His girlfriend Kay said he 'never looked well'. He had 'a rather pale dry skin, as if he'd been dried up by the Burma heat'. Deep wrinkles are etched from nose to chin, like parentheses in stone. He rolls his own 'deplorable cigarettes' from cheap shag and chain-smokes them; his cough is constant, unsettling, he is careless with the ash. His voice is high and thin, a lazy cut-glass drawl.

Orwell thinks of himself as ugly, though no one else does. As early as his twenties he considered himself to be 'wearing badly'. But his eyes are 'marvellous', a pale, piercing blue. 'They were absolutely clear and glittering, and they had humour in them. They were the most vital part of his face. He could look amused or serious with his eyes,' one woman said. 'He's the only person I've ever known who looked absolutely straight and full at you. Sometimes it was a little disconcerting.' When he smiles, 'he *really* smiled. It was like the sun coming out.' Orwell wears tailored but dishevelled tweed, as if signalling the remnants of money and class his family lost generations ago. He enters a party like a ragged John the Baptist coming in from the wilderness, and the jolly rich girls quiver in their furs.

What he says at the party the night he meets Eileen is not recorded by Lydia, nor by his friend Richard Rees. But he has 'something charming and winning about him', is 'original in himself; a card, a dear fellow'. Orwell's favourite gambit is to make outrageous or paranoid pronouncements, which he then tries to defend. 'All tobacconists are fascists,' he says, or 'all Scotsmen are liars' or 'all scoutmasters are homosexuals'. These are conversational grenades, lobbed in to provoke a reaction. They are the pre-emptive strikes of a man who feels he rubs up against the world somehow wrongly, and who wants to see how it pushes back. By one friend's account he is 'a gangling, physically badly co-ordinated young man. I think his feelings [were] that even the inanimate world was against him . . . I mean any gas stove he had would go wrong, any radio would break down . . . he was a lonely man – until he met Eileen, a very lonely man. He was fairly well convinced that nobody would like him, which made him prickly.'

Orwell is a man coming at things from a position of outsiderdom, which doesn't square with his posh accent. And he is taking the life gamble of a young writer, whose stake is himself in a bet that he might one day be, as he confided to Jacintha Buddicom, the great friend of his adolescence, a 'FAMOUS WRITER'. All of which might make a deeply intelligent woman who loved literature and hated tyrants intensely curious.

Orwell was born in Burma, where his father, Richard Blair, was a low-ranking functionary in the colonial opium-trading regime. His mother, Ida Limouzin, was quick-witted and engaged with the world, having been brought up in Burma in a lively, cross-cultural household – her mother, Thérèse, was English, her father a French merchant. When Orwell was two Ida moved with him and his elder sister, Marjorie, to England, leaving Richard, who was much older and to whom she seems never to have been close, in Moulmein. Orwell didn't properly meet his father till he was eight, when Dick, a man with a 'deep-seated grudge against life', came back to England to retire.

Ida, who was 'very intelligent with an acute mind', set about organising Orwell's education. He started with a crammer, where he worked hard to gain a coveted scholarship to Eton at eleven. Once there, though, he became 'a slacker'. His family couldn't afford to send him to university, and the school wouldn't recommend him anyway. So young Eric Blair followed his father into the colonial service, spending the formative years of his late teens and early twenties working as a policeman enforcing British rule in Burma.

People there remembered him as happy, though in private he quickly made one of the most fundamental realisations of his life: colonialism is a racist system of 'despotism with theft as its final object'.

His first novel, *Burmese Days*, came out of this experience. Flory, Orwell's narrator, describes life in the colony, with its soul-killing hypocrisy of racism and, consequently, his coddling of private rage:

> It is a stifling, stultifying world in which to live. It is a world in which every word and every thought is censored . . . even friendship can hardly exist when every white man is a cog in the wheels of despotism. Free speech is unthinkable. All other kinds of freedom are permitted. You are free to be a drunkard, an idler, a coward, a backbiter, a fornicator; but you are not free to think for yourself. Your opinion on every subject of any conceivable importance is dictated for you by the pukka sahibs' code.
>
> In the end the secrecy of your revolt poisons you like a secret disease. Your whole life is a life of lies. Year after year you sit in Kipling-haunted little clubs . . . eagerly agreeing while Colonel Bodger develops his theory that these bloody Nationalists should be boiled in oil. You hear your Oriental friends called

'greasy little babus', and you admit, dutifully, that they *are* greasy little babus. You see louts fresh from school kicking grey-haired servants. The time comes when you burn with hatred of your own countrymen, when you long for a native rising to drown their Empire in blood . . .

. . . So he had learned to live inwardly, secretly, in books and secret thoughts that could not be uttered . . . But it is a corrupting thing to live one's real life in secret.

Orwell saw the horror of colonial racist politics up close because he was part of its instrument. He was one of the 'louts fresh from school'; he admitted he'd kicked his servant – though he was fond of his houseboy, whom he taught to wake him by tickling his feet. An American who once watched him supervise the brutal interrogation of a local man walked away distressed, saying, 'I wouldn't care to have your job.' Orwell was a white man ruling over Burmese workers and suppressing dissent, but he seems never to have mentioned, anywhere, that his own family was part Burmese. Both an uncle and a great-uncle on his mother's side had partnered with Burmese women; his cousins were mixed race. His grandmother Thérèse adopted Burmese dress, gave big mixed-race parties (taboo at the time), and at the end of her life 'disappeared' into Burmese society. Her death was never recorded.

Part of colonial power was sexual power. Sex with local women was such an intrinsic perk of working for the Empire that when the governor's wife campaigned for British men to marry their concubines or stop sleeping with them, the response, in writing, was 'no cunt no oil'. Orwell frequented the waterfront brothels of Moulmein, where an impoverished teacher had set up with three of her sixth form.

To read early Orwell is to watch a young man from a female-led, mixed-race family coming to manhood in a world where women and other races must be denigrated so as to make white men central. He lived in a regime of hypocritical tyranny that was at the same time politically repulsive and personally intoxicating. And he was becoming the man with the searing insight into power in his time: the Empire was a despotism designed to plunder. He saw that it relied on racism, a 'vast system of mental cheating' in which colonised people are thought of as not fully human, so their work, goods and lives can be stolen.

In this system the oppressors can imagine themselves innocent of crimes against a people, not by denying the crimes, but by denying the equal humanity of the people.

When I read how Flory feels, sitting in that club burning 'with hatred of [his] own countrymen', it is to James Baldwin's extraordinary words, written a generation later, that I turn in order to understand what is going on here:

> [I]t is not permissible that the authors of devastation should also be innocent. It is the innocence which constitutes the crime.

Orwell was becoming the man who would give this mental state of false innocence its name, and so coin one of the most famous neologisms of the twentieth century: doublethink.

But his insight into the rapacity of power in the colony never extended to relations between the sexes. Orwell stayed blind to the position of women, though he'd been buying girls for a few rupees a time.

Five years before meeting Eileen, Orwell returned to the UK. He was nearly twenty-five, back at his parents' house in Southwold. He found tutoring jobs that allowed him to write. He would have liked a girlfriend, or a wife. He visited Jacintha, the love of his adolescence, but she wouldn't see him, for reasons he seemed not to recollect. He had an affair with Eleanor Jaques, the girlfriend of his friend Dennis Collings, and they used to make love in the woods. But Eleanor didn't want to marry him because he was 'too cynical or too sardonic'. He stalked a local girl named Dorothy Rogers and had to be shooed away by her fiancé on a motorbike.

He fell in love with Brenda Salkeld, a 'forthright, intelligent and independent-minded' sports teacher, the daughter of a clergyman. Brenda refused to sleep with him but they spoke about his writing, and wrote intimate letters. 'We talked about marriage,' she remembered, 'and he said he wouldn't want me to have anything to do with my brothers. I said, "Don't be ridiculous, I'm devoted to my brothers."' She laughed, but decades later she remembered this strange impulse towards control by isolation. '[N]ever write about people,' she told him, 'you don't understand them. Even about yourself you haven't a clue.'

Orwell relied on women at every turn. He asked his friend the poet Ruth Pitter for help with his poetry, and she found him a flat in London, where he was so hard up he used to warm his hands over a candle flame. Once there, he began his sorties 'underground', disguising himself as a tramp to research the conditions of life of working-class East Enders, itinerant labourers, hop pickers and vagrants. In early 1928 he left to spend eighteen months in Paris, where his Aunt Nellie, his mother's flamboyant, glamorous older sister, lived. Nellie, an actress, suffragette, socialist and Esperantist, helped him financially, and connected him with an agent and publishers. He tried his hand at journalism and reportage, and worked as a *plongeur* – dishwasher – in a fancy hotel. These experiences formed the basis of his first book, *Down and Out in Paris and London*.

After Paris he returned to his parents at Southwold, where he met Mabel Fierz on the beach. Mabel and her husband, a steel executive, had a holiday house in the town. Thirteen years older than Orwell, Mabel was well off, literary and connected. She advised him to move back to London if he wanted a chance at a serious writing career, and she put him up at her Hampstead home there while she introduced him to the world of agents, publishers and magazines. At one point, dispirited by the rejection of *Down and Out in Paris and London*, Orwell flung the manuscript at her saying, 'Burn it, and keep the clips.' Instead, she sent it to Leonard Moore, an agent she knew. When Moore also rejected it she brought the manuscript back into his office and 'badgered' him to read it again. Moore then took Orwell on and became his agent for life.

Down and Out in Paris and London was published in 1933 under the name George Orwell – to spare his father the shame if it failed, he said. Mabel then found him a place to live at her friend Rosalind's, and after that another place where, unbeknown to him, she paid part of his rent. At some point in their friendship, they became lovers. He confided secrets to her that he seems to have told no one else.

As an old woman Mabel gave interviews to Canadian broadcasters. On tape she sounds confident, liberated, clear-sighted. But in the biographers' eyes all her work, love, generosity and connections are minimised, and she is reduced to 'a vivacious and opinionated middle-aged woman, [who] considered herself something of a talent-spotter', an 'Egeria' (a Roman nymph), or even 'a wee bit of a crank'.

Not long before he met Eileen, Aunt Nellie found Orwell a job in a socialist bookshop in Hampstead owned by friends of hers. He had the afternoons free for writing, and was working through the material of his life. He worked hard. His second novel, *A Clergyman's Daughter* (drawing on the relationship he'd tried to have with Brenda), was coming out. And he had started publishing reviews in the left-wing magazine *The Adelphi*, owned and edited by the wealthy, kind, radically self-deprecating bachelor Richard Rees – the other tall, moth-eaten man draped over the fireplace that fateful night.

Richard Rees

Rees is here at the beginning, and he will be here till the end. He never marries. His interests seem to be literature, politics and, for reasons he never articulates, redemption. Rees's manner is gentle; he saves his lacerations for himself. The product of a dysfunctional family, Eton and then Cambridge, he attributes 'it to a kindly providence rather than to any of them that I was not recognisably a cretin ...' Rees has become a socialist, believing, 'with moronic simplicity', that he can help change society, something he later saw as 'no more than a symptom of my own maladjustment'.

Rees could hold his friend's flaws in mind at the same time as his love. He considered Orwell 'on the surface the easiest and most affable of men. Pleasant, humorous, witty, considerate, gentle; but unpredictable. Below the surface,' Rees observed, 'it was conceivable that he might be "awkward". Actually,' he thought, 'below the surface he was extremely reserved and undemonstrative – exceptionally endowed with *pudor*' (shame, something Rees, again, leaves unexplained). Despite his love for Orwell, 'I could never feel that he was at all a reliable judge of character,' Rees wrote. 'He was, or appeared to be, somewhat obtuse about what was going on inside the minds of those nearest to him.' This was, perhaps, because he 'never really looked at another human being'.

. . . and who is she?

Eileen really looks at other human beings. She observes them 'as if their faces and manners were glass', a novelist friend later writes of a character based on her. 'What she sees are their feelings.'

Lydia writes that she was 'Sophisticated, fastidious, highly intelligent and intellectual, . . . perhaps no less gifted, though in different ways, than the man she married.'

> Physically, she was very attractive, though rather gawky in the way she moved. She was tall and slender, and had what is commonly regarded as Irish colouring: dark hair, light-blue eyes and delicate white and pink complexion, though the colour in her cheeks, she told me, was due to her using rouge. 'Must you put it on?' I protested. 'If I didn't I'd look as if I were about to pass out,' she replied. She had what George called 'a cat's face'.

He wears 'proletarian fancy dress' as a provocation, but she genuinely doesn't care what she wears, which is usually good-quality but 'shabby and unbrushed clothes, generally black'. Despite being 'rather unkempt' she has a particular grace, 'a body beautifully poised on her legs'. Eileen is 'very thoughtful, very philosophical'. And she is an extraordinary listener, taking her time to respond, 'because her sense of life was so intense that she got the full impact of anything that turned up and saw it not isolated but with all its connections'. When she speaks it's thrilling, funny, worth waiting for. People wait.

'When she told you something amusing,' Lydia remembered, 'her eyes would dance and the whole of her features become suffused with laughter ... You knew that she habitually embroidered her stories, that things did not happen quite as amusingly or unexpectedly as she described; nevertheless, you never questioned the accuracy of her accounts – it did not seem to matter. Her exaggerations were rarely malicious ...'

But sometimes they are. Earnest Lydia finds that her friend can 'lash with her tongue'. Eileen doesn't suffer fools, and she doesn't spare anyone. 'Her stories were often told against herself,' Lydia said, 'or against the members of her own family. She talked of her family with what seemed to be an utter and deliberate frankness, revealing their relationships with one another as if she were discussing people in a book. Later on, she talked in the same way about herself and George.'

A person who can describe her relationships with an 'utter and deliberate frankness', as if 'discussing people in a book', is someone with a novelist's instinct for what it is to *be* another. Eileen could distil herself and others, human and animal, into characters with lives – and therefore plots – of their own. All her life she turned her experiences into stories, which involved seeing those around her more clearly, in many cases, than they saw themselves. But this ability to imagine yourself into the skin of another can be an openness to the other so radical it leaves you unprotected; it can be a sign of someone who may not even be on their own side. Eileen's elusiveness, her whimsy, her lack of self-care and her untended intellectual brilliance lead Lydia, eventually, into paroxysms of protective frustration.

Eileen comes from a 'mad gay' Anglo-Irish family from the north of England, more securely upper middle class than Orwell's, whom he famously labelled 'lower-upper-middle' (meaning upper middle class without money). While Orwell was in Burma she won a scholarship to Oxford, where she read English, focusing on Chaucer and Wordsworth. J. R. R. Tolkien was one of her teachers; the poets Auden, Spender and MacNeice her contemporaries.

Eileen would have liked to stay on at Oxford and teach, but she failed, 'through one of those vagaries of chance', to get a first. According to Lydia, '[t]hat failure had removed the ground from under her feet, had deprived her of impetus, had made her feel no effort was worth making'. At no other point in her life does Eileen seem to have felt she deserved more than she got. Something unjust, annihilating, something she couldn't accept appears to have happened, but she never said – at least to anyone who recorded it – what it was. It might have been that the dons didn't give women firsts then – certainly none were given in her course in 1927, the year she graduated. Women had only been allowed to take degrees *at all* for the previous five years. If I were writing a novel I would invent a character to enact that kind of sexism, invisible and ubiquitous as air. It might look like a hand – hairy or pale, ringed or unringed – on her thigh, an unspoken demand for a kiss-for-credit, or something worse. Or, it might have been that she simply corrected a man – as she did later in her psychology class – and so infuriated him.

In any event, from this point forward her efforts to put writing at the centre of her life are displaced. She will not write academic work on literature. She will not persevere with the poetry she has been writing. Now, her literary talents will be sublimated into helping other people realise theirs.

Career paths for women in the 1920s were severely limited and usually ended at marriage, unless you went into the paid version of domestic service. After graduating, Eileen tried different jobs. She spent a term at a girls' boarding school, 'engaged mainly', according to Lydia, 'in making a humorous study of the species of female who own and staff such schools'. She was a reader for elderly Dame Elizabeth Cadbury of the famous Quaker chocolate-making family. She published some feature pieces in newspapers, and delivered two series of lectures at the Workers' Educational Association. Though she didn't tramp with down-and-outs, she worked in their interests with the Archbishops' Advisory Board for Preventive and Rescue Work; one Orwell biographer puts this as 'presumably social work among prostitutes'. And she worked at a typing agency for 'a formidable businesswoman' who was 'neurotically sadistic' and 'revelled in reducing all her female staff to tears'. Eileen watched how this woman 'took pleasure in humiliating her employees, criticising their work in a most severe, destructive way and keeping them under a permanent threat of dismissal'. After a few months Eileen gathered all the staff behind her and led a successful 'revolt of the oppressed' against the tyrant before 'walking out in triumph'.

In 1931, somehow, whether with savings or family money (no one seems to know), Eileen bought a secretarial business. She employed a bright fifteen-year-old, Edna Bussey, as her assistant, or 'oil rag'. They grew so close they seemed to 'know each other's thoughts and sometimes even the next moves', Edna remembered. Edna said Eileen never made much money 'as she was too generous and I fear most unbusinesslike . . . She was untiring in her efforts to help people. I well remember a Mr Tereschenko, a White Russian, who was writing a thesis for his professorship, being taken under her wing. She literally re-wrote his thesis for him, and I have always felt that it was she who earned the professorship.' Eileen saw something in Edna too, and offered to take her in to tutor her for university entrance. But Edna's jealous mother wouldn't allow it.

Years later Edna told an interviewer, 'Probably you think I am biased – well I am. I am sure you too would have been under her spell.' Edna saw what Eileen had put at the centre of her life, if now at one remove. 'Writing was her love, I think.'

In 1934 Eileen finally found a qualification perfectly suited to her keen insight, her empathetic gift and her steel-trap mind – a Master of Psychology at University College London. Her head of department was Professor Cyril Burt, a 'short, brisk, eloquent' man who had begun his career in 1912 with a thesis proving that girls had equal general intelligence to boys (a question that says a lot about the 'general intelligence' of 1912). In any event Burt considered Eileen to have a 'more than ordinary aptitude.'

When Orwell meets her, Eileen's subjects make him nervous. They include 'word association', 'reliability of eye-witnesses' and 'psychopathology'.

When Eileen meets him, she finds her next project.

Had Eileen somehow known that it would be Lydia – and not her best friend, Norah, nor her writer husband – who would leave one of the clearest pictures of her in words, she might have been surprised, because Lydia is someone she sometimes tries to avoid. Lydia is the person who will tell you not to do the thing you want most to do because it's dangerous, which is precisely why you want to do it. None of that do you want to know at the time; not that it is dangerous, and not that that is what attracts you to it – or him.

With Lydia's help I can see Orwell and Eileen standing at the mantelpiece in Rosalind's Hampstead flat that night, swapping stories about the 'species' of people who run small private schools, or tin-pot tyrants in the colonial service and in secretarial agencies. I see them talking about the poor and their lives – vagrants, tramps, hop pickers and prostitutes – as individuals they've known, and as victims of an unjust social system. I see them noticing, and taking comfort in, each other's gawkiness: she's all elbows; his own slips off the mantelpiece and he rains ash everywhere. He stoops to pick up the coal pan and brush to sweep it up; she watches as he rubs it further into the carpet. Orwell was secretive about his own work and wouldn't have talked about it, but I imagine them discussing literature, especially poetry. He'd set out initially to be a poet; her favourites were the Lake Poets. She might have mentioned a poem she'd written the year before, projecting a future of telepathy and mind-control in 1984. Or how she liked to take herself off to Oxford from time to time 'with a suitcase full of poetry' to roam the Bodleian Library for solace and pleasure. He might then have complained that success in the highbrow literary world in London could only come by 'kissing the bums of verminous little lions'. She would have laughed, then made him justify the remark.

Whether Orwell saw it that evening at Rosalind's or later, Eileen's unshakeable integrity and her independent mind, her gift for storytelling and her ability to prick the absurdities of those around her clearly delighted him. Eileen was the embodiment of the 'fundamental decency' of human beings Orwell treasured. Over his career he came to realise this was the single most important quality that could save us from mindless capitulation to power gone wrong – to the structures that oppress us while selling themselves on keeping us 'safe'. It was a quality he would have liked to have had.

Southwold

It's dark outside now and dinner has been cleared. She slides back again behind the desk by the window, pulls the letter from her pocket. When she unfolds it some sand falls out. She brushes it away. There is more to tell Norah, but she doesn't know how to say it in a way that wouldn't be laying it on too thick. It's all true, of course, but also, when you put it down in black and white, too much.

As a wedding present someone in the village gave them a jar of marmalade, solid and golden. That first morning when she put it on the table he was aghast – he wanted it decanted into a pot. She laughed, but she did it. He'd wanted the two of them to dress for dinner, too. When she called that an 'affectation' it was his turn to laugh with delight and say, 'Yes, I suppose it is', so they didn't. Other times his sensitivities were overwhelming. When the lavatory backed up, overflowing muck all over the seat and into the box, he said he simply couldn't do anything about it. (It was true he wasn't well, but no one would be faced with *that*.) There was no money for a plumber. She'd put his waders on, done it with garden gloves and a bucket. That she really can't tell Norah. Or her brother. Or Lydia. She doesn't know if she is protecting him or herself by not telling.

She wants to finish this letter. She wants to tell Norah
about the important things, which are not marmalade
and rain and the overstaying Aunt, but sex and work and
Spain.

The sex is strange. Perfunctory. Or performative. It
doesn't seem to be an act of communication at all, or of
passion. She has always liked sex, hopes it'll change and
grow as they do. She wonders about his other girlfriends.
She's met some of them. Mabel, an older, married woman,
seems sensible, energetic. Kay, an easygoing literary type
he'd met in the London bookshop, had laughed when
telling her how he'd never 'go Dutch' in a restaurant, always
insisting on paying after complaining the whole lunch
about how poor he was. There were a couple of unrequited
loves – Brenda the schoolteacher, and Sally, another
bookshop friend. She hasn't met either of them. In Burma
he'd been in love with an officer's wife, a cultured woman.
And of course there were the girls in the brothels there, and
in Paris. So whatever it is, it's not for lack of practice.

These are the things she knows. About men she doesn't
know – 'the usual fagging' at school, she assumes, whatever
that involved. His pleasure in being undressed by his
houseboy in Burma. 'Sodomy', he always spits the word,
was 'rife' in the down-and-out kips when he went tramping.
Possibly, she thinks, he lives in a zone where desire and
disgust mingle, a place where she is not.

And now, he's off to the trenches.

He'd come into the kitchen at the cottage when she was washing
up. Said it as casually as if he were walking out for cigarettes.

'I thought I'd go to Spain.'

Something had thudded then, twice, at the back door. She'd wiped her hands on her apron and opened it. The goat, Nellie (named secretly, wickedly, after the Aunt – she can't tell Norah *that*), had come untethered, looking for company. She'd patted the soft head, then led her back to the shed. When she'd turned around George was at the door, hands on hips, waiting for his answer. She saw then that to him she belonged here with the animals and the house and the garden.

'Spain is a good idea,' she'd said, reaching the back step. 'I'm sure we could be useful.'

He'd looked startled. 'But I'll be at the front. There'd be nothing for you to do.'

She'd just let that sit. Plenty of women had gone to help the anti-fascist side. Did he really think he was her only cause?

'And all this?' He'd spread his arms about. 'We'd need to find someone to take over.'

'Yes,' she'd said. 'We', she'd thought, is me.

And here he is now, leaning on the doorjamb, a hand in his pocket, looking apologetic. 'Av says they need a fourth for bridge,' he shrugs. His eyebrows are raised, he's telling her he's sorry for the interruption, and, also, that they are in this together.

She folds the pages of her letter, licks the envelope. It's impossible, anyway. She can't explain these things in a way that will not lead Norah to descend upon her to rescue her. Or in a way that leaves room for the hope she feels when she's with him. She is so curious to see where they will go, what will be written.

'All right,' she says. 'Deal me in.'

⌒

Free

Autobiography is only to be trusted when it reveals something disgraceful. A man who gives a good account of himself is probably lying, since any life when viewed from the inside is simply a series of defeats. However, even the most flagrantly dishonest book . . . can without intending it give a true picture of its author.

George Orwell, 'Benefit of Clergy: Some Notes on Salvador Dalí', 1944

I am making dinner. The TV in the kitchen shows the US Senate Judiciary Committee vetting a nominee for the Supreme Court. My son, who's nine, watches as a woman who looks like his mother cries, her face contorted in pain as she tells of an assault long ago. Then a man is behind the microphone, his face rigid with outrage as if her account is not just false but the breaching of a taboo so fundamental he has no words for it: how he treats women should have no bearing on how he is perceived as a 'decent' human, suitable for high judicial office. It is a face that says ten thousand years of patriarchy gives him the right to deny what he did thirty years ago, regardless of the facts. It is a face that says, Get back in the black box.

My little boy turns to me. 'When did it all start?' he asks.

'When they were in college, I think,' I say.

'No, I mean men doing this to women?' I see in his pale, open face a horror that this might be part of being a man. I tell him it's not necessarily so; his father is not like that, most men are not like that.

And then after the dishes are put away I go back to my text, trying to unravel the web we're all caught in, this house of wax.

Patriarchy has existed for somewhere between five and ten thousand years. Before that, in some other times and places, it is thought there were different ways of seeing and valuing each other, in societies organised around bringing up the young, or valuing maternity, or 'female choice' of sexual partner. Simone de Beauvoir links patriarchy with war, writing that 'it is not in giving life but in risking life that man raises himself above the animal; this is why, throughout humanity, superiority has been granted not to the sex that gives birth, but to the one that kills'. Still, she knows it doesn't really make sense. 'The world has always belonged to males,' she writes, 'and none of the reasons for this have ever seemed sufficient.'

There is no logic for this portion of our knowledge.

Eileen's notebook from Oxford, c.1924.

In political philosopher Friedrich Engels' view, patriarchy developed when nomadic hunter-gatherer societies settled and claims were made, to land, animals, women, progeny. Borders (black boxes, ring fences) became important: whose land was it? Whose animal? Whose child? Men wanted to exert control over the reproduction of children, so women's sexuality was controlled by the institution of monogamous marriage, and inheritance made exclusive to sons so as to keep wealth male. 'The overthrow of mother-right was the world-historical defeat of the female sex,' Engels writes. 'The man took command in the home also; the woman was degraded and reduced to servitude, she became the slave of his lust and a mere instrument for the production of children.' In *The Creation of Patriarchy* historian Gerda Lerner puts it this way: 'women were the first slaves'. Domesticated, along with the animals. In 1938 Virginia Woolf wrote, 'Behind us lies the patriarchal system: the private house, with its nullity, its immorality, its hypocrisy, its servility . . .'

What lies ahead of us?

Though my mother never met my daughter, she would have enjoyed watching her lick peanut butter off a knife and question my bona fides.

When she started work in the 1960s my mother's pay was half that of a man. When she married, the law forced her to stop working. Later, after she got her PhD, she – perhaps unsurprisingly – spent her life researching the economic situation of women in patriarchy, especially divorced wives. This involved the then radical idea of putting a dollar value on the work wives do. Generations of us, it seems, have been trying to get our heads around wifedom.

My mother came from a long line of Irish Catholics in Australia, which gave the following story, told sometime in the 1990s – late in her short life – an element of sectarian surprise. One of our forebears, she said, was the younger, wayward son of the archbishop of Canterbury, the leader of the Church of England. This young man, disgraced for reasons no one remembers, arrived in nineteenth-century Melbourne equipped with only a part of the family silver and a letter

of introduction to the governor, a man named Darling. My forebear
was at a loss as to how to go on with his life. He did not know how,
without much of a stipend, to live. He called on Darling, who advised
him, 'Advertise for a maid. Choose the prettiest one – and marry her.
That way,' and here my mother's voice went low and wicked, 'you get it
all, for *free*.'

My mother, a psychologist, told this story from a range of motives.
One was to tell an anti-colonial fairy tale in which the canny maiden
used her power at the moment of betrothal to insist that future
generations be raised Catholic. Another was the pleasure in finding
a moment in which the unspeakable truth – unspeakable because
so common as to go without saying, but, once spoken, unspeakably
bad – was said: a wife was an unpaid sexual and domestic worker.
I should be warned.

Having now become both a writer and a wife, I find myself
envying the titanic male writers, those unthinking 'mid-century
misogynists' (insert almost any big name here). I don't envy them for
any personal reason or anything much to do with their work/travel/
gun-toting/sexual antics, etc. – or maybe I do. What I most envy
are their conditions of production. So many of these men benefited
from a social arrangement defying both the moral and the physical
laws of the universe in which the unpaid, invisible work of a woman
creates the time and – neat, warmed and cushion-plumped – space for
their work.

We know that a male writer's time to write was traditionally
created for him by liberating him from the need to shop, cook, clean
up after himself or anyone else, deal with mundane correspondence,
entertain, arrange travel or holidays, care for his own children
(except as a 'helper' who is thanked, as if it were not his job, or not his
children) and so on. Time is valuable, because it is finite. So, as with
all other finite commodities, there is an economy of time. Time can
be traded, bargained for, snuck and stolen. A weekend is finite – as

any parent trying to juggle space and apportion time within it with a spouse will tell you. A life is finite. The more I looked at Eileen and Orwell's life together, the more I felt the long-ago dynamic reverberate, disconcertingly, in my own. Access to time, as to any other valuable good, is gendered. One person's time to work is created by another person's work in time: the more time he has to work, the more she is working to make it for him. To examine a marriage of eighty years ago involves the faux-comfort of distance (*surely* we are more evolved than that?) along with a frisson of horror: things have not changed nearly enough. I can count on one hand with fingers to spare the number of heterosexual relationships I know in which the man creates the domestic and other conditions for the woman to enjoy her time in life to an equal extent as she does for him. Things in the rear-view mirror are closer than they appear.

To benefit from the work of someone who is invisible and unpaid and whom it is not necessary to thank because it is their inescapable purpose in life to attend to you, is to be able to imagine that you accomplished what you did alone and unaided – whether you wrested a fortune from a conquered isle, or words from the void. Invisible workers require no pay or gratitude, beyond perhaps an entire, heartfelt sentence in a preface, thanking 'my wife'.

It is a phenomenal advantage to the writerly imagination to think this way. The first task of the imagination, for a writer, is the creation of the writing self. It's quite a job, and it helps to have two of you at it: she, believing in you, so you, too, believe in yourself. This nurtured self is then mother to the work. And the work, in turn, becomes evidence of a self: I made, therefore I am.

And in that sentence, she disappears.

Writers are notoriously unstable elements, lacking a sound core, and are prone, without support, to falling into our own empty centres. If you have someone in your orbit, you feel like the nucleus. If there's an audience, you must be the star.

For this bolstering of male centrality and of the male imagination to make the work, it is crucial that the supports to it remain invisible. A high-wire act is not awe-inspiring if you can see the wires. Invisible and unacknowledged, a wife is the practical and often intellectual wiring that allows the act to soar; and for it to be truly astonishing, the wires, and the wife, need to be erased both at the time, and then over time. Her work is barely acknowledged by the man whom it benefits, and she is later erased by his biographers from his achievement. One might think of this as millennia – or in Orwell's case nearly a century – of male pattern blindness.

It's hard to live in someone's blind spot. And it's hard, then, for history to find you. But not impossible.

As a writer, the unseen work of a great writer's wife fascinates me, as I say – out of envy. I would like a wife like Eileen, I think, and then I realise that to think like a writer is to think like a man. It is to look from his perspective at what he needed and see how he got it. But as a woman and a wife her life terrifies me. I see in it a life-and-death struggle between maintaining her self, and the self-sacrifice and self-effacement so lauded of women in patriarchy, which are among the base mechanisms by which our work and time are stolen. What did she give and what did it cost her? I find this question so chilling, coming out of twenty years of intense life-and-home-making, that I prefer to think it does not apply to me. I live in a different age, in which women are said to be equal, despite doing an unfathomably disproportionate load of the adults' work in households, caring for the generation to come and, in many cases, the one before. The gap between what is said to be and what is, is the gap we collude in making by keeping all this work invisible. And it is a gap into which you can fall.

I am a privileged white woman and though I know that patriarchy is a planetary Ponzi scheme by which the time, work and lives of women are plundered and robbed, my unearned privilege makes me uncomfortable talking about it, for two reasons. The first is because I live in a rich Western country, which struggles with shocking racism, poverty and class prejudice – struggles my privilege can blind me to. I know that other women and men here and elsewhere in the world have much harder lives. But what makes it impossible to stay silent is that everywhere, among every race and class, women do more unpaid work in the home and earn less outside of it than men. Statistically, there is an irrefutable, globally intransigent heterosexual norm that pervades across ethnicity, colour and class. There is not one place on the planet where women as a group have the same power, freedom, leisure or money as their male partners.

Apparent class equality, or, on the other hand, wealth, haven't changed the unequal load, anywhere. Despite the rhetoric about women's equality in communist countries, women remain responsible for household and care work and are barely to be seen in leadership positions. And in democratic capitalist societies money doesn't seem to equalise it among couples either: affluent women are still responsible for the work, even if they can pay for others, usually women, to do some of it. Every society in the world is built on the unpaid or underpaid work of women. If it had to be paid for it would cost, apparently, US$10.9 trillion. But to pay for it would be to redistribute wealth and power in a way that might defund and de-fang patriarchy.

There are many individual exceptions to this situation. Single parent households where one person (most often, a woman) does it all. Heterosexual and homosexual couples in which the work of love and life is shared more equally. And we live in an age in which the gender binary (along with what it is to be a 'good' woman, or a 'real' man) is being challenged. Maybe a more fluid understanding of gender will eventually also free us not only from the fictions of what it is to be female and what it is to be male, but also from the assumptions about work and care that those definitions secretly, and not so secretly, carry.

The other reason it's hard to talk about is because my husband and I think of ourselves as equals. To draw attention to the gendered load feels like driving a wedge between us – though in truth the wedge is *already* there, imposed by an unseen patriarchal bargain neither of us signed up to. So many women I know feel the same, but we talk about it *sotto voce*. We avoid conflict, thinking instead that each of us has failed, individually, to fix her life properly, and under the righteous resentment there's a shame that keeps our voices down. I pretend I am equal while I am: walking the dog/doing the grocery shopping/waiting in the orthodontist's/commiserating about mean teens/folding laundry. I pretend I am equal when I am chopping vegetables/organising the counsellor or the hospital or the solicitor/de-griming the fridge. Actually, I mind none of it. This is my real life, with my real loves. I know that when I'm old I'll envy my younger self her busyness, her purpose, her big-hearted whirligig life. But still, the distribution of labour is hard to make equal, because so much of it is hard to see, wrapped up in the definition of what it is to be me. Pretending I am not subject to modern versions of the same forces Eileen was, by 'practising acceptance' or 'just getting on with it', is a kind of lived insanity: to pretend to be liberated from the work while doing it.

Over the years of writing this, almost every woman I spoke to nodded, laughed, rolled her eyes and had stories of her own that popped out as we stood in the corridor at work or school, in the shopping or COVID-testing queue. One mother of two, an eminent historian, told me that what she could no longer manage on top of family/house/career was the garden she loved. A briar rose trailed over her front door, and she had quietly stopped pruning it, waiting to see if anyone else would, or if, continuing to ignore the work she'd been doing, they'd simply enter the house through an ever smaller and thornier space. Another friend, a powerful journalist married to a famous, and famously depressed, writer, had to write some of his screenplays when he was low, for which he didn't credit her. 'I am losing myself,' she said. Another, a lawyer with a triple black belt in karate, described herself as 'grout'. For some reason she is the only one who can see, as she passes the drying rack, that the laundry needs putting away. She is, she said, 'what holds it all together'. They tell me all this quietly, as if it were something that should have been fixed long ago, and as if it were up to each of them, alone, to sort out. Another item on their to-do list: birthday present for Saturday/get chairs fixed/anti-fungal/dog: leptospirosis vaccination/make work and self visible/fix patriarchy.

You might think that, as privileged women in professions, we'd have the tools to liberate ourselves. But we don't, or at any rate we haven't. To talk about this level of inequality between a woman and a man who live together doing the work of care and love was for a long time taboo: you risk being seen as 'complaining' or, because this work has insidiously been made part of what it is to be a 'good' woman, a bad one. Reams of women's magazines offer advice to overburdened women on 'self-care' or 'juggling the load', as if the problem is personal, and can be solved by yet *more* effort on our part – leaving the system that makes us and takes from us untouched.

I am married to a man who's emotionally astute, deeply engaged with our children. Craig and I share the financial load, we think we share most things in our lives. This was not enough to protect me. The patriarchy is too huge, and I too small or stupid, or just not up for the fight. The individual man can be the loveliest; the system will still benefit him without his having to lift a finger or a whip, or change the sheets. This is a story I tell against myself. And against the system that made this self, as well as my husband's, and put her into his service.

Wifedom is a wicked magic trick we have learned to play on ourselves. I want to expose how it is done and so take its wicked, tricking power away.

Passive, Tense

Never use the passive where you can use the active.
George Orwell, 'Politics and the English Language', 1946

How is a woman made to disappear? Orwell's biographers start with fundamental omissions, such as his cultural and intellectual inheritance, which came through his mother's side. You can read them all and understand only that his father's family had had money generations before from slaves, and that Dick was a lowly sub-agent in a backwater of the opium-trafficking Empire. You would not learn that his mother, Ida, was a Fabian socialist and suffragette, educated in England. Nor that her sister, Nellie, had been on the London stage, demonstrated for women's suffrage with the Pankhursts (and been imprisoned for it), and belonged to the Women's Freedom League which advocated against censorship, for equal pay and to revolutionise the relations between the sexes. Nellie was connected in both Paris and London with important writers and thinkers, including G. K. Chesterton, Henri Barbusse, E. Nesbit, and Orwell's hero, H. G. Wells. These links are not made, because it is impossible, apparently, to attribute to women the environment of ideas and politics that made him.

The biographers are helped by Orwell himself erasing or obscuring the women in his life. He writes, for instance, to his teenage love, the wealthy, literary young woman Jacintha, saying that she 'abandoned

him to Burma', leaving out that after their last meeting – a 'walk' in
the countryside – something happened that made her run traumatised
into her family's house with 'a torn skirt and a tear-stained face like
thunder'. It's not that he didn't know how she felt: she'd written to
him afterwards, 'telling him of her disgust and shock that he should
try and FORCE her to let him make love to her ... He had held her
down (by that time he was 6' 4" and she was still under 5') and though
she struggled, yelling at him to STOP, he had torn her skirt and badly
bruised a shoulder and her left hip.'

One of the more flamboyantly inventive instances of erasure
of a woman is Orwell's own. In *Down and Out in Paris and London*
he recounts being robbed of all he possessed in his lodgings by a
'swarthy Italian with side-whiskers'. The truth was that he was
cleaned out by a woman, the 'little trollop' he adored, whom he'd
picked up in a café in Paris and installed in his hotel room. Suzanne,
a streetwalker and con artist, was the woman he 'loved best' of all the
girls he'd known before Eileen. He told Mabel, 'She was beautiful,
and had a figure like a boy, an Eton crop and [was] in every way
desirable.'

But Suzanne can't be given the power to con him because
that would reduce his own, and therefore shame him. So Orwell
transforms her into a male foreigner, complete with sideburns and
a fulsome fictional backstory for verisimilitude. Suzanne becomes
a 'compositor' the landlady instantly distrusts and from whom she
requests rent in advance. Orwell needs to describe the robbery, because
it plunges him into the poverty that leads him to take the infamous
dishwasher job and be treated in the hospital for the poor. But this
itself obscures another woman – Aunt Nellie again, who was living
in Paris the whole time, who gave him meals and money, connected
him with editors and intellectuals, and, with her radical-socialist
life partner, Eugène Adam, introduced him to the ideas of the anti-
Stalinist left.

And then there's Spain – but that's a whole other story.

The methods of omission started to fascinate me as I came to recognise them. When women can't be left out altogether, they are doubted, trivialised, or reduced to footnotes in 8-point font. Other times, chronology is manipulated to conceal. What a woman does, or what is done to her, is only mentioned pages *after* the events themselves, which are described without her. This separates her actions from their effects, her bravery from its beneficiaries, her earnings from the man who lived from them, her suffering from the people who caused it. And when none of that works, women are imagined to have consented to what was done to them – in Eileen's case, to a completely fictitious '*ménage à trois*' or an invented 'open marriage'.

The most insidious way the actions of women are omitted is by using the passive voice. Manuscripts are typed without typists, idyllic circumstances exist without creators, an escape from Stalinist pursuers is achieved. Every time I saw 'it was arranged that' or 'nobody was hurt' I became sensitised – who arranged it? Who might have been hurt?

Once I knew who should be in the text but wasn't, the biographies seemed like oddly collaborative projects between biographer and subject, as if they belonged to the same unnamed club, the first rule of which is: don't give women main roles. Don't talk about what we (or our hero) might owe them (as mothers, teachers, editors, mentors or financiers), nor what we do to or with them (as girlfriends, prostitutes, lovers, wives and mistresses).

The more I saw these hidden methods, the more they seemed like the methods of patriarchy in microcosm, laid out in ink.

Patriarchy is a fiction in which all the main characters are male and the world is seen from their point of view. Women are supporting cast – or caste. It is a story we all live in, so powerful that it has replaced reality with itself. We can see no other narrative for our lives, no roles outside of it, because there is no outside of it.

In this fiction, the vanishing trick has two main purposes. The first is to make what she does disappear (so he can appear to have done it all, alone). The second is to make what he does to a woman disappear (so he can be innocent). This trick is the dark, doublethinking heart of patriarchy.

As I read the biographies, I began to see that just as patriarchy allowed Orwell to benefit from his wife's invisible work, it then allowed biographers to give the impression that he did it all, alone. The biographers are choosing the facts for his story in a world that has *already* sifted them in his favour. The narrative techniques of patriarchy and biography combine seamlessly so as to leave the women who taught and nurtured Orwell, influenced and helped him, like offcuts on the editing floor, buttresses to be removed once the edifice is up.

And so I write, as Orwell put it, because there is some lie that I want to expose, some fact to which I want to draw attention. Or, as it happens, a person.

Engagement

When Eileen starts seeing Orwell she is living with her mother. It can be a bit tense, so she often stays at Laurence and Gwen's. Eileen and Orwell walk a lot, and go riding at nearby Blackheath. They discover one another. He liked to have sex in parks and woods; maybe they did.

Lydia 'could not believe she had fallen in love with Eric Blair: I did not find him at all attractive'. No biographer uses this. Nor this: 'I admired her and thought she deserved someone better than an unknown and impecunious writer, "moth-eaten"', she says again, 'and obviously not in the best of health. I was sure she could inspire devotion, and I wished her to have a secure and comfortable life.'

It's impossible to know whether Lydia conveyed her misgivings to Eileen. She was in the classic bind of a good friend: do you risk the friendship to warn against someone? You could be totally wrong. And even if you're not, up against desire words lose their power; a person in love can mute the whole world.

After they've been in a relationship for some months, Orwell moves out of Rosalind's flat. Their other flatmate, Janet Grimson, a medical student, had found herself having words with him about (not) sharing the housework. When he was gone Rosalind and Janet discovered a 'family of mice' living in his wardrobe, presumably on the half-finished boxes of biscuits he kept stashed there. Orwell moves into a flat – organised, again, by Mabel – in 'resolutely working class' Kentish Town. This one he shares with two younger men: Rayner Heppenstall, who was starting his writing life, and Michael Sayers, a young Irish poet who was carrying on a 'torrid' affair with his cousin Edna.

Lydia visited once for supper. Other people enjoyed food Orwell prepared on his 'bachelor cooker', but Lydia couldn't bring herself to. 'He must have cooked the meal himself,' she writes, 'and it must have been something hardly edible – for he was no cook.'

No biographer gives a reason for the move, which was into a less convenient area. The closest one of them gets is to suggest that he moved to 'gain more privacy', because there must have been 'difficulties in having his fiancée's fellow-student as a landlady'. What sort of difficulties could these unspoken ones be? All three of them were educated, liberated people in their late twenties and thirties. Rosalind had been married before; none was prudish about sex. What was it he wanted to do in that 'privacy' from Rosalind? Not one of the biographers links what he was actually doing (the facts) with why he might change his living arrangements to suit them, because it's uncomfortable.

But if you untangle the evasions and establish the chronology they have concealed, the reason becomes clear. 'Meanwhile,' one biographer writes, as if referring to events running parallel, entirely unconnected with the move, 'Orwell continued to sleep with Kay during the week, reserving weekends for Eileen . . .' And he was also seeing another woman, Sally, who was refusing, so far, to sleep with him. None of the biographers wonders whether Eileen knew this was going on. In order for her to continue to be in the dark about it, it can't keep happening in Rosalind's flat, because Rosalind might tell her. It would be off-putting to discover that your suitor is sleeping with someone else and trying to sleep with yet another person the whole time he is, apparently, falling in love with you. It would, perhaps, be a sign.

In January 1936 – Orwell and Eileen have known each other ten months now – Orwell goes north to the poor mining town of Wigan, to investigate the lives of the coalminers for what will become the wonderful *The Road to Wigan Pier*. When he returns in March he decides to move even further away from society, to Wallington in Hertfordshire, a tiny village of a hundred people forty miles north of London. There, his Aunt Nellie is about to give up a cottage she's been renting. It's cheap and very isolated. The front room was once a grocery store, and Orwell thinks he might reopen it to make some money, though the locals all shop elsewhere. He plans to grow vegetables, raise chickens, and write up his book on the living conditions of the poor. And to get married.

Running

A couple of months before the wedding Eileen and her family – old Mrs O'Shaughnessy, Laurence and Gwen – visit Wallington. Lydia comes too. They cruise up in Laurence's magnificent black car. The cottage is three hundred years old, with two rooms downstairs and two upstairs, no light, a camp stove and only one tap.

Lydia is grumpy. She's worried Eileen is going to abandon her MA. They have their meal downstairs 'somehow', she recalls, 'managing to squeeze ourselves round the gate-legged table'. After lunch Orwell leads them on a walk around the local manor house, through market gardens and fields dotted with golden corn stacks, then towards home, past the abandoned school. There's talk of how the smattering of local children are bussed each day to school in the next village. 'When I heard this,' Lydia writes, 'I smiled a little bitterly at Eileen's assurance that she would continue her research – which involved giving intelligence tests to a large, unselected sample of children.'

'The object of my concern, Eileen herself,' Lydia continues, is 'unusually silent during that walk.' Orwell is talking to Laurence. Lydia is walking with Eileen's mother. Eileen walks with calm, sensible Gwen, who, as a doctor, has a professional life of her own. 'Then suddenly Eileen began to run. We all stared after her, wondering what was the matter. The two men then resumed their conversation.

Old Mrs O'Shaughnessy was the only one to murmur some remark on her daughter's eccentric behaviour.'

To me, it looks as though Eileen is bolting from all the things that are not being said; from the unbearable awkwardness of being with your whole family as they're 'inspecting' the outwardly unprepossessing prospective husband. For Orwell, his writerly poverty might be a sign of ambition, of dedication, or of failure, but for a wife it is, as Lydia forensically foresees, a portent of hard labour, physical and mental.

The moment one introduces a lover to one's family is inevitably uncomfortable. Who we choose reveals more about ourselves than we can know, about what we want and what we need, and the gap between self-revelation and self-knowledge is a chasm of vulnerability. Eileen's attraction to Orwell perhaps discloses more about her to her family than she can stand: her fatalism and her utter disregard for material things, a passionate commitment to writing along with the foreshadowing of the fact that this writing – given her wit, her renowned storytelling gift and her education – will not be her own.

When the others reach the cottage Eileen is nowhere to be seen. She has run way beyond it. Eventually, she comes back. 'She looked defensive and somewhat out of breath, but she did not say anything and no one made any comment,' Lydia reports. 'Some time later she told me spontaneously: "I just couldn't bear it any longer ... I had to run."' Lydia doesn't ask what it was she couldn't bear: 'I thought I understood.'

Eileen may have been running from her family's inspection of her suitor, but she may also have been running from Lydia and her 'bitter' smile. Clearly, to marry Orwell and live here will mean to abandon her studies and any possibility of an independent professional, intellectual and financial life. What kind of diffidence or masochism might lie under such a decision? Was it the standard kind, required of wives at that time, in which your own ambition was incompatible with wifedom: you could be yourself, or you could place that self in the service of another. Or did it, even for the times, go too far? Either way, there was no protecting her.

Around this time Kay stops sleeping with Orwell. She isn't interested in being a wife. In fact, she and her friends 'rather despised marriage', she later tells a radio interviewer, laughing. She says that Orwell, though he 'liked women well enough', never 'really regarded them as a force in life. They were very secondary.' Kay had said to him all along, '"well now look if you find someone else don't hesitate to say so because I don't like these dragged out things" . . . and actually, he was the *only* one that ever said "look, I've met a girl I want to marry."' Though he left it till quite close to the wedding day.

Kay saw clearly the cost to Eileen of her decision. 'I thought it was rather tragic that she should give it all up,' she said about her degree and career. 'I don't think I would have.'

Slipstream

When we were in our twenties, my friend was in a relationship with an old rock star, a man whose fame united a subculture of smacked-out, leather-clad cognoscenti, and was exaggerated in his own mind because he lived in the eternal present tense of alcohol and heroin. It's strange that I have no memory of what happened, particularly because I know it was a sudden tongue down my throat.

But she tells me she's grateful that I told her. It's a horrible position to be in – to wreck your friend's happiness or keep from her your knowledge of its unstable foundations. I chose her, I suppose, over her happiness then. I'm lucky she forgave me for being the bearer of bad news. It was easier, I think, because she knew his pounce had nothing to do with desire, but with ego and opportunity, the rampant rock-star self.

Now, she tells me she liked being with him because, 'there was something nice about being the sidekick of such talent. Reflected glory.' There was a basking pleasure of being found worthy of being in his orbit. But the thing that comes with that is the abandonment of your own talent, and the centrality to yourself you must claim in order to feed it. We were young lawyers, searching around for ways to leave our black-letter lives, and, eventually, we did.

I wonder if Eileen was doing something like this when she put Orwell in the place where her own ambition had crashed and burned.

And once he was there, she couldn't leave him. His work was her purpose. He and it were in the place where she and hers should have been. She was in the slipstream of him.

Deleting Obscenities and Drawing a Blank

The wedding is scheduled for 9 June 1936 at the tiny church of St Mary's in Wallington. The month before, Orwell writes to a friend:

> *I am getting married very shortly . . . This is as it were in confidence because we are telling as few people as possible till the deed is done, lest our relatives combine against us in some way & prevent it. It is very rash of course but we have talked it over & decided I should never be economically justified in marrying so might as well be unjustified now as later. I expect we shall rub along all right – as to money I mean – but it will always be hand to mouth as I don't see myself ever writing a best-seller.*

Orwell's sister Avril said that secretiveness ran in the family: their father was exactly the same. But even so, it seems extreme to imagine a conspiracy of relatives preventing the wedding, especially as they are all invited, and they all come. The person who would most like to prevent it is Lydia and she is, conveniently, abroad. Lydia seems to have known that her antagonism had been felt because later she doubted whether, even if she'd been in Britain, she would have been invited.

The truth of what Orwell is saying to his friend is not in his words, but in what he means, which is: I can't believe no one is stopping this.

Orwell is getting away with something. He can barely afford to keep himself, and yet he is going to get another person's labour, for life, for *free*.

The morning of the wedding he is still keeping up with correspondence, even of the non-urgent kind. He writes to an old school acquaintance who has recently returned from America and been in touch after many years:

> *Dear King-Farlow,*
>
> *Of course I remember you . . . I'm afraid I can't possibly come along on the 11th, much as I would like to . . . Curiously enough I am getting married this very morning – in fact I am writing this with one eye on the clock and the other on the Prayer Book, which I have been studying for some days past in hopes of steeling myself against the obscenities of the wedding service.*

The wedding is a small affair. Orwell's parents and sisters come, Eileen's mother, Laurence and Gwen. There is no nervous waiting at the altar for Orwell – the couple walk together from the cottage to the church. And then, in a flamboyant and joyous gesture, Orwell vaults the churchyard wall, picks up Eileen and carries her through the gate.

When they get to the altar there is a surprise for him. Eileen has organised the wedding, including for the O'Shaughnessy family vicar to come down from the north to conduct the ceremony. And she has dealt with at least one of the 'obscenities' of the wedding service. The next day Orwell reports to his unrequited love, Brenda, 'We were married yesterday in correct style at the parish church here but not with the correct marriage service, as the clergyman left out the "obey" clause among other things.' The obey clause is the traditional one in which brides promise to love, cherish and obey their husbands, but grooms don't reciprocate the 'obey' part. Clearly, Eileen was not having *that*. But as far as Orwell and the biographers and posterity are concerned, the vicar left it out unprompted. No one, then or now, can credit Eileen with identifying the 'obscenity' of 'obey' and deleting it.

After the ceremony Orwell fills in the parish register, 'Eric Arthur Blair. Age 33. Bachelor', and signs it. In the box next to 'occupation' he writes 'Author'. Eileen's side reads: 'Eileen Maud O'Shaughnessy. Age 30. Spinster.' And next to occupation, she draws a line.

The little wedding party has lunch at the pub. Eileen later tells Lydia that 'old Mrs Blair talked without stopping, while Avril, who was famously blunt, said not a word the whole day'. Before they leave, the Blairs give the couple part of the family silver as their present. And then, '[a]fter lunch,' Lydia writes, 'the families drove away and the couple were left on their own – George to get on with his writing and Eileen with her housewifely duties . . . and the shop.' Orwell had been wanting to open the shop, but he waited till Eileen was there to do it.

Wedding certificate, June 1936.

Idyll

It does not do to leave a live dragon out of your calculations, if you live near him.

J. R. R. Tolkien

For Orwell, the first months of marriage are idyllic. 'However enigmatic she may ultimately have been, however ineluctable her qualities,' one biographer writes, 'there is widespread agreement among Orwell's friends at the time that Eileen cheered him up, took him out of himself, gave him confidence in his abilities.' One friend said, 'the only year that I ever knew him really happy was that first year with Eileen'. Writing in the early 1970s, Orwell's earliest biographers, Stansky and Abrahams, agree. Living as a newlywed in the primitive cottage he's the happiest he's ever been. 'In any study of Orwell's life,' they write, 'the summer of 1936 must occupy a unique place. His health was good, his spirits high; he was able to work as he wished; he had the pleasure of living in the country, which he had long wanted to do; above all, the pleasure of being married to Eileen, of being with her, week after week, untroubled by illness or absence ... Indeed, only in that summer of 1936 would there be such a combination of elements and circumstances as to fulfil an ideal of happiness for him.'

For a writer, the conditions of production are the conditions of happiness. Even if you're writing in penury and misery (or, as Orwell is, broke and bronchitic in a hovel), at least you're writing, and to write is to wrest the happiness of production from your life by putting a word count between yourself and oblivion. It is the difference between action and entropy; between life and psychic death.

Orwell's 'combination of elements and circumstances' which mean he can work as he wishes are, apparently, happy accidents rather than a situation tailor-made for him by someone else's labour. These conditions appear to exist without a creator, because the passive voice has made her disappear.

But as we know, Eileen is there, working. And managing her impulses towards murder or separation when George doesn't want his work interrupted by life.

All writers – though perhaps not their spouses – would have some sympathy here. In his last notebook Orwell put it this way:

> . . . [all my writing life] there has literally not been one day in which I did not feel that I was idling, that I was behind with the current job, & that my total output was miserably small. Even at the periods where I was working 10 hours a day on a book, or turning out 4 or 5 articles a week, I have never been able to get away from this neurotic feeling, that I was wasting time.

But he isn't wasting time. Eileen is making more of it for him than he could ever have if he had to manage his own life. She deals with much of his correspondence, including with his agent. She organises their social lives, does all the shopping (involving a bus ride to the village of Baldock three miles away) and much of the cleaning (there is, intermittently, a 'char'). Eileen's working conditions are difficult. According to one biographer, the sixteenth-century cottage is 'very small and very narrow . . . built of lath and plaster, with a badly fitting front door, low, head-knocking oak beams and an ugly

corrugated-iron roof that made a terrific racket whenever it rained . . .
oil lamps provided dim illumination . . . The outdoor privy, freezing
in winter and none too comfortable at other times, was at the end of
the garden.' When Orwell falls ill Eileen 'got stuck with the most
disgusting jobs, including cleaning out the whole privy when the
cesspool backed up'. A friend found the conditions 'hazardous . . .
The sink would be blocked. The primus stove wouldn't work. The
lavatory plug wouldn't pull. The stairs were very dark . . . and they'd
put piles of books on the staircases at odd places, so there were lots
of traps, and the place was rather dusty.' Eileen herself describes,
hilariously, 'battalions of mice, shoulder to shoulder on the shelves,
pushing the china off'.

Eileen has been a financially independent woman for many years.
Now that she is working for free, she is coming to understand what it
means to be 'completely broke'. Certainly there is vastly more physical
labour for her than she has ever done before – in the house and garden
and shop – as Lydia predicted. And, even if she doesn't admit it to
herself, she's probably intuiting that she'll have to give up any idea of a
career of her own. She is starting to live the blank she'd drawn on her
marriage certificate.

In her first letter to Norah, written at Orwell's parents' in Southwold, Eileen is amusing about Orwell's neediness and manipulation,
but there it is, on the page. How else is he going to get so much
work done? Which continues apace. Three days after the wedding
Orwell submits the essay 'Shooting an Elephant', and in the next
six months he writes *The Road to Wigan Pier*, twelve reviews of
thirty-two books, and two articles: 'Bookshop Memories' and
the lengthy 'In Defence of the Novel'. While he writes Eileen
deals with the 'dreadful' resident Aunt (there for *two months!*), the
flood, the cesspit, the shop, the house, the garden, his illnesses, the
chickens, the goat and the visitors. She makes thwarted attempts to
take a (working) break with her brother, who needs her help editing

his scientific papers. There hasn't been time to get her head around it all; there hasn't even been time to write a letter to her best friend.

Under the list of slapstick misfortunes she delivers up to Norah lies the dawning realisation that not only her career, but also her life, is going to come second to her husband's work. She tells Lydia, though, that she can rely on her brother. 'If we were at opposite ends of the world and I sent him a telegram saying "Come at once", he would come,' she says. 'George would not do that. For him his work comes before anybody.' Lydia is not reassured.

Eileen relates the facts of her newly-wed life to Norah as if by identifying them she might withstand them. But it is not true, much as we might wish it to be, that named dragons are tamed dragons. They are still out there – or upstairs, wanting their dinner.

Confessions of a Gendered Soul

I feel the need to say – though of course I shouldn't have to – that I am not writing this from a position of high domestic standards. Once, when we were away on holiday, my brother and his wife had to drop something into our house. 'Oh my god,' my sister-in-law said, 'they've been ransacked.' 'No,' my brother sighed, 'this is how they live.'

Nor am I the world's most assiduous mother. This is a wish list of things my bored ten-year-old once wrote on my office whiteboard, while she waited for me to stop working. It includes the predictable 'camp', 'clothes' and '$$$' but, close to the top: 'medical attention'. I have kept it there, to remind me of things I might not see.

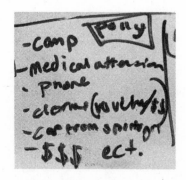

I write this as a confession, as if the house were mine to keep tidy. My house might look like I have killed Virginia Woolf's Angel in it, but she lurks here somewhere still, making it my job to straighten cushions and hide random kid-debris before people come over. For Woolf, who lived far from the work of maids or of mothers, it was a different Angel she had to kill, the one who 'must charm ... must conciliate, ... must – to put it bluntly – tell lies if [she is] to succeed'. This model of Angel-in-the-house womanhood makes it impossible for a woman to express 'what you think to be the truth about human relations, morality, sex'. 'Had I not killed her,' Woolf writes, 'she would have killed me. She would have plucked the heart out of my writing.'

But you can't kill an angel who is also a mother because our job is, somehow, to interpret the madness and injustice of the world to our children in a way that does not make them despair. We 'conciliate', we make sense, we console when sense can't be made. To what extent this involves lies that harm both us and them, I don't know. This book is a risk: to show you the injustice of the world might harrow and harm you.

Or, it might arm you against it.

Mint Humbugs

Back in class Lydia longs for Eileen. She goes to Wallington to stay for a weekend.

Lydia has made peace with none of it. 'I came in a mood still barely resigned to the fact of her marriage, vaguely antagonistic to her husband and ready to be critical of his attitude to his wife.' What she finds at the cottage appears to be some kind of masochistic rustic fantasy in full swing, an experiment in living on the breadline and suffering for someone else's art.

The cottage is cold. There's a fireplace in the living room but it 'smoked dreadfully whenever a fire was lit' so the choice, apparently, is between freezing or being cured like meat. One time Orwell opens the door to visitors with a completely blackened face, blue eyes staring out of it, as if this were a normal consequence of trying to heat a house. There's one paraffin lamp, otherwise just candles. They are camping, with walls and a tin roof.

Lydia remembers being too cold to sleep properly. And then, 'you were startled into wakefulness in the early morning by Eric Blair's incredibly loud alarm clock. The sound reached you through two closed doors and a room between. It was to rouse Eric in time to give the hens their feed.'

When Lydia protests – about the hour, the loudness – it 'only brought forth a humorous crease at the corners of Eric Blair's eyes and a reply: "Hens want their food at the same time every morning. They don't know it's Sunday."' He knows Lydia isn't telling him not to feed his hens. She's asking him not to wake her doing it. He then dares her, with that look in his eyes, to assert her needs. She doesn't, or can't.

But what she can do is report, later, on his pleasure in making others uneasy. 'The space between the corrugated iron roof and the ceiling of the guest-room was full of stirrings and sounds, especially at dusk and at dawn. "People think they're rats," Eric Blair remarked with a smile of satisfaction, anticipating a reaction of horror from me, but I did not oblige. "In fact," he said smiling, "they're birds nesting or just roosting in there."'

Eileen, unafraid of dirt or mice, might have found such a remark a reflection of Orwell's rat phobia, or a humorous dig, but Lydia can't see it that way. She wants to protect her friend from her husband's seedy pleasure in discomfort, and his pleasure in discomforting others. She recognises something like sadism under the thin moustache and the 'smile of satisfaction', and she sees what Eileen doesn't yet: the masochism it will demand of her to survive it. Orwell is taunting Lydia. 'See how much she loves me?' is the subtext here. 'I can make her live anywhere, in any conditions I choose. Nothing you can do about it.' Lydia's fuse is lit. Unless she can somehow make Eileen see what she sees, and quickly, she will never come between them: they will fit together like lock and key, shutting her out. 'In this partnership,' she writes, 'Orwell's needs always came first.'

However, 'That did not mean that she was a dumb, adoring wife, subservient to and uncritical of her husband. Quite the contrary . . .' Lydia remembers an exchange at the cottage when Orwell offers a provocative conversational sally, and Eileen edits him, in real time:

> . . . she was a clear logical thinker who immediately pounced on any 'nonsequitur' of his during a discussion. One particular instance remains in my memory. We were having eggs and

bacon for breakfast when George remarked that every villager ought to have his own pig and cure his own bacon. 'But,' he added, 'they are not allowed to keep pigs unless they satisfy a set of complex sanitary regulations. Bacon manufacturers had seen to this . . .'

Eileen gave me a quick glance and a smile. 'Now what made you say this?' she exclaimed. 'Isn't it rather a sweeping statement to make?' The look on George's face showed that he was both amused and a little embarrassed but he stuck to his guns.

'It is in the interests of bacon manufacturers . . .' he began.

'Yes, I know, but have you any evidence to show that they were responsible for the sanitary regulations?' He had not, and she added: 'That's the kind of statement an irresponsible journalist would make . . .' George had enough sense of humour not to mind this kind of challenge, and Eileen often challenged him in these ways.

'I am certain,' Lydia continues, 'that her logic, her feeling for accuracy in the use of words influenced him, perhaps without his being aware of it, in improving his style of writing, which in earlier years had a certain crudity and calculated exaggeration, detracting from its power to carry conviction.' Or perhaps he *was* aware of it, and knew Eileen would make his work better.

Richard Rees, too, noted 'an enormous change' that took place in Orwell's work in 1936. But he couldn't put cause and effect together to explain why his writing before marriage 'did not have the grace and charm and humor that were to adorn so much of his later work'. 'There was such an extraordinary change in both his writing and his attitude,' Rees said. 'It was almost as if there'd been a kind of fire smouldering in him all his life which suddenly burst into flame at that time. But I can't understand it or explain exactly what happened; I just don't know.' Some of the biographers see it more clearly, writing that 'it is not just coincidence' that 'the major phase of Orwell's career . . . should coincide with the beginning of his marriage . . . There is an uncramped expression of feeling, a generosity and humaneness, an acknowledgement of the complexity of seemingly simple experience that had been absent from his earlier writing and that would be present in his work thereafter, which can be attributed at least in part to the influence of Eileen . . .'

Lydia stays all weekend. 'My impression was,' she writes, 'that he was taking her too much for granted. Any man, I thought, ought to treasure such a wife – most attractive to look at, highly intelligent, an amusing and witty talker, an excellent cook. Yet I did not detect any fond glances or small gestures of attention from him to her. Eileen did all the work, prepared the meals and served them and answered the shop bell when it rang. After lunch Orwell withdrew upstairs and we heard him using his typewriter. I helped Eileen to wash up; then we went for a walk.'

Eileen talks about writing a children's book with a cast of hens in leading roles, but then laughs about having barely twenty-five minutes between clearing up one meal and starting preparations for the next. And she's still telling Lydia she's going to finish her thesis, though there are hardly any children in the village and the nearest school is three miles away. 'Eileen might have been able to cycle there, but her domestic duties and "minding the shop" hardly left her enough time for anything else.' And she's thin and pale. At some point Eileen began to suffer what seems to have been endometriosis; later she was anaemic. Already, Lydia thinks she was not 'strong enough . . . for bicycle rides of any length'.

But Eileen works out a way to lure the children to her, whether as experimental subjects or as company, or both. 'They soon discovered that "the lady" at the shop sold them four sweets for a half penny while they got seven for a penny elsewhere.' So they do the maths and pop in and out for liquorice allsorts and mint humbugs. One of them, a shy ten-year-old called Peter, is considered 'backward', but Eileen tests him and finds he has a high IQ. 'She then volunteered to coach him in reading and arithmetic for several months, which resulted in his winning the coveted scholarship.' As Eileen had done before, with the Russian émigré and with the 'oil rag' Edna, she found someone whose life she could change. 'Her success,' Lydia reported, 'gave her much pleasure: she was as proud of Peter as if he were her own son.'

For Lydia this is not nearly enough use of her friend's 'doubtless considerable, psychological gifts'. But perhaps Eileen has already understood something Lydia doesn't, which is that her next and most ambitious project is upstairs, working. Eileen has been reading and typing *The Road to Wigan Pier*. At first, Orwell is wary of her suggestions, so she doesn't give many.

Eileen begins keeping Lydia at a distance. She writes to Norah to arrange a time to meet in London. *I want passionately to see you*, she says. She is trying to time her trip so as to avoid Lydia *descend[ing] on me in wrath*. The trip never eventuates.

Too Much Sex

He was as secretive about his private life as any man I ever knew.
Fredric Warburg, Orwell's publisher

At the time Orwell met Eileen, his first biographers, Stansky and
Abrahams, write, '[h]is experience of women thus far in his life –
he had celebrated his thirty-first birthday in June – seems to have
been meagre and belated . . .' After his marriage, they add, 'at least
he had a well-regulated sex life'. Thirty years later, in 2003, another
biographer writes: 'The couple's physical intimacy was evident and
they seemed happy enough in their rural idyll. Eileen certainly
seemed to enjoy helping George with the shop and the animals, and
even helped clean out the foul garden latrine. But,' he continues,
'the idyllic picture taken away by his friends concealed a problem
that had arisen between the couple.' Eileen told Mabel, George's
older, married friend, that she thought George had had 'too much
sex' before marriage. The biographer glosses this by writing that
Eileen 'complained' to Mabel, as if she were 'hinting perhaps at a
less than delicate performance in bed'. Another puts the opposite
interpretation on it: 'She presumably meant that after a time he'd
become jaded and unresponsive.' None of them mentions another
reason Eileen might have had for discussing her sex life with Mabel,
which was that Mabel had been sleeping with Orwell for years.

The idea of women conferring about sexual issues appears to be unthinkable for the biographers. So they don't think it. Instead, they say things like his prior sexual experience was 'meagre', when the evidence from his wife, who would know better, is that it was 'too much'—whatever that means.

For a long time I was queasy about delving into their intimate life. It felt like an invasion of privacy of a kind he'd have hated – anyone would. But the more that in looking for her I felt I was invading his privacy, the more I realised that not to go there would be to accept, when weighing up the right to privacy against the right to decent treatment, that male animals are more equal than others.

And in his work, if not his life, Orwell is on my side. He delved into the living conditions of the colonial oppressed in Burma, of northern English miners, of British tramps and French dishwashers. His desire to expose hidden people from under society's hypocrisies that keep us blind to them is so admirable, and so exciting. The project of good writing (to reveal to us the world we thought we knew) is perfectly combined with a political project (to reveal the world we thought we knew so we can change it).

Orwell's friend the writer and satirist Malcolm Muggeridge felt that 'there was in him this passionate dedication to truth, and refusal to countenance enlightened expediency masquerading as it; this unrelenting abhorrence of virtuous attitudes unrelated to personal conduct'. But in patriarchy, bizarrely, 'personal conduct' does not mean behaviour towards women, or at home. If the conventions of patriarchy weren't so totalitarian – by which I mean so total, allowing of no other reality – Muggeridge might have thought to consider his friend's conduct in the private sphere. And if those conventions hadn't been so beneficial to Orwell, he might eventually have gone 'down and in' to investigate the living conditions of women and wives, even his own.

After all, this 'private' world of women was deeply familiar to him. Orwell was raised in a household of politically engaged women – one biographer calls Ida 'almost a *femme libre*' – and was especially close to his sexually liberated political activist Aunt Nellie. In another notebook passage written in the last year of his life he remembered:

> The conversations he overheard as a small boy, between his Mother, his aunt, his elder sister and their feminist friends. The way in which . . . he derived a firm impression that women *did not like* men, that they looked upon them as a sort of large, ugly, smelly and ridiculous animal, who maltreated women in every way, above all by forcing their attentions upon them. It was pressed deep into his consciousness, to remain there until he was about 20, that sexual intercourse gives pleasure only to the man, not to the woman. He knew that sexual intercourse has something to do with the man getting on top of the woman, and the picture of it in his mind was of a man pursuing a woman, forcing her down and jumping on top of her, as he had often seen a cock do to a hen. All this was derived, not from any remark having direct sexual reference . . . but from such overheard remarks as "It just shows what beasts men are." "My dear, I think she's behaving like a perfect fool, the way she gives in to him." "Of course, she's far too good for him." And the like. . . . It was not till he was about 30 that it struck him that he had in fact been his mother's favourite child.

In adulthood, the family conversations about relations between men and women came to include him. In the only surviving letter from Nellie to him, from 1933, she enclosed money, a subscription to a magazine, and the news that she is reading Machiavelli and *Les Dogmes Sexuels*, 'a refutation,' she tells him, 'of the generally accepted ideas on sex as regards the contrast between the male and female and

[it] is based on biology'. Seventeen years before Beauvoir's *The Second Sex*, Adrienne Sahuqué's work outlines how there is no basis in science for the social inferiority of women in patriarchy, which nevertheless remains 'so permanent and universal an error'. Looking for the reasons, she examines 'sexual dogmas', or ideologies, which are 'a rationalisation of masculine supremacy, secured through war and the rape of women slaves'. There's no knowing whether Orwell ever read it, but it's clear that the family interest in politics included sexual politics. And it's also clear that he's known all his life that women can feel, as he put it, 'maltreated in every way', and, since he was a young man, that they expect pleasure in sex. But, in the life he is embarking on, he will ignore the first, so he can benefit from his wife's work, and the second too, perhaps because he has no choice.

Though Orwell might not be feeling sexual desire in these newly-wed days at the cottage, at some level he's thinking about it. Just after his wedding Orwell reviews his friend Cyril Connolly's novel, trashing it for its glorification of 'sodomy', pleading, 'The fact to which we have got to cling, as if to a life-belt, is that it *is* possible to be a normal decent person and yet to be fully alive.' Orwell wants to be 'normal' and 'decent', by which he seems to mean heterosexual, but that may not be, for him, 'fully alive'. It's a harrowing cry.

No biographer deals plainly with the possibility of Orwell's homosexuality. 'Misogynistic he was not,' write Stansky and Abrahams. 'He was a late starter, but from the time of his return from Burma women would always be necessary to him.'

When I first read that sentence, I found it funny. Then I went looking for the joke. I set off on a mental journey back in time, trying to reach the point when respected biographers, their editor, publisher and reading public could swallow a sentence which effectively erases any charge of misogyny with a screw. I nearly made it, but not quite. Unless misogyny was code for homosexuality, the sentence has to mean that as long as you're having sex with women, you must like and respect them. Which is not what the biographers are trying to say.

The more I thought about this strange sentence, the more women being 'necessary to him' sounded like a plea for his heterosexuality. Numerous friends of Orwell thought his virulent homophobia odd. His friend the poet and critic William Empson remarked on his 'deep internal revulsions' and connected them with 'his firmly expressed distaste for homosexuality'. It's a revulsion Empson doesn't share. 'At that time,' he noted, 'or when we were both a bit younger, many young gentlemen who loved the Workers did it practically.' Empson thought 'Bodily disgust, or rather a fear that a good man may at any moment be driven into some evil action by an unbearable amount of it, is deeply embedded in his best writing . . .' Connolly, who'd been at school with Orwell, remembered that he considered himself too ugly for the 'call-boy arrangements prevalent at boarding schools', though he once slipped Connolly a note begging him to leave a boy he loved to him. In the all-male share house he moved to before he was married, Orwell famously bashed his drunken flatmate Rayner Heppenstall with a shooting stick, causing Mabel, who had helped set up the household, to console the injured man, telling him, 'I think it's disappointed homosexuality.' The other flatmate, Michael Sayers, was ten years younger. Each morning Orwell used to bring him tea in bed. The older man's feelings towards him were, Sayers felt, 'very close, very tender, even homoerotic'. Sayers had the 'overwhelming impression' that Orwell was aware of 'something inside himself that was repellent and dangerous to him'. Jack Common, a writer also living at Wallington and a close observer of Orwell's married life, thought his marriage to Eileen 'was not a true one', and 'that it seemed somehow wrong for them to be together'.

At the end of his life Orwell raised a doubt about his homophobia himself, again in his last literary notebook and again in the third person: 'Like all men addicted to whoring,' he wrote, 'he professed to be revolted by homosexuality.' And as for whoring, he described the falseness of its pleasures by comparing them to a man in a gallery 'telling himself' he was enjoying the art. Orwell was trapped in a homophobic world that may have separated him from his truth. His sexual experience was not 'meagre'. It was not 'belated'. And it may not have been what he really wanted.

In an age in which homosexuality was horrendously vilified and illegal, but also common – in schools and kips and high society – Orwell might have experienced this split at a level so deep it was

Orwell in the churchyard at Wallington,
possibly on his wedding day.

hidden even from himself. Perhaps it gave him access to the space between what was desired and what was possible, what was true and what could be said. Perhaps this split led him to see the world in its doublethink contradictions, and to speak them.

I can sense in his 'neurotic' struggle, as he described it, the gargantuan effort he put into mining his own seam of brilliance, while animating forces inside him remained, as they do for so many of us, unexamined.

There is no knowing how much of any of this Eileen knows, or wants to know, in these early days of marriage. Mabel might, or might not, have told her that she thought 'he went to bed with women as if to prove his masculinity and virility'. Perhaps she wonders, speaking to Mabel, how many of the other women she meets are former lovers of his. Perhaps it's easier to think he's had 'too much sex', whatever that means, than that he doesn't want to have it with you.

Mistletoe

Lydia hears the news when they are all at dinner at Laurence and Gwen's. Orwell is going off to fight in the war in Spain.

'My first reaction was one of dismay,' she writes, 'then of anger – at Eric Blair', for leaving his new wife.

It gets worse. When it comes time to leave, Orwell approaches Lydia to say goodbye. Giving her a 'wry smile', he says, 'Shan't be kissing *you* under the mistletoe this Christmas . . .' Lydia bristles. Kissing her is a pleasure he's been thinking about, apparently, but will have to forgo, for now. 'I must have given him an unfriendly look,' she writes, 'for I felt he was behaving meanly to Eileen, and I did not like his joke about the mistletoe.'

Laurence walks Lydia to the station. She 'pours out' her indignation about Orwell's treatment of his sister, 'going off to Spain so soon after Eileen and he had settled down in the country'. She doesn't mention anything about him flirting with her. She wonders aloud 'how Eileen was going to support herself: she had told me that their income from the shop amounted to half-a-crown a week!'* Laurence is calm, as ever, remarking only that Orwell has 'a warrior's cast of mind'. Possibly, the bond between the siblings is so strong he

---

* About £25 at the time of writing.

thinks he will be enough support for Eileen, even if she has to live remotely and alone. Perhaps Eileen thinks so too.

Eileen makes the arrangements for Orwell to leave, kitting him out with boots, a torch, long johns, tobacco, writing materials, a penknife. And she arranges the funding for his trip, taking the Blair family silver they'd been given as a wedding present to hock at the pawnbroker's. 'We panicked at the last moment that he hadn't enough money with him,' she told a friend, 'so we pawned all the Blair spoons and forks.' After he leaves she manages the final edits of *The Road to Wigan Pier* and sends it to the publisher.

In fact, as Lydia knows, Eileen would have 'dearly liked to go to Spain with him, but this could not be arranged at the time'. Eileen must stay to look after the shop, the animals, the vegetable garden, his publication schedule, proofs and all correspondence. A wife gives a man a double life: one to go off in, and another to come back to.

He leaves shortly after their visit to his parents at Southwold. She goes back to Wallington.

Alone at the cottage it seems even colder. Perhaps, she thinks, one less human body lowers the temperature? The pipes have frozen. Old dishes are immured in the sink, like bones in a glacier.

After feeding the hens, planting the potato crop and dashing up and down to answer the shop bell, she sits in the evenings mostly unwashed, freezing and smoking, living on eggs and black tea. Depending on what happens in Spain, this may be a very short marriage.

Tonight the fire is smoking quite a lot. She is ignoring it, reading by the light of the paraffin lamp. Though also ruminating. Chewing the cud with her mind. She is trying not to behave like an animal, but of course she is one; some are just more so.

She gets up and holds a piece of newspaper in front of the fireplace to try to get the smoke to draw upwards, instead of into the room. She'd asked the vicar to take 'obey' out of the marriage vows because it's a ridiculous thing to say, a relic from when the slavery of the arrangement had been explicit. The vicar, pale lashes behind his wire-rimmed glasses, didn't blink; he'd known her for her whole life. George was startled, but then quickly said he'd no objection. He's not a Neanderthal. Yet here she is, obediently corralled with the other domesticated animals, without anything having needed to be said.

There is a way of feeling alone that is not about being alone. But these are not things to write to Norah.

The chickens are asleep. Outside, the dark has seeped into everything and silenced it.

II

INVISIBLE
WARRIOR

A Plague of Initials

Orwell is excited to be going to war. He wants to 'kill fascists', to fight for 'common decency' and to write about it.

Homage to Catalonia is Orwell's account of his time in battle – and then fleeing for his life – in Spain. Orwell bares all: he'll tell you he's scared, that his Spanish is 'villainous', that he's a terrible shot, and that legions of lice are breeding down his inseam and crawling over his testicles. His vulnerability and honesty cleave you to him. I've loved this book since I was a teen.

As soon as he arrives at the Lenin Barracks in Barcelona Orwell experiences a moment of intense attraction to a young Italian, 'a tough-looking youth of twenty-five or six, with reddish-yellow hair and powerful shoulders . . . Something in his face deeply moved me. It was the face of a man who would commit murder and throw away his life for a friend . . . I hardly know why, but I have seldom seen anyone – any man, I mean – to whom I have taken such an immediate liking . . .' Orwell greets him gamely 'in my bad Spanish'. Then the man 'stepped across the room and gripped my hand very hard. Queer, the affection you can feel for a stranger! It was as though his spirit and mine had momentarily succeeded in bridging the gulf of language and tradition and meeting in utter intimacy.' Sex and death are close in war, closer than Orwell will let himself think. He's going 'down and out' again, into another, all-male world, where intimacy is with men and sex means prostitutes.

As lovely and lucid as his prose is, Orwell's poems are leaden – as his friend, the poet Ruth Pitter put it, 'like a cow with a musket'. But he used them when prose would have been too direct, as here:

> The Italian soldier shook my hand
> Beside the guard-room table;
> The strong hand and the subtle hand
> Whose palms are only able
> To meet within the sound of guns,
> But oh! What peace I knew then
> In gazing on his battered face
> Purer than any woman's!

He's newly married. But here among men is where he wants to be.

The revolution in Spain happened just six months ago. Orwell writes that he finds it 'startling and overwhelming' to be here, 'where the working class was in the saddle'. Land has been given to smallholders and industry collectivised – even the bootblacks and the prostitutes. He is especially struck by the scrapping of the class system. 'Waiters and shop-walkers looked you in the face and treated you as an equal . . . Nobody said "Señor" or "Don" or even "Usted"; everyone called everyone else "Comrade" and "Thou". The revolutionaries quickly outlawed tipping, the capitalist custom by which the undertaxed get to feel generous at whim in a world of the underpaid. It was all 'queer and moving. There was much in it that I did not understand, in some ways I did not even like it, but I recognized it immediately as a state of affairs worth fighting for. Also I believed that things were as they appeared . . .'

In 1936 it looks as though Europe is falling to fascism, under strong-men dictators. Hitler is in power in Germany, Mussolini in Italy, and in July a right-wing Catholic commander, General Franco, had tried to seize control over Spain. In Catalonia a motley group of unions and their barely armed militias had succeeded, miraculously, in overthrowing the feudal-clerical despotism that had held power there for centuries.

Now, the revolutionaries are fighting Franco's forces, to retain their new socialist order. They don't want capitalist democracy – which the local Anarchists consider 'no more than a centralized swindling machine'. They want something fairer. But while Hitler and Mussolini send men and munitions, gunboats and planes to Franco, the Republican resistance is virtually unarmed and alone. Only Mexico (in a minor way) and Russia (in a disastrous one) give any assistance. So, droves of idealistic individuals have come to help Spain resist fascism. Writers are arriving too, some to report, and others, like Orwell, to fight.

Orwell thinks he's here to defend 'civilization against a maniacal outbreak by an army of Colonel Blimps in the pay of Hitler'. He doesn't care under whose banner he fights. As for 'the kaleidoscope of political parties and trade unions, with their tiresome names – P.S.U.C., P.O.U.M., F.A.I., C.N.T., U.G.T., J.C.I., J.S.U., A.I.T.,' he writes, 'it looked like Spain were suffering from a plague of initials'. The initials he chooses are ILP, for the Independent Labour Party, which he knows through Aunt Nellie's connections.

The ILP was the sister party of the Spanish POUM, the Partido Obrero de Unificación Marxista, or Workers' Party of Marxist Unification. Stalin despised the POUM because he considered it to be allied with his nemesis, Trotsky. Nearly twenty years earlier Trotsky had been one of the leaders of the Russian Revolution, but he had independent ideas about it, ideas which Stalin wanted to eradicate, by eradicating him. By the time Orwell gets to Spain Trotsky has fled for his life to Mexico City and Stalin has begun his 'purges' at home – the summary executions, mass killings, rigged show trials, arbitrary imprisonment and exiling to Siberia of political opponents, intellectuals, entrepreneurial peasants and ethnic minorities.

Now, Stalin is setting his sights on 'Trotskyists' abroad. Just as Orwell arrives and joins the POUM, Stalin declares his intention to liquidate it. 'In Catalonia the elimination of Trotskyites and Anarcho-Syndicalists has begun,' the dictator announces. 'It will be carried out with the same energy as it was carried out in the Soviet Union.' That is, in a murderous frenzy. Orwell has stepped into the most vicious fight in Europe. It's not the one he thinks – between the Republicans and the fascists. It's between the supposed anti-fascist allies: the independent Spanish POUM and Stalin's communists.

It was this insidious battle that would most mark him. *Animal Farm* is a parable of Stalin's betrayal of the Russian Revolution and his persecution of Trotsky. *Nineteen Eighty-Four* is steeped in Orwell's

Lenin Barracks, Barcelona, 1936. Orwell can be seen at
the rear, fully a head taller than the others, 'mostly boys
of sixteen or seventeen from the back streets'.

experience of Stalinism and surveillance in Catalonia. It was here that he came to understand that surveillance and betrayal are *the* methods of terror, and terror is the basis of totalitarian regimes. It bit deep. For the rest of his life and even in the remotest of places, he remained petrified that an undercover communist would hunt him down and kill him.

After training for just a couple of weeks the order comes for the men to leave for the front in the Sierra de Alcubierre. The ragged, barely armed men and boys march in a torchlight procession past ecstatic crowds to the station.

That same day in Moscow Stalin commands his people in Spain to 'launch a campaign among the masses and in the press against Trotsky and Trotskyists as terrorists and saboteurs . . . spies liaising with the German Gestapo'. Orwell can't know it, but as he boards the train for the trenches he's being accused of collaborating with the enemy he's off to kill.

When they get to the mountains the men climb on foot into the hills of Aragon. They walk behind their leader, a fat man on a horse. This is Georges Kopp, Orwell's 'stout Belgian *commandante*'. From the rear Kopp is triangular in the saddle, his beret at a jaunty angle, a cigar clamped permanently between his fingers. Kopp is blond and dimple-chinned, decisive, optimistic and immensely brave. He's also a man with a fabulist's charm and a fictionalised view of his personal history. Born in Russia (which for some reason he covered up, along with much else), he'd lived mostly in Belgium, where he hadn't let incomplete training as an engineer stop him from working as one. When the war broke out he'd left his ex-wife with their five children and come to Spain. Kopp is a bon vivant, a lover of food and women, a man without acid or irony, unembarrassed to express his feelings –

the polar opposite of the thin, funny, truth-loving, self-punishing Englishman. But in the battles to come each would be prepared to throw his life away – for the cause, and for the other.

As they approach the battlefront Orwell hears bombs and machine guns and confides, 'In secret I was frightened.' But once they get into the dugouts the problem is boredom, not bullets. 'I was profoundly disgusted,' he writes. 'They called this war! And we were hardly even in touch with the enemy!' The men live in frozen caves hollowed into the side of a hill, looking over at the fascists frozen into their own hill – seven hundred metres away, practically out of range. Orwell is so bored he starts popping his head up above the level of the trench. Soon enough, 'a bullet shot past my ear with a vicious crack and banged into the parados behind'. He disappoints himself. 'Alas! I ducked. All my life I had sworn that I would not duck the first time a bullet passed over me; but the movement appears to be instinctive, and almost everybody does it at least once.'

In three weeks he fires just three shots. 'They say it takes a thousand bullets to kill a man,' Orwell laments, 'at this rate it would be twenty years before I killed my first fascist.' Kopp strides through the dugouts flapping his arms, binoculars banging around his neck. 'This is not a war!' he cries. 'It is a comic opera with an occasional death.'

Orwell fills the time writing, leaning against the mud wall. He takes down details of men, food, cold. He terrifies the others by crawling out into no man's land foraging for firewood or potatoes, risking enemy fire. The water, carried up on muleback, is so disgusting he resorts to shaving in wine. They live with the smell of their waste – rotting food, unwashed human bodies. There is a ravine latrine behind them but sometimes men defecate in the trench, 'a disgusting thing when one had to walk round it in the darkness'.

Most horrific of all, the whole scene is a rodent party. Orwell hates rats. In the trenches they nibble the leather in your cartridge

Georges Kopp, Catalonia, 1937.

belt, the kitbag you are using as a pillow. Once, he wakes to find a fat rat gnawing at the boot – on his foot. He grabs his pistol and aims – at foot and rat – missing both. A friend in the muddy cave with him remembered the noise vibrating all over the front. '[T]he fascists thought this is the attack,' Bob Edwards recalled. 'Shells came over, bombing planes came at us. They blew up our canteen and blew up our buses and everything.' The destruction Orwell has brought down on them is beyond even his capacious self-deprecation and this episode doesn't make it into *Homage*. Perhaps he doesn't even tell Eileen about it. As Edwards said, 'It was a very costly shot at a rat, that was.'

In mid-February the men are moved to positions outside the fascist-held town of Huesca. Here, the battle is raging close.

Sierra de Alcubierre. Reconstructed trenches at Orwell's first posting, looking across to the fascist position outside Huesca.

'It was the first time that I had been properly speaking under fire,' Orwell writes, 'and to my humiliation I found that I was horribly frightened . . . You are wondering all the while just where the bullet will nip you, and it gives your whole body a most unpleasant sensitiveness.' Still, he keeps sticking his head up. 'Get your head down!' the others cry, but he won't.

Miracle, Manicure

It's mid-February. The world is a palette of grey and the cold is in her bones.

She sits on the bench near the back door to pull on her wellingtons before walking the goat. They used to put a leash on her and take her through the village together each afternoon. George doesn't give a damn what the villagers say. She knows it's eccentric, but she has kept doing it. Poor Nellie lives her life tethered in a small orbit so as not to devour the vegetable crop. It seems only fair to keep taking her out.

She pats the pockets of her coat: cigarettes, matches, handkerchief, coins, sweets for any children she might meet. Though she can see with her rational mind how she got here, it still doesn't add up. She puts her hands on her thighs, breathes deeply.

He's been gone for weeks. She did not sign up for goat-walking, alone.

She wants to go to Spain, but for them to have a home to come back to she'd have to replace herself here. Though who would possibly live like this and do all this work, for free?

The goat's lead isn't on the hook. She looks under the bench where it must have fallen – in the corner there's a mass of red wool. She pulls it out gingerly – it could be full of baby mice. It isn't – it's a frayed old knitted hat, the Aunt's. She takes it with her to the shed and pulls it over the animal's head, draws her caramel ears gently through the holes. With any luck a behatted goat might lure the children out. Nellie is probably happier than the woman she's named after. Poor Aunt. Her common-law husband, the Esperantist and socialist 'L'Anti', has abandoned her and disappeared to Mexico. She's back in the UK now, tail between her legs.

As she closes the gate – of course! Aunt Nellie is the perfect person, the only person.

When she gets back she writes to her. The heedless enthusiast who'd crashed their newly-wed existence, ageing actress, socialist, salonnière. Maybe now she can add 'tenant farmer' to her qualities.

It worked! She's in London! On her way to Spain! At Laurence's desk now, on the first floor overlooking Greenwich Park. She dips the nib of her fountain pen into the ink bottle, fiddles the lever to suck it up. She can't believe she's leaving tomorrow.

Aunt Nellie, poor woman, had written straight back. Then she'd turned up, broken-hearted but game, happy enough to be instructed on how to manage the shop, look after chickens, hoe and sow potatoes and spinach, and milk the goat. She didn't tell Nellie the goat's name. The goat doesn't answer to it anyway.

A rustle-and-scrape sound of metal; she stands up to look. The warden, a scarf pulled over his nose, is closing the park gate. Street lamps are lit, a bright, extravagant arc of them.

She sits back down. To come here is to resurface into light and civilisation: a heated house, a cook and maid. All the benefits of money and class they are fighting to eradicate in Spain. Lydia says if you don't *pay* for a servant, you *are* the servant. Lydia says that the revolution in Russia liberated workers from bosses, but not women from men. She takes a sheet of paper from the drawer. Perhaps these things will sort themselves out in *this* revolution. Or not. Still, the amount of time she has here is *unbelievable*.

No idea what the date is. Somewhere in the middle of February, so she'll put the 16th.

Dear Norah.

She rolls back her sleeves and stretches her arms. How to begin? Her hair is newly washed and keeps falling onto her face, stray lazy curls. She puts it behind her ears. It strikes her as a small miracle, what she's about to describe. Of her own making. She's more excited than she can ever remember being.

When Ida and Avril came to the cottage to say their goodbyes, and to see Nellie installed there, it was a close call. She served them all tea – but not with the family silver. They asked where it was. She had to think of something on the spur of the moment, so she drew breath, looked from one to the other and said, 'It seemed a good opportunity, George being away, to have the family crest engraved on it.'

She smiles to herself now at the neat wickedness of her story. It's a private joke, a tale crafted using real people as characters and finding small, secret narrative comeuppances. After she got home with the cash from the pawnbroker she'd remarked to George how ironic it was to be funding his foray into socialism with the remnants of a vanished fortune made in slaves. But even more delicious, it seems to her now, was her cover story to fob off the class-conscious relatives: a fiction about the etching of lost privilege into precious metal.

She lights a cigarette. It was another narrow escape when the boy Peter came to the gate with a bucket of 'scraps for Nellie' as they were leaving. She hopes the Aunt didn't hear. She won't tell any of this to Norah, who is nicer than she is and sometimes troubled by acerbity. Really, though, the silver was George's only way out, and the story was hers.

She takes up the pen again.

A note to say that I am leaving for Spain at 9 am tomorrow (or I think so, but with inconceivable grandeur people ring up from Paris about it, and I may not go until Thursday).

The inconceivable grandeur, she suspects, conceals disorganisation. She has managed to get herself employed – though without any pay *of course* as *a kind of secretary perhaps* to the ILP, *which in Barcelona consists of one John McNair who has certainly been kind at long distances but has an unfortunate telephone voice and a quite calamitous prose style in which he writes articles that I perhaps shall type.* No matter, she tells Norah, *If Franco had engaged me as a manicurist* she'd have done that fascist's fingernails to get herself to Spain.

Then she remembers – her last letter said nothing about George going to Spain. It had seemed too much.

By the way, she adds, *I suppose I told you that George was in the Spanish Militia? I can't remember. Anyway he is, with my full approval until he was well in. He's on the Aragon front, where I cannot help knowing that the Government ought to be attacking or hoping that that is a sufficient safeguard against their doing so.* She wonders if her conviction that reality generally outstrips what can be imagined will protect him there: if she predicts it, it won't come to pass.

The gong sounds from downstairs. Dinnertime already? There's more to say, there's always more to say.

Supposing that the Fascist air force goes on missing its objectives and the railway line to Barcelona is still working, you'll probably hear from there some day . . . I am staying at the Continental too to begin with . . . After getting George over there, there's hardly any money left, so Lord knows how long she'll be able to stay at the hotel. She might, she thinks, end up *doing what the Esperantists call sleeping on straw and as they are Esperantists they <u>mean</u> sleeping on straw.*

As she reaches over to adjust the green glass shade of the desk lamp she thinks of the poor Aunt, living now by candlelight. A jilted Esperantist milking her nephew's goat. What would the Esperantists call *that*? Still, she feels bad. The narrative justice of installing the overstaying thespian as hovel-and-goat-minder is not convincing enough, it would appear, for her conscience. She stretches her shoulders back, rubs her right wrist. But it's done now.

She asks Norah to write to her over there – does she sound nervous? She doesn't want to sound nervous. She asks her to write *because I think it likely that I may loathe Barcelona, though I'd like to see some of the excitements that won't happen.* She's uncertain how long she'll stay. *Unless George gets hurt I suppose he'll stay until the war* qua *war is over—and I will too unless I get evacuated by force or unless*

I have to come and look for some money . . . The dinner gong is going. Is it not touching to think that this may be the last dinner unrationed for
        Pig.

～

Anything can happen in a war, they both know it. Eileen plays it down – she's constitutionally incapable of placing herself at the centre of the action. Which is, as it turns out, exactly where she'll be.

Backwater

The gun battles turn out to be rare. Orwell is in a boring backwater of the war for over a month. But despite the cold and shit, the rats and lice, there are some comforts. The food is 'good enough'. So is the wine, and there are cigarettes. Oh, and 'By this time my wife was in Barcelona and used to send me tea, chocolate, and even cigars when such things were procurable.'

Yes, she's in Barcelona. That's where he's sending her all his observations in letters, notebooks, on the backs of mud-smeared envelopes. She is there, typing them into one long document that will be the basis for his book. And, apparently, spending the rest of her time finding little luxuries to send to him at the front.

I had read *Homage* twice and never registered that Eileen was in Spain. No one I have ever asked remembers her. How can you read a book and have no memory that a person was not in a place alone, but with their spouse? Perhaps, I thought, if all she did was live in a hotel, type his notes and send him supplies from time to time, that might be all the mention that's fair?

I went back to the biographers. One says that she went to Barcelona 'to take up a volunteer's post in John McNair's office' and stayed, thinking 'her husband's interests were best served by the supplies of tea, chocolate and, when procurable, cigars'. Another writes that 'she decided that she would go out to Spain too, not for political reasons (though her sympathies were entirely with the Republic) but simply because she wanted to be near him . . .' Not much to see there. Though I sympathise with the biographers, because Orwell seems to have written her out of the story himself. So, as was my habit by now, I scoured the footnotes and went back to the sources to find what – and who – had been left out.

Eventually, I pieced together Eileen's war. I saw where she had been and what she had done for the cause, the troops and for Orwell. It was clear that she had saved lives. When I read *Homage to Catalonia* again, it was with a sense of bewilderment that she was nowhere to be seen. This lucid, honest and self-deprecating book now felt like a half-truth.

That's when I went to Barcelona.

I arrived from London by train and caught a taxi to the hotel, winding the window down for the ride up the Ramblas. The air tasted different here – a tang of salt from the sea, the aroma of chickens roasting in window rotisseries. The sun was different too – more golden, less afraid.

I came to travel through Catalonia with two men in their seventies, the heirs of this story. Richard Blair, the son Eileen and Orwell adopted in 1944, and his friend from infancy Quentin Kopp, the son of Orwell's commander, Georges Kopp. As history – this story – would have it, these men grew up almost as cousins. Together they now lead the Orwell Society.

Quentin looks like his father. He's a cheery man with blue eyes and a wide smile – unflappable, ample, practical. He's as great an organiser of tour groups as, I imagine, his father was of troops. Richard is dark-eyed and elegant, wearing a pinkie ring and a white fedora with a black band. He's a retired employee from Massey Ferguson, a tractor company. At various places on the tour – on the roof of the Poliorama building, in the trenches, at the town of Huesca – Richard read the parts from *Homage to Catalonia* about the place where we stood and what his father, or Quentin's, had done there. It was moving to be in this company, to measure time – or its opposite, closeness to the past – on the bodies of these sons.

We were a dozen people with an interest in Orwell, or the war he fought. We stayed together in a hotel in the heart of Barcelona, and walked the streets in thick May sunshine. We travelled to the stubbly hills of the battlefront at Alcubierre, bent ourselves into the dark mud dugouts Orwell lived in. We went to small ragged towns where there were no children, fowls busy behind stone walls.

The war Orwell fought was lost; Spain spent almost forty years under a right-wing dictatorship, from which it only emerged on Generalissimo Franco's death in 1975. There have been generations of silence here.

At Huesca we visited a memorial, opened in 2016, honouring locals who had died trying to defend the town from the fascists.

Memorial to those shot in Huesca, between 1936 and 1945.

It was a small gap in the brick wall of the cemetery, on the outside of which many people had been shot. Inside the slit the names of 548 dead were inscribed, though in a way so as to be barely visible. Remembering the past is hard when the past is here.

Spies and Lies
Barcelona, 1937

⟳

In Barcelona she arrives by train at Sants Estació, catches a
taxi to the Hotel Continental. As the car moves along the
Ramblas she winds the window down, looks up through
the blur of bare plane trees to the high sky behind.

She places her suitcase and typewriter down in the
room, unslings the satchel from her shoulder and looks
around: bed, wardrobe, desk, radiator, bathroom with
hot and cold taps. There is a gilded mirror between the
windows to the street. For a moment she stands before
it – open-collared shirt, grey trousers, wild hair. Parts of
her are blurred by cloudy spots in the old glass. She opens
casement doors to the balcony, leans over the wrought-iron
balustrade. The whole Ramblas extends beneath her, a lane
of traffic on each side of a wide median strip, a news kiosk
festooned with newspapers, their headlines (¡Victory in
the East! ¡Nin announces free bread!) between exclamation
marks each way up. She needs to get to work.

She washes her face, grabs her satchel and goes
down the carpeted stairs, through the lobby and the
rotating door and onto the footpath. The office of the ILP
turns out to be only a hundred yards down the street in
another ornate Art Nouveau hotel, the Rivoli. She dashes

up four flights of stairs to the door with the International
Labour Party poster tacked on it. Behind it stands a
neat man at a desk – nearly fifty, large brown eyes, sleeve
garters, small hands.

'You must be Mrs Blair,' he says. 'Come, come lass,
welcome.'

So this is John McNair, her boss.

⌐⸺⸗

John McNair is a long-term bachelor who left school at thirteen to
be an errand boy, and has spent his life involved in socialist politics.
These past twenty years he's lived in Paris, working in the leather trade,
coaching boys' football teams and giving lectures on English poetry.
Now, he is the director of the ILP in Spain. He talks as if everything is
always, equally, urgent – football, food, paper, guns, money.

Money actually *is* urgent. As soon as she starts work Eileen
discovers that the entire ILP, including its leader, is broke. *Living is
very cheap here*, she writes to her brother, *but I spend a lot on the ILP
contingent as none of them have had any pay & they all need things. Also
I've lent John 500 ps because he ran out.* Eileen's job was described as a
French-English shorthand typist, but it turns out to be much more.

The first part of it is logistical. The ILP has thirty-one men at
the front. She organises all their letters, telegrams and parcels
between the trenches and home. She finds them clothes, money,
tobacco, treats (chocolate, margarine, cigars). And medicine: at one
point she convinces Gwen to load the family car full of medical
supplies obtained through her practice and drive it from London to
Barcelona. Gwen is practical and intrepid, but Eileen is nevertheless
relieved when a young volunteer, David Wickes, hitches a ride
and shares the driving. Being a 'secretary', Eileen discovers, means
running the supply, communications and banking operation for the
entire contingent.

The other part of her job is working with Charles Orr, an American, in the propaganda department of the ILP. Together they produce the party's English-language newspaper and its radio program, taking the truth from the front and turning it into the news. Orr is an urbane and cultured economist in his late twenties. Before the revolution he'd been working with the International Labour Organization in Geneva. He's just married Lois, a nineteen-year-old college graduate from Kentucky. Lois has the freshness of a teenager commenting on the folly of the world. When she meets Eileen she thinks her 'nice but very vaguish when she talks and . . . eternally smoking cigarettes'.

While Orwell is struggling to find a bullet to hit him, battling mainly boredom and vermin, Eileen is at the heart of the operation.

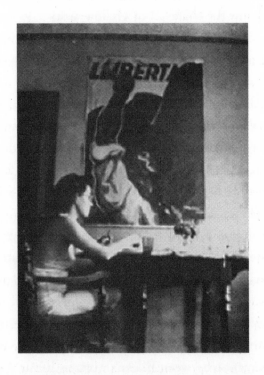

Lois Orr, in Barcelona.

She knows from all their despatches and the visits of Commander Kopp exactly what's happening – when the men come under fire, how few munitions they have, that they have only three greatcoats between them which they have to swap when they take turns at sentry duty. And she knows how this woeful situation is being spun into glorious propaganda about the advancement of the POUM-led anti-fascist effort, because she and Charles are writing it and she's typing it.

It's Charles Orr who leaves the closest portrait of Eileen's working life in Spain. Eileen, he says, was beautiful, outgoing and gregarious. 'Everyone liked her, women as well as men.' When Charles discovers she's an Oxford graduate trained in psychology he admires her for being 'not too proud to accept a job as a secretary-typist . . . The reader may think I over-idealize her, but working in the same office every day one comes to know the character of a fellow-worker. When I compare her with the refugees, reformers and revolutionaries who made up our office staff, and others in our political milieu, Eileen stands out as a superior person.'

Charles feels compelled to write about her because '[i]n *Homage to Catalonia* [Orwell] scarcely mentions his wife'. And it isn't only at the office that Eileen makes an impression. Another friend describes how, after settling in, Eileen becomes 'very much a figure in ILP quarters, holding what in other circumstances . . . would have been called "a salon" in the Hotel Continental'.

In war, as in spying, distinctions between personal and work life, between private and public, dissolve. At the point of death or betrayal they cease to exist. In a trench there is no private life, and dying is what you're paid for. In an office a spy befriends you for their work, enters your private life to play with it, betray you with it. Just as trench life is part of fighting, personal life is part of spying. As the war goes on, there is no distinction between Eileen's working life at the office, and her life a hundred yards up the street at the Hotel Continental.

The Continental is a hotbed of revolutionaries, idealists, spies and journalists from all nations. Some are working for the revolution and against fascism. Others are working for Stalin, to scuttle it. Some are reporting to newspapers around the world. Others to their handlers. Doors open and close along carpeted corridors buzzing with news, rumours, intrigue. The opulent lounge with its mirrored walls and mock-medieval ceilings is a gilded backdrop for militiamen, mercenaries, operatives. When shells burst on the street the chandeliers shudder and people take cover under tables. The Continental is home, but there is no way of knowing who, exactly, you are living with.

Eileen herself has inadvertently helped bring a spy into the office. David Wickes, the young 'language teacher' who drove over with Gwen, is a trained communist spy. As soon as he arrives he starts briefing Soviet intelligence on Eileen, McNair and Charles Orr. His reports go straight to Alexander Orlov, Stalin's man in Spain, who's assembling his kill list. Orlov is waiting for the order from Moscow to begin the elimination operation.

In the office Eileen talks about Orwell a lot. She 'just could not resist talking about Eric – her hero husband, whom she obviously loved and admired', Charles writes. She counts the days they've been apart (115, apparently), and he has to listen. As a fellow newlywed he's sympathetic, but it wears a bit thin. 'It was my privilege,' he notes wearily, 'to hear about him day after day. Not that I paid much attention. He was still just an unknown would-be writer who, like others, had come to Spain to fight against fascism.'

When Charles meets Orwell he finds him 'tall, lean and gangling, to the point of being awkward ... he was tongue-tied, stammered and seemed to be afraid of people'. Orwell, he thinks, 'needed, no doubt, a socially extrovert wife as a window to the world. Eileen helped this inarticulate man to communicate with others. Though married for less than a year, she had already become his spokesman', indeed, his 'outreach to the world'.

Eventually, Orr comes to respect Orwell, 'this husband of my secretary, this militiaman – in his baggy, tan coverall uniform'. But this, too, is 'because of Eileen herself. A man who could win a woman of such quality must have some value. The man she revealed to me was a good man, a profound man, not just some blundering adventurer.'

The Go-Between

Charles Orr isn't Eileen's only admirer. Orwell's commander, Georges Kopp, travels to and from the front in his huge staff car bringing news of the men, and taking back supplies and mail. He is a go-between for the office and the trenches, and for Eileen and Orwell. Kopp falls deeply in love with her, a love that shapes his life, and lasts till the end of it.

Charles describes Kopp as 'a big, heavy, ruddy, blond Belgian, jolly, not very sophisticated, but an educated man. Everyone liked him.' Except, perhaps, for straight-talking, finicky young Lois, who calls him 'gross' and 'pot-bellied'. But Eileen likes him. He strides into the office with flowers and chocolates for everyone, and, for her, with stories of the man she loves. She and Kopp often eat together, alone or with others. When Lois joins them she's bored witless by their passion for and endless discussion of the food.

As time goes on Eileen realises that Kopp is, as she writes to Norah, *more than 'a bit gone on' me*. It makes her uncomfortable. Later, she tells Norah she is very fond of him because of his *quite remarkable courage* and because he cherished Orwell *with real tenderness* on the battlefield. But *It was always understood that I wasn't what they call in love with Georges—our association progressed in little leaps, each leap immediately preceding some attack or operation in which he would almost inevitably be killed . . .*

Kopp likes Orwell, but he's besotted with Eileen. He must have proposed at some point because afterwards Eileen tells Norah that she *only ever once missed the opportunity to tell him that nothing on earth could induce me to marry him.* That 'once' comes later in this story, when he is about to be executed.

Another British spy, this one working undercover as a journalist in the office, reports back to the Stalinists that he is '90% certain' that Eileen is on 'intimate terms' with Kopp. Many of the biographers would like to think that Eileen slept with Kopp, not so much for reasons of historical accuracy (they can't possibly know), but because one revolutionary tryst would transform the Orwells' marriage to an 'open' one in which infidelity was the deal. It wasn't.

Eileen knows her life is riddled with spies but feels she can manage it. Around the office there are, as one observer put it 'nondescript hangers-on with nominal jobs or none but who nevertheless seemed to be in some mysterious way, "on the inside"'. She and Lois are targeted by reporters (real and faux) who buy them 'swell dinners at all the fine places', Lois remembered. The 'newshounds' ply them with wine and food and 'pump them' for information but they, 'of course', tell them nothing. One of them, Giorgio Tioli, is a debonair anti-fascist who has fled Mussolini's Italy. He hangs about the office a lot, 'pretending', as Charles realised later, 'to be a journalist'. Tioli is charming. Even Lois approves, finding him an 'elegant, spare, Italian gentleman, immaculate in his white linens'.

Tioli targets Eileen. He claims to be a child psychologist, so as to have more in common with her. He moves into the hotel room next to hers. He and Eileen and the Orrs spend weekends picnicking or rambling in the hills outside Barcelona, having long lunches with wine. Eileen and Giorgio bond over their shared mock-horror at what Lois calls the 'screwy but nice' Catalan language, and they all plan fantasy escapes to Mexico. Whether the friendship is real or not is impossible to know.

But the spying is real. Tioli, as Charles said afterwards, was 'the most intriguing of the Communist agents'. He, too, was reporting on Eileen, McNair and both the Orrs directly to Stalin's people in Spain.

Tioli and Wickes pay Eileen a lot of attention, as does at least one other spy. Deep interest in everything you do and say and think can be love, or spying – or both.

In letters home Eileen plays it all down. She makes being at the epicentre of what was on the surface an anti-fascist civil war, and beneath it a Stalinist elimination purge, sound like summer camp, with bombs. She writes:

> *Dearest Mummy,*
>
> *Tuesday we had the only bombardment of Barcelona since I came. It was quite interesting . . . Not that there was any real emergency but the bombs fell closer to the middle of the town than usual & did make enough noise to excite people fairly reasonably. There were very few casualties . . . I had a bath last night—A great excitement . . . I have coffee about three times a day & drinks oftener . . . Every night I mean to go home early & write letters or something & every night I get home the next morning . . . !*

She apologises for this letter, perhaps in a nod to the fact that the mail is being censored or intercepted by spies: *it is a dull letter again I think. I shall do this life better justice in conversation—or I hope so.*

In mid-March Eileen convinces Kopp to take her with him when he returns to the battlefront. Charles comes too. They ride in the big staff car through the bare terrain of Catalonia, ribbons of road through a dun-coloured landscape yet to wake up. Eileen hasn't seen Orwell since before Christmas.

The British 'Tom Mann' Centuria, with Giorgio Tioli
kneeling at the front wearing a watch.

She spends three nights at the front and loves it. *I was allowed to stay in the front line dugouts all day*, she writes. *The Fascists threw in a small bombardment and quite a lot of machine gun-fire, which was then comparatively rare on the Huesca front, so it was quite an interesting visit—indeed I have never enjoyed anything more.* The men are grateful for everything she's done for them and warm to her immediately. One biographer obscures her professional role, describing Eileen's work for the troops as taking a 'motherly interest' in them. A photo is taken of them all in a trench, gathered around the machine gun. Orwell stands behind her, tall as a cypress. She crouches at his feet, smiling at the camera. Kopp is not in this photo; Quentin thinks his father must have taken it.

At the Huesca front Eileen and Orwell sleep in the outbuildings of a rambling farmhouse, La Granja, that's serving as a barracks. Kopp

Eileen at the battlefront. Orwell is fifth from the right,
behind her. Harry Milton is third from the left, kneeling.

arranges things so the couple can have at least part of the third night together. *We went to bed at 10 or so,* Eileen writes to her mother, *& at 3 Kopp came & shouted & I got up . . .* She stumbles into the night, alone. *I emerged in black dark & waded knee deep in mud in & out of strange buildings until I saw the faint glow . . . where Kopp was waiting with his car . . . George went to sleep again I hope.*

Despite Orwell's usual attention to detail this visit is not mentioned in *Homage.* You'd think it might be – it was when he was reunited with Eileen, who revealed herself unflappable under enemy fire. But it's as if it never happened. She was never there.

It was April 2017 when our little group visited La Granja, the walled complex of 'strange buildings' Eileen and Orwell stayed in. It's back to being a working farm. I walked towards the carriageway gates Eileen emerged from that morning in 1937 to meet Kopp's car. There were still bullet holes in the outside walls. Inside them there was a small chapel (used as a latrine during the war, for both practical and anti-clerical reasons, but now finely restored), a low-roofed house, and outbuildings across a courtyard strewn with disarticulated farm machinery, flowers and tall grass triumphing thinly through the metal.

The granddaughter of the Republican leader, Andreu Nin, who was assassinated in 1937, had joined our group for the day. We sat down at a long table in the farmhouse with our hosts, to celebrate a resistance that had been vanquished, forcibly forgotten for forty years, and now found again. A woman in a worn white apron brought out a huge tureen, fragrant with garlic and thyme. As its contents were ladled into wide bowls I heard the clink of bones, and then something louder, like metal or stone. When the plate reached me I saw the thin stew was of rabbit and snail. Three shells big as mice lay in my bowl, two upright and one sideways. Time spiralled and collapsed.

She drives away from the front with Kopp and Charles, dawn rising over bald hills, the sleek car chewing up the road. Back to friends and colleagues, spies and chancers popping into the office, inviting her to lunch, and swimming through the gilded corridors of the Hotel Continental.

The rotating door spits her into the foyer, off-balance because of the rucksack on her back. She nearly crashes into a woman in green suede pumps being led by a teacup poodle on a chain. Someone grabs her arm.

It's John McNair. His shirt is rumpled and he's unshaven.

'Put your bag in your room. We're going out. To talk.'

She's just spent seven hours in a bouncing car.
She wants a shower.

'We can't talk here?'

'No.' He keeps scanning the room over her shoulder.
His breath is terrible.

He won't go to a café. So, they walk down the median
strip of the Ramblas, under the trees to the sea and back.
He starts talking and he doesn't stop.

Last night, he says, he was with a young Quaker friend
in a big café when the police came in and arrested them at
gunpoint, making a big fuss about it so everyone saw. They
were hustled into a waiting car and 'taken at breakneck
speed through the dark, back streets'. He thought the two
of them would be 'finished . . . off quietly and . . . our bodies
thrown anywhere'. Instead, they were taken to a prison
where he brandished his British passport and kept shouting
at his interrogator 'asking him who the hell he thought he
was, detaining two perfectly innocent British citizens'. The
two of them were kept overnight and released at dawn this
morning. He has been waiting for her for hours in the lobby.

'Saved by making a good old ruckus,' he says, as they
reach the waterfront.

'Perhaps,' she says, squinting into the sun to look at him.
They both know that's unlikely. It was a catch-and-release
operation, toying with prey. 'I'm glad you were, anyway,'
she adds. A little girl with matted hair and two front teeth
missing beckons them over to the shoeshine. McNair waves
her off, already turned around to walk back. Eileen slips
three coins into the small palm.

As they approach the hotel he tells her, 'I'm going to
Paris for some meetings. Till things cool down. A week or
so. You can run the office, can't you? With Charles?'

'Yes.'

'I just want you to be careful.'

She nods.

He stops. They are right out the front now, by the news kiosk, watching the rotating door of the Continental. He gives a little shrug. 'There's nowhere to hide of course,' he adds.

She's grateful for that acknowledgement of reality. 'I don't suppose there is,' she says. And they go in.

In the shower the water sluices off her body down the plughole. She takes deep breaths. She understands from McNair's story that the Stalinists have taken over the civil police. Now, through them, the Russians can do anything to anyone. There is no civilian authority. This is a reign of terror. Soon any law, any passport, anyone you know will be worth nothing.

She opens the window in her dressing gown to the warm afternoon. Sits at the desk to do something normal. Write to Mother. *I thoroughly enjoyed being at the front,* she begins. Then she realises it is true. There, the enemy is clear. It's simpler than what's going on here.

All the mail, she knows, is intercepted by spies. She keeps her letter anodyne. *I am enjoying Barcelona again,* she tells Mother, as though she'd needed a change, for reasons she doesn't say. Now, things are even tougher, also for reasons she can't say. *Even I fall into the universal habit of yearning over England,* she stops. She can't, of course, tell Mother why, so she'll just tell her how, *when our waiter lit my cigarette the other day I said he had a nice lighter & he said 'Si, si, es bien, e Ingles!' And he handed it to me, obviously thinking I should like to caress it a little.* She asks her mother to deal with *the Aunt* who has not communicated with them at all, and who Eileen suspects may be *very sad about living in Wallington.*

She puts her pen down. The revolution is coming unstuck. Wealthy people are showing themselves again in the hotel and no one dares call them 'comrade' or 'thou'. People are afraid of things they can't see and can't name. Everyone is whispering, 'There's going to be trouble before long.'

Her fingers are still outlined in neat arcs of dirt under the nails. She goes back to the bathroom to scrub them.

Terror

At this point Richard Rees, Orwell's closest friend, turns up in Barcelona. He's 'in a mixed state of exaltation and despair and wearing a brand-new ambulance driver's outfit in which a cynical friend in London had pretended to mistake me for one of Hitler's Brownshirts'. His exaltation, he writes, 'sprang from the thought that I was preparing to risk my life for socialism, and my despair from a more down-to-earth appreciation of my motives'. It's impossible to know what he is not saying here; perhaps he wanted to prove to himself he was not the 'lamentable milksop' he felt himself to be.

Rees comes straight to Eileen. He finds her changed, almost beyond recognition. 'I called on Orwell's wife, Eileen, at the POUM office where she was working, and found her in what struck me as a very strange mental state. She seemed absent-minded, preoccupied, and dazed.' He assumes she's consumed with worry about Orwell at the front. He wants to take her out to lunch. She refuses. He presses; she says she just can't. Rees is bewildered at this 'curious manner'. Then she asks him, quietly, to step out of the office. In the corridor she explains: she's under surveillance – to be seen with her will put *him* in danger. Gradually the penny drops, as 'she began talking about the risk, to me, of being seen in the street with her . . .'

Eileen knows she is a target. Who in her life will turn out to be Stalin's henchmen, she doesn't know. But something is about to happen. 'I realized afterward,' Rees writes, 'she was the first person in whom I had witnessed the effects of living under a political terror.'

One biographer invents a different reason for her state. 'It could equally have been the fear of an amorous Kopp appearing suddenly and embarrassing her in front of an old friend of George's,' he writes. In this way an overlay of implied sexual innuendo conceals Eileen's political work, and trivialises her value as a target of Stalin's terror.

A few days later Orwell comes back to Barcelona on leave. He is shocked at the change in the city. The streets are full of beggars again, hungry children clamour for scraps. Waiters and shop assistants are 'cringing in the familiar manner. My wife and I went into a hosiery shop on the Ramblas to buy some stockings. The shopman bowed and rubbed his hands as they do not do even in England nowadays, though they used to do it twenty or thirty years ago. In a furtive indirect way the practice of tipping was coming back.' The revolution is fading away, undermined by forces unseen.

Eileen tells him what has happened here: they have been turned into enemies. McNair's overnight imprisonment was a salvo to show that any of them can be made to disappear, at any time. She tells him of the surveillance she's under, that there may be a communist spy, probably several, in her office. There are certainly any number of them in the hotel. They dine with Giorgio Tioli, 'a very good friend of ours' as Orwell calls him, and they probably talk about it with him.

The next day, Tioli brings another British 'war reporter', David Crook, to the office to meet Eileen. Crook is twenty-six with dark hair in waves off his forehead, a chiselled jaw, bright wide smile. He was educated at elite schools in the UK and at Columbia University, volunteered for Spain, and recently took three bullets in the leg. While recuperating in Madrid, he tells Eileen, he'd socialised with writers – Martha Gellhorn and Ernest Hemingway, Mulk Raj Anand and Stephen Spender. What he doesn't tell her is that he'd also been trained there by the Russians. Crook has just finished a crash course in sabotage, covert violence and surveillance techniques with the master, Raymond Mercader, who will later go on to assassinate Trotsky. Crook's target is the ILP; 'in particular', the 'major ILP figures working with the POUM: McNair, Kopp and the Blairs'.

As an old man, after a long teaching career as a communist in China, David Crook told an interviewer that he was not proud of his role in crushing the POUM. Which is not to say that he wasn't good at it. He was.

Soon, Crook has the run of the office. While the others are out at long lunches he stays back under one pretext or another. Each day he walks out of there with hidden files, takes them to a Russian safe house on Calle Muntaner, photographs them, and returns them before anyone gets back. Within a week the Russians have copies of everything. Crook also writes detailed reports on Eileen, Kopp and McNair, delivering them to his handler, another British communist. Sometimes they meet in a café, and he passes the files over in the folds of a newspaper. When he needs to be more discreet he hides them in the hotel bathroom for collection. It is Crook who reports that he's '90% certain' that Kopp and Eileen are on 'intimate terms'.

After his months in the trenches Orwell wants to have a good time. 'I had a ravenous desire for decent food and wine, cocktails, American cigarettes, and so forth, and I admit to having wallowed in every luxury that I had money to buy.' Presumably he and Eileen go out on the town; he doesn't mention being with her. But he's funny about himself. '[T]hanks to over-eating and over-drinking, I was slightly out of health all that week. I would feel a little unwell, go to bed for half a day, get up and eat another excessive meal, and then feel ill again.' He's 'obsessed', he says, with buying a revolver. And he's so sick of being in a backwater of the war, so desperate to get to the Madrid front, that even though Eileen has explained everything he *still* wants to join the communists.

For Eileen, this is dangerous. Like McNair, she is a target because of her work at the ILP headquarters – whereas Orwell, an infantryman at the front, is not yet in their sights. She tells her brother of Orwell's plans but notes, cryptically, that *Madrid is probably closed to me*, adding, *Of course we—perhaps particularly I—are politically suspect.* It's the only time she ever puts herself 'particularly' in the centre of anything: here, of a communist rifle-sight. But still, she goes along with Orwell's desire. To organise his transfer to the frenemy they speak with the communist recruiter. They tell him *all the truth* of their situation, and the man, she says, *was so shattered that he was practically offering me executive jobs by the end of half an hour, & I gather that they will take George . . .*

David Crook, Spain, 1937.

There's no record of what she said that was so 'shattering' about the truth of their situation. Presumably it included that her boss was kidnapped, that there are spies in the office, that she might be bundled into a dark car at any time. What charm did she have, what high, quiet interpersonal intelligence that she could tell a communist recruiter of her terror at their hands and be offered a job within the fold, so as to protect her?

Or, perhaps, Crook and Wickes' reports about her were as good as a reference?

Looking for a Fight
3 May 1937

It's somewhere between three and four o'clock. Orwell is walking down the Ramblas near the Continental when bullets fly in front of him. Trams stop, their drivers and passengers flee, shopkeepers snap down steel shutters. Hell is breaking loose. 'I thought instantly: "It's started!"' he writes, '... I realized that I must get back to the hotel at once and see if my wife was all right.'

But he doesn't. A passing acquaintance convinces him to go the opposite way, down to the Hotel Falcón, 'a sort of boarding house' for POUM members near the port.

At the Falcón there are masses of people either sheltering from or looking to be involved in the street fighting – young men, old women, women with babies. He tries to find a weapon but, as this is the impoverished POUM, of course there are hardly any. He'd like to get back to the Hotel Continental, he repeats, but 'Everyone said that it was impossible to go up the Ramblas' and then, 'there was a vague idea floating round that [their building] was likely to be attacked at any moment and we had better stand by ...' But he doesn't stand by – he goes out to dinner: 'my friend and I slipped out to his hotel'. When he gets back he tries to call the Continental to let Eileen know he's alive, or that he's not coming home. 'I could not make contact with my wife,' he says, 'but I managed to get hold of John McNair.' McNair, back from Paris, tells him that 'all was well, nobody had been shot'.

Then Orwell finds a spot to sleep in an abandoned theatre in the building. He takes out his knife, rips down a stage curtain and rolls himself up in it. He sleeps fitfully, disturbed by the thought of the shoddy anarchist bombs in his pockets 'which might blow me into the air if I rolled on them too vigorously'.

Now that I have read *Homage* backwards and forwards, knowing what happened when, who was there but isn't in the text – this feels like a moment to unpack. A moment when Eileen can be glimpsed, if in a negative way, like dark matter that can only be apprehended by its effect on the visible world. The way the text buckles and strains to avoid her is the way I can see the shape she left.

When Orwell calls Eileen he reaches McNair. How? Most likely, when she's not in their room he calls her boss. Orwell can't tell us how, in looking for Eileen, he calls her boss, because he can't tell us that she has a job. Or an office. And he particularly can't tell us that she has a political job with the POUM Executive. He is calling buildings near where the battle has been raging, but he can't say that either because it would reveal that she was in danger and he had run the other way. Much later in the text (we're now the day *after* his night spent wrapped in the curtain at the Falcón), so as to separate his concern for his wife from the dangerous situation which provoked it, he mentions that 'The day before' an attack had been mounted on 'the POUM building' (her office). '[T]wenty or thirty armed Assault Guards'* had seized the Café Moka next door and been shooting at people on the street. When he finds out that 'all was well, nobody had been shot', he is finding out that Eileen is okay. 'Nobody' is her.

---

* The Assault Guards were special police and paramilitary units created by the Spanish Republic in 1931 to deal with urban and political violence. At this point they were coming under Stalinist control.

Reverse-engineering the book's chronology felt like untangling a cobweb. Reconstructing cause and event from the point of view of an invisible person showed me how the disappearing trick is done. Once you recognise the techniques, the patri-magic doesn't work and you can see her, right there – at the heart of the action.

Café Moka, Barcelona, 1930s.

In the Fight
3 May 1937

The office window is open and the desk calendar flutters:
3 May 1937. It's somewhere between three and four o'clock.
The others are still at lunch. George is out and about
somewhere. She'd like another coffee.

It's a flat staccato sound she doesn't recognise, then
she does. She moves quickly to the window. Things appear
stuck, the tram is stopped – tac-tac-tac-tac it goes on – then
the deeper thunder of an explosion somewhere to the right.
Opposite, a woman in the side street crouches in a doorway
shielding a child with her body.

McNair flies in, sweating and puffing, the air swirling
around him in panic.

'Assault Guards have taken the Moka next door!
Barricading themselves in! Machine guns!'

'How did you get in?' she asks. She's leaning on the
desk, her back to the window.

'The rear entrance.' McNair throws his jacket on a chair.
'Where's Charles? The boy?'

'At lunch I think,' she says. The boy is Stafford Cottman,
on leave from the front – eighteen, keen, though fairly
useless in the office.

McNair is pacing. 'They'll probably cut the phone lines!'

She picks up the receiver and puts it to her ear. 'Not yet,' she says.

'We only have two guards on this building!' He won't sit down, is giving the impression of action without any, the impression of thinking probably without—

'I've got to go and see about reinforcements.' He picks up his jacket.

'We'll need to get things out of this office,' she says, gesturing around her. 'Correspondence, passports, maps, codes.'

'Yes, yes,' McNair says, waving the back of his hand in her direction as he walks to the door. 'See to it, will you?' She moves to the door and closes it behind him, leans her forehead against it.

She turns around, takes a deep breath. Her eye runs along the bookshelf till it meets McNair's copy of Hitler's *Mein Kampf*. Even though it's in French as *Mon Combat*, it would *not* look good for them in a Stalinist raid. As she takes it down, a slimmer thing, almost a pamphlet, falls out: Stalin's 'Measures for Liquidating Trotskyists and Other Double Dealers'. That wouldn't look good either. She makes a pile on the desk of materials about the fascism they're fighting, which could now be used to make them look like fascists. She lives, she thinks, in a zone of dangerous irony, if there is such a place.

She turns quickly and hunches down to the safe, undoes the combination lock from memory and takes out the passports of the men as well as her own and Orwell's – thirty-three altogether. They make a blue heap next to the typewriter. The typewriter! She can't leave it here – they'll barely exist as an organisation without a typewriter. But she can't very well saunter out of the building under the eyes of the enemy with a typewriter case under one arm and the most vital contents of the office they're laying siege to under the other. She looks around the room: four desks, two safes, filing cabinets and bookshelves along the walls. This needs to be a process of elimination – an elimination operation! She shudders at her own joke, but must think clearly, slowly now, about what, exactly, to save. She wonders how and when the men will attack from next door – she doesn't get as far as thinking what will happen to her if they do. Her heart is a bird in a box.

She scans the room again for cases, bags, anything. There's a wine crate with banners in it – useful, but not enough. Then her eye catches a flash of tartan in the back corner behind the door – the shopping cart! A canvas thing on wheels she has barely used. Perfect. There are three string bags inside – even better. She grabs the brown paper roll they use for sending packages and swiftly wraps the passports in three bundles. Then she pulls out maps, files, books and wraps them too, stuffing them into the shopping bags like portions of cheese, rolls of sausage. She puts the typewriter in its case, then tries to lower it into the cart. It won't go, but without the case it just fits – she covers it with brown paper parcels. The string bags are heavy. It'll take two trips – but what if they seize the building before she gets back?

She picks up the receiver and calls Lois. There's no answer, so she calls Giorgio. Then she sits on the desk looking out the window – at nothing. The Ramblas is empty. Right when so much is happening there's nothing to see.

When Giorgio arrives he takes it all in at a glance. A woman on a desk between bulging string bags. 'I help you with your shopping!' he claps. He is impeccable. Does the man never sweat?

And so they walk out in broad daylight, a slight woman pulling a chequered shopping cart, and a tall Italian in a linen suit with a bulging briefcase under one arm and his shopping in the other. No one shoots.

After Giorgio leaves her room she takes each item out of the cart, then lifts the typewriter onto her desk. She stands on the red carpet with the parcels of passports in her hands and turns slowly – bed, wardrobe, desk, radiator, bathroom . . . She wedges them behind the toilet cistern. So obvious, but it will have to do.

In the lounge she looks for someone to eat with, someone she trusts, or the least slippery person available. The hotel has been declared neutral ground in the fighting, so it has filled to the brim with a most extraordinary collection of people. She sees foreign journalists she knows, political suspects of every shade, an American airman in the service of the government and in the corner as usual a fat, sinister-looking Russian nicknamed Charlie Chan wearing, attached to his waist-band, a revolver and a neat little bomb . . .

Fat sinister Russians are easy to spot. The problem with spies is that the best ones are the most charming; that's part of their arsenal. Lois is at a table by the window. Thank God.

As she sits the light catches her glasses. Filthy.

'Where's Charles?' Eileen asks, pulling her handkerchief from a pocket in her dress. When she starts to polish the lenses she must steady her wrists on the table.

'You're shaking,' Lois says.

'They're preparing an attack on the office. You need to tell Charles not to go in.'

'And you,' Lois says, signalling the waiter, 'need whisky. Where's George?'

'I don't know. Out looking for a fight – I think,' Eileen says.

'Pretty safe then,' Lois grins.

'Though maybe not.' But Eileen smiles too, biting her bottom lip. When she puts her glasses on everything snaps back into focus. 'I do hope so. I have no idea where he is, he's been out all afternoon. I keep hearing gunfire and hoping he's far from it.'

In the office the phone starts to ring – it rings out. Then it rings out in her room.

Eileen and Lois eat marinated artichokes, sardines, and lemon sorbet with mint. Then she goes up to bed, waiting for him to come back, or at least to call to say he's safe.

The Telephone Exchange was raided today. Perhaps it has stopped working. She has had so many nights alone in this bed not knowing whether he was alive or dead at the front that tonight shouldn't be any different. Though it is. Because the fighting is here.

At dawn she wakes to more gunshots. Rushes to the balcony in her nightdress – it's coming from her office.

For a long moment it's a still tableau: a man in the green uniform of the Assault Guard – the enemy but also an auburn-haired boy – lies on the footpath. His cap is five feet away from his head, which is perfectly intact. A pool of blood blooms under him, the only moving thing.

Then life starts up again – the POUM guards run from her building on to the median strip and drag one of theirs – she hadn't seen him lying there – back into her building.

A man in uniform, too short to be George.

That same morning Orwell wakes up and untangles himself from the theatre curtain at the Hotel Falcón. He hasn't been blown up by the bombs in his pocket. He decides he'll now risk getting back to the Hotel Continental – he can hear gunfire, but reckons it's further away. It's not. As he passes the covered market a shell explodes, its glass roof shatters and everyone scatters. He goes in anyway and buys a coffee and 'a wedge of goat's-milk cheese which I tucked in beside my bombs'.

As he approaches Eileen's office he sees the enemy in position all around it. Terrified POUM shock troopers are inside defending it. Both sides are shooting. An American caught in crossfire on the median strip hides behind the news kiosk, his head, for all intents and purposes, 'like a coconut at a fair'. But Orwell slips past unharmed. 'I went up to the Continental,' he writes, 'made sure that all was well, washed my face, and then went back to the P.O.U.M. Executive Building (it was about a hundred yards down the street) to ask

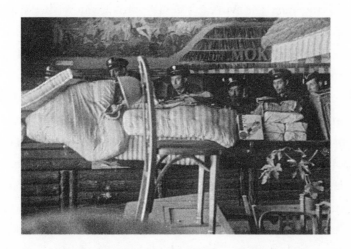

Inside the Café Moka, May 1937.
'The Assault Guards in the Café Moka had drawn down the steel curtains and piled up the café furniture to make a barricade.' *Homage to Catalonia*

for orders. By this time the roar of rifle and machine-gun fire from various directions was almost comparable to the din of a battle.'

Again, when he says he 'made sure all was well', it's a way of telling the reader that he checked on his wife without naming her, or saying why she might have needed checking on. He doesn't say why his wife is at the hotel at this point and not at work in the POUM Executive office. He doesn't have to because, as we know, he's never mentioned that she works there.

At Eileen's office Kopp has taken command. Everyone's jittery. There are hardly any weapons. Suddenly they hear 'appalling crashes'. 'Kopp glanced out of the window,' Orwell writes, 'cocked his stick behind his back, said: "Let us investigate," and strolled down the stairs in his usual unconcerned manner, I following.' Outside, POUM boys are 'bowling bombs down the pavement as though playing skittles'. They are exploding near the Moka, 'twenty yards away with a frightful, ear-splitting crash which was mixed up with the banging of rifles.'

Only now does Orwell tell us why everyone is so terrified. 'Early in the morning they had attempted to come out, shots had been exchanged, and one Shock Trooper [POUM] was badly wounded and an Assault Guard killed.'

Kopp comes out with raised hands, facing the machine gun turned his way from the café. He sees his car, which has been riddled with bullets and its windscreen smashed by bombs. Kopp places his gun on the ground, then walks to parley with the terrified Shock Troopers, a thing, Orwell says, 'I would not have done for twenty pounds.'

An unstable ceasefire is reached, after which Kopp posts Orwell to the roof of a building opposite, the Poliorama. Orwell spends three days there, mostly bored, reading Penguin paperbacks. He smokes, goes over to the Continental for lunch.

One time he comes in 'tired, hungry, and dirty after a night on guard' to find 'a couple of men from the International Column [communists] sitting in my room at the hotel'. He writes, 'Their attitude was completely neutral. If they had been good party-men they would, I suppose, have urged me to change sides, or even have pinioned me and taken away the bombs of which my pockets were full; instead they merely commiserated with me for having to spend my leave in doing guard-duty on a roof.'

Sometimes omission makes things weird, as the text strains to occlude her. Why would he enter 'my room' at the hotel to find two communists sitting there? Have they broken in? Are they lost, sitting by accident in an empty room? It can only be because Eileen is there, talking with them. Possibly, she is discussing Orwell's desire to fight with them. Or possibly they are trying to get information out of her about the POUM. Who knows? Because he just won't say she's there.

The next day, 5 May, Kopp tells him 'with a grave face', that the POUM is about to be outlawed. They will be hunted like animals. The men barricade themselves into Eileen's office building and prepare to be attacked from next door, a battle, Orwell feels, 'in which I should presumably be killed'. 'My wife', he tells us, 'had come down from the hotel in case a nurse should be needed.' He lies down on a sofa for half an hour's rest before the fighting begins. 'I remember the intolerable discomfort caused by my pistol, which was strapped to my belt and sticking into the small of my back. And the next thing I remember is waking up with a jerk to find my wife standing beside me. It was broad daylight, nothing had happened, the Government had not declared war on the P.O.U.M. . . . and except for the sporadic firing in the streets everything was normal. My wife said that she had not had the heart to wake me and had slept in an arm-chair in one of the front rooms.'

So 'my wife' comes down to be a nurse. It's still not possible to say that they are at her workplace, that they are in her office, that she might need to retrieve something from a desk, secure a safe, show people the way to the cleaner's cupboards for more buckets, or find the key to the back stairs.

The next day it's all over. Thousands more Assault Guards flood the streets to end the revolution on behalf of Stalin and in the interest of Franco. There's a 'horrible atmosphere produced by fear, suspicion, hatred, censored newspapers, crammed jails, enormous food queues and prowling gangs of armed men'. And the rewriting of history begins: this was a POUM uprising, because they are working *with* the fascists to scuttle the revolution. So, now, they must be eliminated.

The Continental is a place of terror. The police are after Spaniards and foreigners alike, men and women, combatants, civilians, office workers, wives – anyone with an association with the non-Stalinist left is an 'illegal' and to be disappeared. A wounded British friend of Orwell's is seized on the street and spends eight days in 'a cell so full of people that nobody had room to lie down'. Wives are being arrested to lure their husbands out into the open. 'You had all the while a hateful feeling that someone hitherto your friend might be denouncing you to the secret police,' Orwell writes. His nerves are shot. 'I had got to the point when every time a door banged I grabbed for my pistol.'

So, he escapes. He goes back to the front with his old contingent, which has dropped its now criminal name of POUM and become the 29th Division of the Popular Army.

Leaving Eileen at the epicentre of fear, suspicion, hatred and prowling gangs of armed men.

⌒

The fighting is over.

At dawn she carries the naked typewriter back down the street, held in front of her chest. Cigarette butts and empty cartridge cases litter the pavement, make a trail up the stairs to her office. The desk is still there in the window. There are boot prints on it – dusty giants have been dancing here. She puts the typewriter down.

She has no idea if the typewriter will be safer at the office or in her room, but it is POUM property, so *she* may be safer if it is not in her room.

In the desk drawer there's still paper. She runs her forearm over the seat of the chair, sits. Spools a sheet into the machine. It's a letter she probably won't get to send. It's a letter that cannot contain what she wants to say. She breathes in, and starts anyway.

Dear Norah,

War is fun so far as the shooting goes and much less alarming than an aeroplane in a shop window, but it does appalling things to people normally quite sane and intelligent—some make desperate efforts to retain some kind of integrity and others make no efforts at all but hardly anyone can stay reasonable, let alone honest.

The sun is up now, filtering through the green leaves of the plane trees on the Ramblas, making filigreed patterns on the ground. The kiosk man pushes up the steel shutter with a metal pole, preparing to sell papers full of lies to men who might have shot her yesterday.

She reads over what she's written. It sounds hysterical. Perhaps that's how she's feeling? Norah will see through it. She'll see that *she* is making her own desperate efforts to retain some kind of integrity – and she'll wonder why that is. She is rattled by the Davids – Wickes and Crook – who hang about her. They agree with everything she says before she's finished saying it.

And then of course there are the Georges. Right outside that filthy window, between her office and this hotel, they went about saving each other's lives in a way that was – horrible. Though George had not then noticed that Georges Kopp was in love with her. Sometimes, she thinks, no one ever had such a sense of guilt before.

There's no way to put this in a letter she knows will be opened by spies and authorities of several nations. She pulls it out of the typewriter, folds it into her dress pocket. It's quiet here, like the devastated path of a hurricane.

That same dawn Orwell is at the front. He stands 'head and shoulders' above the parapet, a black silhouette against the pale world. It's the changing of the guard. He's lit a cigarette, is regaling the boys with stories of his exploits in the brothels of Paris, of how cheap it was, actually, to install the 'little trollop' in his hotel. The bullet goes clean through his neck.

Harry Milton is the man next to him as he falls. 'He had bitten his lips, so I thought he was a goner. The speed of the bullet had seared the entrance of the wound. I put his head in my arms, and when I put my hand under his neck there was a puddle of blood.'

For Orwell 'it was the sensation of being at the centre of an explosion . . . I felt a tremendous shock – no pain, only a violent shock, such as you get from an electrical terminal; with it a feeling of utter weakness, a feeling of being stricken and shrivelling up to nothing . . .'

'Cut open his shirt!' Harry cries. Orwell wants to get his own knife out to help, but then realises he can't move. 'This ought to please my wife,' he thinks, 'she had always wanted me to be wounded, which would save me from being killed when the great battle came.' He manages to ask where he's been hit. 'In the throat,' Harry says.

As soon as I knew that the bullet had gone clean through my neck I took it for granted that I was done for. I had never heard of a man or an animal getting a bullet through the middle of the neck and surviving it. The blood was dribbling out of the corner of my mouth. 'The artery's gone,' I thought. I wondered how long you last when your carotid artery is cut; not many minutes, presumably. Everything was very blurry. There must have been about two minutes during which I assumed that I was killed. And that too was interesting—I mean it is interesting to know what your thoughts would be at such a time.

His thoughts go to her. 'Please tell Eileen that I love her,' one of the stretcher bearers reports him saying.

In the version she later typed, he put it more diffidently: 'my first thought, conventionally enough, was for my wife', he writes, as though shy of expressing a love that might sound unoriginal. But at the time it was real, and it was urgent. 'My second was a violent resentment at having to leave this world which, when all is said and done, suits me so well.'

Moments later he's reassured by horrendous pain:

for I knew that your sensations do not become more acute when you are dying. I began to feel more normal and to be sorry for the four poor devils who were sweating and slithering with the stretcher on their shoulders. It was a mile and a half to the ambulance, and vile going, over lumpy, slippery tracks. I knew what a sweat it was, having helped to carry a wounded man down a day or two earlier. The leaves of the silver poplars which, in places, fringed our trenches brushed against my face; I thought what a good thing it was to be alive in a world where silver poplars grow . . .

He is outside of himself. He thinks of his stretcher bearers' pain, he feels the caress of silver poplars and experiences a rush of love for his wife and the world he might be leaving.

Orwell reports in slapstick detail the trips from hospital to hospital in the backs of trucks, the wounded men like bloody rag dolls tumbling off their stretchers. He's taken to the field hospital (a wooden shack) and given morphia, then transferred to a hospital at Siétamo, then the following day to another at Barbastro, and the next to a bigger hospital at Lérida where he spends five or six days. After that, he's transferred in a jolting third-class train carriage with other 'corpse-like forms' to a hospital at Tarragona, where he says he spends another three or four days. As his strength returns, so does the energy to complain, mostly about abysmal amateur nursing care.

Finally, he's moved to the Sanatorio Maurín, the converted mansion of 'some wealthy bourgeois' on a hill in the outskirts of Barcelona, now a hospital for men of the POUM. He's recovered enough that he can get on a tram and have lunch in town, as 'My wife was still staying at the Hotel Continental, and I generally came into Barcelona in the daytime.'

Eileen, it would seem, had been 'still staying at the Hotel Continental' the whole time he was shot and shunted about like a bag of bones, surviving blithe doctors and bad nursing and fickle trains.

But that's not how it was. As soon as she got the news, Eileen was in a car with Kopp to the front. She arrived within forty-eight hours of the injury. She was with him 'every minute' for the days at Lérida and at Tarragona. She nursed him, travelled with him, dealt with the doctors and organised his transport to the Sanatorio Maurín. She had Kopp draw a diagram of the throat wound to send to Laurence for his opinion – in fact she had him draw two and sent them by different mails, knowing that they'd likely be intercepted by spies. (She was right – one of the diagrams has been found in Orwell's KGB file in Moscow, 'presumably,' one biographer tells us, 'lifted by Moscow's own man about the ILP office, Crook'.) The other reached Laurence, who set about organising Orwell's care for when he came home.

And Eileen telegrammed his parents in classic, understated style:

ERIC SLIGHTLY WOUNDED. PROGRESS EXCELLENT. SENDS LOVE. NO NEED FOR ANXIETY. EILEEN.

Orwell spends over 2500 words telling us of his hospital treatment without mentioning that Eileen was there. I wonder what she felt, later, as she typed them.

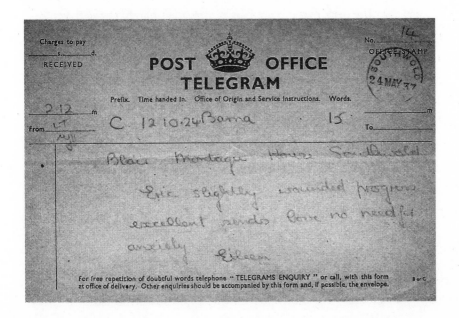

⌒

Once he's safely in care at the Sanatorio Maurín she
goes back to her room at the Continental, into what she
thinks of as a lunatic asylum – though who are the mad
and who the warders is entirely unclear. As George said,
it's as if some huge evil intelligence is brooding over the
town. She lies on the bed, looks at the curly plaster vine
trapped in the ceiling. She can't rest. Can't think. Giorgio's
typewriter is cla-cla-clacking next door. She leaves for
the office.

She and Charles and John have discussed whether to
keep using the office. In the end they decided that if the
police want to arrest them they will find them anywhere, so
there's no point hiding. She's still managing the boys' affairs
at the front. Charles comes in most days, and Wickes and
Crook. Though today, no one's here.

The desk has a green baize inlay, she's barely noticed
it before. Someone must have tidied up. Then she sees
a letter resting on the typewriter addressed to her. It's
from David Wickes. He says he thinks he should go
with the strength – that's with the communists – and so
should she. He won't be coming into the office again,
so 'we won't be seeing one another any more', he says,
as if that's what they'd been doing. At the end he asks
for her forgiveness, which is when she knows for sure.
A match strikes.

Crook is in the doorway. 'What's that?' He exhales,
cigarette between index finger and thumb, bent back into
his palm. He's insanely handsome, his dark hair in unruly
curls, eyes crystalline blue, Adam's apple under soft skin.
It's distracting.

'A letter from David. He says he won't be back.'

'*Adieu, mon amour?*'

'Hardly.'

She thinks of everything Wickes knows about the work of this office, and about her, and who he's telling it all to now. And the outrageousness of implying that he loves her, which is why she should forgive him for it. She feels sick.

'I always thought he was a bit . . . slippery,' Crook says. 'Are you all right?'

'Fine. Absolutely.'

'Lunch then?'

On the way to the hotel restaurant they walk through the lounge. The fat Russian, grenades slung from his belt, has cornered a militiaman.

'Look at that,' Crook says. 'OGPU agent for sure.'

'I think,' she says slowly, 'it's the first time I've seen someone whose *profession* it is to tell lies,' she smiles. 'Apart from journalists, of course.'

It's a microsecond – but still a microsecond – before Crook laughs.

After lunch she goes back to her room. The moment she puts the key in her door Giorgio pops out of his.

'Oh, good,' he says, 'I've been hoping to see you.' He has important maps, *incriminating* maps in his possession, he tells her. He's worried about them being found in his room.

'Found?' she asks.

'Well, I feel vulnerable,' he says. 'Can I keep them on your balcony, in case they come to search my room?'

She lets the silence sit for a beat.

'And if they come to you first I'll hear, and I'll just reach over from my balcony and grab them back.'

Just?, she thinks. Charles says in spycraft that's what they call a 'tell', the unwitting revelation of a lie. Giorgio's eyes are liquid pools, his breath smells of peppermint.

'Of course,' she says. Though anything might happen. He might be anyone.

He goes into his room and brings them back. It's a cardboard cylinder.

'Thank you, *cara*,' he says.

She places it on the balcony.

After he's gone she moves to the pile of typescript on the desk. It is the sum of all George's writing from every notebook, scrap of paper and toilet tissue he sent from the front, which she's typed on foolscap into one continuous document, now tied with red twine. Aside from themselves, this is the most important thing to get out of here. She knows that it is not safe in this room.

The next day George comes in on the tram from the hospital. His neck is bandaged and his right arm is in a sling. She's pleased, so pleased he's here.

Barcelona's streets are laid out like a spider's web, a maze of irregular diagonals. She takes him down narrow alleys away from the hotel. They pass a fresh poster on a building – it's a POUM member pulling off a mask to reveal a wicked face with a swastika on it underneath.

'Slander!' Orwell says, trying to rip it down with his good hand. Only part of it comes off. 'Do you have a pen?'

She takes the cap off as she passes it to him. He scrawls 'iVisca Poum!' over what remains of the poster.

As they walk on he's shaking his head. 'Calling us fascists! The communists are giving themselves reasons why they attacked us.'

'Tear off the mask!' Communist propaganda poster,
Barcelona, 1937.

'Yes,' Eileen says. She stops at the dark recessed door of
the restaurant. 'But why go to so much trouble if it's over?'

The doorway opens into a narrow bar, leading to a
cavernous restaurant behind. The bar mirror reflects them
as they pass: a tall man with a broken wing; a woman with
a dandelion head. They walk under haunches of *jamón*
hanging hoof down, dripping fat into tiny paper cornets.
It's only noon, there's hardly anyone here. They find a table
among barrels of red wine at the back.

She tells him that something else is coming. 'Wickes
has jumped ship to the communists,' she says, 'perhaps his
handlers.'

He is frozen, listening.

'Giorgio is so afraid of searches he's given me documents for safekeeping – which makes no sense. John is edgy as a cat.' She tells him that the street battles were just the prelude. First the propaganda makes you an enemy, then they get rid of you.

'But I'm still here,' he says.

She looks at him for a full three seconds.

'This is an elimination operation,' she says, her tone very even. 'Russian-style. We need to be careful.'

'I'm not much use here now,' he says, shrugging the shoulder that works. He looks like a patched scarecrow. His eyes are very blue, and to her, despite everything, unbelievably innocent. 'Let's go home.'

In the morning he leaves early, back to the front to get his discharge.

She sits on the edge of the unmade bed, her bare feet on the red rug. They are tanned, with white stripes from her sandals. Badger feet. The ashtray on the bedside table is full. She lights another cigarette. She is more alone than she can ever remember being. She stands up, shakes it off. Picks up his notebook finished last week on the roof opposite here, and sits down to type.

⌒

Orwell could leave the country on his British passport, dressed as a bourgeois tourist and pretending never to have fought. But he wants to get a discharge so he isn't deserting. To do that he has to go back to a medical board at the front, then to each of the hospitals where he was treated and finally to the POUM militia headquarters to get all those papers stamped. He leaves Barcelona on 15 June 1937.

For five nights he sleeps roughish – sometimes in a hospital, other times in a lodging house, or a ditch. Eventually he gets his discharge, 'stamped with the seal of the 29th Division, and the doctor's certificate in which I was "declared useless"'.

Once again, Owell misses the action. The day he leaves, Stalin gives Orlov, his man in Barcelona, the order to liquidate the POUM, and Orlov instructs the Spanish police to carry it out. The terror begins.

Eileen's office building is raided this time. No defence is possible. The entire executive of the POUM and its leader, Andreu Nin, are arrested and thrown incommunicado into police cells and prisons, and when they're all full, into hastily repurposed villas. Many are tortured, some are killed. They are going after foreigners, combatants, women, civilians, anyone.

⌒

She is typing on her old machine in her hotel room when there's a knock at the door. McNair rushes in before she can speak.

'Thank God you're here. They've raided the office.' His forehead is beaded with sweat – he seems held together only by his braces and the garters on his shirtsleeves.

'They've taken everyone to prison – or somewhere. They've got Nin.'

The words make sense, but she doesn't yet know what they mean.

McNair holds one wrist in the other hand and twists it as he walks about. 'We have to get all the boys out of Spain. Every one of them. In civilian clothes. You have the passports?'

'Yes.' She's thinking fast now. 'And I think I can get clothes.'

'Good lass. When they come back from the front the exit visas will need to be in the passports. From the Police Prefecture. We have to lodge them then at the consulate.'

'Yes, of course,' she says. 'We', she thinks, means me. The Police Prefecture, she also knows, is where they come from to arrest you.

McNair is moving to the door. 'I'll find the others. If they're still free. We shall meet back here at three this afternoon.'

She nods, but he's gone already.

She takes a finished page out of the typewriter, adds it to the pile of George's manuscript, now more than an inch thick, and re-ties it. Then she goes into the bathroom and retrieves the passports from behind the toilet cistern. Takes their chequebook out of the desk drawer and adds that to the pile. It's Sunday, the Police Prefecture will be closed. Once again, nowhere in this room looks safe. She lifts the mattress and sees a mess of springs. She takes a folded newspaper and slides it over them, puts all the documents there and settles the mattress back down.

She lunches with Lois, though neither of them has much appetite. It amazes her that kitchens keep functioning while the world outside implodes.

Giorgio joins them for coffee – cream suit, pale blue shirt, no tie. He pulls the chair out from the table quite far, places an ankle across one knee in a pose of studied calm. He speaks quietly, smiling casually, as if for an audience.

'If you were arrested tomorrow what would you like to have somebody bring you?'

He's asking both of them. It might be a joke.

Lois laughs. 'That's the funniest thing yet,' she says.

Eileen is watching him. 'My toothbrush,' she says.

Giorgio turns to Lois. 'You?'

'That's so silly. I can't think of anything.'

'No, really,' he says, 'tell me.'

'Is this a thought experiment?' Eileen asks.

'*Sì*,' Giorgio says, 'a thought experiment. Exactly.'

'Then peaches,' Lois says. 'I'd like some peaches.'

Five Days, Five Nights

Something – not this, but essentially this – must have happened.

⌐◦

At three o'clock they are in her room – she and Charles and McNair. She has sent Cottman out to buy underwear for the men. McNair has asked David Crook to join them and they are waiting for him.

McNair can't sit. There are damp half-moons under his arms. Charles has moved the desk chair to the window so he can look out over the balcony. He's leaning forward, elbows on his thighs, one heel quietly tapping. The sun catches his head; for the first time she notices his hair is thinning. He seems very calm, though he has just come back from the gathering outside the police station where they've taken Nin. It's a long June afternoon, a pale innocent sky.

Music starts up.

'Good Lord,' McNair says, 'the organ grinder's still here.'

Eileen smiles. 'The monkey doesn't know there's a war on.' She turns to Charles. 'Where's Lois?'

Charles has taken off his little round glasses and his eyes are suddenly smaller, grey-green and undefended.

'In the bath.'

'It's a talent.' She remembers being nineteen, the invulnerability of it, thinking that the world's foolishness does not apply to you.

A rap on the door and Crook enters. 'Sorry,' he says. 'Got held up.' He smiles like nothing's happening, lips so full, teeth so even. He settles into the armchair and starts discreetly cracking his knuckles.

'Good,' McNair begins. 'We can keep this brief. You may have heard – there are warrants out for our arrests.'

'All of us?' Crook asks. He pulls one hand through his thick curls.

'Me, Eileen and George. Though they are arresting plenty without warrant too.'

'I don't know why they bother with them then,' Crook says.

McNair takes a handkerchief from his pocket and pats his face. 'There's nothing for it. We must all go underground. But as you well know, the POUM has no safe houses. It means sleeping rough.'

Charles turns to Eileen. 'That means you too.'

'I—' She stops. Starts again more forcefully. 'I can't. George will come back and walk into a trap.'

Charles hooks the wire rims of his glasses back behind his ears.

'You are in a trap *here*,' he says, looking at her as if there's no one else in the room. 'As soon as George walks in they'll simply grab both of you. Eileen—'

'I can't leave George to walk in and be taken away,' she says. 'I'm staying.'

Charles puts his hand over his eyebrows and pulls them together. He swallows hard and keeps his hand there. Crook looks at McNair, says nothing.

'John.' Eileen gets up from the bed, picks up the typescript of Orwell's notes and approaches McNair, who has come to rest for a moment at the balcony. As she passes she touches Charles on the shoulder by way of apology, or comfort. To McNair she says, 'If you're disappearing, can you take this with you?'

'Christ,' Charles mutters under his breath. 'You'll save that but not yourself.'

She ignores him.

'And this.' She gives McNair a roll of waxed-paper trench plans and troop movements outside Huesca that Kopp has entrusted to her for safekeeping. 'You can fold those if you need to.'

McNair takes the manuscript, folds the waxed-paper plans and puts them all in his satchel.

Crook coughs. 'I might have somewhere you could all go,' he says. 'An anarchist tailor I know near the docks has a room above his shop.'

'Thank you,' McNair says, 'but young Cottman and I are staying at the lodging house on Plaça Macià for tonight.' He puts his satchel over his shoulder. 'After that, we'll see.' He turns to Eileen. 'You have all the passports?'

She nods. 'I'm taking them to the Police Prefecture tomorrow.'

'Good lass,' he says, and then he's gone.

Crook excuses himself and goes to the bathroom. Eileen leans on the desk and rolls a cigarette. Charles sits in silence. They hear the door to the next room open and shut.

Charles clears his throat. 'I saw Giorgio today, actually,' he says softly. 'Outside the police station. There was a big crowd there with Mrs Nin, demanding they release Nin.

Giorgio came up to us – it was the queerest thing. He promised to bring us blankets when we too would be in prison.' The music coming from the street stops. Charles drops his voice, almost to a whisper. 'A joke, do you think?'

Eileen shakes her head. 'He asked Lois and me what we wanted brought to us too. She wants peaches. I said a toothbrush.' She blows a smoke ring out the window. 'Perhaps a warning?'

Charles nods. 'Do you think he's working for them?'

She shrugs. The idea is shocking when she hears it in words, though she's half thought it before. 'No way of knowing. But the strange thing is, it didn't occur to either of us to ask him what *he* wanted.'

Charles is scratching at the cuticle on his thumb with a forefinger. The toilet flushes. He stands up.

'Eileen . . .' He removes the cigarette from her hand and places it in an ashtray. This contained, professional man is now holding her shoulders. 'Lois and I are going underground from tomorrow. She says we are rats leaving a sinking ship. I say that's better than disappearing into one of these godawful jails.' He holds her gaze. 'There's a boat for New York on Thursday.'

'That's three nights on the streets.' Her voice changes not a whit, though she has never heard this tone from him before – almost begging. 'I might be able to help you with tickets.'

Charles closes his eyes and breathes in deeply through his nose. 'I don't want you to help me. I want you to help *you*.'

Crook comes out of the bathroom. Charles lets go. He is dignified as ever, beyond embarrassment. Turns to Crook.

'And you – will you disappear too?' Charles asks him.

Crook shakes his head. 'I need to keep filing about this for as long as I can.' He puts his hat on. 'Let me know if either of you want that room.'

'Thanks,' Charles says. 'Let's talk tomorrow.'

'You?' Crook says to Eileen.

'No, thanks. Not yet.'

'*Adéu* then.'

~

That night, hiding out in a room of the lodging house where Cottman stays, McNair can't sleep. It's unbearably hot and he's terrified about the 'incriminating documents' in his bag. He decides to burn them. 'I tried with the tracing paper but it would not burn, it only smoked and melted a bit . . . I took the documents to the W.C., tore them into little pieces and pulled the chain to flush them down, but there was no water. I went into the kitchen and got a bucket of water to flush them down. Then I went back to bed.'

At 1.30 a.m. 'Six burly guards rushed in, seized me in my thin pyjamas and threw me on the bed.' They bark questions. McNair doesn't make a ruckus this time. Instead he yawns, pretending to be 'a tired, phlegmatic British traveller. '"I am here helping the Republicans,"' he tells them. The police open his satchel and find Orwell's manuscript, see the words 'POUM' and 'Huesca' in it. McNair bluffs: 'The POUM's one of the small parties isn't it?' he says. 'Of course this great writer needs to tell of all the little parties in this great struggle against fascism . . .'

After the men leave, he's shaky. He goes down the corridor to wake Cottman. They decide to flee at five in the morning and go 'on the run'. Later that day he 'saw the Stalinist morning paper and read that a warrant had been issued for the arrest of one John McNair, who had stolen fifty million pesetas. A good whopping lie, one of the sort that sticks.' He is, he feels, one step ahead of the story.

Others are not. That morning as Kopp strides into the Hotel Continental the concierge picks up the telephone. Armed guards emerge from nowhere, shuffle him through the doors and stuff him into a car.

Moments later Crook is arrested in the lavatory off the lobby. He is placed with Kopp in the same makeshift prison – to keep spying on him.

And at 8 a.m. they come for Lois and Charles. Eight men – 'four plainclothes men of the SIM* and four Assault Guards' – enter their flat and stay there for two hours. They search it 'to the bottom of the garbage can,' Charles reports, so thoroughly they found 'things that we had lost and could not find ourselves'. Then they take them both to jail.

At midnight the prisoners are marched out into the street, two guards flanking each one. Lois is 'sure my end had come'. At the very least, she thinks, they should be singing revolutionary songs, 'something, so that we didn't just let them extinguish our lives silently, in this utter darkness'. Nobody sings.

Charles and Lois are taken to the 'magnificent home of a fascist', now a jail, and put in windowless rooms, the men separated from the women. They are held for nine nights in cramped and horrible conditions, overseen by bewildered left-wing boys who can't understand why they are locking up their own comrades, nor why there's a Russian upstairs ordering them around. The prisoners are on starvation rations: watery soup with mouldy bread twice a day. There are no beds, but bedbugs crawl about. They try to keep their spirits up with songs, or by scrawling slogans on the walls. One of the women, they suspect (correctly, as it turns out), is a spy. They call Lois '"the baby"', she says, 'because my life story was so short'.

---

* SIM was the Servicio de Información Militar, the political police of the Republic.

Lois is brought before a Russian to have her fingerprints taken – five times, for five different forms. The man speaks excellent English. He 'frightened me to death', Lois remembered, 'by telling me what was to happen to each of these forms. "One goes to Moscow, one to the FBI in Washington, one to the Valencia government, one to the Generality police, and one we keep here," he said. "You will never be able to escape from your crimes."'

The next day the prisoners read in the communist press (the only paper they're given) 'the full accusation against us', which is 'a classic GPU frame-up: The secret network of foreign agents working for Franco and Trotsky would be brought to trial in specially created espionage courts.' This propaganda is reproduced around the world. Even the *New York Times* carries a piece, complete with photos, about the Orrs being members of a 'fascist spy ring'.

Outside, Eileen is 'working overtime' to keep informed about where they are, and what they need. This is almost impossible because Barcelona is now a network of secret prisons. But someone has told the American consul exactly where they are. Not only does the consul come to the correct secret prison, but he also brings the correct gift – peaches for Lois, 'but no toothbrush', because whoever is informing him – it must be Giorgio – knows Eileen isn't there. The American is refused access, but the peaches are, surprisingly, passed on. The women divide them up carefully so they get 'two bites apiece'. Lois is so grateful for a sliver of hope she can't join the dots to see it is Giorgio's betrayal that has put her here.

In Lois's home town in Kentucky a senator reads the *Times* piece naming her as part of the 'fascist spy ring'. As a long-time family friend he knows she's no fascist. The senator immediately contacts the American consul in Barcelona, who tries again to see her. When the Russians tell him Lois doesn't want to see him, he says he needs to hear that from her. She is 'hauled upstairs into a little room' where he is. 'I was never so happy to see anyone in my life,' she said.

At four o'clock the next morning Lois and Charles are released into the street. A week later they are in Paris.

Eileen is now truly alone. The only person left is Giorgio – a fact which may be of no comfort at all.

In Plain Sight

⌣

The office is disbanded. Everyone's in prison. George is
away somewhere, getting his discharge papers.

She sits most of each day and into the night in full view
in the hotel lobby. She changes chairs, drinks tea, orders
food she doesn't eat. She smokes and smokes.

George will get off a train from the front, push his
ragged frame through those gilded doors – and be arrested
before he can blink.

Every chair she sits in must have a view of the main
entrance. It's not much of a plan, but it's all she has. He will
walk in, she will get up and walk him out again. Hardly a
plan at all. For all she knows she may be luring him into a
trap. One of the reception staff seems friendly, but you can
never tell. Every time he picks up the phone she gets a stab
of terror in her belly and looks to see if the guards at the
door are coming for her.

The nights are the worst. If he is dead already, there's
no office left to let know. She wonders how long the news
would take to reach her. She could be here night after night
for no reason.

Very late on the fourth night Giorgio comes and stands
before her.

'You miss him?' he asks.

'I do.'

He leans down, touches her forearm. 'You should get some sleep, *carissima*. Really.'

What is he saying? The simplest things might mean something else. This place is insane.

She goes up to bed. Before she lies down she checks under the mattress: their passports and chequebook are still there. Then she settles in, like a hen on precious eggs.

It's hard to sleep. She watches her thoughts as they come in; it's Psychology 101, it's her trick not to be overwhelmed by them. What she thinks now is that there are two fictions protecting her. The first, that nothing ever happens to Pig. This brings Norah's gentle, smiling face near. The second is the illusion that because she's done nothing wrong she cannot be imprisoned. But democracy, like money, requires everyone to believe in it. Otherwise the law is just flimsy paper, same as the chequebook and passports she's lying on.

She drifts off thinking of Kopp and Crook, of Charles and Lois, all rotting in some cellar. If they are still alive. She hopes McNair and the boy have found a safe ditch or soft graveyard to sleep in. And she waits for the knock on the door. It might be George. Or it might be—

There it is. She sits up. She must have slept, but there's no light yet between the curtains.

The knock again. Not him then.

She hopes Giorgio has heard it next door. Putting her feet on the floor she calls, 'Coming,' quite loudly, in English, and hopes Giorgio hears that.

She opens to a blur. Six of them. Uniformed. Three carrying crates. She puts her hands to her neck, the tie of her nightie is undone. As they wordlessly take up positions, she inches back slowly onto the bed, rests against the headboard. Slips her feet under the covers. Her chest thumps, blood in her ears.

An older man with a thick neck and grey in his moustache is barking orders. Another, just a boy really, a spray of pimples on his cheek, sneaks a look at her. She gestures to the nightstand. Then slowly she reaches over, picks up her glasses, puts them on.

'*Buenos días,*' she says. She sits a little straighter on her pillows, one stacked up behind the other.

She listens for noise on the balcony. Nothing. Sucks in air, and holds it. What she knows, as they maintain their prearranged spots around the room, is that there is nothing here of value to them; they have everything they need already from office raids and spies, whoever they are. The purpose of this search is her terror alone. She has a part to play.

The men are moving, lifting, patting. The boy's hands are in her underwear drawer. He barely fills out his uniform, and here he is in a woman's bedroom, at dawn, riffling through her smalls. The other men sense his shame and want to eliminate it. She pretends not to see but she does – it shames them to see themselves reflected in the boy's black eyes, this boy who has not yet learned to distinguish a fascist from a POUM member, an order from something beyond the pale, a woman from an enemy of the cause—

'Desk drawers,' the commander barks at him.

One of the others is in the bathroom. She glimpses him feeling behind the cistern, bending to look under the bath, then hears him opening the cabinet, the clink of bottles being tipped into the basin. Another has upended the wastepaper basket under the desk and is examining the contents – mandarin peel, typewriter ribbon, crumpled paper. A third is sounding the walls, God alone knows what for. Then he stands on a chair, feels along the curtain rods. The one with the wastepaper basket finishes and starts rolling up the carpet. A fourth has opened the wardrobe and is putting his hands in the pockets of Orwell's trousers and her cardigans, taking a flesh-coloured slip out and holding it up to the light. The commander is examining the piles of books and manila folders on the desk and around the floor while the one who was in the bathroom now walks behind him, putting things in crates.

The commander stops. 'This, fascist,' he says. He is holding up McNair's copy of Hitler's *Mon Combat*.

'*Sí*,' Eileen says. '*Para saber.*' In order to know.

He keeps going. Stops again. She watches him pull out Stalin's pamphlet 'Measures for Liquidating Trotskyists and Other Double Dealers'. The commander puts it in the crate without comment.

The boy has worked his way through the desk drawers, pulling out pens, ink, paper, rubber bands, stamps, some letters, two notebooks, a matchbook, a torch, some wick rope, cigarette papers. A bloom of red is spreading up the back of his neck. The commander snatches the letters and notebooks and puts them in his satchel.

'The cigarette papers,' he says. 'Check them.'

There's half a second before the boy turns to the packet in his hands. His eyes meet hers. Then he looks away at her neck, her chest rising and falling.

'*Puc?*' May I? She gestures again to the bedside table where her cigarettes are, reaches and lights one.

The boy pulls out one cigarette paper, then another, till there's a fluttering white pile on the desk.

The men are there for two hours. She does not leave the bed.

The three bearing crates go through the door first, the commander leaves last. '*Senyora*,' he says as he passes her. He doesn't close the door.

Something rises in her throat. Every single thing in this room, every article and surface, has had their fingers on it. She goes to the bathroom and retches. Then she comes back, closes the door and thinks.

⌣

Orwell describes this scene twice in *Homage to Catalonia*. Once to account for how he lost his notebooks and some fan mail (and to apologise for not replying). The second time, he does it in a way that lets us hear, I believe, Eileen's voice telling him what happened (though he doesn't, of course, say it's her). The police, he writes, 'were thrown into ecstasies of suspicion by finding that we possessed a French translation of Hitler's *Mein Kampf*. If that had been the only book they found our doom would have been sealed.' But the next moment 'they came upon a copy of Stalin's pamphlet . . . which reassured them somewhat'. In the two hours that they were there, '*they never searched the bed*. My wife was lying in bed all the while; obviously,' and here I can hear Eileen again, 'there might have been half a dozen sub-machine guns under the mattress, not to mention a library of Trotskyist documents under the pillow'. Orwell makes no mention of his wife's courage, indeed he obscures it by saying 'our doom' would have been sealed – when it was she who was facing danger. For him, the episode is all about the men. 'Yet the detectives made no move to touch the bed, never even looked underneath it. I cannot believe that this is a regular feature of the OGPU routine. One must remember that the police were almost entirely under communist control, and these men were probably Communist Party members themselves. But they were also Spaniards, and to turn a woman out of bed was a little too much for them. This part of the job was silently dropped, making the whole search meaningless.' The episode becomes, for Orwell, a 'queer little illustration' of the 'generosity, a species of nobility' of the Spanish.

Orwell's notebooks are gone. The Spanish are decent. But 'my wife' is barely there.

The night after the raid she resumes her position in a wing-back chair in the lobby. She hasn't been able to eat today. She feels she has been turned inside out like a glove, defiled like the pockets of her cardigans. But there is nothing else she can do. She sits in the lobby, lit up for all to see, waiting for Orwell to walk through that door. She's sure she'll miss him when he comes – be in the loo, or distracted by someone talking to her, blocking her line of sight.

But she doesn't.

He comes through the revolving door like a revenant. Her heart races but she forces herself to move slowly. Smiling while everything inside her is screaming. She puts her arm around his neck, her mouth to his ear, and walks him back out the door.

This is Orwell's version:

It was late when I got back to Barcelona ... I made for the Hotel Continental, stopping for dinner on the way ... When I got to the hotel my wife was sitting in the lounge. She got up and came towards me in what struck me as a very unconcerned manner; then she put an arm round my neck and, with a sweet smile for the benefit of the other people in the lounge, hissed in my ear: *'Get out!'*

'What?'

'Get out of here *at once*!'

'What?'

'Don't keep standing here! You must get outside quickly!'

'What? Why? What do you mean?'

She had me by the arm and was already leading me towards the stairs . . .

'What the devil is all this about?' I said, as soon as we were on the pavement.

'Haven't you *heard*?'

'No. Heard what? I've heard nothing.'

'The P.O.U.M.'s been suppressed. They've seized all the buildings. Practically everyone's in prison. And they say they're shooting people already.'

So that was it. We had to have somewhere to talk. All the big cafés on the Ramblas were thronged with police, but we found a quiet café in a side street. My wife explained to me what had happened while I was away.

⁓

She leads him away from the hotel, through the fractal maze of streets to a café they've never been to before. They take a booth at the back. Eileen tells him to empty his pockets. She goes through his papers, says he should destroy his POUM card and some photographs of himself at the front. He won't part with his discharge papers, even though they might incriminate him. He folds them and places them back in his shirt pocket.

She tells him what she knows: the legless body of Nin, the POUM leader, has been found dumped on the steps of the parliament building in Madrid. Charles and

Lois – if they are still alive – are in a prison somewhere.
Kopp was arrested in the lobby and taken away, Crook too.
McNair and Cottman are on the run.

It's almost too much for Orwell to take in. He's
exhausted, his arm is sore, his throat is sore, he's still jangly
from being in the back of a truck. She puts her hand around
his neck, her forehead to his. She can feel the bullet hole
in his skin under her right fingertip. He just wants a bed.
He just wants to sleep.

'If you sleep in the hotel, my love, they'll have us both in
prison by tomorrow. No beds there.'

'It makes no sense. Why would anyone want to arrest
me? What have I done?'

'It doesn't matter. They've declared you're guilty of
"Trotskyism", and that's enough.'

'You're being patient with me, aren't you?' he smiles.

She kisses him. 'I'll put you in touch with McNair. I'm
meeting him tomorrow at ten near the consulate. You can
sleep under the stars with him and Cottman. The exit visas
should be ready in two or three days. After I've got them we
can try to leave.'

⌒

'Meanwhile,' Orwell writes of this time of mass arrests and killings,
'they had not "got" my wife. Although she had remained at the
Continental the police had made no move to arrest her. It was fairly
obvious that she was being used as a decoy duck.'

He imagines that Eileen's value to the Stalinists is because she
will lead them to him, a militiaman who's been off at the front. But
her value to them would have been much higher, because she knew
everything about the ILP and POUM from having worked at the
epicentre. He can't see it, or at least he can't say it.

For forty-eight hours Orwell, McNair and Cottman wait for Eileen to get their visas. At night they sleep rough. By day they pretend to be British tourists, eating in posh restaurants, getting a shave and having their shoes shined.

Eileen, meanwhile, sleeps alone in the defiled room, under surveillance. She goes in and out of the hotel past the guards who have arrested her friends. She needs to obtain the three stamps in their passports so they can get out of Spain. This is a complicated process, involving the risk of arrest at each step. Orwell describes it without mentioning her: 'It would probably take a couple of days to get our passports in order. Before leaving Spain you had to have your passport stamped in three separate places – by the Chief of Police, by the French Consul, and by the Catalan immigration authorities. The Chief of Police was the danger, of course.' That is the danger 'of course' because the police chief has just sent his officers to raid her room and arrest her friends.

The biographers, following Orwell's lead, don't mention that Eileen has to face that peril to save them. One, for instance, notes the danger and urgency of the task, without mentioning the person doing it – and implying they did it together: 'Had Orwell and Eileen remained in Spain they would almost certainly have been shot. Meanwhile they were stuck in Barcelona with time running out and a complex series of protocols to negotiate before they could escape.'

And even if they have all the right stamps in their passports their names will probably be on arrest lists at the French border. Everything will depend on the mañana nature of the Spaniards, and their communication – or lack of it – with the border guards.

On one of the two days while they wait for their passports, Eileen goes with Orwell to see Kopp in prison. This is a mad gesture of loyalty because visitors to 'Trotskyist-fascist' prisoners are, perhaps unsurprisingly, sometimes arrested as Trotskyist-fascists as soon as they walk in. They enter a smallish space, formerly the front of a shop.

It's filled with nearly a hundred people, standing room only. The light is crepuscular because the metal shutter is pulled down to the street, and the place has 'the beastly stench that you always get when crowds of people are penned together without proper sanitary arrangements'. When Kopp sees them, Orwell writes, he 'elbowed his way through the crowd to meet us. His plump fresh-coloured face looked much as usual, and in that filthy place he had kept his uniform neat and had even contrived to shave.' Kopp 'seemed in excellent spirits. "Well, I suppose we shall all be shot," he said cheerfully.' He tells them a massacre of 'Trotskyists' is expected. There is, though, one thing that might save him: a letter from a commander vouching for his bona fides as an engineer and requesting his presence at the eastern front. But that letter has been confiscated by the police.

Orwell dashes off to the Police Prefecture to try to get it back, a quest that astonishes several of the biographers in its bravery, though not one comments on Eileen having just been to the exact same place.

She looks up at Kopp's face. With George gone they are suddenly in a strange zone of silence, despite the prison din all around them.

'I hope they don't arrest him,' Kopp says.

'I was there yesterday,' she says. 'They seem pretty disorganised. Is your eye all right?' His left one is bloodshot.

'It's fine.' He takes her hands. His are large and warm and hers, small and cold, disappear.

'It's not fine!' she laughs, but hot tears spring up. 'I don't want to leave you here.'

He shrugs, still holding her. 'What will happen, will happen. Or not.' He bends close to her ear. She smells soap. 'If I get out of here we should marry. I can look after you.'

Her face is streaming but he has her hands and she can do nothing. She nods.

'I love you,' he says. He squeezes her hands tight, '*Je t'aime*, Eileen.'

She knows it's true. He has said it before. How can someone be so alive here, breathing in her ear, and then not. She wants to kiss him.

It's impossible. Over his right shoulder Crook appears and the room is full of noise again. Kopp lets her hands fall. Crook is unshaven, a dirty red bandana twisted around his neck.

'Lovebirds?' he smiles. He's shifting his weight from foot to foot.

She feels a surge of – hatred. Wipes her face with both hands.

'We were making arrangements,' she says. 'I can get letters out for you too, if you like.'

'Thanks,' Crook says. 'I'll have one for you tomorrow, if I can scrounge some paper.'

Then a guard is here, taking her by the elbow.

'Tomorrow then,' she says to Kopp over her shoulder, though they both know it's not true.

~

Eileen didn't get back to the prison, though Crook, as a career spy for Russia, needed no help to get letters out.

Kopp does write one. It's shortly afterwards, when he thinks he's about to be executed and this will be his last letter. It's to Eileen, in Britain. When Crook offers to get it out somehow, Kopp is suspicious. He manages to make another copy, and smuggles it out some other way. One of them, addressed to Eileen, reaches the UK (it seems Eileen destroyed it). And one, thanks to Crook, ends up with the secret police in Moscow.

Orwell doesn't manage to retrieve Kopp's letter from the police. There's nothing more he and Eileen can do for him except leave money with a local woman who will bring him food for as long as she can, or for as long as he is alive.

Seen

Eileen is still sleeping at the Continental, under the eyes of the enemy-authorities. The plan is for her to join Orwell, McNair and Cottman at the station for the 7.30 p.m. train to France. She is to be packed with everything of theirs – cases, bags, satchel, typewriter – and have a cab waiting so she can quickly pay the bill and get away before the hotel staff realise she's fleeing and call the guards. But when Orwell arrives at the station that evening he finds to his bewilderment that the train has left early. He manages to contact Eileen, who reverses her steps and stays another night in the hotel. He and the others sleep in an anarchist café owner's spare room.

The next morning she makes it to the station without being arrested: 'my wife slipped out of the hotel successfully', as Orwell puts it, without mentioning any danger she might have been in. The four of them board the train, sitting apart from each other, pretending to be wealthy tourists. 'I remember,' McNair writes, 'I was reading Wordsworth, Cottman my copy of John Masefield and Orwell was getting on with his book. It was a very slow train ...' Eileen doesn't rate a mention, though without her they'd probably not be there.

Two detectives come through the carriages taking down the names of foreigners, but 'when they saw us in the dining car they seemed satisfied that we were respectable', Orwell writes, so they leave them alone. The last check is at the passport office at the French border where 'they looked us up in the card-index of suspects', which must have been terrifying. But 'thanks to the inefficiency of the police our names were not listed, not even McNair's. We were searched from head to foot, but ... the *carabineros* who searched me did not know that the 29th Division was the P.O.U.M. So we slipped through ...' Orwell notes drily that 'The Spanish secret police had some of the spirit of the Gestapo, but not much of its competence.'

When they arrive in France the first thing McNair does is buy a newspaper from a kiosk near the station. He opens it to find a report of his arrest on charges of espionage, the newspapers having been fed the future by the powers that be. Once again, he is one step ahead of the story.

He and Cottman go to Paris. Eileen and Orwell have a few desultory nights in Banyuls-sur-Mer on the Mediterranean. Then they travel back to London through southern England, which seems to him, suddenly, to be 'the sleekest landscape in the world'.

After I had pieced together Eileen's time in Spain I still puzzled over how I could have read *Homage to Catalonia* twice before and never understood she was there. Eileen had worked at the political headquarters, visited him at the front, cared for him when wounded, saved Orwell's manuscript by giving it to McNair, saved the passports, saved Orwell from almost certain arrest at the hotel, and somehow got the visas to save them all. How is it that she remains invisible? I scanned through the electronic text of the book. Orwell mentions 'my wife' thirty-seven times. And then I see: not once is Eileen named. No character can come to life without a name. But from a wife, which is a job description, it can all be stolen.

Stalin's people, though, could see Eileen perfectly clearly. As Eileen and Orwell are arriving in the UK an indictment for treason against both of them is issued. Had they been caught, they would have been killed. The indictment is based on information from Crook, Wickes and Tioli. (Tioli disappeared around this time – no one knows how he perished. Perhaps, as Charles Orr thought, he was punished for trying to warn or comfort them, with blankets and peaches and toothbrushes.) And the Stalinists could name her (if with a lot of errors and typos):

> Tribunal of Espionage & High Treason, Barcelona 13 July 1937.
> ERIC BLAIR and his wife EILEEN BLAIR
> Their correspondence reveals that they are rabid Trotskyites.
> They belong to the I.R.P. [sic] in England . . .
> One has to consider them as ILP liaison agents of POUM.
> They used to live in the Falcon Hotel supported by the POUM executive committee.
> Credential of the POUM executive committee signed by Jorge [sic] Kopp (its nature leads one to suppose that it is a credential which was valid during the events that took place in May) and made out in favour of Eileen B.
> Eric B. Took part in the events of May . . .
> Eileen B. was at the Huesa front on 13. 3. 37 . . .

In Barcelona the streets hold their secrets. I walk up the Ramblas, past the Mercado de la Boquería where, during the fighting in May 1937, Orwell bought his wedge of goat's milk cheese. Past the stinking prison Kopp was held in, now a chain fashion store. When I reach the Hotel Continental, the grand entrance Eileen watched for Orwell to come through is no longer there; the street level has been sold off for shops. The entry is now a door to one side, opening on to a marble staircase that was once for the concierge, the staff and the policemen. The stairs are white and soft and cool, worn concave from the passage of countless feet.

From the lobby windows I look over at the Poliorama, where Orwell sat on the roof for three days. He would have been able to see Eileen's room. When the fighting stopped he had to get his rifle back over here without attracting attention. He put it down the leg of his trousers and walked it over, Monty Python style. Maybe she watched, laughed.

I walk a hundred metres down the street to the Hotel Rivoli.

Here is where Kopp's black staff car was shot up.

Here is where the boy lay dead that morning.

I look behind me. Up there is the balcony she could have seen it all from.

The plane trees are so beautiful, throwing their shapes around. The kiosk man smiles hello.

III

INVISIBLE
WORKER

Wallington
New Year's Day, 1938

There's still no electricity at the cottage. With the last of the daylight she stops typing. She's at the part where he decided, after being away to get his discharge during the mass arrests, disappearances and killings, to have dinner between the station and the hotel where she was. Her friends were all in prison. She had been waiting for him in the lobby of the hotel night after night, smoking and lit up for all to see.

She reads it back again: he stopped to have dinner and had a conversation with a 'very fatherly waiter' about copper jugs. Too much detail. She doubts that's what happened, but what did happen she doesn't want to know. When she types the part about the 'high-class brothels' being de-collectivised as the revolution was quashed, is when she particularly does not want to know.

He's upstairs, also typing. It's freezing. She puts her typewriter on the wobbly card table to be as close to the fire as possible. They're out of candles, or at least she can't find any down here. She has cut the fingers out of her gloves – much better for smoking, and typing. Her hands look like a tramp's, like Fagin's. She'll write to Norah, conjure her up for company. First, a cigarette. The match-burst of flame a breath of sulphur, comfort. She rests it in the ashtray.

The Stores, Wallington

New Year's Day

You see I have no pen, no ink, no glasses and the prospect of no light, because the pens, the inks, the glasses and the candles are all in the room where George is working and if I disturb him again it will be for the fifteenth time tonight. But full of determined ingenuity I found a typewriter, and blind people are said to type in the dark.

The dog lies sideways on the hearth, dreaming.

I found a bit of a letter to you, a very odd hysterical little letter, much more like Spain than any I can have written in that country.

She found it in a dress pocket when she unpacked, and it lies crumpled in front of her. Hopefully this fresh one will make more sense. She puts the cigarette between her lips and types with one eye closed.

So here it is. The difficulty about the Spanish war is that it still dominates our lives in a most unreasonable manner because George (or do you call him Eric?) is just finishing the book about it and I give him typescripts the reverse sides of which are covered with manuscript emendations that he can't read and he is always having to speak about it and I have returned to complete pacifism . . . .

She puts the cigarette down and looks at the crumpled letter. Then starts typing again.

War is fun so far as the shooting goes . . . but hardly anyone can stay reasonable, let alone honest.

She thinks of David Crook – beautiful, slim-hipped, raven-haired creature. It seems, mysteriously, that he's out of prison. Though poor Georges Kopp is still in some godawful cellar. She doesn't know if it can be explained, any of it. A tangled tale of love and bullets, spies and raids,

only part of which appears in the manuscript here on
the desk.

The abandoned cigarette has turned itself into a sleeve
of ash. She stubs it out. Lights a cigarillo. Picks up the
typewritten manuscript pages on the table, holding them
towards the firelight. Yes, here it is: 'Meanwhile the police
were arresting everyone they could lay hands on who was
known to have any connexion with the P.O.U.M. . . . the
police were adopting the trick (extensively used on both
sides in this war) of seizing a man's wife as a hostage if he
disappeared.'

She had told George about the wives being seized
because that was what she was risking in the hotel lobby
night after night. She sees now that her experience in
Spain has become separated from herself. It has become
his general knowledge, unattributed and unrelated to her.
When 'the police were arresting everyone they could',
those were her colleagues. The rumours that were flying,
and the Russian spy striding through the lounge with a
fringe of bombs on his belt – these are things she told
him. She herself has become generalised too, as 'my wife'.
Everything she is and does and knows seems to be his for
the taking.

There are not really words for this that she can find.
She stares at the pages of his book, her scrawl all over
the margins. She's in this story only in a way no one
will ever see, like scaffolding, or a skeleton, something
disappeared or covered over in the end result. The habit
of self-effacement, she thinks, only works if you still
exist, insisting on the smallness of your role as a sly way
of drawing attention to it. Self-effacement shouldn't be
literal, but there it is.

She places the cigarillo in the glass ashtray. She wonders if anyone, ever, will find her here, between the lines she is typing.

She'll just stick to telling Norah about the war.

The Georges Kopp situation is now more Dellian* than ever. He is still in jail but has somehow managed to get several letters out to me, one of which George opened and read because I was away.

Mary, their mutual friend from Oxford days, had asked her to come and visit her, urgently, on health grounds. She wishes George hadn't read the letter, in its curly European hand, its French 'I send you *pensées choisies*' and 'love to you' and mere 'shake hands' to him. George said he'd opened it because Kopp might have needed urgent help in prison, which was real enough. But so was his tight jaw as he said it. She felt she had nothing to explain, and yet it was the case that if a man wanted you, suddenly you did. His desire is your fault. Maybe it will make more sense on the page.

He is very fond of Georges, who indeed cherished him with real tenderness in Spain and anyway is admirable as a soldier because of his quite remarkable courage, and he is extraordinarily magnanimous about the whole business—just as Georges was extraordinarily magnanimous. Indeed they went about saving each other's lives or trying to in a way that was almost horrible to me, though George had not then noticed that Georges was more than 'a bit gone on' me. I sometimes think no one ever had such a sense of guilt before.

The typing upstairs stops. A cough. It goes on and on until he can draw breath and she hears him hitting the

---

* No one seems to know what she means by 'Dellian'. Possibly, it describes a three-cornered love affair they both knew of at university, or one in which someone called Dell pursued her.

keys again. She looks at her last sentence. The guilt, she
thinks, is not so much about what happened – or didn't –
between her and Georges. She was never in love with
him. It's more because Georges might have behaved
more sensibly if he hadn't been in love with her. Though
that's ridiculous – he'd still be in prison. She starts typing
again, to make something clear to herself as much as
to Norah.

*It was always understood that I wasn't what they call
in love with Georges—our association progressed in little
leaps, each leap immediately preceding some attack or operation
in which he would almost inevitably be killed, but the last
time I saw him he was in jail waiting, as we were both
confident, to be shot, and I simply couldn't explain to him
again as a kind of farewell that he could never be a rival to
George. So he has rotted in a filthy prison for more than six
months with nothing to do but remember me in my most pliant
moments. If he never gets out, which is indeed most probable,
it's good that he has managed to have some thoughts in a way
pleasant, but if he does get out I don't know how one reminds a
man immediately he is a free man again that one has only once
missed the cue for saying that nothing on earth would induce
one to marry him.*

Enough. What is there to do? Absolutely nothing. She
turns to the present tense, this farm and all its characters,
human and animal.

*We have nineteen hens now—eighteen deliberately and
the other by accident because we bought some ducklings
and a hen escorted them. We thought we ought to boil her this
autumn so we took it in turns to watch the nesting boxes to
see whether she laid an egg to justify a longer life, and she did.
And she is a good mother, so she is to have children in*

*the spring. This afternoon we built a henhouse . . . There is
probably no question on poultry-keeping that I am not able
and very ready to answer. Perhaps you would like to have
a battery (say three units) in the bathroom so that you
could benefit from my advice. It would be a touching thing
to collect an egg just before brushing one's teeth and eat it
just after. Which reminds me that since we got back from
Southwold, where we spent an incredibly family Christmas
with the Blairs, we have eaten boiled eggs almost all the
time . . . We also have a poodle puppy. We called him Marx
to remind us that we had never read Marx and now we
have read a little and taken so strong a personal dislike to
the man that we can't look the dog in the face when we speak
to him . . .*

She pats her leg. Marx dislodges himself from the
hearth, pads over. His tail wags involuntarily; his base
setting is joy.

*The dog is meant to be silver, but is black and white and,
at 4 months, greying at the temples; he is meant to be
miniature but is larger . . . and has a remarkable digestion.
I am proud of this. He has never been sick, although almost
daily he finds in the garden bones that no eye can have seen
these twenty years and has eaten several and a number of
chairs and stools . . .*

She tells Norah about her visit with Mary, whose
young son David *is very intelligent and makes me slightly
jealous because I should like a son and we don't have one.*

*Mary and I summed up human history in a dreadful way
when I was there—I was in the throes of pre-plague pains,
which had happened so late that I was wondering whether
I could persuade myself that I felt as though I were not going to
have them, and Mary wasn't having any pre-plague pains at*

Marx

all and was in a fever and going to the chemist to try to buy some ergot or other corrective.

Her friend wants an abortifacient. But for her, hope bleeds out every month.

The last candle is guttering, and there isn't any good way out of this letter.

She gets up and puts another piece of wood on the fire – it's late, but otherwise there'll be no light at all. She longs to go to Bristol to see Norah.

I am supposed to be having a holiday when the book is finished, as it will be this month, only we shan't have any money at all . . . I don't know whether I can get away even for a day because the book is late and the typescript of the final draft is not

*begun . . . and I keep getting his manuscript to revise and not
being able to understand anything at all in it—but if you <u>were</u>
coming to the sales these things would all be less important to
Pig.*

Before she can take the paper out of the typewriter he's
standing behind her, a dark shape coughing and talking.
She has no idea what time it is.

When he goes back upstairs she adds:

*Eric (I mean George) has just come in to say that the light
is out (he had the Aladdin lamp because he was Working) and
is there any oil (such a question) and I can't type in this light
(which may be true, but I can't read it) and he is hungry and
wants some cocoa and some biscuits and it is after midnight and
Marx is eating a bone and has left pieces in each chair and which
shall he sit on now.*

She winds the paper out of the machine. Then she goes
and makes the cocoa.

Eight weeks later and the book is done. It's early March,
still cold. They are by the fire in the front room. George
starts to cough, he coughs till blood comes out of his mouth.
So much blood, it seems prepared to go on forever. She calls
an ambulance, she calls her brother, she calls their friend
Jack Common in the next village to come and look after
the animals. George lies on the sofa with ice on his head, a
towel on his chest that is sodden, maroon, horrific. He says
he's sorry, then he says, 'Christ, what a mess.'
She rides in the ambulance to the hospital.

Laurence meets them there, thank God. He examines
George with his stethoscope, taps his white chest, orders

X-rays and sputum tests. He decides he wants George in his care at Preston Hall in Kent where he consults, so he orders another ambulance.

George is sedated for the trip. He falls asleep, propped up on pillows, his head dropped at an angle. She looks at his mouth, cleaned up so you'd never guess the horror that came out of it. She knows Laurence will tell her whatever the science says – TB, lesions, treatment options, the number of years and months left – and she will understand it. But at the same time – George's breathing is so calm, unruffled, his face sunk into its folds – she feels something in her split from science into hope and magic: she wants him to live no matter what the facts say. She feels herself enter a zone of will and unreality, love, and what used to be called prayer.

That night she stays at the Greenwich house with Laurence and Gwen. In the morning she writes to clever, kind Jack to thank him for coming to the cottage in the pouring rain to look after the animals. She tells him *they've stopped the bleeding, without the artificial pneumothorax* they were going to have to insert. The ride from the local hospital to Preston Hall was

in an ambulance like a very luxurious bedroom on wheels . . .
so it was worth while. Eric's a bit depressed about being in an
institution devised for murder but otherwise remarkably well.
He needn't stay long they say, but the specialist has a sort of hope
that he may be able to identify the actual site of the haemorrhage
and control it for the future . . . This was really to thank you for
being so neighbourly from such a distance, in such weather. One
gets hysterical with no one to speak to except the village who are
not what you could call soothing. I'll let you know what happens
next. I have fearful letters to write to relations.

Yesterday's panic embarrasses her now that it's over.
You write to find out what you feel; she only sees how alone
she is in the village now she's written it. She can't tell Jack
that the specialist is her brother – it will look to him, a
working-class man, like special treatment for the middle
class. Which it is.

Jack has left before she gets home to the cottage. When
she turns the key in the door Marx is ecstatic, jumping up
and whimpering, turning shaggy pirouettes. He has chewed
the cushion stuffing out of a striped armchair, which is
bad, even for him. Nellie has pulled out the stake she was
tethered to and devoured the entire spinach crop. Her udder
looks painful; first thing to do is get the pail and milk her.

Tongue Kiss

For the six months that Orwell is at Preston Hall sanatorium Eileen lives alone. Every fortnight she visits him. The trip from Wallington to Kent is expensive and takes five hours. It's a three-mile walk to the bus, then a train, then the underground, another train, another bus and another walk. She'd have preferred to live with Laurence and Gwen – and it would have been closer – but she must tend to the goats (they have two now), the ducks and chickens. She brings Orwell food, flowers and stories of the Scheherazade hen, who has saved her own life by laying.

One time she asks Lydia to go in her stead. Living in London, Lydia is closer. 'I was to take George some home-made scones and a bunch of cowslips, of which they both were very fond,' Lydia writes.

The sanatorium was some way out of Maidstone and was surrounded by a large park. I found George fully dressed sitting in a deck chair outside; on my arrival, he got up and suggested we should go for a walk in the park. We did not go very far. When we were out of sight of the buildings, we sat on the grass and he put his arms around me. It was an awkward situation. He did not attract me as a man and his ill health even aroused in me a slight feeling of revulsion. At the same time, the fact that he was a sick man, starved of intimacy with his wife, made it difficult for me to repulse him. I did not want to behave like a prude or to treat the incident as a serious matter. Why should I push him away if kissing me gave him a few minutes of pleasure? I was convinced that he was very fond of Eileen and that I was in no sense a rival to her.

When Orwell had murmured, that Christmas before leaving for Spain, 'shan't be kissing you under the mistletoe', Lydia had sensed immediately a sexual approach designed to undermine Eileen. This is where it has led – to a tubercular tongue kiss. And then Lydia leaps into the eternal female doublethink, which is automatically to see things, including oneself, from the man's point of view. She anticipates the insult 'prude' if she rebuffs him. It would be humourless of her to 'treat the incident as a serious matter'. She is trapped in a way she can't quite articulate that makes it somehow easier to kiss her beloved friend's sick husband than not to, though she knows that the kiss is a betrayal of Eileen and, possibly, the kiss of death. Just as Eileen had felt herself to be a comfort she couldn't withhold from Georges Kopp who might have died any day in Spain, Lydia feels herself to be a pleasure Orwell deserves.

A kiss – especially a first kiss – is not just a kiss. It is a situation a woman must navigate. The options for her are prude/slut or humourless bitch/accomplice, and the slash that divides them is the slimmest of terrains in which a woman might first find, and then satisfy, her own desire.

As the months roll on Eileen and Orwell's funds deplete, so she takes in typing to keep them afloat. At the end of his stay, the medical recommendation is to go to a milder climate so he can recover further. They are practically broke, but an anonymous benefactor – actually the novelist L. H. Myers – gives them £300* so they can go. Orwell hates to accept so much money, but Laurence persuades him it's medically necessary. They board the SS *Stratheden* for Marrakesh in northern Africa in September 1938.

Before they leave, things are a blur. *For myself,* Eileen writes, *I don't remember the last few weeks in England except that they were spent almost entirely in trains. People had to be said good-bye to & things (including Eric) collected from all over the country & the cottage had to be handed over to the Commons who are spending the winter there & mustering the goats etc . . . .*

She takes Marx to stay with Orwell's sister Marjorie in Bristol, but for some reason – is there not time, or is she not there? – she doesn't manage to see Norah.

---

*   About £20,000 at the time of writing.

On Becoming Visible and Invisible, *à la fois*

Quicksand

When I was small we lived in France. Just before we came back to Australia – I was six – we went to Mont-Saint-Michel on the Normandy coast. To get there we drove along a causeway across a landscape of wet sand through which the sea was rising unseen. The tide, we wide-eyed children were warned, came in faster than you could run. The Mont itself was from a fairy tale, a castle on a hill of underling underbuildings. When we got out of the car we were told that the sand was in fact quicksand, so I stepped into it immediately. My leg sank in to the knee. I had to be hauled out, but it was something I wanted to know.

Back in Melbourne my mother enrolled me at the Alliance Française to keep up my French. After the first class, the teacher, a man with a black beard, took me aside and asked me when my birthday was. I told him and he leant down. 'And then,' he said softly into my face, 'I will give you *une bise*.' I understood what he meant, and I also understood it would not be a normal birthday kiss. I said nothing to my mother, only that I didn't want to go back. For the first – and I believe only – time in my life, she didn't make me persist with something. That still surprises me. And what's more surprising is that she never asked me why.

I have conflated – in the way of dreams, of memory, of the swift, subterranean imperative of narrative – this first experience of sexual threat, the sadness of how I knew it in my bones at six – with the galloping tide at Mont-Saint-Michel. The fabulous and freaky haste of the world you might be curious about and then, if only just, able to outrun.

Point de Vue

A later stay in France, this one a holiday as a pre-teen. I lie around, reading my father's Simenon and Ross Macdonald detective novels, and adjust myself to seeing the world through the eyes of the private dicks. It is a world where women are foreigners, there to be desired. My father and I and the teenage boy staying with us walk along the beaches of Hyères. At the first one the women wear bikinis, at the second they are topless and in the third bay they are naked. My father, a kind man, says light-heartedly to the boy – he's fourteen – 'You can look, but don't touch.' They laugh, and I realise I'm not even there, topless with my small feet in the sand.

Later, in the middle of the night, we children are laid out asleep. The boy starts to caress my leg from the toe, moving ever higher up my thigh. I pretend to be asleep. His hand moves, always stopping before it gets where I want it to go. He hadn't listened to my father. Neither had I.

Mushrooms

I was about twenty. A party at the family home. It was quite early in the evening – still light, people still sober. I was standing with my parents and another couple, he a professor of medicine, like my father. Apropos of nothing, while the conversation continued, the professor leant across, grabbed my wrist, and pulled my hand to his crotch. He may have said something, made some kind of joke, but I don't remember anyone noticing anything at all.

Afterwards I described it to my mother, who had been there. I can't believe she didn't see – was she somehow distracted? Dealing with the food? Disciplining the crazy dog? I told her, 'It felt like a bag of mushrooms.' She laughed because she liked similes. And that, as they say, was that. I wasn't traumatised. The situation was so public there was no threat in it. The shock consisted in realising that a man could feel free, or compelled, or both, to do that in front of his wife and my parents, in our house, and that he would get away with it. Invisibility feels like mushrooms, sounds like a titter.

Morocco

Orwell and Eileen spend their first night in Marrakesh in a hotel. It *may have been quite good once,* Eileen writes to her mother-in-law, but *lately it had changed hands & is obviously a brothel. I haven't much direct knowledge of brothels but as they offer a special service they can probably all afford to be dirty & without any other conveniences.* They stay anyway, *partly because Eric didn't notice anything odd about it until he tried to live in it & partly because my temperature was by that time going up about one degree an hour & I only wanted to lie down, which was easy enough, & to get drinks, which were brought to me by a limitless variety of street Arabs who looked murderous but were very kind. Eric of course ate out & this is very expensive in Morocco so we moved here as soon as possible . . .*

They have found a villa for rent, five kilometres out of the city.

Once installed, she writes to Norah. She wants to make sense of how they got here, but there is one crucial thing she obscures, both telling her and not.

Eileen tells Norah that the doctors had kept Orwell in the sanatorium for months after they'd decided he *didn't* have TB. This is odd, because he was in fact suffering from the disease. Orwell was evasive about his illness all his life, perhaps not wanting to focus on it, given that there was no cure. He often didn't tell people around him — it's a small miracle more of them didn't catch it. Sometimes he called it 'bronchiectasis' (a less serious lung disease). Mostly he just ignored it. Eileen and Laurence would have known exactly what the situation was from the X-rays, so she might have been covering up the severity of the situation to spare Norah's feelings.

But despite writing that Orwell didn't have TB, Eileen almost reveals the truth when, describing her brother's insistence on a warmer climate, she says, that Laurence *was unable to think of any more lies about the disease*. And Eileen and Orwell both know his life will likely be cut short. *Of course we were silly to come but I found it impossible to refuse & Eric felt that he was under an obligation though he constantly & bitterly complains that by a quite deliberate campaign of lying he is in debt for the first time in his life & has wasted practically a year out of the very few in which he can be expected to function.*

But for the moment he is working and they are both well enough. The house is beautiful, she tells Norah, if isolated. It's in the middle of *an orange grove & everything belongs to a butcher who cultivates the orange-grove but prefers to live with his meat. The only neighbours are the Arabs who look after the oranges . . .* One of the locals, Mahjroub, keeps house for them. The villa is furnished with grass-and-willow chairs, a prayer mat, *two charcoal braziers for cooking, about a third of the absolutely essential crockery & some chessmen.*

She has bought a bicycle and likes to ride into Marrakesh. The city has pink walls, she tells Norah, and is full of *beautiful arches with vile smells coming out of them, adorable children covered in ringworm and flies . . . The markets are fascinating if you smoke (preferably a cigar) all the time and never look down.*

Eileen brought the flies to life in a letter to another friend, observing that *The Arabs favour bright green* [shrouds] *& don't have coffins which is nice on funeral days for the flies who leave even a restaurant for a few minutes to sample a passing corpse.* Orwell used her observations for the opening of his essay 'Marrakesh', transmuting them this way:

As the corpse went past the flies left the restaurant table in a cloud and rushed after it, but they came back a few minutes later ... What really appeals to the flies is that the corpses here are never put into coffins, they are merely wrapped in a piece of rag and carried on a rough wooden bier on the shoulders of four friends.

Eileen is pithily alive to all the characters in her sentence – Arabs, flies, even the corpse, which, in '*passing*', has something to do. The contradictions are where her humour lives: the shroud is '*bright*', the lack of coffins is '*nice*', the flies can ponder their choice between sampling restaurant food and a corpse.

In Orwell's version the corpses are somehow being mistreated: 'never' put into coffins, 'merely wrapped in a piece of rag' and taken on a 'rough wooden bier'. There are no Arabs, and no choosy flies. One biographer notes the similarities, saying this 'suggests that key ideas in his later work may have emerged from mutual observations and discussion with the poetic Eileen'. The biographer is pointing ahead, I think, to *Animal Farm*. I would put it more clearly, and say that it shows how ways of seeing other characters and creatures of all kinds – more vivid, more humane, more humorous – came from her.

This morning she went into Marrakesh to buy Christmas presents to send home. George haggled (badly, he's too generous) for a brass tray fully four feet across which will doubtless dominate them for the rest of their lives. She found an exquisitely worked leather box for Norah.

Now, she rests in the house, the tiles cool under her bare feet. Mahjroub has just washed the floor, so for the next ten minutes it'll be free of grit. She can hear him at work in the kitchen, moving backwards on his hands and knees with the bundle of wet rags. She sends him home in the evenings now, because he'd spent them sitting on the back step, leaping up and down intermittently to wait on them at the table. George didn't notice, but Mahjroub's anxiety was unbearable to her. He is wizened and watchful and deferent in a way that puts distance between them, but they still talk. He was recruited as a child soldier by the French. She wonders if he knows there's another war coming.

The typewriter clacks from the small observatory on the roof. George is writing a novel he's calling *Coming Up for Air*, about a man with a nagging wife and a couple of brats who lives in a miasma of middle-aged disappointment. She thinks it's good. She also thinks he's expiating some terrors.

In the corner of the room one of the pair of doves they bought craps succinctly then struts off. She'll have to call Mahjroub back for that. She adjusts the hot-water bottle on her abdomen, and then the belt that holds the cloth between her legs. The bleeding has been painful, but it should be over soon. It's nothing like the violent headaches – along with the additional achievement of food poisoning – she survived in the first weeks in this country. Mahjroub has made her mint tea with water she asked him to boil for twelve minutes, though he shook his head about the waste of gas.

Outside, the sun has baked the ground gold. The washing she hung on the line this morning – sheets, underpants, shirts – flaps like live things, or a semaphore of surrender.

She takes a fresh piece of paper from the ream and starts to write. The news to relay to Norah about family at home isn't great. People are finding it hard to know how seriously to prepare for war. Orwell's sister Marjorie is buying gas masks for her children but calling her husband a 'lunatic' for digging a bomb shelter in their yard. Old Mr Blair is dying of cancer and not making a fuss of it. But what's really on her mind is that *Georges Kopp proposes to come & stay with us in Morocco (he has no money & we had heard the day before by cable that he was out of jail & Spain. Eric's reaction to the cable was that Georges must stay with us & his reaction to Georges's letter announcing his arrival is that he must <u>not</u> stay with us, but I think the solution may be that Georges won't find anyone to lend him the necessary money).*

She doesn't really want to see Kopp. She suspects that, shorn of the drama of war, the high-stakes life that turned the unlikeliest of men into heroes, he will seem wet and unreliable. She realises with a pang of shame that she was happy in Spain to take florid French hyperbole as real; it seemed to match the situation there. She doesn't even know what he reads. Hopefully, he won't come. Perhaps she should suggest he goes to Laurence and Gwen in the UK instead.

Eric [George] *however is better . . . & doesn't cough much (though still more than in England) so I think he may not be much worse at the end of the winter abroad than he was at the beginning. I expect his life has been shortened by another year or two but all the totalitarians make that irrelevant . . . now that we're hardened to the general frightfulness of the country we're quite enjoying it. Eric is writing a book which pleases us both very much. And in a way we have forgiven Brother Eric* [Laurence] *who can't help being a Nature's Fascist & indeed is upset by this fact which he realises.*

She sits back, lights a cigar. Norah knows Laurence is a socialist; she will understand that she means he's authoritarian about his medical pronouncements.

The doors here are all open. Outside, Mahjroub is humming as he wrings the washrags in the trough.

He has been worried lately because he never can remember the French for fish but this week he's really learnt it—it's oiseau.* We understand each other very nicely now (he often calls me Mon vieux Madame) though I seldom know whether he is talking French or Arabic & myself often speak English. He does the shopping & pumps the water & washes the floors . . . & I do the cooking & curiously enough the washing. The laundries are very expensive . . . We also have two doves. They don't lay eggs but if they think of it will doubtless nest in our pillows as they spend most of the day walking about the house—one behind the other.

Eileen has a favour to ask. Marjorie has written to her saying 'Marx is being perfectly good except for such natural wickedness as will never be eradicated', a sentence that at first struck Eileen as funny, but now she feels the poor pup might need rescuing. Eileen would like Norah to check on him, and pay a diplomatic visit to George's sister. *Deep in my heart I dislike Marjorie who isn't honest but I always enjoy seeing her.* And Marjorie's children – Jane fifteen, Henry ten, Lucy seven – are fun.

She's late choosing a Christmas card for Norah's mother. She hasn't told Norah she's been in hospital here with a fever, migraines and extended bleeding, but she can tell her now because it's as good as over.

. . . a fortnight ago I suddenly got violent neuralgia & a fever. Normally I go into Marrakech on a red bicycle made in Japan for someone with very short legs & the biggest hands in the world, but for this occasion I had a taxi to go for an X-ray.

*   Bird.

It seemed obvious that I had another cyst—indeed I even packed a bag in case I had to go into hospital again. There was nothing whatever the matter with my jaw & the fever just went away two or three days ago & today I went out for the first time with a handkerchief round my head . . . it's too late for Christmas cards so give your mother my love instead for the moment and all the other relatives & yet uniquely Norah is loved by
                    Pig.

She hips a large wicker basket off the kitchen floor. As she steps out towards the washing line she hears, carried on the wind, the five o'clock call to prayer. Mahjroub is gone to his vespers.

Eileen in Morocco – most likely taken by George, whose shadow is on the wall.

Break

After he's finished *Coming Up for Air* and she has edited and retyped the manuscript, they go for a break to Taddert, high up in the Atlas Mountains. It's a village of tiny, flat-roofed stone dwellings nestled like a cubist apparition on a bare, snow-dusted expanse.

⁓

They find an inn, sit on cushions to eat mutton stew, drink tea from small glasses. Outside, the townspeople go about robed in hooded garments that reach the ground; the women wear silver bracelets and line their eyes with kohl. Their chins are tattooed. George is fascinated by the girls. She feels his gaze linger on them, and she sees that he doesn't care that she sees.

They use their right hands to eat, as they have learned to do. George asks the young daughter of the innkeeper for a spoon and is given one. After the meal he leans back.

'I've been working so hard, Mum,' he says, in a schoolboy voice, fumbling in a trouser pocket for the lighter he brought back from Spain, with its long yellow wick.

'You have, dear.'

'I deserve a treat,' he says, blowing a thin stream of smoke away from her.

A small thing inside her turns to stone. He doesn't mean

her. She forgets to breathe, then does. Closes her mouth. He says he wants one of these Berber girls, 'just one'.

'And from me you want?' she says.

'I just thought I should tell you.'

She waits that night alone in their small room, looking out a window without glass over the village into deep blackness. A red cloth dangles on one side of the opening – some kind of curtain. Waiting in rooms seems to be a part of marriage. It is a thing she does now; she hadn't anticipated so much waiting in rooms. She smokes, paces. Reading isn't working. She tries to examine her thoughts, then decides she must not. There are no proper thoughts anyway; in their stead is a hollowness, a wretchedness. Something is happening that will change her place in her life.

He is at the door, red fag ember between his fingers. There are, of course, no bathrooms here, no washing facilities beyond a jug. One bed.

This will not go in a letter to Norah. There are no words for this, this being put to one side.

⌐

I am imagining these details, but because this is what happened, there must have been some kind of scene. I use evidence most of the biographers omit; when they can't, they slip it into footnotes and throw doubt on it as well, hoping to transmute a fact to a rumour. Their efforts betray a difficulty squaring 'decent' Orwell with his actions.

Sometimes a male source does the doubting for them. Tosco Fyvel and his wife, Mary, became good friends of Eileen and Orwell later, during the war. At a lunch at their house, Orwell, presumably out of Eileen's earshot, reminisced to Mary about his sexual exploits in Morocco, perhaps by way of indicating to her that he had 'permission' to stray – and seeing if she did too.

Tosco recalled, 'I can also remember his talking to Mary about the time he and Eileen spent in Morocco. He said that he found himself increasingly attracted by the young Arab girls and the moment came when he told Eileen that he had to have one of these girls on just one occasion. Eileen agreed, and so he had his Arab girl. True or imagined? It did not matter.'

I bet it mattered to her. And there is other evidence, again from Orwell's own lips. And again, often relegated to a footnote. At the end of the war Orwell dined with the wealthy gay writer and scholar Harold Acton in Paris. Acton remembered their conversation.

> . . . I prompted him to reminisce about his life in Burma, and his sad earnest eyes lit up with pleasure when he spoke of the sweetness of Burmese women . . . He was more enthusiastic about the beauties of Morocco, and this cadaverous ascetic whom one scarcely connected with fleshy gratification admitted that he had seldom tasted such bliss as with certain Moroccan girls, whose complete naturalness and grace and candid sensuality he described in language so simple and direct that one could visualize their slender flanks and small pointed breasts and almost sniff the odour of spices that clung to their satiny skins. A description worthy of Gide, I mused, and equally sincere.

The biographers try to excuse Orwell's behaviour. One claims that 'this evidence is very hard to handle', and then reveals just how hard he finds it, by writing 'The Moroccan admission, even if actually said, is unlikely – and Orwell knows whom he was talking to and may have been trying to embarrass him. (Even Dr Johnson once debated whether intercourse with a Duchess would give, in principle, more pleasure than with her serving maid.' It's clear the biographer wants to throw doubt on it, referencing Acton's homosexuality in a veiled way and then invoking literary luminary Samuel Johnson's help to justify Orwell sleeping with someone assumed to be of a lower class. Other biographers, writing together, try to schedule this tryst out of existence, by adding in a footnote: 'Masculine pride, of which Orwell had his share, accounts for much . . . and almost certainly for [this] curious conversation . . .' Then they monotonously list travel dates, stress how hard he was working on *Coming Up for Air*, that he was ill for three weeks after their mountain holiday and that the couple then set out for London, as if to give the impression that he was simply so *busy* before and after his break in the mountains that he would have had neither the time nor the energy to procure himself a Moroccan girl while there.

Another biographer tries to minimise Orwell's cruelty by implying it was a mutual arrangement. He writes that 'in the end Eileen had allowed him to have one' of the 'teenaged Arab prostitutes in Marrakesh' (though the conversation with the Fyvels is sometimes reported to be about the innkeeper's young daughter in Taddert). This, he continues, 'lent an odd gloss to an otherwise conventional relationship, the thought of shadowy, secret recesses stretching away beneath the surface of their public lives'. But the 'shadowy recesses' were not behind 'their' public lives; they were behind his. The biographers are trying to save their subject from himself, giving him his agency and his innocence at the same time. Or, in this case, his 'Moroccan girl' and his decency, despite the evidence. It is done by reducing the act, and so the woman (or girl), to a boast, a scheduling impossibility, or a mutual arrangement.

Orwell is not too busy to be planning his sex life upon his return to England. He has been secretly writing to Lydia, letters which make her deeply uncomfortable:

So looking forward to seeing you! I wonder who your young man is now? I have thought of you so often – have you thought about me, I wonder? I know it's indiscreet to write such things in letters, but you'll be clever and burn this, will you?

Lydia read that letter 'with mixed feelings':

I was looking forward to seeing Eileen again but not George, especially as the tone of his letter suggested a renewal of the amorous behaviour I had been too soft-hearted to repel at the Maidenhead hospital. Nor did I like the phrase 'who your young man is now?' – as if he had played that part before they had left for Marrakesh. I had several men friends at the time whom I found far more attractive than George, and his masculine conceit annoyed me. Least of all did I want to disturb his relationship with Eileen, or have anything to conceal from her. I was determined to remain passive as far as 'keeping dates open' was concerned and to avoid making things easier for him.

But in her flat she is a sitting duck.

As the dates he had mentioned approached, I went about my affairs as usual, and one afternoon found a card had been dropped through my door on which he had scribbled:

Dear Lydia,

I knocked on the door of your flat and was very disappointed not to find you at home. I gathered from the hall porter that you were not actually away from London. I've got to go down to-morrow and see my parents for the week-end, but hope to see you when I get back about Tuesday. Meanwhile, if clever I may be able to look in for an hour tomorrow morning, so try and stay at home in the morning, will you?

Love, Eric.

Lydia avoids this visit:

> I do not remember whether I went out that morning, or did not
> answer the telephone, knowing it would be George announcing
> his arrival, but whatever I did, was done deliberately. I was
> annoyed by his assuming that I would conceal our meetings
> from Eileen, revolted by deception creeping in against my
> wishes. I wanted to avoid meeting him when I was in that
> hostile mood, capable of pushing him away if he tried to
> embrace me.

As it happens, he can't get to London as planned, so Lydia 'was spared
this particular experience'. But not the repercussions of daring to avoid
him. He's angry.

> *Dear Lydia,*
>
> *You were mean not to stay at home this morning like I asked you.*
> *But perhaps you couldn't. I rang up 3 times. Are you angry with me?*
> *I did write to you twice from Morocco, and I don't think you wrote*
> *to me. But listen. I am coming back to town Monday or Tuesday,*
> *and Eileen is going to stay down here a bit longer. I shall have to be*
> *in town several days to see to various things, so we can arrange to*
> *meet – unless you don't want to? I'll ring up.*
>
> *Yours ever. Eric.*

A few days later another letter arrives explaining that he wasn't able to
come this time either, because of illness:

> *. . . but in not many days I'll have to come up to town on business, and*
> *we'll meet then. I'll let you know beforehand. So sorry it didn't come off*
> *this time.*
>
> *Best love. Eric.*

Lydia gives in. Instead of feeling annoyed or 'mean', she'd prefer to feel humane. It seems easier, but it's not really.

> I felt sorry too – not about our failing to meet, but about him falling ill so soon after he had spent several months in Africa, at considerable expense, for the sake of his health. My annoyance with him was extinguished by compassion. So when we met at last, I could not be unpleasant to him. He, no doubt, chose to think that I let him kiss me because I liked it. I did not. He was not merely failing to attract me as a man, but the fact of his being a sick man vaguely repelled me.

It gets worse when she realises *why* Orwell wants to be sexually involved with her.

> ... I was further disturbed by his relating to me with some amusement how he had 'slipped up' by almost blurting out to Eileen that he was going to meet me in London. He was in bed when she brought him my letter, a reply to his last one and, as he opened it, he said, spontaneously: 'A letter from Lydia!' Then, suddenly realizing that she might ask to see it and discover that he had written to me more than once in the last few days, he promptly told her something of its contents. Luckily, he said, Eileen showed no curiosity about the rest, and he was so clearly pleased about his success in this bit of concealment that it made me angry again. The unwelcome, the positively repellent role of an accomplice in deceit was thrust upon me. And why should I deceive my friend Eileen, whose friendship I valued much more than his? Why did he want to make love to me? A sick man, losing confidence in his attractiveness to women, needing reassurance, needing comforting ...?

Eileen would most likely have recognised the handwriting on the envelope, or the return address on the back of it. Perhaps she showed no curiosity because she wasn't suspicious of Lydia, or perhaps she did not want to give Orwell the satisfaction of his cruel power game. Lydia, for her part, wants to avoid being angry or prudish. She wants, strenuously, to feel compassionate.

> That was how I saw his insistence on treating our relationship as an amorous affair, though I resisted throughout it becoming a love affair. I felt very guilty about having to conceal from Eileen my meetings with her husband – but what was the use of telling her? I feared her discovering it, because she might not have believed that I was an unwilling accomplice.

When Orwell had moved to a flat with two men during his engagement and continued sleeping with Kay, it seems as if he wanted to remove himself from the world of women who might tell Eileen about it. Then he had isolated Eileen further by moving to Wallington. There, he fell ill just about every time she tried to leave to see Norah or her brother. Now, it seems, he wants to isolate her from her persistent friend Lydia too, using sex as a weapon to divide them.

Orwell could have had sex with any number of other women not known to Eileen. He frequented brothels – he could have gone to one. The attraction of Lydia was perhaps that sex with her would do maximum harm to Eileen. Going for your wife's close friend is an act calculated to undermine your wife. That way she will be all the more totally alone, and so all the more yours.

Lydia felt cornered. Was she wedged into silence by that first unwanted kiss, by which she was forced to betray her friend? Or was it something else?

At the end of her life Lydia wrote in her private diary, 'My main memories of [Orwell] are tactile . . . the sensation of bristly short hair at the back of his head, the touch of his lips on mine, a slight whiff of a faint sweetish smell from his mouth (his damaged lung?).' Was she curious about what Eileen had? Did her love for Eileen extend, in some psychic triangle of desire, to wanting to sleep with the same man she did? There's no knowing; possibly she didn't know either. But it's important to believe what she says, and I do, when she describes herself as 'an unwilling accomplice'.

⌣

They've been home from Morocco a month. George is visiting his parents at Southwold. She is at Wallington, alone again with the animals. After the chores are done in the mornings, she goes for long walks in the countryside, coming home through the village.

When she sees young Peter, the boy she tutored, tapping an old bicycle wheel along with a stick, her heart lifts. She ups her pace towards him. He is a gentle boy, hazel-eyed and cowlicked, and now he is at the grammar school he will have a life that will suit him. He catches the bicycle wheel in his left hand and beams. They stop together in the middle of the street.

Suddenly, she says she must go home, mutters some excuse about goat mush. She turns quickly away, fumbling in her pocket for cigarettes before she's even at the gate. When she pulls it something catches the skin of her hand and she recoils. She sucks her finger on her way up the path, shoves the house door open with one shoulder.

She'll have to apologise to the dear child. All he'd said was that he saw Mr Blair too, last week, with the other lady teacher, walking towards the woods.

⌣

Lydia is living with the terror of deceit. One day Eileen comes to her flat, arriving 'in a state of great frustration and anger against her husband'.

> She began by telling me that after their return from Morocco their relationship had been unusually harmonious; then, all of a sudden things began to go seriously wrong.
>
> 'I know why!' she said impulsively and with such uncharacteristic harshness and determination that I felt shaken, expecting to be charged with being the cause of her unhappiness. 'It's that woman!' she continued.
>
> 'What woman?' I asked weakly.
>
> 'The woman he went to meet in the wood the other day . . . He knew her before he married me. She's a schoolmistress, or something. The village people saw him meeting her. This affair goes on because she wouldn't sleep with him. If she had, it would have been finished long ago.'
>
> As she went on talking, furious, unforgiving, fear released its grip on me . . . Clearly, George needed a lot of reassuring and comforting! And it amused me to hear Eileen say that 'the woman' had such a hold on him because she would not sleep with him. Could this be the reason for his being so persistent with me?

When she confronts him about meeting Brenda for a walk in the woods George defends himself by saying he hasn't slept with her.

> 'I know. You wouldn't be this obsessed if you had.'
>
> 'So . . .' he smiles. 'What if I wished it – just twice a year? Get her out of my system.'
>
> 'That's hardly out of your system,' she says, her voice stony.

Mind the Gap

He felt as though he were wandering in the forests of the sea bottom, lost in a monstrous world where he himself was the monster.

George Orwell, *Nineteen Eighty-Four*

Craig and I are at our son's third-grade parent–teacher interview. We sit on the miniature chairs, our knees just fitting under the laminex desks. The classroom is festooned with pictures, paintings, geography and maths projects, hanging from every wall and pegged on strings crisscrossing the air above us. But the central sign hangs in pride of place off the teacher's desk. From my perch on the low chair it is exactly at eye level, and it is what nine-year-olds most need to know, possibly what we all most need to know: 'INTEGRITY: Doing the right thing even when no one is looking'. Eileen called it 'honesty'. Orwell called it 'decency'. And in that moment I see how the concepts of privacy and decency, so fundamental to Orwell, can be opposites in patriarchy. In the privacy of his own home at that time a man was legally entitled to behave in ways that would not be considered decent (or legal) outside it, that would be an affront to his own sense of integrity if he behaved that way to anyone else. He can behave that way, in fact, to women in or out of the home because our silence (enforced, traditionally, by shame) guarantees his privacy.

How can a society live with a concept as contradictory as the decency of the unaccountable private patriarch at its heart? Orwell said it best:

> DOUBLETHINK means the power of holding two contradictory beliefs in one's mind simultaneously, and accepting both of them ... The process has to be conscious, or it would not be carried out with sufficient precision, but it also has to be unconscious, or it would bring with it a feeling of falsity and hence of guilt ... it is a vast system of mental cheating.

Patriarchy *is* the doublethink that allows an apparently 'decent' man to behave badly to women, in the same way as colonialism and racism are the systems that allow apparently 'decent' people to do unspeakable things to other people. In order for men to do their deeds and be innocent of them at the same time, women must be human – but not fully so, or a 'sense of falsity and hence of guilt' would set in. So women are said to have the same human rights as men, but our lesser amounts of time and money and status and safety tell us we do not. Women, too must keep two contradictory things in our heads at all times: I am human, but I am also less than human. Our lived experience makes a lie of the rhetoric of the world. We live on the dark side of Doublethink.

Doublethink is so effective men can be bewildered by this vast world, invisible to them, which has upheld them. And so women are more equal than others, when it comes to recognising it.

How is it Orwell comes to see the world as split between decent and indecent, conscious and unconscious? Perhaps his ability to see both sides comes from experiencing splits in his own life. He passes as posh at Eton, though he's an outsider noticing the tics and traits of a class he's not born to. He goes to Burma to enforce colonial rule in a rapacious racist system, but he comes from a mixed-race

French/English/Burmese family himself. He chases woman after woman and is homophobic to a degree his friends find remarkable, though his desire, hidden perhaps from himself, may have been for men. Living a split life enables him to see reality as a cover story and go looking for the other one. But it makes it harder to think of himself as the same inside and out or, as he put it, 'decent'.

We want people to be 'decent' and we want our writers to be too. Orwell engaged with this question of good work coming from flawed people. Does it also require doublethink to admire the work and ignore the behaviour of the private man? The question arises for him thinking about Dalí, Dickens and Shakespeare – and, tellingly, how they treated their wives. Reading Dalí's flamboyant autobiography, Orwell calls him a 'dirty little scoundrel' who 'boasts that he is not homosexual, but otherwise he seems to have as good an outfit of perversions as anyone could wish for'. Orwell is gruesomely appalled by Dalí's necrophiliac urges, his fascination with excrement and his sadism to his wife. But Dalí, he thinks, is also a great artist. How can he hold these two things in mind at the same time?

In an essay on Dickens, Orwell argues explicitly that an author's mistreatment of a woman in private life should not affect how we read his work. He dismisses a novel about Dickens as 'a merely personal attack; concerned for the most part with Dickens's treatment of his wife'. 'It dealt,' he writes, 'with incidents which not one in a thousand of Dickens's readers would ever hear about,' – nor should they, he implies – 'and which no more invalidates his work than the second-best bed invalidates *Hamlet*.' (Shakespeare willed his 'second-best bed' to his wife, a fact which has spawned centuries of agonised – and inconclusive – examination of whether it was an act of testamentary bastardry or something else.) For Orwell, it is possible to think of Dickens completely separately from his work because 'a writer's literary personality has little or nothing to do with his private character'. A man should be free to write as if he were one person, and behave like someone else altogether. What happens to the woman in the box doesn't count.

Which leaves completely open the question of how much the dark furnace inside Orwell – inside any of us – is the place from which the work comes. No great artwork feels as though its author is unacquainted with this place. After all, it is the invisible world we want art to show us.

But it is a world in which you might be the monster. 'The point is,' Orwell writes of Dalí, 'that you have here a direct, unmistakable assault on sanity and decency . . . in his outlook, his character, the bedrock decency of a human being does not exist.'

For Orwell, human decency is the ultimate test of a person. Decency is what will save us from totalitarian and other cruel instincts. It is the quality in the animals of *Animal Farm* and in the 'proles' of *Nineteen Eighty-Four* that provides the only glimmer of hope. But is it real, or a manhole cover on another life?

Sometimes, as I sign books for people after an event, I channel the novelist Richard Ford. I once heard him explain why he feels he is always, inevitably, a disappointment to readers when they meet him. 'I put my best self into my work,' he said, opening out his hands, 'and I am not my best work.' In the gap between his hands I saw the gap between an author and their work. This is not an empty space. It's full of dark matter, matter that holds together the writer, the work and the reader.

Signing queues are a chasm of intimacy. People, not at all unreasonably, would like you to be the person they think you are from your work. You can see in their kind, open faces that these total strangers *already* know you, as the person they have intuited on the basis of the book. In the intimate, imaginative fusing that is reading they will have brought a lot of themselves to her. So the 'you' they want you to be is a hybrid, an amalgam of you both.

Writers pull from themselves things they know and things they don't, and put them out there for the world to see. At a book signing you are being asked to be worthy of the work you have written by matching yourself to a reader's imagined version of you, as if you are a key meant to fit into a lock-shaped space in someone else's mind. If it fits, you will be the guarantee that authenticates the work. And if it doesn't (I mean, if I don't), what then?

These anxieties of authenticity exist because when words go inside a reader, they make magic. They fizz and pop and conjure. They change minds. Your words may cast a spell on the reader but they cannot be felt to be a con-artist's trick, for then the reader will feel defrauded. All the reader wants is for the avatar sitting behind the table to match their inner picture. It's not much to ask, surely – and there they are, standing shyly, patiently, expectantly in line, book in hand, sticky-note marking the spot to sign the deal.

But on the page, as Virginia Woolf put it, '"I" is only a convenient term for somebody who has no real being.' That written 'I' is flexibly, creatively capacious, outrageous, furious. She evades gender expectations. She owes no one anything. She is not managing the Household List; she is not worried she'll hurt her husband, or offend her friends, or neglect or shame her children. She is not, in Woolf's words, 'harassed and distracted with hates and grievances', legitimate and important as those might be. That inner 'I' is both known and unknown to a writer. She may be similar to the one psychoanalysis tries to recover – remembered or created on the page or in the consulting room. Like the force behind crop circles or the tides, the self leaves traces in other phenomena – our dreams, our writing, our children – but remains out of sight. None of us is who we think we are. None of us may be 'decent'.

To my mind, a person is not their work, just where it came from. To want the two to be the same, on pain of 'cancellation', is a new kind of tyranny. And from there, no art comes.

If Orwell were sitting behind a table signing books today, a fan in the queue would see the man they know from the work, who is the man they want to see: a skinny fellow in an ancient, battered sports jacket too short for his arms, chain-smoking roll-ups and coughing, acute blue eyes, high-pitched Etonian drawl, a bit of a stutter. They would see the grand wizard of plainspeaking, of decency, of the underdog. They would see a self-deprecating man who investigated the lives of the poor, who risked his own life to fight fascists in Spain, and who denounced hypocrisy in essay after brilliant essay. A sympathetic mensch who, clearly, from the look of him, had no thought for himself.

And then, if you were a young woman, standing shyly, patiently, expectantly in line, he might ask you, if you could spare the time, though of course you probably have better things to do – cough, cough – to go for a walk in the woods.

Any writer could fall into the gap between what a reader imagines of them, and who they think they are. And a woman might live there.

Editing,
in Real Time

⌒

They are at Greenwich because her bleeding has been getting more painful each month and she's come to London to see a doctor. She's pale as the sheet she lies on.

When she opens her eyes there's light between the curtains. He's already up, probably downstairs typing in the drawing room. She's surprised, because he came home so sozzled last night from a magazine party.

Yesterday she was in pain, and now that it has mostly receded she wants to sleep more. Here at Greenwich she can; there are no animals to get up for (bless dear Jack and Mary Common, who are looking after them). She rolls over and closes her eyes.

It could be five minutes later or it could be midday when he comes back in. He's holding the draft of an essay he'd typed himself. She handwrote emendations on it yesterday.

'Are you all right?' he asks. She sees there's something frightening and unmentionable to him about her pain, this ability to bleed without dying.

She nods, pulls herself up. 'I'd be better with tea.'

He smiles. 'I'll get Lorna to bring some up.' Lorna is the girl.

He pulls the cord near the door.

'I can't read your writing,' he says, handing her the essay. He turns the chair at the desk around and sits down. She picks up her glasses from the bedside table and looks at her comment on the back, then turns the paper over to the typed side.

'"Dalí,"' she reads, '"grew up in the corrupt world of the nineteen-twenties, when sophistication was immensely widespread and every European capital swarmed with aristocrats and rentiers who had given up sport and politics and taken to patronizing the arts. If you threw dead donkeys at people, they threw money back."' She looks up, eyes glittering. 'That's very funny.'

'Thanks.'

She looks back at the page. 'But that's not it. Ah, here we are: "If Shakespeare returned to the earth tomorrow and if it were found that his favourite recreation was raping little girls in railway carriages, we should not tell him to go ahead with it on the ground that he might write another *King Lear* . . . One ought to be able to hold in one's head simultaneously the two facts that Dalí is a good draughtsman and a disgusting human being. The one does not invalidate or, in a sense, affect the other."'

She turns the page over again to check what she wrote. '"Disarticulate". Yes, very cryptic of me, sorry.' The light is behind him so he's a silhouette of hair, ears, shoulders. But she knows from experience that he's listening closely. This, right here, is where they meet.

'What I mean,' she readjusts the pillows at her back, 'is that there are two ideas here, run together. The first is about whether the raping of little girls in railway carriages – or whatever you might have your genius do – somehow *fuels* him to write his masterpiece.' She looks up at him, pushes her glasses up the bridge of her nose with a finger.

'The second is about how we think about the masterpiece *afterwards*, when we realise its creator is this "disgusting human being", as you put it. Or even,' she looks at him, 'just an ordinarily flawed one. Do we accept the price, you see?'

He seems to find it almost a physical feeling of warmth, this basking in her attention. He fiddles the wedding ring around his finger.

'I just meant,' he says, 'that if Shakespeare *had* done that, *King Lear* still stands.'

'But that's not what it says here.' She holds up the page. 'You're implying that if a genius needs to rape little girls in railway carriages that shouldn't affect how we think about his work. And afterwards we can enjoy the work and disregard its price. Everyone gets what they want.' She holds his gaze, shrugs. 'Except, I suppose, the little girls.'

'That's not what I'm saying.'

'Well, that's how it reads. And it's not a bad question, either.'

He puts a fist to his mouth and coughs. 'Psychoanalysis is all I need.'

She smiles. 'Clearly not – where do you take a potshot at it?' She looks back at the paper. 'Ah, here – the "complex" Dalí might have in his "phobia for grasshoppers". *Reductio ad absurdum.* You talk of grasshoppers and rape in railway carriages so as to make phobias and bad behaviour seem outrageous. When they're both, in their way, commonplace.'

This would be the moment to ask him whether fucking other women fuels his work, or his sense of himself as man enough to do it. This is the question both of them know is here, standing shyly, patiently, expectantly between the bed and the chair, waiting to be asked.

'Terrifying as it is, of course,' she says, 'as soon as one puts pen to paper one always reveals more than one thinks.'

He waits.

She looks past the black outline of him. Over the park a plane pulls a thread through the sky.

A knock. Lorna enters, flame-haired and timid in her black dress, white apron, carrying a tray.

'Here, ma'am?' she asks, reaching the desk. It has a typewriter on it, and papers scattered about. The tray is heavy, with hot things that could slide. The girl stands, waiting.

'Thank you, Lorna.'

George is thinking of something else; at any rate he makes no move. He needs direction, she thinks, like an actor in a play.

'Dear, would you?' Eileen says.

'Yes, of course.' He gets up and moves the typewriter. Lorna puts the tray down. She is red now, neck to scalp.

'Shall I pour, ma'am?' she asks.

'No, Lorna,' Eileen smiles. 'We'll manage.'

As George pours the tea, she looks back at his essay.

'You have here, for instance, that Dalí's work is "a direct, unmistakable assault on sanity and decency; and even – since some of Dalí's pictures would tend to poison the imagination like a pornographic postcard – on life itself."' She looks up. 'You don't think your pornographic postcards poisoned your imagination, do you?'

He makes a noise that is part laugh, part grunt of surprise. Puts the teapot down.

'Well, I don't.' She smiles as he passes her a cup of black tea. 'They were much too mild to have done it.'

He laughs. She knows editing is a thrill to him, the dangerous pleasure of having someone see you more clearly than you can.

⌐◡

Strawberries

It's summer, 1939. They are back at the cottage. Orwell wants to stay here through the winter, though Eileen thinks that's a terrible idea. His chest is bad, and when everything freezes outside it freezes inside too.

And war is coming. Orwell says if the ordinary people knew, they would rise up against it. Eileen disagrees, telling him that if the government declared it, they'd all get behind it. This is when she is struck by his 'remarkable political simplicity'. He makes a note of her insight in his diary.

To stay or to go. There must have been a moment to decide.

⌒

She places the huge metal pot in the sink and turns on
the tap. Lights a match and puts it to the primus. Lights
another for a cigarette, which dangles between her lips as
she takes off her watch and places it on the windowsill.
This week she has made apple sauce, pickled cucumbers,
and peaches in syrup. She hasn't agreed to live here for the
winter; the provisions are for him if he insists on it. She's
going to stay at Laurence and Gwen's in London, and
then see. This work of boiling glass and vats of fruit over a
flame under a tin roof is like something from a fairy tale,

the master upstairs coughing, trying to spin gold from ink. Possibly this boiling vat is just a distraction from what is happening between them.

Today, strawberry jam. She picks up the white enamel bowl and goes out through the back door. The sun is bright and high and makes her blink. The garden is a riot of late summer pinks and purples – dahlias, stocks, roses – nodding in a perfumed haze. The insects are drunk. The chickens gossip, intermittently outraged. As well they might be – they live with *thieves*.

She's in old cut-off trousers tied with his belt. In the shed she takes the hessian sack from its nail and lays it down by the strawberry bed. She will gather, in 'that field of light,/ New pleasure, like a bee among the flowers'. Beloved Wordsworth, sweet William. She kneels and finds the strawberries, glossy red pincushions hiding under their dark green shields. She puts one in her mouth – a shock of pleasure.

Three years ago they set this teeming life in motion. Every garden bed built up and trench dug, every flower and fruit seeded was a down payment on a dream. Back then, their arguments were couched in laughter; they were on the same side of the wheelbarrow/trench/shovel/sink/axe. Their disagreements had seemed to be about the trivialities of how to live – dressing for dinner ('at the cottage??' she'd exclaimed), decanting marmalade for the table. But now she sees that those wrangles were really about who would do the work: who would gift the other time. They have congealed in her memory into a single fight about him stopping her leaving Wallington when she wanted to see Norah, or when her brother came for her. They usually ended with George trudging upstairs, leaving her to the dishes and ashtrays.

The strawberry bowl is full. She wipes her fingers on her trousers. As she turns towards the house the light catches the upstairs window. He's working up there, but she can't see him.

The Wallington cottage from the end of the garden.
Someone can be glimpsed in the window.

Cleaning the latrine had been the highlight – or lowlight – of all that. He hadn't felt well enough to do it. One moment is etched in her mind. Midway through he'd opened that window and called to her. She extracted herself cautiously, pulling her boots out of the dark muck

flowing over the seat, the suck of it so disgusting, the
stench making her gag. She took four steps towards the
window so she could hear what he was saying; stood there
in his green fishing waders, gloved hands held out from her
sides, covered in shit.

'Tea time, don't you think?' he'd said.

Her blood was ice. Not for a split second had she
thought that he meant he'd make it for her.

She puts the bowl of strawberries down on one side of
the sink under the window. She starts washing and rinsing
jars under the cold tap. As her forearms goose-bump to
the elbow, she realises that she has always thought that
to know something is to understand what it will feel like.
But she has underestimated experience itself, which can
freeze your blood before your head has understood what is
happening. She could not have predicted the lurid detail of
it – that he would ask her 'permission' for sex with others.
She wonders if it's the sex with them that makes him feel
powerful, or if her humiliation does the trick. The only way
she can manage not to be humiliated is to pretend it doesn't
matter. And to do that – she places the last rinsed jar on the
tea towel next to the others – is to pretend that *she* does not
matter. She turns off the tap. She needs, sweet William, to
'fix the wavering balance of her mind'.

She lowers the jars carefully into the boiling water.
There are six of them, and six round glass lids, six metal
clasps and six orange indiarubber rings to seal them.
Double, double toil and trouble. She'd like a cup of tea, but
must wait now till this sterilising operation is over because
there's only the one burner. 'Ah, that's better,' he's given
to saying after the first sip. He says it too as he rolls off
her. 'Ah, that's better,' as he extracts himself. What was it

Mabel told her about the girl he'd installed in his room in Paris? She had a flat chest, an Eton bob, and was in every way desirable. Mabel slept with him for a while too, and she thinks he's homosexual. So does his friend Heppenstall. Possibly, dear man, no woman is what he wants. Why should she stay?

She checks the strawberries for insects, wiping them with a tea towel. Then she takes the paring knife from the drawer, removes their green hats and starts to chop. The problem is that she can see past what he does and love what she finds. The making of anything truly *good* – she puts the knife down, pushes hair off her forehead with a damp wrist – is in the edit.

She glances at her watch on the windowsill. She's boiling the jars for twelve minutes, till they're sterile. Which is another thing. In three years she has not become pregnant. When she suggested they go to doctors to investigate the problem he'd said, 'I'm sterile. That's the problem.'

They'd been walking the goats on leads down the village street. Three boys, about eight years old, were playing marbles in the dirt, oblivious to them.

'But how do you know?'

'I just know. I've never got anyone pregnant.'

'You might not know. A girl in Burma. Or Paris.'

'I just am,' he said.

She watched the road ahead. Her throat grew tight.

'But you've always said how much you want children.' She touched his arm to stop walking. 'When did you think you would tell me?'

He lit a cigarette, shielding the flame with one hand.

'I'm telling you now.'

She would like him to go to a doctor but he refuses. Any investigation of him, he says, would be too 'disgusting'. Her doctor has said that, despite all her monthly pains, the problem is not with her.

As she reaches for the tin of sugar on the shelf there's a scuttle. Down the other end another canister is knocked off, spilling flour all over the floor.

'What's that?' comes the voice from upstairs.

'Nothing,' she calls back. 'I just dropped something.' He's completely phobic about mice. She is not; she imagines them as company, cancanning lines of them dancing on the shelf. She moves to get the dustpan and brush from behind the door.

More coughing. She stops.

Then the typewriter starts again. She exhales, sweeps up.

She removes the pot of jars from the burner and replaces it with a saucepan of strawberries and sugar. When that is simmering nicely she goes to take a book from the pile on the stairs and just then a cascade of them topples down from above. Next thing he's standing there, handkerchief to his mouth, blood all down his old blue shirt.

'Ice,' he says. His eyes are panicked.

She dashes to the icebox and hacks some off. Faced with blood and death she finds herself firmly on his side, and other women, girls, vanish.

The ambulance comes and takes him away again. She stays here to finish the jam, put the chickens in the henhouse. She will follow by bus. The place feels so empty.

In the kitchen she picks up the ladle and plunges it into the dark red mass in the pot. It's still way too hot to be doing this safely but she can't think of anything else to do. Marx leans into her shin, he won't sit till she does. She wonders if a haemorrhage can have a psychological cause – the fear that she might leave him, even just for the winter. She should ask Laurence if this has been investigated.

She hadn't expected to live with so much blood, his and hers. His comes almost painlessly, despite the coughing and spurting, though it's more horrific for what it signifies. Hers is silent but agonising, disguised as something that should signal the potential for life.

'We're a bloody mess,' she'd joked once.

He'd made a moue of distaste.

'That reminds me,' he said, 'perhaps don't hang those rags on the line in full view.'

She has stopped mentioning her own pain to him.

When the jars are cool enough to touch she seals them and stacks them with the others behind the back door. A spectrum of green to red – the deep green pickles, paler apple sauce, the golden peaches, and now these red ones, glutinous as specimens. She doesn't know if they will be too few or too many.

She sits at the table. Her heart appears to have made another decision on its own: she will stay in this marriage. She will keep him alive, and see what can be written.

The next day she goes to the hospital by bus and train, carrying a bunch of white tuberoses wrapped in newspaper, a cone of scent. Dr Morlock is another colleague of her brother, a breezy extrovert in morning dress and a cravat with a pearl pin. He tells George 'not to worry about coughing up blood; it might even be good for you'.

It's grotesque, she thinks, this deceiving of the patients, though George's eyes light up. He is emboldened to ask 'how many good years' he has left – he doesn't want to know, no one would, how many years altogether. Morlock says, 'as many as you need, old man'. The doctors have no idea, she sees, their whole method is cajoling and placebo, sleight of hand. As he leaves the room, Morlock dons a black silk top hat.

Orwell fiddles with the twine she'd used to tie the flowers.

'How long is a piece of string?' he smiles softly.

She bursts into tears.

It's evening when she gets back to the cottage. She collects the eggs she didn't get to this morning (eighteen today), to sell to the butcher. They have no other money, as her typing work has dried up. They are, as he says, 'living a hand-to-mouth existence'. The money situation is becoming 'completely unbearable'. Aside from freelancing, he has no work and no prospect of any. Thank goodness Morlock is treating him for free as a favour for her brother. She puts the kettle on, lights a cigarette with the same match and sits down.

She stubs out the cigarette. She must earn some money.

While George is recuperating in the sanatorium, and then at his wealthy friend L. H. Myers's luxurious home, she visits a friend from her Oxford days who works at the War Office in London. Nothing has been declared, but war is creeping in unannounced. Trains are full of affluent people leaving the city. Schoolchildren are being walked in lines along the streets, practising evacuation. The War Office itself has been sandbagged. Her friend tells her that war is 'almost certain'.

The morning of 3 September they are both staying in Greenwich. They gather around the wireless with Gwen and Laurence. It is what they have long expected, but still it hollows them out. The prime minister's voice is sombre. The Germans will not agree to withdraw from Poland, he says, so, 'consequently, this country is at war with Germany . . .'

A look passes between Laurence and Eileen. He turns to Gwen as he says it, though she probably knows already too.

'I'm joining. Medical Corps. Do what I can.'

'I'll come with you,' George says. Laurence nods, though no one imagines he'll be accepted.

Laurence insists on being sent to the front, where he feels he can be of most use as a surgeon. Gwen will stay in London with their one-year-old son, also called Laurence, and keep practising from the surgery

Laurence at Greenwich.

at home. She is a woman of science, not prone to premonitions. So when she has one about her husband, she is both more unsettled by it and more dismissive of it. She tells no one but the nurse who works with her.

As he leaves for France Laurence asks Eileen if she would mind staying at Greenwich from time to time, to keep Gwen company. Perhaps he's also thinking of his sister having a reprieve from another bitter winter at the cottage.

Propaganda

Eileen must stay in London anyway because a job has come through. It's a quite highly placed position in the newly formed Censorship Department of the Ministry of Information, which is responsible both for issuing censored news about the war and censoring what is reported in the media. Her office is in Senate House, Bloomsbury. Orwell said that she got the position through Oxford connections, because of 'somebody who knew somebody etc., etc.,' as if it were a prize she didn't deserve, not a way to keep them both alive. The biographers

Senate House

never make it clear that she supports them both financially for the next two years. Orwell himself played it down.

Orwell is rejected by the military on health grounds. He goes back to the cottage for the winter, doubly humiliated by being unable to fight and having to live on his wife's earnings. Alone in the winter of 1939–40 the goats are poor company and the potatoes he plants rot in the ground. What happens when he next haemorrhages no one wants to think about. Eileen visits every second weekend.

London is hunkering down, waiting to be attacked from the air. Every night in the city there is a blackout, though the skies are still empty. Windows are covered with cardboard or paint. Tube stations are rechristened 'air-raid shelters'. Sandbags stacked to ceiling height surround St Paul's. In the park opposite Laurence and Gwen's a vast barrage balloon floats in the sky above the Observatory, tethered by a web of wires to trap enemy aircraft.

Despite the danger, Eileen would rather be in London than at Wallington. She feels 'it would be wrong for her to stay in a safe place while the rest of her family were exposed to the danger of air-raids'. Lydia thinks she 'seemed almost to welcome the dislocation the war brought into her life, for her it was a new, dramatic experience'. More than that, Eileen had, in her view, 'an unconscious *wish* to risk her own life'. Whether this was some kind of fatalism, or desperation for adventure, it was something, I believe, she shared with Orwell.

Just as her job in Spain had done, this one puts Eileen at the epicentre of a war, on the line between what was happening and what could be said about it. It might have sounded interesting on paper – working in an office dealing with classified government information, suppressing news from the front and managing press censorship at home. Instead, it turns out to be a job of long hours and hard work, she writes to Norah, of *inconceivable dullness*. Her colleagues barely know the difference between the socialist *Daily Worker* and the fascist *Action*.

And her boss is a vacillator, *almost as frightened of me as he is of taking any decision on his own.* Worse, consumed by the detail of the work, it's hard to get the full picture of what's going on. Some of the intelligence is trivial; early on Eileen reports drily that she's learned that Oswald Mosley, the leader of the British Union of Fascists, is 'a masochist of the extreme type in his sexual life'. Orwell comes to believe that upper-class appeasement is continuing, as there are 'halfwits and profascists filling important jobs' who are 'more likely to betray Britain than defend her'. More interesting to Eileen might have been the possibility of finding out what was really happening to the troops battling Hitler on the Continent, where Laurence is.

It's impossible to know exactly what kind of censorship Eileen was involved with in Senate House. Possibly, Orwell was inspired and informed by her work there, erasing certain truths so that some unalloyed version of the nation could replace them. He probably took the building as his model for the Ministry of Truth (i.e. lies) in *Nineteen Eighty-Four*.

At Wallington Orwell is finishing a book of essays, *Inside the Whale*, but barely managing on the life front. Again the dishes freeze in the sink. Again the toilet breaks. At the end of January Eileen goes up to help him pack and get out. They lug suitcases and his typewriter through three miles of snow piled to head height to the next village to get the bus. At one point they abandon the road and set out over the fields, waist-deep in drifts, unsure of their footing. Orwell, unruffled, has enough energy to be delighted by nature, noticing 'flocks of hares, sometimes about 20 together', lolloping over the snow. Unsurprisingly, he is ill for six weeks afterwards and has to be nursed at Laurence and Gwen's. But in mid-March he goes straight back to the cottage. Jack Common, their local friend, is shocked when he sees him, the wind blowing his corduroy trousers about his skinny legs.

Orwell lasts only a few more weeks on his own. In the spring of 1940 the chickens are sold, the dog and the goats put into the care of villagers. After living apart for more than six months (the third time in their three-and-a-half-year marriage), Orwell moves to London.

He and Eileen now look for their own place, one they can afford on her salary and his occasional freelance earnings. They find something in Baker Street called Dorset Chambers, described by one biographer as 'the most miserable two-room fourth-floor flat, above shops, backing on to garages in a mews, with no lift, little light, cheap second-hand furniture, gas water-heater and shared bathroom'. They furnish it with Orwell's Burmese swords, the Blair family Bible, and a portrait of an ancestor, 'Lady Mary'. Lydia says it was 'from the point of view of safety in air-raids, the least that could be desired'. This doesn't worry them at all.

There is no record of how Eileen feels each time she leaves her brother's magnificent home in Greenwich, with its cook, nanny, maid and 'odd jobsman', for weekends of farming, cooking, cleaning, nursing, editing and typing at the cottage. Nor is there a record of her feelings on moving into the dingy flat in Baker Street. Now, she's on a triple shift, working by day at the Ministry; doing all the housework, shopping and cooking; and editing and typing his work in the hours that are left. She left no complaints – a good friend of hers later said she seemed 'unruffled' by their 'gypsy lifestyle'. Perhaps she considers the triple load to be the price of the choice she made to link her life to a writer, in the hope that the satisfactions of his work will satisfy her too. Perhaps, even, she sees what he will never say, which is that his output requires the work of two.

Orwell is at a low ebb. He's ashamed to be on the streets of London when he's clearly of enlistment age. He doesn't want his 'yellow ticket' exemption from service, though he knows 'half the men in this country would give their balls' for it. And it's hard to write. The world might be ending any day now, with Britain being invaded and turning fascist.

Then, as one biographer writes, 'Unexpectedly, he was offered steady work reviewing plays and films for *Time and Tide*.' Another writes that this book reviewing 'offered by' *Time and Tide* would 'give him the chance to finance cheap lodgings in London and be with Eileen', eliding the fact that he was coming to London because he couldn't manage the work of the cottage alone, and that her salary was and would continue to be their main support. Having learned to read under the passive voice I'm immediately wary of phrases like 'was offered' and 'came up'. Male editors Orwell wrote for are named, but in this case it was Lettice Cooper, a novelist who was at that time an associate editor of *Time and Tide*, who offered him the job. It didn't turn out terrifically well, she remembered, as 'I don't think he liked going to the theatre much, especially to "any bloody play". He was apt to be suddenly indisposed before a first night, and I had to nip in and do it for him.' Here the biographers' language hides the woman who not only gave him the job, but then did lots of it for him.

This job isn't full-time. Eileen seems to have found him some freelance work at her Ministry, though again, a biographer constructs his sentence so as to avoid mentioning that she works there and probably got him the job: 'He found occasional work for the Ministry of Information (Britain's answer to Goebbels' Ministry of Propaganda), which had its headquarters at the University of London's Senate House – one source for his Ministry of Truth in *Nineteen Eighty-Four*.'

Orwell is happier when he starts writing for *Horizon*, an influential publication of the 1940s edited by his friend Cyril Connolly. He begins 'to move, however imperceptibly, in a more glamorous literary world', a world of 'delightful parties' and a 'succession of well-bred young secretaries'. The biographer adds, 'And there was something else. On one of his visits to the office he would certainly have come across Connolly's editorial assistants. Among them was a striking dark-haired girl named Janetta Woolley, one of whose first jobs was to ink out by hand the swear-words' in a short story, and another, a 'fresh-faced blonde woman in her early twenties . . . Her name was Sonia Brownell.'

This is how affairs, the 'something else', are hinted at, in sentences that describe the women solely in terms of their 'well-bred' bodies. There is no helpful verb here to cover Orwell's meeting them, only that he 'came across' them. These are sentences designed to convey with a silent wink a meaning which can be plausibly denied by their author. In this way, the affairs Orwell is thought to have had, or wanted to have, with Janetta and Sonia are simultaneously inferred *and* covered up.

Eileen and Orwell don't own a radio so they go to the pub to listen to the nine o'clock news. The windows are covered, the place is soupy with smoke and chatter. When they ask the barmaid to turn on the wireless she says, 'Oh we never turn it on. Nobody listens to it, you see . . . they've got the piano playing in the other bar, and they won't turn it off just for the news.' But she does it for them anyway. The politicians' speeches are rousing and vague at the same time. When Orwell complains that they say so little, Eileen says uneducated people like grand speeches even if they don't understand them – they catch the stirring feeling, and that is more important to them. This strikes Orwell as true, and he makes a note of it in his diary.

Speeches that say nothing are necessary because the facts are terrifying. Hitler's troops have taken Denmark, Norway and now Luxembourg. France will be next. Fascists are overrunning the Continent in an unstoppable spread of black and red. Every night the blackout is earlier.

⌒

There has been no mail from Laurence for weeks. At home she can't concentrate, can't sit, can't read. At work she can't make sense of the news – or the pieces of it that come across her desk. One evening George is out so she goes to the pub alone. Again she has to ask the barmaid to turn the wireless on. She listens between the lines for what is not being broadcast. She remembers writing propaganda in Spain that bore the slimmest connection to what was going on at the front, as if it were a story inspired by events for a whole other purpose – which is exactly what it was. She listens now for underlying facts, gleans only that Belgium has fallen and that, by implication, Britain has been let down by the French, who have failed to defend themselves properly. As Hitler rolls over Europe, Europe rolls over.
He will be here any day.

At the office someone talks about the planes Hitler is sending over France, strafe-bombing lines of refugees in carts and cars and on foot, people trying to flee on roads and through fields. She is terrified for her brother. He is there somewhere, and taking cover is not in his nature.

⌒

People are connected in ways no one can see. Lydia senses it with Eileen and Laurence. 'I was at the flat with Eileen one afternoon after the fall of France when the news of Dunkirk began to come through. She had just made tea, but neither of us was drinking it. Eileen paced up and down the room, smoking one cigarette after another. "I just don't know what we shall do with Mother," she was saying, "I'm sure he is dead . . ."'

Orwell is distressed too. He goes to the train stations at Waterloo and Victoria to search for Laurence among the wounded arriving home.

The platforms are a mess of frightened refugees and soldiers with war in their eyes. He approaches several of them to ask about a doctor they might have met – medium build, blue eyes, dark hair, square jaw – called O'Shaughnessy, known as 'Shock'. But the men have been ordered not to speak and are quickly whisked away.

Shock

It is just before the evacuation, when the British fleet and every imaginable private fishing and sailing and leisure vessel will set out in a ragtag flotilla, a crazy armada over the Channel, to retrieve Allied forces fleeing Hitler, who has conquered France.

Laurence has arrived in Dunkirk early; the other doctors in his group are still making their way along dangerous roads. German planes buzz overhead. His colleague George McNab is here too, racing around town asking shopkeepers to allow their cellars to be used as bomb shelters. Then the bombing starts. McNab spots Laurence in a café, 'making no attempt to take cover'. McNab shouts at him to get into the cellar. Laurence won't move. McNab is distraught – Laurence 'repeatedly refused . . . to go down into the cellar for shelter as the bombs began to fall'. He stays sitting there as the town blows up around him. When a bomb hits the café the force of it throws McNab into the cellar. As he plummets he glimpses his friend – catastrophically injured. Once the raid is over McNab 'went up and found [poor old Shaugh] obviously *in extremis*, demanding morphia and water, which I gave him'. McNab calls to some others to help carry him to another cellar, then 'I went off to find an ambulance . . .' Everything is on fire: buildings, dust, air.

When McNab gets back he goes down into the cellar to bring Shaugh up 'but . . . Shaugh was moribund'.

No one could understand why Laurence wouldn't take cover. Perhaps he didn't want to be sheltering when the rest of his contingent was still on the road. Perhaps he just wanted to be where he said he would be. There is something twisted and forlorn about pitting yourself against the universe, daring its godless self to take account of you. Others who were there in Dunkirk put it more simply: Laurence had died from stubbornness.

Eileen never heard McNab's story, nor how her brother died. But she might have intuited it, because she shared his brave and brazen fatalism, that perverse defying of death by courting it.

⁓

She has come to Greenwich to be with Gwen, as Laurence had wanted. Her hands on the green basin in his bathroom. The cabinet open in front of her face. It contains tooth powder, a Gillette safety razor in a white mug, whiskers still caught in the blade. She closes it. Looks in the mirror from one eye to the other. There are blue veins under her skin. She seems to have singed some of her hair at the root.

She has bought all the newspapers she can find. If she reads it, she might believe it.

In *The Times*:

MAJOR LAURENCE O'SHAUGHNESSY, M.D., F.R.C.S., R.A.M.C., who fell in Flanders, was one of the more eminent younger surgeons of the chest and heart . . .

In the *Irish Times*:

. . . Mr. Laurence O'Shaughnessy, who has been killed in action, was one of the most brilliant surgeons in

Harley Street. The moment war broke out he left his work to rejoin the Royal Army Medical Corps ... His wish was to be right at the front so that he might deal at first hand with war wounds in the chest ... a pioneer surgeon, an Irishman quick and determined. He was a scholar ... whose spiritual master was Professor Saarbruck, Hitler's doctor.

Hardly Hitler's only doctor. Sauerbruch is surviving over there, Laurence says – said – by threading his Hippocratic oath through the eye of the needle of a dictator keen to experiment with mustard gas on prisoners. Sauerbruch is hardly an enemy. He had come to England, after all, to operate on the King. Laurence had arranged it. She breathes in.

Laurence, photographing Gwen holding baby Laurence.

'Killed in action'. She wonders whether the obituaries have been run through her Ministry, the Department of Euphemism. There has been time; it is well over a week since he died. Is there a special division for obituaries? In a crypt perhaps? Or the basement?

Summer, 1940

This is how the shattered world comes inside her.

'Eileen's own grip on life,' Lydia writes, 'which had never been very firm, loosened considerably after her brother's death. She told me more than once that her brother was the only person on whose immediate help she could count absolutely whenever she was in difficulties.'

Orwell writes not a word in his diary about Laurence's death or Eileen's sorrow. He thinks 'Everything is disintegrating', but he barely mentions the death to anyone. There are accounts from two others, though, of how she is that summer.

From time to time Eileen and Orwell go to lunch at Scarlett's Farm, the country place their friends the Fyvels and the Warburgs have taken. Overhead, planes circle close, then away. Sometimes they are RAF planes, at others the Luftwaffe's. What will later be called the Battle of Britain has begun as a deadly game of tag in clear summer skies. 'As I write,' Orwell notes, 'highly civilized human beings are flying overhead, trying to kill me.' They stay where they are in the garden.

Eileen is incapable of speech. She sits outside, Tosco Fyvel remembered, 'sunk in unmoving silence while we talked. Mary, my wife, observed that Eileen not only looked tired and drawn but was drably and untidily dressed.' Her hair is unbrushed. Mary tries to coax her to talk, but she 'seemed to have become completely withdrawn'. No one asks anything, no one explains. 'Since both Orwell and Eileen were reticent to a degree,' Tosco writes, 'it was only after her second or third visit that we learned that her brother Lawrence, who was serving as a doctor with the British Forces, had been killed . . .'

Margaret Branch is a psychotherapist friend of Eileen's who had been an ambulance driver in the Spanish War and is about to leave to become a secret agent in the French Resistance. In Margaret's view Eileen is 'severely depressed' for eighteen months. She is 'facing her dark night of the soul. Nobody could get through to her.' Margaret's diagnosis goes deep. 'To marry Orwell and share his curious life-style at Wallington, she had to have a streak of mystical dream,' she wrote. Now, 'her dream of life [had been] disturbed'.

What does it mean to be a 'dreamer' in the way Eileen is? The word makes me flinch, which is how I know it is hitting a truth I don't want to see. We are part flesh, part fiction, even if that fiction is made, like the one on this page, of real materials.

Is it to think like an artist who hitches their life to a dream of work to be made, living in the service of something they will leave behind? Unlike life, with chickens and bombs and no fixed purpose, this dream has one: every book is a deposit on immortality. Orwell has his eyes fixed on becoming a FAMOUS WRITER, and to be the person who can accomplish that, he needs Eileen. He needs her storyteller's gift of untangling causes and effects, characters and fates from the streaming mess of life. He needs her gift of seeing life at a distance of irony when you can't change it, and metaphor when you want to put it together. She could give it all to him when she had Laurence to remind her who she was. But he is gone. Laurence's death killed for her a dream of life, which, like all dreams, is hard to re-enter.

She has told Lydia numerous times that she could always rely on her brother, knowing that for George, the work comes before anybody. Every time she tries to understand that the work is more important to him than she is, she puts Laurence in the sentence to be there with her. Though you might write it or say it to a friend, it is another thing to be left so alone in a marriage. You cannot be rescued from the cause of your trouble by the cause of your trouble.

Treat

The Germans are coming. His wife is catatonic. But Orwell has other things on his mind. It's his birthday, and he wants a person as a present. This is too much for one of the biographers, who writes, 'Astonishingly in the circumstance of his wife's bereavement, Orwell was openly hankering after Brenda.' On 25 June, his thirty-seventh birthday, he pens a letter to his unrequited love, the smart and savvy sports teacher who won't sleep with him, with a proposition:

> I've tried so often to forget you but somehow didn't succeed . . .
> You are such a big piece of my life. Do you remember . . . that
> beautiful walk we had last summer just before the war began? I
> couldn't explain then abt [sic] you & me & Eileen, you didn't want
> me to, & of course such a relationship [as] was between us was unfair
> and impossible for you. Eileen said she wished I could sleep with you
> abt twice a year, just to keep me happy, but of course we can't arrange
> things like that. It's a pity though we never made love properly. We
> could have been so happy. If things are really collapsing I shall try &
> see you. Or perhaps you wouldn't want to? I've no rights over you . . .
> I've been longing for months to write to you & compelling myself
> not to. But today is my birthday & Eileen said I was to give myself a
> birthday treat. Write, if you feel like it, to the above address . . . Take

care of yourself, dear love, take cover when the air raids start, & try
& be happy.
    With love
    Eric.

Several biographers read this as a 'rather clumsy attempt to establish a *ménage à trois*', which would be funny if it weren't such a clumsy attempt by biographers to manufacture the innocence of their hero by inventing Eileen's consent. They want to include Eileen in this infidelity so as to make it seem less of one. It is unimaginable that Eileen, bereaved to the point of being mute, wants to have sex with the 'schoolteacher or something' she'd so angrily told Lydia about. And it's clear that she doesn't want Orwell to be in a relationship with her either. When Orwell wants to 'explain about you & me & Eileen' – and Brenda shuts him down: 'you didn't want me to' – he is not saying 'how about you & me & Eileen?' He is spinning Brenda a story of permission she almost certainly knows is a lie and so doesn't want to hear. It's embarrassing, watching someone lie to your face. So now, in this letter, he puts it to her again: 'Eileen said she wished I could sleep with you abt twice a year, just to keep me happy'. And then for good measure: 'Eileen said I was to give myself a birthday treat'. He leaves it nicely ambiguous as to whether the treat is the writing of the letter or Brenda herself. She said I could, he's saying to Brenda. But you said I could, he'll say to Eileen.

I don't imagine Eileen sincerely 'wished' for him to sleep with her. I can imagine her saying, 'Why don't you just have sex with her twice a year if that will keep you happy?', meaning 'Stop wheedling and nagging and mooning about in front of me lusting after your schoolteacher.' Eileen had told Lydia that the only reason he was pursuing Brenda was because Brenda refused to sleep with him. She understands that for Orwell the pleasure is in the hunt, not the sex itself, and she wants this conquest to be over. Eileen perhaps thinks that if they have sex he'll stop wanting to sleep with Brenda, or that Brenda will stop wanting to sleep with him (if, indeed, she wants to now). Orwell slyly represents Eileen's words to Brenda as permission, when it's more likely she's saying, Just do it and shut up. Do not come to me for 'permission'. Do not make my pain part of your pleasure.

As for Brenda, her considered view was 'He didn't really like women'. Whether she meant women as people or sexual partners, or both, is unclear. Brenda explained it in a passage no biographer uses: 'He was a sadist and that was why he had this feeling towards women.' For her part, she may not have liked men all that much either. Though Brenda stayed in touch with Orwell till the end, she remained single her whole, long life (she lived to be a hundred and one), never marrying and always refusing – as far as is known – to sleep with him.

Self-Arming

While Eileen is working full-time at the Ministry and full-time at home, Orwell has time on his hands. So he joins the Home Guard in St John's Wood, a chapter of the 'Dad's Army' of volunteers created to back up the regular army when the Germans invade. The Nazis have prepared lists of the names of British left-wing intellectuals who are to be sent to concentration camps. An acquaintance says that there's a specific instruction in the event of an invasion, for the Home Guard in Cornwall to 'shoot all the artists' – which Orwell quips wouldn't be such a bad thing. In his mind the Home Guard is the 'revolutionary militia of the impending insurrection' against the Nazis after they get here, some native defence against what he is gloomily predicting to be the 'inevitable move towards Fascism' in the UK.

The St John's Wood volunteers are a motley group of ten men too unfit or too young or too old for active service. The commander is a grocer, the second-in-command a garage owner; there are two 'wealthy bourgeois', a Selfridges van driver, a teenager named Denzil Jacobs, and Fred Warburg, Orwell's erudite, genial friend who will later become his publisher. They meet twice a week on top of a garage in Abbey Road. Orwell is proud of his long experience with weaponry but Warburg, who likes him, nevertheless thinks he 'represented a greater danger than anything they had to fear from the enemy'. At one point Orwell loads a Spigot mortar with the wrong kind of bomb and fires it, 'knocking out one man's teeth and putting another one in hospital'. Orwell brings lots of weapons back to the tiny flat. 'I can put up with bombs on the mantelpiece,' Eileen says drily, 'but I will not have a machine gun under the bed.'

Orwell loves the uniform, and has it nicely tailored to fit him. Sometimes the men stay up late playing poker. Jacobs, the teenage boy, remembered Orwell losing ten shillings at a game, standing up and declaring, 'That's my lot', and then, as one biographer describes it, 'taking the boy off to chat ... Behind their conversation,' as he puts it, 'lurked the shadow of the dark horse.' It's unclear what the biographer is implying here. So often when the sense shimmers, or a metaphor blurs, or a bit of stray Latin or French is introduced, what is being hidden is sexual. As with the innuendo about secretaries in the *Horizon* offices, or calling Mabel an 'Egeria' or Ida a *femme libre*, the smudging of language here is a way of hinting at something Orwell was doing or wanted to do, without it being said. It is a way of telling the truth and covering it up at the same time.

In September 1940 a long letter from Georges Kopp arrives for Eileen. *How you must have suffered during this war Eileen dear*, he writes. Kopp has suffered too. After escaping from the Stalinist prison in Spain he went to France and joined the Foreign Legion. When the Germans invaded he was taken prisoner again. Then he somehow escaped that too, though losing a thumb and the use of two fingers in the process. He has reached Vichy France, from where he writes this letter. Kopp is working undercover for British Intelligence (which he doesn't say) and hoping to get to Britain (which he does). He writes to Eileen of things she might like. *The country is splendid*, he says of Provence, *hills with parasol-pines like in Catalonia, on the road between Montserrat and Barcelona, on which we sped in the coach back from*

Lerida . . . I would love to come here someday with you . . . They make little pies, fluffy and stuffed with anchovies, which you would like and [chocolate rolls] I am sure you would be crazy about. As he comes to the end he writes *Must I tell you what a joy it will be for me to see you and hear you . . . you know all that. You even know what sort of pensées choisies I am sending you.* He signs off *with love, George.*

It's clear that he loves her, though equally clear from her letters to Norah that she doesn't love him. But it must have touched a nerve to have a man think about what she might like, what she might feel, what she might be suffering. Eileen didn't send him an answer but she kept this letter, when she threw away almost every other one.

Blitz

At the end of summer, 1940, the war that killed her brother comes across the Channel to kill them. Hitler begins his 'Blitz', raining bombs down on Britain. At first they are targeted to destroy roads, docks and airfields, but from mid-September it's wanton bombing to slaughter civilians. The aircraft come in swarms, hundreds of them in the sky shitting thousands of bombs. Anti-aircraft sirens start up before you see any glint of the planes, then the wail merges with the low-thrumming thunder of the bombers as they come into view. When the missiles start to fall you can hear them too, a screaming whistle as they come close. The single note, bizarrely, gives you time enough to get to a cellar, or find shelter in the Underground. If you're too close you won't hear it and you'll never know. Orwell and Eileen hold one another in bed. Orwell can tell when the bombs are close because her heart beats faster. Thirty thousand people will be killed in London alone.

Eileen no longer cares if she lives or not. 'Whenever the sirens let out their warning wail,' Lydia remembers, 'Eileen would put out the lights in their top floor flat, open the window and watch the happenings in the street. I do not think she ever used an air-raid shelter herself...'

Contrails in the sky over London, 1940.

The couple walk past bomb craters and piles of rubble, streets cordoned off. It is disorienting to turn a corner towards home when the corner itself is gone. The horror has eclipsed what can be spoken: a child's head in a tree, an old woman's hand and wrist under rubble. When missiles land close to their flat the walls shake out layers of plaster dust and they come home to everything covered in a pall of grey, like lime.

Bombs fall every single night till November. Any night could be your last, any time you see a friend could be the end. In the morning people emerge homeless and dazed, clutching suitcases of belongings, going nowhere. Soot-smeared firemen stand exhausted, holding hoses against towers of flame.

They have acquired a new vocabulary: V-1, V-2, barrage balloon, anti-aircraft gun, Stuka, parachute bomb, air-raid shelter, incendiary canister, Heinkel, tracers, Luftwaffe. People wield these words in sentences shorn of surprise, suddenly familiar with the mechanics of the apocalypse. Life, Orwell says, consists of 'insanities'.

Some weekends they go to Wallington. In the countryside the street signs have been removed or turned the wrong way to confuse the invaders; farmers have strewn old machinery in the fields to stop enemy planes landing. Over it all, the German bombers soar. Someone reports that in Cardiff a ship has been hit and 'bodies brought up in pails'. There are now eleven evacuees in the village.

This summer Trotsky was assassinated in Mexico, by Mercader, the NKVD agent who'd been active in Barcelona. Orwell is jumpy now – about Nazis, who might be parachuting down, but also about the communists he imagines are still after him. Any unexpected knock on the cottage door could be an ambush. Every time he hears one he grabs his rifle, jumps behind the door and gets Eileen to open it. It's never an assassin. One time it's Lydia, who's had to evacuate after a parachute bomb plunged through the roof of her building, snagging just before reaching the ground; it hung, unexploded and terrifying, in the stairwell. At Wallington she finds a domestic scene, defiant in its ordinariness. After Orwell puts his gun away, Eileen serves up some of her 'very nice apple meringue pie'.

In London Eileen still stays with Gwen from time to time, to keep her company. One evening Orwell is there too when the sirens start up, so they leave the house for the crypt beneath the Greenwich church. About two hundred and fifty people are packed in there. He finds the stench 'insupportable' and is deeply upset by the sight of children playing in a vault full of corpses.

Other times, when he remains in their London flat, Eileen cooks for him before going to Gwen's. Once she leaves shepherd's pie warming in the oven and puts out boiled eels for a cat they've adopted. Orwell eats the eels, notices nothing untoward.

The horror is so persistent, it's almost banal. From the flat one evening he calls her at Greenwich and hears 'a tremendous crash' in the background.

'What's that?' he asks.

'Only the windows falling in,' Eileen says, and continues the conversation.

The Greenwich church is bombed, with people sheltering inside. Another bomb, undeterred by the barrage balloon, hits near the Royal Observatory. Tracts of the park opposite are gone.

Barrage balloons over London.

She wants to write to Norah but the question is, can she get out of bed.

She is ill, so they've given her a month's sick leave from the Ministry. She's staying at Greenwich with Gwen. Little Laurence, not yet two, has been sent with his nanny to Canada. Life has turned into a choice of harms, a child's game of 'What would you rather? Would you rather be a boy on a boat in a sea of warships, or a boy in a house under bombs?'

She has been in bed for weeks. Every day new parts of this city are craters of stone and bones.

Each morning since Laurence died, when she wakes, a dull thud has knocked her down. But today it didn't. Tomorrow it will again, probably, but not today. Now, the part of her that went with her brother is coming back. That split-second of feeling whole when she opens her eyes is how she knows. There's a fresh stab of grief as she leaves him behind.

She says nothing to anyone. Everyone has their losses, bears them bravely or histrionically – mostly bravely, which means in hidden ways. But the bleeding and dizziness, the abdominal pain and general wretchedness, have been harder to hide. A month ago Gwen ordered her to bed. Sometimes she is just a curve under a sheet, holding her abdomen as the knives shoot through it. Poor girl who comes to take the bucket of sodden rags for washing. The smell of her own body makes her gag.

She gets out of bed – a triumph! Sits in her dressing gown at the desk. She hasn't seen Norah for such a long time she is almost a fiction, an imaginary soulmate who can see her under her jokes. She rummages for a new nib in the drawer.

No idea what date exactly. It doesn't matter anyway.

This is to accompany a Charming Gift but I don't know what the gift is yet because it will be bought this afternoon. Or so I hope.

This letter is to tell Norah that she has her in mind, as she sets out. Of course, when Norah receives it the journey will long be over, the mission – possibly – accomplished. Or it might end in a bloody mess, or under a pile of rubble. But that is not the point . . .

The pen has leaked ink, so blue it's almost black, on to her middle finger. The point – she caps it – is the power of holding someone in mind. The point is to plant their future thinking of you. If they will be thinking of you in two days' time when they receive this letter, you should still be here

(so the irrational magic goes) to think about. She hopes
that this magic works in the forward direction too, and that
Norah herself is still there now, to receive this letter. The
bombs have rained down on Bristol, the destruction and
death have been beyond imagining. Though of course this
does not make it into the newspapers.

I have been ILL. Ever so ill. Bedridden for 4 weeks &
still <u>weak</u>. You know or Quartus does perhaps though it's more
than all my local doctors do. They diagnosed cystitis and then
they diagnosed nephrolithiasis & then they diagnosed Malta
fever with ovarian complications & then they went all
hush-hush while they diagnosed a tuberculous infection so that
I couldn't possibly guess what they were testing for. They haven't
yet diagnosed cancer or G.P.I. [general paralysis of the insane],
but I expect they will shortly. They're in a great worry because
nothing can be found wrong with my heart as that was assumed
to be giving out very soon. Meanwhile a perfectly sweet little
pathologist like a wren did an ordinary blood count & found
the haemoglobin down to 57%. This is much despised by the
clinicians but in fact they can find nothing else. So now I hear
I'll be cured when I weigh <u>9 stone</u> [57 kg]. As my present weight
is 7st 12 [45 kg] with my clothes on I think perhaps they'll lose
interest before the cure is complete.

She takes a breath and looks out over the park. The
barrage balloon, that great friendly whale tethered in the
sky, is gone, because the Observatory was hit a few nights
ago. This house used to be the Royal Astronomer's; perhaps
he had his desk here too, so he could sit, practically astride
the prime meridian, on zero longitude itself. This place has
always felt, she thinks, like the centre of something – which
is no doubt why Hitler wants to obliterate it and make it
his, resetting the world on his terms from Zero Hour, Zero

Place. On the footpath below, a woman pushing a pram stops and takes off her shoe. She balances one hand on the chrome bar as she taps out a stone.

She wants to go back to work on Monday *as all this is just silly, but I can't go back without a health certificate & the wretched man won't sign one. However I am now allowed to go shopping on medical grounds though the financial ones aren't so good. How is your paint?* She has no idea whether Norah's been hit or not. Whether she's alive or not—

I had arranged a long weekend (which I was going to spend with <u>you</u>) because the pain was worse but then it got a lot worse & the long weekend was merged in sick leave. Which she spent typing George's little book 'The Lion and the Unicorn', *explaining how to be a Socialist though Tory.* It had to have an extra ten thousand words inserted so Warburg could double the price and *Some of the later ones look like being good ... I hope you have a tolerable Christmas. We're having the Dinner on Boxing Day, theoretically for lonely soldiers but they are so lonely that we don't know them yet.*

The thought of soldiers brings her perilously close to thinking of Laurence. She wrote to Norah when he died of course, but she doesn't have any more words for it. And Mother is unwell too, from grief, or at any rate nothing diagnosable. Men are being blown up or drowning or vanishing all around them, and here they are, she and Mother, just waning like moons.

Georges Kopp, whom I had also assumed dead, was captured with two bullets in his chest & part of his left hand shot off. Later he escaped to unoccupied France & he's now trying to get here but his letters take about two months to come so one can't know much of what is happening ...

Nothing to add there. She'll deal with him somehow if he ever makes it here.

Now I must go shopping being as ever a Devoted Pig.

She shops without incident. No bombs, no bleeding or collapsing. When she gets back she adds:

Having walked twelve or fourteen miles to find mother soft slippers with heels, I had to buy everyone else hcfs [handkerchiefs] in a horrible shop. Last year's gift was identical I believe but you will have a nice stock of white hcfs for the cold days.

Mother may be fading away, but she is still Mother.

A week later she's still not well, but goes back to work. There they are saying that the invasion is expected sometime in the next thirty to sixty days, probably involving gas. It hasn't come by March, which is when Mother dies. She takes one day off for the funeral, then goes back to the office. They need the money.

The quiet feels like time she owns. George is out at the *Horizon* office. She has plain toast with marmalade for tea – he ate her portion of butter as well as his this morning, absent-mindedly. He has no idea of the size of rations.

She last wrote to Norah two weeks ago, about Mother. Her death is sad, but the world was already rent. She is writing, now, to impersonate herself. If she can find that voice maybe she can find that self.

There's a paper shortage, so she's using waste paper she's brought home from work and straightened out. It's still slightly creased, which is oddly perfect. She feeds it into the typewriter.

The semi crest means that the paper was waste before it
Flowered. The same is true of my time as a government servant.
There is not much paper, so to sum up:

Physical condition – much improved by air raids, possibly
because I now sleep several hours a night longer than ever in
my life;

Mental condition – temporarily improved by air raids
which were a change, degenerating again now that air raids
threaten to become monotonous;

Events since the war – daily work of inconceivable dullness;
weekly efforts to leave Greenwich always frustrated; monthly
visits to the cottage which is still as it was only dirtier;

Future plans – imaginings of the possibility of leaving
a furnished flat ('chambers') that we have at Baker Street &
taking an unfurnished flat north of Baker Street to remain
in George's Home Guard district, with the idea that we
might both live in this flat – probably to be frustrated by
continued lack of five shillings to spend & increasing scarcity of
undemolished flats & perhaps by our ceasing to live anywhere.
But the last is unlikely because a shorter & no less accurate
summing up would be

NOTHING EVER HAPPENS TO
Pig.

She lights a cigarette. Perhaps she could tell Norah how she
can't smoke for the whole fifteen minutes of each day that
they have to spend wearing gas masks around the office,
turning them all into demented horses of the apocalypse.
Or that her TB tests keep coming back negative –
miraculously. But that's not it. Not what she wants to say.

She looks over the letter. A thought experiment: what
would you write if the end were coming? A whistling letter

of em-dashed news and anomie while death rained down in
500-, 1000-, 4000-lb canisters all around you?

When she puts her hands over the keys the payload is
there before she can think.

*Please write a letter. The difficulty is that I am too
profoundly depressed to write a letter. I have many times half
thought I could come to Bristol but it is literally years since a
weekend belonged to me & George would have a haemorrhage.
I suppose London is not a place to come to really but if you do
ring NATIONAL 3318. My departmental head is almost as
frightened of me as he is of taking any decision on his own &
I can get Time off. Meanwhile give my love to everyone. E.*

'[D]uring the war,' Lydia wrote, 'I had an uneasy feeling that Eileen
did not expect to live and so hardly cared about, or planned for the
future.' Eileen used to say, 'I don't care if I live or die.' Not as a way to
attract attention, but as if to spare her friends grief if she were killed.
It spared them nothing.

Dissociating

His wife has disappeared into grief and illness. She's still working full time to support them as well as keeping the house, provisioning it and doing the cooking, but he needs more. Orwell starts another relationship.

Inez Holden is an 'entertaining' woman of 'fragility of feature' and 'consumptive charm', a novelist and journalist. She's friends with one of Orwell's literary heroes, H. G. Wells, and is living for the moment in the flat above his garage. After a visit to the zoo Orwell takes her back to his place 'for tea'. He excuses himself. When he reappears he has changed into his Home Guard uniform. Then he 'pounced' on her. Inez is 'astonished' by his 'intensity and urgency' in sex.

The next day, he meets Inez and 'explained to her about his marriage . . .' '[D]oubtless,' one biographer notes, 'the same story as to Brenda – as long as what he did made him happy, Eileen did not mind.' Inez finds his explanation (whatever it actually was) 'helpful and clarifying'. The biographer then goes a step further with his fiction of consent to an open marriage. Orwell's story seemed 'to confirm', he writes hopefully, 'that by now he and Eileen had worked out some form of open relationship – at least Orwell thought they had'.

The evidence shows something different. That evening, Orwell and Eileen go to dinner with Inez. Far from 'not minding', Inez finds that 'There was rather an atmosphere of submerged strain'. And then, as if the situation weren't weird enough, she notices something even stranger. '[A]lmost subconsciously, [Orwell] seemed to have disappeared as if to disassociate himself from the whole story.'

Inez saw him 'several times a week for about ten years'. They would go to lunch while Eileen was at work, and then back to the flat – presumably, for at least some of that period, for sex. For a biographer this takes some explaining. 'Whatever Eileen knew about their relationship she was obviously prepared to tolerate,' one writes, 'but whether she suffered because of it is unknown and Orwell himself never hinted at knowing or even caring.' The biographical glosses override her feelings, just as her husband did. The tolerating is 'obvious'. The suffering is 'unknown'. And Orwell couldn't care less.

But I can imagine something else, because I am not trying to exonerate my hero. Instead, I'm trying to understand things from her point of view. Why does she stay with him, working to support him financially, psychologically, intellectually, and in every other way – let alone go out to dinner with his new lover, fresh from their bed? Many of her friends were divorced, she could have left him, lived with Gwen and worked to support herself. I know that leaving a bad relationship can be harder than staying – but staying doesn't equal permission.

Fidelity is a peculiar promise. To some people it's fundamental; to others it's a matter of lip service, of 'don't ask, don't tell'. In my own life, I feel pretty strongly that other people's affairs are exactly that – theirs, and none of my business. But I would feel differently if my husband were pouncing on women in hospitals and parks and after parties, making assignations with fans, going to brothels, and hanging around publishers' offices trying to 'chance upon the luscious, Rubenesque Sonia'. I would feel that it said something about him. Loyalty and love would be cratered, one woman at a time, and the devastation would dominate the conditions of my being.

I'm back at the door of the black box, not wanting to rummage around in someone's 'private' life. But I have no choice: in there is where she lived. Not to look would be to turn a blind eye to the quintessence of patriarchy: he can have his sex, paid and free, consensual and 'pouncing', year after year with anyone he 'comes across', and yet no one will speak of it. And history will let him have his decency too.

Because the biographers would like to believe that Eileen and Orwell agreed to an open marriage, they must try to find evidence of Eileen taking lovers. But aside from Kopp's love for her (and no one knows if they slept together) there are none. I find myself wishing that there were, but there's only a friend of her brother who admired her, and vague, single-source rumours of someone high up at the BBC. But there are almost innumerable affairs and 'pounces' or attempted rapes on Orwell's part.

Sometimes Eileen is severely distressed by his behaviour. And at least once she told him she would leave him if he didn't break off a relationship. To be okay with something that harms your deepest selfhood seems to be the epitome of female conditioning in patriarchy. We are supposed to collude in a system that uses us and then makes us say we agreed, or we didn't mind, or even asked for it. In any event, we are 'obviously prepared to tolerate it' and whether we suffer will remain unknown.

Prey

The night of 10 May 1941 they wake to sirens, ungodly crashes, people shouting. Their building has been hit. Instead of moving down to safety, Eileen and Orwell go up on the roof to watch. The world is on fire.

They don't move till the smoke drifts over them, by which time it 'was thick enough to make it difficult to see down the passage', Orwell writes. Back in the flat they 'slipped on some clothes, grabbed up a few things and went out.' In the stairwell Orwell stops to comfort an old woman cowering in fear, 'kneeling on the floor by her,' Eileen told a friend, 'looking like Christ and putting his hand on her head and his arms round her shoulders and comforting her'. This friend thinks Orwell is 'compassionate, though more so to strangers than to people in his immediate entourage, including his wife'.

It turns out their building has been spared, it's the garage out the back that was bombed. Nevertheless, they walk through the pitch-dark streets to stay the night at a friend's place. When they get there Orwell remarks on Eileen's blackened face. 'What do you think your own is like?' she replies.

Eileen has been the 'bread-winner', as Lydia puts it, for two years. But she is ill with frequent uterine bleeding. She is still grieving and hates her job. It is hard to sustain along with the housework, hosting relatives and bombed-out friends, looking for new accommodation, and doing all Orwell's editing and typing and shopping and cooking and caring for him when he is ill. In June 1941 she can't go on. She resigns from the Censorship Department.

Although the biographers do not like to mention that she was supporting him, they like to credit him with saving her from it. 'It seems at this point,' one writes, 'that he decided that Eileen was overworking and urged her to resign. By June she was again a free woman.' To be fair, the biographer is taking his lead from his subject, who writes, 'I have induced her to drop it for a while as it was upsetting her health.' Not one of them cites the real reason she could stop working for money, which is that he had finally found a full-time job, at the BBC.

To Orwell the BBC is a 'mixture of whoreshop and a lunatic asylum'. As the bombs fall he produces talks on the arts, politics and the war for broadcast to India and South-East Asia. He is cranky about the job and his voice is too thin and flat for him to read much on air, but he does good work – so good, in fact, that one Orwell expert 'felt sure Eileen must have helped with at least some of them'.

Some colleagues like him, finding him 'unworldly' and 'of a rare moral dignity', a person who in another era might have been 'burned at the stake'. Others feel he is 'a rather withdrawn and preoccupied person giving an impression of being generally bored with what he was doing'. There are, though, consolations in the crazy whoreshop. The secretaries, one biographer writes, 'all seemed young enough'. Another writes, 'The social life was not entirely uncongenial to him. B.B.C. gossip from those days insists that he had a brief affair with a secretary – rather as if out of a sense of duty or as if he thought it a normal part of office life.' Here in one hilarious sentence are all the elements of patri-magic designed to exonerate him by erasing a woman. Orwell's affair is doubted as 'gossip', trivialised as 'brief', and the woman has no name. And then follow swiftly the excuses by which his innocence is manufactured: he felt obliged to have the affair, out of 'duty', or the need to fit into 'normal office life'.

Whether or not it's the same woman, another biographer reports an affair with a secretary as being more significant: 'An affair with a young BBC secretary is said to have become quite serious, and he may also have had a close relationship with the Jamaican poet, Una Marson, "a dear creature"', whose slave owner he played in a radio play (no recordings survive).

Yet another affair at the BBC he took more seriously, and the biographers have to as well, because this woman has a voice. Henrietta (Hetta) Crowse was a 'beautiful, high-spirited South African and committed Communist' and a writer and sculptor. According to Hetta, Orwell was so smitten 'he said he would even leave Eileen for her', and so upset when she married their colleague, William Empson, that he refused to attend the wedding.

As well as Inez, the unnamed secretary/ies, the Jamaican poet and Hetta Crowse, at this time Orwell 'was close to Stevie Smith', another writer who was submitting scripts to the BBC. Smith, one biographer writes, 'may have been a victim of the Orwell "pounce" – she is said to have hinted at "a fling"'. Another biographer throws doubt on this affair as 'male literary gossip' aired at a 'masculine lunch *à trois*' (the French seems to make it both more secret, and more sexy, *à la fois*). It would have been real enough for the person he pounced on.

One biographer writes of a 'curious anecdote' around this time, in which Orwell asked his friend the writer Anthony Powell, 'Have you ever had a woman in a park?'

'No – never.'

'I have.'

'How did you find it?'

'I was forced to.'

'Why?'

'Nowhere else to go.'

Perhaps Eileen was at home ill, or it was when they were staying at Gwen's and he couldn't bring other women there. 'The name Stevie Smith has, in male literary gossip, been persistently linked with this tale,' writes the biographer. These things are removed from the realm of fact to become a 'curious anecdote' and 'gossip', as if, once again, the men can't face squarely what they do. But Stevie Smith saw things clearly.

Smith portrayed Orwell in her 1949 novel *The Holiday*. She said, 'I had the idea at the time that splitting George into two might lessen the danger of libel.' One half of him is Basil Tate, a homosexual Spanish Civil War veteran who 'thinks that women are biologically necessary and resents the necessity, he is like a twelve-year-old boy, he thinks that "girls are no good"'. Basil lusts after the other half of Orwell's personality, represented by 'lanky melancholic' Tom Fox, who is 'murderous [and] mad'.

Perhaps Orwell's affair with Inez was cooling, because she too writes him into an unlikeable character, 'the survivor of an awful prep school where the boys were all "snob-brats", using a tinder-lighter acquired while fighting in Spain, recovering from a wound in a squalid Paris hospital . . . and working in filthy hotel kitchens'. Orwell was not amused. Worse, it was for a radio story he'd commissioned from her.

This kind of material is hard for the biographers. '[U]nfamiliar images of him appear' as one of them puts it – Orwell through the eyes of 'keenly perceptive but put-upon women'. The word 'but' here qualifies what comes before it: the women's keen perceptions are somehow lessened because they are 'put upon', meaning that their good nature has been taken advantage of. I would say that being pounced on dilutes no one's perceptions. To be someone's prey is to see them up close, fang and prick and underbelly.

Eat

After quitting her job Eileen has a few months off, trying to recover her health. But in December 1941 women without children are conscripted to work, and though she's still frail she takes a position at the Ministry of Food. And with it she finds a life of her own.

Lettice Cooper, the novelist who'd been Orwell's editor at *Time & Tide*, was already working there. 'She walked into my room at the ministry forty years ago,' Lettice wrote in 1984, 'and I can see her as clearly as if it had been this morning. She was of medium height . . . very pretty . . . blue eyes and near black hair. She moved slowly, she always looked as if she was drifting into a room with no particular purpose there . . . I never saw her in a hurry, but her work was always finished up to time . . .' Lettice, eight years older than Eileen, had taken a classics degree at Oxford in 1918. Later, she described the Ministry of Food as like *Yes Minister*, but with a more intelligent minister.

The Ministry of Food makes a radio program with the BBC, broadcasting recipes to women cooking for their families with rations. Six days a week *The Kitchen Front* promotes the motley ingredients of wartime – egg powder, dried cod, a *lot* of parsnips – in amusing skits voiced by radio stars. Eileen is a producer. She writes and commissions scripts, vets recipes and deals with the intricate politics between the Ministry and the BBC. She fields keen home cooks submitting recipes, and actors and radio stars clamouring to perform. The program becomes hugely successful, despite promoting such dubious dishes as 'murkey' (a turkey dinner without the turkey). It's the perfect job for Eileen, with her wit, her writing talent and her political nous. *The Kitchen Front* ends up with an astonishing five million listeners a day. And the British people, apparently, have never been healthier, before or since.

If their work is done Lettice and Eileen nip out for coffee each morning (which is not allowed). If they don't get to go for coffee, they go to lunch. 'We lurched around fairly energetically and humorously to find what was the best cheap buy, whose corned beef, quick fritters or shepherd's pie was the best that week,' Lettice remembered. Often, they end up at the Selfridges coffee bar across the road, 'so we had a sort of continuous conversation going on all the time'.

Lettice is single, clever, and Eileen can tell her what she really thinks. She makes jokes about the self-delusion of some of the people who want

Lettice Cooper

to be on the show. 'I have no confidence in people who feel sure that we should find them useful,' Eileen says. And, 'Women who write, like women who act, often make rather a cult of cooking.' When a directive comes out requisitioning even bones for 'munitions of war', Eileen writes a spoof pamphlet for her colleagues' amusement about what to do with a bone. 'First scrape all the meat off it, the first soup, then the second soup, then give it to the dog, then wash it, then take it to salvage.' She doesn't even like the 'potato, salad and vitamin' dishes they have to promote, Lettice said. 'She liked meat, eggs, cheese, wine.'

Though they are close, something about Eileen remains mysterious – some breadth and depth of vision about people that's hard to square with the ragged, absent-minded sylph squinting over a script, a fag hanging forgotten in the corner of her mouth. Lettice takes Eileen as the model for the character Ann in her 1947 novel *Black Bethlehem*.

It's a realistic portrait. Ann 'drifts' into the office 'like a leaf blown in at the door'. Often she hasn't had breakfast because all the food has gone to her husband, or to people staying over. Other women at work can't pass a mirror without checking their hair and make-up but Ann 'hardly looks at hers because her mind is always intent on something she is going to say or has just been thinking about'.

> When you speak to her she generally looks at you for a minute before answering, and then answers very slowly, as though anything you said to her needed careful consideration and was of the greatest importance. At first we thought her affected, and were impatient of waiting for her comments. Later we realised that everything was important to her because her sense of life was so intense that she got the full impact of anything that turned up and saw it not isolated but with all its connections. I find it very difficult to put down what I mean about this, but I think that most people skim over most things ... Perhaps they have to be

like that to get through the day in this crowded world. Certainly
Ann finds it hard to get through the day. She does her work very
well, but she almost always stays late to finish it. She goes home at
night without meat or vegetables which she meant to buy in her
lunch hour, but had not bought because she had not finished what
she was saying at lunch. In the flat when she cooks and cleans
for her brilliant, erratic husband and their friends, she is generally
washing up at midnight . . .

Though Ann and her husband are poor, she's not afraid of being
'sacked tomorrow'. When their boss represents the women's work as
his own, she confronts him about it because 'her passion for justice
does not exclude justice to herself'. But she does it with such sympathy
and tact that the man still comes to her with his problems. Other
men in the department are charmed by her because 'she looks a dear
little thing'. But they are afraid of her too, because 'Ann is a firm
believer in protests and in joint action'. When a colleague is unfairly
dismissed, she tries to get the others to 'resign in a body', but it doesn't
work. 'Honest men,' Ann says afterwards, 'are always a menace to
dishonest men. They shake their nerves.'

This episode is based on something that happened at the Ministry.
Perhaps for Eileen it brought back memories from her twenties,
when she had organised her co-workers against their 'sadistic' boss
at the typing agency. But this time it didn't work, just as it doesn't in
Black Bethlehem.

Lettice saw that Orwell had 'an immense charm that was very
difficult to define', which caused him to be 'surrounded by adorers,
male and female'. Though 'he was in many ways a very ingenuous
and almost stupid man'. (This was too difficult for one biographer,
who simply left out the words 'almost stupid'.) 'I knew he was
kind,' Lettice recalled, and 'I wasn't frightened of him at all – some
people were . . . He was a bit funny somehow – you wanted rather

to laugh at him.' But his generosity, she thought, was real. Eileen once mentioned she was giving Lettice a pound of sugar out of their rations. 'Why?' George asked. Eileen was surprised, and said, 'We've got plenty, you don't mind, do you?' 'Good God,' George answered, 'I didn't mean that, I meant why didn't you give them all we'd got?'

'In a sort of way,' Lettice said, 'I don't think he was very clever . . . there was a . . . sort of innocence too. Naivety.' Eileen, she said, used to laugh telling stories about him. She told Lettice that once when she was bedridden he brought her a 'breadboard with bread and cheese on it and put it down on my chest in bed'. Lettice thought both of them were careless about their health, though he was 'entirely careless about hers'.

Lettice reported that 'Stevie Smith and Inez Holden both fell in love with [Orwell] and sobbed out their troubles to Eileen when he would take no notice of them'. How does a wife console her husband's lovers? Lettice thought Eileen had 'an affectionate, amused, somewhat sceptical love of [Orwell]'. And it helped that Eileen was as free from 'jealousy or rancour . . . as anybody I have ever known'.

Working at the Ministry of Food Eileen is the happiest she has been in a long time. But she is thin, anaemic and often too ill to go in. Overworked at the office and at home, she is trying to ignore what is going on inside her, as well as the bombs that keep randomly obliterating parts of her world. And, somehow, she is dealing with Orwell's extramarital sex life, manoeuvring her heart through the maze set by the Minotaur at home.

While they are at friends' for dinner one evening a bomb explodes nearby and the windows fall in. Eileen is sick of it. 'No, no – not *again*!' she says, as if the terror, so frequent, is now banal. She tells Lettice, as she has been telling Lydia, 'Don't mind if I am alive or dead nowadays.' Not occasionally, but 'all the time'. Lydia thinks it's a death wish, but it could be simply an acknowledgement of what the skies are telling them: no life is special enough to be spared.

Ann dies when a bomb falls on their flat one night while her husband is out. Lettice's narrator thinks, 'I felt her spirit near me, with its wide and sympathetic delight in the whole flow of human lives, its deep instinctive experience, its gentle wisdom. I felt her saying to me that life was short, and the people one loved were most of it that mattered . . . She feels that 'people like Ann, whose love moves out in a widening circle, are rare. Under what star was she born? Why is it that so few of us are like her?'

Fun

The Germans, apparently, have now set a date to invade Britain: 25 May 1942. After the bomb damage to their place Orwell and Eileen are between flats, so they stay for a time in the one Inez has vacated above H. G. Wells's garage.

Orwell felt that literary criticism and friendship could be kept utterly separate. He thought friends whose books – and personalities – he eviscerated in print should be able to continue their friendship with him completely unruffled. Reviewing his oldest schoolfriend Cyril Connolly's debut novel, for instance, he wrote that 'even to want to write about so-called artists who spend on sodomy what they get by sponging betrayed a certain spiritual inadequacy', and expected Connolly to take it on the chin. Which he did, more or less, though he may have taken it to heart too: Connolly never published another novel.

But these kinds of splits aren't possible for everyone. If you insult someone's work and self and presume they won't mind, the world will surprise you. At the BBC Orwell broadcasts a talk accusing Wells, the grand man of letters, of descending into insularity and utopianism. At first Wells reacts nonchalantly: 'What can you expect? All public schoolboys in the 6th learn [is] sodomy & side.' ('Side' in this context means pretentiousness and snobbishness.) But Orwell persists, publishing another piece in which he says that Wells has now 'squandered his talents' and become a 'shallow, inadequate thinker'. This angers Wells, who writes to him, 'I've heard what you've been saying about me, you ungrateful swine. Leave my flat by Monday morning.'

Orwell and Eileen find a 'dreary' ground-floor flat in Mortimer Crescent, Kilburn. Eileen confided to a friend, 'If George and I didn't smoke so much we'd be able to afford a better flat.' Though this one has the advantage of a yard for chickens and a basement for his carpentry workshop, with a spare bed for visitors next to the lathe.

Orwell's niece Jane liked it there. They used to eat about nine o'clock, delicious meals Eileen prepared after work 'in a nonchalant way, mixing pastry while joining in the conversation in the sitting room, smoking constantly'. Jane's teenage brother, Henry, came to stay for a couple of months. He also remembered Eileen rolling pastry, keeping her black overcoat on indoors because it was so cold, talking and chain-smoking all the while. When some ash fell she just rolled it in. Eileen was utterly lacking in vanity, so he was all the more struck when sometimes she would emerge dressed up go to out, looking 'dazzling'. Even a teenage boy could see that 'Uncle George didn't make the most of her'. Though Orwell liked dressing up too. On weekends, 'Uncle Eric would appear in full regalia as a sergeant in the Home Guard, boots shining and a rifle at the ready.'

At this time Orwell's old friend, the poet, Ruth Pitter, pithy and observant as usual, thinks Orwell is dying – and Eileen none too well either. And Ruth notices something odd, something new, something she doesn't like: Eileen is 'anxious' to core the apples properly for a pie, because Orwell doesn't like it when he finds any tiny hard bits left in.

It is the tiny hard bits like this that I don't like, though I leave them in.

And yet Eileen still finds there's fun to be had, and then more in the telling. She wants to patch things up with H. G. Wells. 'It's ludicrous you shouldn't be on good terms with H. G.,' she tells Orwell. 'Why don't I ask him to dinner and see if he's forgotten the whole thing?'

Wells responds immediately. 'I thought it was extraordinarily ungrateful of you to leave that flat I gave you above the garage without any notice,' he writes. 'I forgive you. Yes, of course, I shall be delighted to come to dinner.'

Michael Meyer, a young Cambridge graduate, comes to dinner not long afterwards, and Eileen recounts the evening to him. Wells turned up 'full of amiability and began by warning them that he had stomach trouble and could not eat anything rich'.

'Oh dear,' said Eileen. 'I've cooked a curry.'

'I mustn't touch that,' said Wells. 'Just give me a very little.'

He ate two huge helpings, as well as drinking plentifully, and chatted away in excellent form. After dinner William Plomer (or was it William Empson?) arrived. It transpired that he had not eaten, and the curry, thanks to Wells's greed, was finished, so Eileen said: 'All I can offer you is some plum cake.'

'Plum cake?' said Wells, overhearing this. 'I don't think I could manage that.'

'I'm not offering it to you, it's for Bill,' said Eileen, but when it appeared, Wells observed that it looked uncommonly good and took two slices.

Around midnight they put him into a taxi, in the best of spirits, and as he drove off he cried: 'Don't lose touch with me for so long again!'

They congratulated themselves on having repaired the friendship, but a week later they got a furious letter from Wells saying: 'You knew I was ill and on a diet, you deliberately plied me with food and drink,' etc., and declaring that he never wanted to see either of them again. Apparently Wells had been taken violently ill in the taxi and had had to be rushed to hospital; obviously, they had conspired against him in revenge for (he now remembered) the trouble over the flat. I believe they never did see each other again.

⌒

She dials Lettice's number, tucks the phone between her shoulder and ear as she flips through a pile of papers on the kitchen table.

'Listen to this for a thank-you note,' she tells Lettice, finding Wells's letter. "Why do you attack me in this way? Is it some perverted jealousy or some insane political machinations. Read my early works you shit."'

Lettice chuckles. 'Poor man,' she says. 'Probably thinks you were trying to kill him.'

'Yes,' Eileen says. 'Death by plum cake.' She puts her stockinged feet on the kitchen table. 'You know, I'm told Wells is going about calling George "that Trotskyist with big feet".'

They both chortle.

'I shouldn't laugh,' Eileen says. 'George is upset.'

⌒

Friendly Memories

In November 1943 Orwell leaves both the BBC and the Home Guard and takes up a position as literary editor of *Tribune*. He only needs to go into the office on the Strand three days a week and he wants, in his newly spare time, to work on a book.

But he's not suited to the role and he knows it. 'The fact is,' he writes, 'that I am no good at editing. I hate planning ahead, and have a psychical or even physical inability to answer letters.' He is too kind-hearted or irresponsible to reject even the weakest submissions. 'Somebody has written his heart out,' he tells a friend, 'and I just didn't have the courage to send them back.'

Paul Potts, a 'desperately poor, half-starved' Canadian poet, is a lost soul who hangs about the office. Potts recalled seeing Orwell slipping money – sometimes even a pound note – into an envelope to someone whose manuscript he was rejecting. 'My most essential memory of that time,' Orwell admitted, 'is of pulling out a drawer here and a drawer there, finding it in each case to be stuffed with letters and manuscripts which ought to have been dealt with weeks earlier, and hurriedly shutting it up again ...' When Tosco Fyvel visits he finds Orwell sitting 'sadly eyeing a pile of new books for review like a set of enemies'. After sixteen months Orwell gives up the job to Fyvel who discovers, on his first day, 'a whole mass of unrejected literary rejects' in desk drawers, filing cabinets, precarious stacks on the desk.

'Still,' Orwell wrote, 'I have friendly memories of my cramped little office looking out on a back yard, and the three of us who shared it huddling in the corner as the doodle-bugs came zooming over, and the peaceful click-click of the typewriters starting up again as soon as the bomb had crashed.'

And there are benefits. 'In the meantime,' one biographer writes, 'he seems to have embarked on yet another affair ...', this time with his secretary at *Tribune*, Sally McEwan. 'Again he succumbed to the compulsion to enjoy a clandestine encounter, no doubt accompanied by the story that his wife understood ...' But when Eileen finds out about it she is hugely distressed. They have a 'fiendish row' and she threatens to leave him.

Lydia often stays at Wallington to be safe from the London bombing. At this time, she remembered, 'after a row with [Eileen] in London, [George] declared that he was going to me at Wallington Cottage'. When he arrived, 'to my great annoyance, George came to my room and got into bed with me ... I had to spend the next half hour wrestling to ward him off from forcing himself on me.'

Afterwards, Lydia said, he spoke of the secretary, 'dismissively, almost contemptuously, in a way I did not like'.

Nevertheless, somehow Eileen stays with him. Perhaps she feels compassion for him because she knows he's not finding, in all these women, what he really wants. And, still, I imagine, she wants to see what can be written.

Other Animals

Orwell decides to write an essay calling Stalin to account for betraying the Russian Revolution and imposing a new autocracy. Eileen thinks it's a terrible idea. Russia is helping them fight Germany, and no one wants to undermine that right now. In their gelid bedroom they talk over what to do. 'Despite the incredibly strenuous life which both of them were leading,' Lydia reports, 'it was at the Kilburn flat that the idea of *Animal Farm* was born.' Eileen suggests it be a novel, an animal fable of the kind she loves, and once wanted to write herself. When he gets started, she sees 'at once that it was a winner', Lettice recalls. Each evening Orwell reads to her what he's done that day, and they discuss it. Every day Eileen goes in to work at the Ministry and regales her friends with the next instalment. '[S]he would quote bits out of it when we were having our coffee. It was very exciting.'

Animal Farm is written in three months. It is a masterpiece of allegory about the Russian Revolution curdling into a murderous dictatorship with a new ruling elite under Stalin. It is also, like the fairytales and fables Eileen had studied under Tolkien, a perfect story in its own right. An old pig called Major – a Karl Marx figure – has a dream in which the farm animals will one day wrest control over their lives from the humans who exploit them, then live in equality and harmony with each other. After his death other pigs – Trotsky and Stalin figures – lead the animals in a revolution to liberate them from servitude. Rallied by slogans such as 'FOUR LEGS GOOD, TWO LEGS BAD', the animals put in enormous efforts to build the new society. But gradually, as the pigs cement their power, they adopt the ways of the humans they displaced. The slogans are altered. History is rewritten. The pigs don human clothes, go about on two legs, smoke pipes. Power is maintained with the help of a vicious secret police of dogs, taken from their mothers as pups and trained to deny their helpful natures. Ultimately, the old power relations are reinstated, only with a pig instead of a human elite, because 'ALL ANIMALS ARE EQUAL BUT SOME ANIMALS ARE MORE EQUAL THAN OTHERS'.

Animal Farm is an outlier in all of Orwell's works. It has an ensemble of characters, rather than a main one who's an Orwell stand-in. A cat is slinky and unreliable, a pretty horse defects for ribbons and sugar. The donkey, Benjamin, is sweetly gloomy about the whole enterprise. A credulous carthorse, Boxer, embodiment of the working class, works himself to death. The political evisceration of the con job pulled on the Russian people, and the viciousness and hypocrisy of Stalin's totalitarian regime, are acute. But the book has a perfect structure and a tone foreign to all Orwell's other works: of close and sympathetic observation of character foibles, of humour and whimsy. The animals are not stupid or paranoid or grim, they're just themselves – seen.

Once again, as after his marriage, Orwell's friends are astonished at the change in his work. Richard Rees can't understand how Orwell has discovered in himself a 'new vein of fantasy, humor and tenderness'. His publisher Fred Warburg is stunned by its brilliance. Though just how this 'writer of rather grey novels, with heroes embodying some aspect of his personal character, had suddenly taken wings and become – a poet', he cannot fathom. 'There was, he writes, 'after all, little in Orwell's previous work to indicate that he was capable of this supreme effort.' Neither man is able to attribute a cause for this remarkable development.

But Tosco Fyvel clearly sees Eileen behind it: 'It has so often been remarked that, unlike Orwell's other works, *Animal Farm* is a supremely well-written little satire . . .' This, he goes on, is because Orwell discussed it 'with his wife as he worked on it. Sequence by sequence, it is said, Eileen and he laughed about it in bed . . . And if *Animal Farm* is a tale so perfect in its light touch and restraint (almost "unOrwellian"), I think some of the credit is due to the conversational influence of Eileen and the light touch of her bright, humorous intelligence.'

But it was not just 'conversational influence'. The form of the book itself – as fable, novel, satire – was Eileen's idea. She steered him away from writing a critical essay on Stalin and totalitarianism, and then, in bed to stay warm while the bombs fell, they worked on it together. In *Animal Farm* her psychological depth and sympathy met his political insights and made a masterpiece.

The strenuous way Orwell tries to bury her involvement is perhaps the most powerful testament to it. Eileen, he tells a friend much later, *even helped in the planning of* the book. This is a theft-and-erasure mechanism: thanking someone for a minimal contribution while erasing a much greater one. One biographer deletes the 'even' without any ellipsis, so as to erase the trace of his own omission, because the 'even' is the 'tell' of the lie – the written equivalent of losing eye contact or scratching behind your ear.

Her friends know the truth but they put it cautiously, so as to take nothing away from his achievement. 'Some people,' Lettice said, 'who knew Eileen feel that the simplicity and elegance of *Animal Farm* may be due in part to her influence.' Lydia wrote, 'I could recognize touches of Eileen's humour in some of the episodes. Whether she had directly suggested them, or George had unconsciously assimilated some of his wife's whimsical ways of talking and viewing things, matters little in this connection. Personally I have little doubt that in a subtle, indirect way Eileen had collaborated in the creation of *Animal Farm*.'

The writing of *Animal Farm* in the 'icily-cold first-floor bedroom' is a joy for Eileen. But as the winter turns to spring, then summer, the rejections pile up. No publisher will touch a novel so critical of Stalin, even in allegory.

Usually, he's the one who falls ill once a book is done. This time, it's her. She's been in bed for two days with a fever.

He comes in with a breadboard, which he seems not to know what to do with. 'Here,' he says, placing it on her chest. She looks down: half a loaf of bread, a knife and some butter.

'Thank you.' She pulls herself up a little, holding onto the breadboard with her thumb on the knife handle. Tenderness is hard for him, but here it is.

He's smiling, teeth a little crooked, a little brown, shifting his weight from foot to foot. His eyes so blue, wrinkled all around now. He doesn't know what to do with his hands. There are moments of connection – very rare – when he is open to her. There seem to be no more words.

'Tea!' he says then, 'and even honey. I'll bring it all in.'

'Just a cup,' she calls to his back as he leaves. A pot could be a disaster.

He's calling the book 'a little squib' to friends, though they both know *Animal Farm* is just about perfect. She understands this is a celebration, possibly even a gesture of thanks.

She sits up higher, against the headboard. They'd laughed so much in this bed as they nutted out the characters, the circular fable plot. How the animals give the hams they find in the humans' house a burial. How the hens, in protest at having the fruit of their labour stolen, flutter up to the rafters to lay, so their eggs smash on the floor.

He's in the doorway, breathing hard, with a cup of tea in one hand and the open jar of honey in the other.

'Jonathan Cape has turned it down too.' He passes her the tea and puts the honey on the board.

'Let's talk to Moore,' she says. 'I agree with him that we should give it to Warburg.'

'All right,' he says.

'I'm sure it will find a home,' she says.

'I hope so.' He sits down on the bed. 'There's something else I want to talk about.'

IV

HAPPY ENDING

Bud

Towards the end of 1944 it is clear the war will be won. Life will start again.

Orwell passionately wants to adopt a son. It must be adoption, and it must be a son. Eileen is not at all sure about the idea. She is nervous, she tells Lettice, 'that she might not be able to give to an adopted child the love and empathy that she felt she could have given to one of her own ... and this would not be fair to the child'. And she could have had one of her own. 'It isn't I who can't have one,' she told Lettice. 'I am anatomically perfect.' When Paul Potts had suggested 'Why not get Eileen to bear a child by somebody else? At least it would be Eileen's child', Orwell had blanched and dismissed the idea out of hand.

Eventually, Eileen agrees. In her obstetric practice Gwen cares for women who are pregnant to men not their husbands – often US servicemen in Britain – and she herself has adopted a baby girl, Mary. One of her patients, Nancy Robinson, had given birth while her husband was away at the front. Gwen arranges for Eileen and Orwell to take her little boy, Richard.

For reasons not recorded anywhere, Eileen has to collect the three-week-old baby from the hospital alone. The biographers obscure the fact that Eileen did this at all, never mind on her own. 'That summer,' one of them writes, 'he and Eileen ... took possession of a three week old baby'. Another puts it this way: 'The paperwork covering his adoption having been completed, he was first taken, aged three weeks, to the O'Shaughnessy family's house . . . until arrangements could be made . . .'

⤙⟶

For some reason George can't come. She touches the clothes in the brown cardboard case – a cotton nightdress, a pale-blue knitted cardigan and bonnet from Gwen. So tiny, for such a big thing. She puts two baby blankets on top and presses the lid down, snaps each metal clasp. She has bought a Moses basket to carry him in. She places the case in the basket and hips it all to take downstairs.

She goes alone across London – a bus, a Tube, another bus – to the hospital. It would have been easier, she thinks, to have them send the baby to her in a basket downriver, Old Testament style. As the Tube approaches Elephant & Castle she remembers Virginia Woolf's character Judith, Shakespeare's imaginary sister, buried here after she found herself with child. On the way back, she's going to be with child herself. She feels her heart jump, thump.

On the Tube platform she sees a blackboard on an easel with sums chalked on it; schoolchildren have been having lessons here. She exits to the tinkling sound of glass being swept. This world, for this baby?

There are forms to sign, but not many. She can't believe they will just hand over a human being. She's had to do more to get rations.

For such a big thing, when you get him he's so small. Suddenly the basket is huge, she has to roll up the blankets to chock him in, one on each side. The stairs down to the platform are steeper now, frightening. The creature sleeps through the movement on the Tube. A fringe of dark lashes,

just the idea of eyebrows for now, below the blue cap. She
waits for him to wake, to scream in outrage at this heist,
but she gets him home in time for the next feed. He is a
mystery, furled as a bud.

She stares at him as he sleeps. Nothing is happening
but tiny bellows inside him opening and closing, opening
and closing. His eyelids part, she sees the slate-grey irises
shunting. She has never watched a human dream. Anemone
fingers open and close, for practice.

When he's hungry he moves his head from side to side,
open-mouthed, looking for a nipple, finds the bottle, sucks
hard. It's shocking, this grasping towards life. As she holds
the bottle in tension with him, firmly in and out with his
rhythm, her heart opens wide, wider. This tiny scrap of life.

When George comes home his joy is beautiful. He can't
sit, he hovers. He wants a blue perambulator with a gold
stripe! He wants to put the baby down for Eton! He picks
up the birth certificate from the kitchen table, holds it to
the tip of his cigarette and burns it. The baby's name was
Richard Robertson. Now, he is Richard Horatio Blair.

She wants to keep working at the Ministry so she stays
with Gwen at Greenwich where there is a nanny, a nursery,
household staff. Sometimes she thinks about the work
the girl or cook is doing, which would, at the flat, be hers.
She thinks of all the ways people have invented to not see
others around them, to stop themselves from spelunking
into the vertiginous cavern of what it is to be another. And
yet this baby, with his frail and stubborn bellows, his eyes
that wake looking for her, depends entirely, precisely,
on this.

A week later there is a new terror in the skies. Gigantic
V-1 bombs, each with its own onboard jet engine, attack

the city. When one of these 'doodle-bugs' explodes near the house she places Richard on the floor and covers him with her body. She makes an arch with her back, her chin on his soft head. She kisses him as the world crumbles so loudly that you can't tell if it's near or far, here or there, now or later.

⌒

The first time Lydia visits to see the baby they are still at Greenwich. She has never seen Orwell and Eileen so content. 'She had bathed the baby and was giving him his bottle. George was kneeling before her, watching, entranced, rather in the manner of an adoring shepherd in a Nativity painting.'

Eileen stops saying that she doesn't care if she lives or dies.

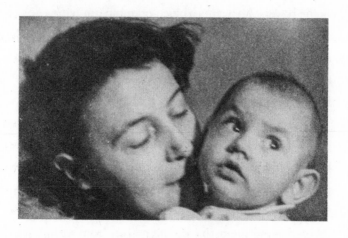

Eileen and Richard, 1944.

Fight or Flight or F---

And yet, for Orwell, the intimacy produces a flight from it, once again. Or perhaps it is sheer force of habit, not squandering the opportunity he sees presented by a woman in a park. One biographer tells of a party at the Empsons' Hampstead flat that summer at which Orwell, who had been drinking heavily, met a young woman he had 'known vaguely' at the BBC. 'Afterwards he offered to walk her home across the Heath and there attempted to make violent love to her. She fended him off by promising to meet him the next day, and when she failed to show up, received an angrily reproachful letter about the iniquity of breaking promises.'

Is being drunk an excuse? Usually, he was sober when propositioning or pouncing on women. The euphemistic 'attempted to make violent love to' is a contorted way of saying he tried to rape her. And his subsequent letter to the young woman leaves me wordless, except to say that it reminds me of his reproaches to Lydia when she would not stay home at the times he'd nominated for sex she did not want. A man is entitled to what he wants, even if that is you.

I hope Eileen never knew.

On 28 June a bomb falls so close to their flat that its roof and ceilings collapse. Again, everything they own is engulfed in soot and dust. Fortunately, they are still staying at Greenwich with the baby. Orwell spends a week going back and forth, salvaging what he can. It's an eight-mile round trip and he walks it with a wheelbarrow. He extracts a typed manuscript of *Animal Farm* from the wreckage, which he submits to T. S. Eliot at Faber, apologising for its 'blitzed' condition. Eliot, along with everyone else that summer, rejects it.

By this time Georges Kopp has arrived in Britain. Eileen had asked Gwen to help him, and he had quickly wooed and married Gwen's half-sister, Doreen. He is now as close to Eileen as he can get; a kind of brother-in-law. The Kopps are living in Canonbury Square with their own new baby. How does Eileen feel about Georges having married into her brother's family? No record remains. How does Georges feel about Eileen? Perhaps he watches her closely, finds her thinner, paler, and yet somehow stronger too, as she corrects or rebuts or laughs with her husband. Georges and Doreen help Eileen and Orwell find a flat right near them, also on Canonbury Square.

The new place consists of five joined-up attic rooms in a 'leprous' tenement, with plaster falling 'in drifts' off the ceiling, 'dark and dingy'. There are gaps under the doors so large that one friend thinks they must have been sawn off deliberately to create draughts. But Eileen is optimistic, writing to Lydia before they move in:

We have a flat in Canonbury Square—at least . . . we shall have it unless the bombs beat us to the post which is rather likely. It's a top floor flat and there have been numbers of bombs in the vicinity though the square itself has lost nothing but a window or two. I rather like it, in fact in some ways I like it very much indeed . . . Disadvantage is that to get to it you climb an uncountable number of stone stairs . . . I don't know how Richard will be managed if the bombing ever stops. I thought we might have a crane and sling and transport him the way they do elephants in the films but George thinks this unsuitable.

Once they've moved in, Eileen resigns from the Ministry of Food. Lydia visits one evening that autumn and finds her in the back garden, where she is trying to bring the pram inside:

> . . . I helped her to get it in, Eileen remarking with a smile: 'He's got to be carried upstairs, but the creature's put on so much weight lately that I just can't manage it . . .' Her remark was one of those warnings one heeds momentarily with a painful contraction of the heart, only to brush aside as unfounded fears. As we drank tea in front of the fire (for which the coal had to be carried up all those flights of steps), and Richard lay on his back on the couch, cooing happily and playing with his toes, his adoptive parents looked more serene, more relaxed and happier than they had done for some time past. The end of the war was near at hand; V-2's still fell on London, but they were few and far between compared with the onslaught of the previous summer . . .

Eileen can no longer put off dealing with her long bleeds, her excruciating abdominal pain and debilitating anaemia. She has 'at last agreed to do something about her health,' Lydia writes, 'for she found she just had no physical strength to carry on with domestic work or the care of the child. She . . . was having a course of injections, yet her strength was not increasing, it was not even being maintained.'

One day Eileen and Orwell are walking in the street when she collapses. Thin and weak, she must stay in bed. Orwell can't care for her – no biographer even raises the possibility that he might have.

Gwen has brought little Laurence back from Canada and evacuated with him and baby Mary to her family house, Greystone, near Stockton-on-Tees. She and a specialist convince Eileen to go there 'where she could have complete rest while Richard was looked after by the children's nurse'.

The court hearing to finalise Richard's adoption is scheduled for 21 February 1945, after which he will be officially their son. Orwell has stayed in London while Eileen and Richard are up north. He has accepted an offer to go to Europe after the hearing, reporting for *The Observer* on the end of the war. He wants to witness the retreat of the Germans from Paris and the advance of the Allies into Germany.

Eileen is feeling a little better. *I've been dressed every day*, she writes to him, meaning that she has been out of bed. Though she's still weak. *I've done very little else except give Richard most of his food and have him for his social* between five and six.* She is looking forward to seeing Orwell at the hearing on the 21st, by which time, she says, Richard will have cut more teeth.

> *I hope you'll be able to do the Court but of course you mustn't mess up the French trip.*
>
> *Could you ring me up on Friday or Saturday evening? It's quite easy—Stillington, Co. Durham, 29. A trunk call of course—you dial TRU & ask for the number. Then we can talk about the plans. Unless of course you're coming up this weekend which would be nice. I'll be home at Greystone on Friday afternoon.*
>
> *Eileen*

---

* The 'social' was the customary hour children otherwise in the care of nannies would spend with their mothers.

No one knows whether he called. But instead of visiting his sick wife, or dealing with the adoption of his son, Orwell takes off abruptly for France on the 15th, leaving her to face the court alone. Was he avoiding the hearing because he feared it would be nerve-racking? Or did he think his own cadaverous appearance might jeopardise it? Perhaps, as he wrote in a column at that time, he was just sick of doing his own dishes.

One biographer conceals Orwell's avoidance this way (the emphases are mine): 'That autumn, six months after their having taken on Richard, *it was necessary* to attend court to have the adoption approved. *All went well.*' And he hides Orwell's abandonment of Eileen like this: 'Three weeks after Orwell left London, Eileen *had become seriously ill* with uterine tumors causing great pain and heavy bleeding.' The grammar dodges and feints here as tenses stretch in an ugly way, because the biographer wants to imply that Eileen only became ill *after* Orwell left. He wants Orwell not to have abandoned a wife who was seriously ill, though both he and Orwell know that he did.

Eileen has to drag herself, bleeding, in pain and alone, into court to appear before the judge. She feels that she and Orwell, both ill and 'old for parenthood', don't make the most auspicious candidates as adoptive parents, so she buys a new honey-coloured hat to distract the judge from her appearance. Perhaps it works; the adoption is approved.

Her husband is not there to celebrate with. So, Lettice remembered, 'She came round to the Ministry with Richard – frightfully proud and pleased. And for the first time in her life she was wearing a hat. She had a neat coat and skirt on – she wasn't generally very neat, and she had bought a yellow felt hat so that the judge should think she was an entirely suitable person to look after Richard, and Richard was fine, very cheerful.'

Alone in London, Eileen even telephones Lydia, who can be so annoying. Lydia comes over, finding her 'serene' as she talks of Richard and his cousins. Eileen needs to finish a letter to get it off in the post. As she puts the date on it she says, out of nowhere, "'I hate writing 1945," and "I should hate even more writing 1946, and as for 1947, I just couldn't bear it ..." We both laughed,' Lydia remembered, 'I treating it merely as one of her whimsical remarks, and even now I do not think it expressed a foreboding.'

Eileen, usually so vague about what day it is, is thinking closely now about dates. This baby is a beginning. Time is starting again. Though it is shunting her away from her beloved brother. As she walks Lydia to the bus stop, 'with sudden intensity of feeling she spoke of her brother ...' Eileen is thirty-nine, the age at which Laurence died, nearly five years ago. 'We kissed each other good-bye,' Lydia writes. 'She seemed much better.'

She knows she's not better. But now, with George gone to Europe and the adoption finalised, she can arrange her own care. She organises a hysterectomy, to be performed by a friend of her brother, Dr Harvey Evers.

She's on a timeline. The operation is scheduled for 29 March. She goes down to London for a dentist appointment and drops in at the flat on Canonbury Square. She flicks through the mail, most of which seems to be letters of demand, or signposts to disasters she'll have to deal with (electricity to be cut off, publishers' queries not responded to). It is the ratcheting-up of the narrative, she thinks, one URGENT termination letter at a time. The phone rings. It's Inez. Strange, or perhaps not, that George didn't tell her he was disappearing either.

She sleeps alone in the cold flat. The next day, in Selfridges, she collapses again. It's a bad bleed, but somehow she gets herself to the Ministry to seek help.

Lettice isn't there. Other friends want to call an ambulance, bring Orwell back from Europe. Eileen is horrified by the idea and refuses.

She stays alone in London for a week before she feels strong enough for the journey back north.

Georges Kopp sees her off at King's Cross station in the evening. She is wan and frail. He puts her suitcase on the rack as she collapses into the seat. If she was catlike before, now she is birdlike – a pale starling chick, bony and fuzzy-headed. Spain was a long time ago.

Money

Years passed. The seasons came and went, the short animal lives fled by.

George Orwell, *Animal Farm*

〜

She is covered in blankets in a wicker chair in the garden. Gwen's housekeeper, Mrs Blackburn, has set up a table with the typewriter on it. Richard and his cousins are inside.

Wednesday 21 March 1945
Greystone
Carlton

Dearest your letter came this morning . . . I was rather worried because there had been an interval of nearly a fortnight . . . one may have gone astray.

Which is what she would like to believe, or to have him say. That there had been a letter in which he asked how the court hearing went, or explained why he bolted, leaving her to do it alone. When he knew she was ill. Never mind, she's out of bed now.

I am typing in the garden. Isn't that wonderful? . . . the
wind keeps blowing the paper down over the machine . . . but
the sun is hot. Richard is sitting up in his pram talking to a doll.
He has the top half of a pram suit on but he took off the rest some
time ago and has nothing between himself and the sky below
his nappies. I want him to get aired before the sun gets strong so
that he'll brown nicely . . . I bought him a high chair—the only
kind I could get.

It was expensive, but she won't mention that – they can't
really do without one, and she has a further purchase to
confess to.

It sort of breaks in half and turns up its tail like a beetle if
you want it to . . . the whole on wheels . . . and I found it very
useful myself on the way up as a luggage trolley.

A high chair is not really a replacement for his help, but
there wasn't a porter to be found at the stations where she
had to change trains. She hasn't told him of her collapse yet,
or the week she spent alone in the flat in London gathering
enough strength for the journey back here.

I came by night in the end so that Georges Kopp could see me
off at King's X which was very nice, but there were no porters at
all at Thornaby or Stockton—and only one at Darlington but
I got him. There is no real news about Richard. He is just very
well. I was sorry to be away from him for a week . . . I bought
him a truck too for an appalling sum of money. I had to forget
the price quickly but I think it's important he should have one.

Mrs Blackburn – she always thinks 'Blackbird', because
of her white apron over a black dress, her deep-set dark
eyes – comes out to say that little Laurence is ready for his
social. Eileen asks her if she'd mind bringing the typewriter
inside. (She wouldn't normally; Mrs B's hands are clawed
with arthritis, but she can't manage it herself yet.)

She reads her nephew a fairy story. Laurence is six now and she tries to see her brother in him, but the boy is impenetrably polite since his time with strangers in Canada. It's heartbreaking.

Afterwards, she's at her desk. Where was she?

. . . an appalling sum of money.

Yes. The first things Orwell had wanted for Richard were a fancy perambulator (they'd used a hand-me-down instead) and to put him down for Eton (undecided as yet). But for most things, frugality rules. So, how about a story he might like, one that Mrs B's husband, who does odd jobs around here, told her this morning:

We're no longer in the garden now. In fact Richard is in bed and has been for some time. Blackburn came and told me all about his other jobs and how [his] . . . predecessor here shot himself. I think perhaps the general shooting standard was rather lower . . . because this man shot a wood pigeon and tried to pull it out of the bush into which it had fallen with his gun (this might be better expressed but you can guess it). Naturally the bush pulled the trigger and there was another shot in the other barrel and the ass was actually holding the barrel to his belly, so he might as well have been an air raid casualty. This convinced me not that Richard must never have a gun but that he must have one very young so that he couldn't forget how to handle it.

She has run out of ways to divert and deflect. She lights a cigarette and reads over what she's written. Takes a deep breath.

Gwen rang up Harvey Evers and they want me to go in for this operation at once. This is all a bit difficult. It is going to cost a terrible lot of money. A bed in a kind of ward costs seven guineas a week and Harvey Evers' operation fee is *forty guineas.* In London I would have to pay about five guineas a week in a hospital but Gwen says the surgeon's fee would be higher. The absurd thing is that we are too well off for really cheap rates—you'd have to make less than £500 a year.*

She must frame carefully the idea of spending money on her health. Work out how to earn it back.

It comes as a shock to me in a way because while you were being ill I got used to paying doctors nothing. But of course it was only because Eric [Laurence] *was making the arrangements. I suppose your bronchoscopy would have cost about forty guineas too—and I must say it would have been cheap at the price, but what worries me . . .*

She stops typing for a moment. Her fingers hover over the keys.

. . . is that I really don't think I'm worth the money.

Her bedroom door is ajar but Gwen still knocks. Her sister-in-law is stolid, wise and kind – she's brought the warmed bottle. Despite all that, Eileen feels a ripple of annoyance; Gwen is not her brother. Irrational, she knows, and unfair. She turns from the typewriter.

'Ten o'clock already?'

'I'm afraid so.' Gwen smiles, standing there in her sensible shoes.

'He's like clockwork. Or his stomach is.'

'It doesn't last all that long.' Gwen passes her the bottle. 'He'll soon sleep through.'

They walk together down the corridor to the nursery.

'You are writing to George?' she asks.

'Yes.'

---

* Seven guineas is about £405 at the time of writing. Forty guineas is about £2,300.

Gwen breathes in. 'But you know the letter mightn't reach him before the operation. I wish you'd let *The Observer* cable him.'

'Thank you, but no. It makes it all seem so dire and urgent.'

They are outside the nursery door. Richard is wailing. It's a miracle the others haven't started up too. Eileen hands the bottle back to Gwen.

'He needs to stop waking for this. He's big enough to sleep through. I'll just pat him.'

Gwen nods. A strand of hair falls forward out of her bun. She seems to have frozen with things she is not saying. Eileen touches her arm.

'What is it?'

Gwen closes her eyes and shakes her head.

'How about we compromise then? You could ask them to cable him when the thing is over.'

'All right,' Gwen says. Her eyes are soft, swimming, she blinks and turns away. Eileen opens the nursery door.

After Richard is sleeping again, she sits back down at the typewriter. This letter is interminable, difficult. Where was she? Ah yes, at money.

She can't unsay it now, and it'd be worse to go back and XXXX it all out, so she'll stick to listing options to convince him: a cheaper, quicker operation; the possibility of selling a house she inherited from Mother (though there's a mortgage over it, so it's not worth much); earning more money herself, somehow. Perhaps by writing – with him, or on her own, who knows?

On the other hand of course this thing will take a longish time to kill me if left alone and it will be costing some money the whole time. The only thing is, I think perhaps it might be possible to sell the Harefield house if we found out how to do it.

I do hope too that I can make some money when I am well—
I could of course do a job but I mean really make some
money from home as it were. Anyway I don't know what
I can do except go ahead and get the thing done quickly. The
idea is that I should go in next week and I gather he means to
operate quickly—he thinks the indications are urgent enough
to offset the disadvantages of operating on a bloodless patient;
indeed he is quite clear that no treatment at all can prevent me
from becoming considerably more bloodless every month. So I
suppose they'll just do a blood transfusion and operate more or
less at once.

Blood, blood, blood. How he hates it. But she must
tell him how sick she is, because it is a thing he doesn't see.
She rubs her face with her hands. Pulls her cardigan sleeves
over her wrists. Can a bloody collapse have a psychological
cause? She's wondered about this before, when he'd
haemorrhage if she was trying to go away.

Last month he'd offered her typing services to a refugee
acquaintance for a bit of extra money, and the manuscript
had to be delivered to his secretary – Sally – at the *Tribune*
offices. She always hated seeing his women – Sally or Inez,
Hetta or Stevie, the women at the BBC. It made her feel
ashamed, as if something had been stolen from her under
her nose.

I set off with it all right, broke the journey to go to the bank
and was taken with a pain just like the one I had the day before
coming North, only rather worse. I tried to have a drink in
Selfridges' but couldn't and all sorts of extraordinary things then
happened . . .

She'd fallen on the floor. The lift boy shot out to cradle
her head, but when he saw the blood on her skirt he'd
called to the girl behind the counter, who dashed to get the

manager, a woman. The two of them lifted her up under the arms and took her to the lavatory. She came out, her skirt all wet, and they put her in a cab.

. . . but after a bit I got myself into the Ministry. I simply could not do any more travelling . . .

Miss Sparrow, who'd been her secretary there, called *Tribune* for someone to come and collect the manuscript.

People from <u>Tribune</u> . . .

She can't say Sally's name, it hurts. Though she was so kind and

rang up in the most friendly way, offering to come and look after me, to bring me things and to get you home. I was horrified. But yesterday I had a phase of thinking that it was really outrageous to spend all your money on an operation of which I know you disapprove, so Gwen rang <u>Tribune</u> to know whether they had means of communicating with you quickly and could get your ruling. They hadn't but suggested she should ring the <u>Observer</u>, which she did and talked to Ivor Brown. He said you were in Cologne now he thought and that letters would reach you very slowly if at all. He suggested that they would send you a message about me by cable and wireless . . . Gwen says he couldn't have been nicer. But I'm not having this done. It's quite impossible to give you the facts in this way and the whole thing is bound to sound urgent and even critical. I have arranged with Gwen however that when the thing is over she'll ask the <u>Observer</u> to send you a message to that effect.

Her mind is going in circles. There's her illness, which is hard to downplay at the same time as setting out reasons for an expensive operation. There's permission. And there's getting him to come.

One very good thing is that by the time you get home I'll be convalescent, really convalescent at last and you won't have the

*hospital nightmare you would so much dislike. You'd more or
less have to visit me and visiting someone in a ward really
is a nightmare even to me with my fancy for hospitals—
particularly if they're badly ill as I shall be at first of course.
I only wish I could have had your approval as it were,
but I think it's just hysterical.*

There's his permission. There's the money. And then
there's her body.

*Obviously I can't just go on having a tumour or rather
several rapidly growing tumours. I have got an uneasy
feeling that after all the job might have been more cheaply
done somewhere else but if you remember Miss Kenny's fee
for a cautery, which is a small job, was fifteen guineas so she'd
certainly charge at least fifty for this. Gwen's man might have
done cheaper work for old sake's sake, but he's so very bad at the
work and apparently he would have wanted me in hospital for
weeks beforehand—and I'm morally sure I'd be there for weeks
afterwards. Harvey Evers has a very high reputation . . .
and I am sure that he will finish me off as quickly as anyone
in England as well as doing the job properly—so he may well
come cheaper in the end. I rather wish I'd talked it over with you
before you went.*

But he left so suddenly, a week early, before the court
appearance.

*I knew I had a 'growth'. But I wanted you to go away
peacefully anyway, and I did not want to see Harvey Evers
before the adoption was through in case it was cancer. I thought
it just possible that the judge might make some enquiry about
our health as we're old for parenthood and anyway it would
have been an uneasy sort of thing to be producing oneself as an
ideal parent a fortnight after being told that one couldn't live
more than six months or something.*

It is cancer, but it's operable. She turns to their future, which she's also organising. He wants to go and live in a disused farmhouse on an island off the far west coast of Scotland, a place it takes two days' travel to reach, first by train then bus then ferry then lorry, the last leg an eight-mile walk.

I'm now so confident of being strong in a few months that I'm not actually frightened as I should have been of living a primitive life again (after all when you were ill soon after we were married I did clean out the whole of Wallington's sanitation and that was worse than emptying a bucket) but it does waste a lot of time.

She looks at what she's just written in parentheses. He probably won't understand it. She is saying-without-saying that he's likely to be so unwell that he'll rely on her, as ever, to do the physical work of the farm and house, the childminding and cooking and quite possibly dealing with cesspits. She will need to be strong.

Georges Kopp hasn't been forwarding mail from their London flat to Orwell as he'd promised to do, mostly because Orwell had failed to give him a forwarding address. But also, she suspects, because Georges is incensed at him for leaving her, ill and alone with a new baby.

I found to my distress that Georges was not forwarding letters to you . . . because he had not heard from you . . .

She herself doesn't even have a firm address for him, and this letter may never reach him.

I can do nothing with this except send it to the Hotel Scribe and hope they'll forward it. It's odd—we have had nothing to discuss for months but the moment you leave the country there are dozens of things. But they can all be settled, or at least settled down, if you take this week's leave when you get back.

Then again, he might not come.

If you don't come next month I'll have to think again . . .

Perhaps he'll come if she arranges some fishing for him at Garrigill nearby, as he'd asked her to.

I don't know about Garrigill. It depends when you come. But at worst you could come here couldn't you? If you were here we should stay mainly in my room, indeed I suppose I'll be there for some time after I get back in any case, and Richard will be available. Mary and Laurence both spend a lot of time with me now but they could be disposed of . . . and if I'm still at the picturesque stage of convalescence you could go out with Blackburn who knows every inch of the countryside or perhaps amuse yourself with Mr. Swinbank the farmer . . .

She needs to let him think that his options are open.

Or you could go over to Garrigill for a weekend's fishing on your own.

She would like to live in the country, if it could be done in a less extreme way, without her being the house serf. London is a bombsite, where she must dodge filth and other women.

I think it's quite essential that you should write some book again . . .

The question is, where?

. . . Indeed if the worst comes to the worst I think [Richard had] better go to Wallington for the summer, but it would be better to find somewhere with more space because you and Richard would be too much for the cottage very soon and I don't know where his sister could go. And I think the cottage makes you ill—it's the damp and the smoke I think.

The idea they've talked about, of adopting a baby girl, thrills her. But that would overload this letter, so long already because:

While this has been in progress I have read several stories
to Laurence, dealt with Richard who woke up (he has just
stopped his 10 o'clock feed), dealt with Mary who always cries
in the evening, had my supper and listened to Mrs. Blackburn's
distresses . . . That's why it's so long. And partly why it's so
involved. But I should like to see you stop living a literary life
and start writing again and it would be much better for Richard
too, so you need have no conflicts about it. Richard sends you this
message. He has no conflicts.

. . . Whether he can keep his certainties over the difficult
second year I don't know of course but he's much more likely to
if he has the country and you have the kind of life that satisfies
you—and me.

Now I'm going to bed. Before you get this you'll probably
have the message about this operation and you may well be in
England again if you keep . . . on the move. What a waste that
would be.

All my love, and Richard's.
E.

She folds it, puts it on the bedside table. Turns off the light.

This is the most terrifying letter, with its dodges and feints by which a
woman plays down her needs to the point where she does not deserve
critical medical care, so that her husband should feel free to either
come or not. She has earned more money than he in the last few years,
and she has inherited more again. Yet the letter is couched as if she
needs his approval to spend it. Self-effacement is a feminine virtue in
patriarchy, but it eventually realises itself and looks like a crime.

Eileen writes to several friends before her operation, asking them
to send letters to the hospital, letters to go to sleep with, letters to wake

up to. To Lettice she writes more directly, and with more detail, than to Orwell. She knows Lettice will see through her brisk bravado, the layers of self-deprecation, and understand what is being asked of her.

~

23 March 1945 or thereabouts
Greystone
Carlton

Dear Lettice,

I'm sorry about the paper and the typewriter but Mary got at both. You practically can't buy paper here so I can't waste that and although I could do something about the machine I am bored with it after about twenty minutes spent in collecting the ribbon and more or less replacing it. A typewriter ribbon is the longest thing in the world. It will go round every chair leg in a good sized house. So I've just discovered.

Thanks for the coat for Richard . . . He's still backward but has great charm which will be a lot more useful to him than talent. And he is not so stupid . . . because he found out about pulling trucks by their strings before he was ten months old and is now investigating the principles of using one object to drag nearer or to pick up another. He's a hard worker.

She's sorry not to have seen Lettice in London, but:

Then I got ill and rang no one up and finished with all kinds of dramas looking for you at the Ministry, but you were out.

How she wishes Lettice had been there that day.

On the way up I went to see a Newcastle surgeon because as Richard's adoption was through I thought I might now deal with the grwoth (no one could object to a grwoth)* I knew I had. He found it or rather them without any difficulty and

---

*   'grwoth' in original.

*I'm going into his nursing home next week for the removal.
I think the question about the hysterectomy is answered because
there is hardly any chance that the tumours can come out
without more or less everything else removable. So that on the
whole is a very good thing. It was worth coming to the north
country because there is to be none of the fattening up in hospital
before the operation that I was to have in London. London
surgeons love preparing their patients as an insurance against
unknown consequences. I think they're all terrified of their
knives really—probably they have a subconscious hope that the
patient will die before getting as far as the theatre and then they
can't possibly be blamed.*

   *In London they said I couldn't have any kind of operation
without a preparatory month of blood transfusions etc. Here I'm
going in next Wednesday to be done on Thursday. Apart from
its other advantages this will save money, a lot of money. And
that's as well. By the way, if you could write a letter that would
be nice. Theoretically I don't want any visitors, particularly as I
can't get a private room; in practice I'll probably be furious that
no one comes—and no one can because such friends as I have in
Newcastle will be away for the school holidays. So if you have
time write a letter to Fernwood House . . . It's a mercy George
is away—in Cologne at the moment. George visiting the sick is
a sight infinitely sadder than any disease-ridden wretch in the
world.*

   *[T]his . . . has taken about a week to write . . . But all
this time we have been thanking you for Richard's present,
he & I.*

   Lots of love
       Emily

The biographers generally ignore Eileen's fears and her worry about Orwell being angry about the expense of her operation. They like to cite *George visiting the sick is a sight infinitely sadder than any disease-ridden wretch in the world* as evidence that she didn't want him to visit her. They use this sentence as if she meant it literally, rather than seeing it for the brave face she was putting on his abandonment. She is even made responsible for him forsaking her: 'she played the whole thing down,' writes one biographer, 'saying, "I really don't think I'm worth the money."' There is something horrifying about a woman supplying an excuse for the man who is neglecting her, and his biographers then taking it up and running with it.

Sometimes she wonders if he thinks of her. Or what he is doing.

Amusing Himself

In Paris Orwell is staying at the Hôtel Scribe, along with a lot of foreign correspondents, including the rich aesthete Harold Acton. They go out to a fancy dinner, which is when Orwell reminisces about the 'sweetness' of Burmese girls, and the 'slender flanks and small pointed breasts' and 'odour of spices' and 'satiny skins' of Moroccan ones. Probably he's back in the brothels of Paris. He's still writing to Sally, his lover at *Tribune*.

He wants to meet Ernest Hemingway, so he goes to his room at the Ritz and knocks on the door.

'Open!'

Orwell sees a bed with two cases on it, and the famous writer, barrel-chested and handsome, standing behind it, packing.

'I'm Eric Blair,' he says.

'Well what the fucking hell do you want?' Hemingway bellows at the skinny Brit with his uniform hanging off him.

'I'm George Orwell,' he says, more diffidently.

'Why the fucking hell didn't you say so?' Hemingway pushes the cases to the top of the bed and bends down, feeling under it. He pulls out a bottle of Scotch. 'Have a drink. Have a double. Straight or with water, there's no soda.'

Orwell tells Hemingway he's frightened of being assassinated by communists, because 'They' are after him. Hemingway thinks he's 'fairly nervous and worried', and looking 'very gaunt and . . . in bad shape'. Orwell asks to borrow a weapon he can easily conceal, so Hemingway hands over a .32 calibre Colt. Personally, he thinks it's pretty useless but he hopes it'll make Orwell feel better. For some reason Hemingway sends friends to 'shadow' Orwell. They report that he 'was quite safe and happily "amusing himself" in Paris'.

Orwell stays in Paris for a month. At the end of March he returns Hemingway's gun and goes to Cologne.

⌒

She hasn't received an answer to her last letter, but then who knows how the post from France is working as the occupying power retreats? Did they have to change the stamps? From Marianne to a Valkyrie, and now back again? She must look at the stamp on his previous letter, wherever she put that. Then, too, there's the fact that she's unsure of his address.

Nevertheless, she's going to assume that he's receiving these letters, so she's not repeating anything about operations, blood, permission.

Greystone,
Carlton,
Stockton-on-Tees

Dearest

    I'm trying to get forward with my correspondence because I go into the nursing home on Wednesday (this is Sunday) & of course I shan't be ready. It's impossible to write or do anything else while the children are up. I finish reading to Laurence about a quarter to eight (tonight it was five to eight), we have supper at 8 or 8.15, the 9 o'clock news now must be listened to & lasts till at least 9.30 (the war reports the last two nights have been brilliant) & then it's time to fill hotwater bottles etc. because we come to bed early. So I write in bed & don't type. Incidentally I did while explaining the poaching laws as I understand them to Laurence make my will—in handwriting because handwritten wills are nearly always valid. It is signed & witnessed. Nothing is less likely than that it will be used but I mention it because I have done an odd thing. I haven't left anything to Richard. You are the sole legatee if you survive me (your inheritance would be the Harefield house which ought to be worth a few hundreds, that insurance policy, & furniture). If you don't the estate would be larger & I have left it to Gwen absolutely with a note that I hope she will use it for Richard's benefit but without any legal obligation. The note is to convince Richard that I was not disinheriting him. But I've done it that way because I don't know how to devise the money to Richard himself. For one thing, there has been no communication from the Registrar General so I suppose Richard's name is still Robertson.

She doesn't imagine the theatrics of Orwell burning the birth certificate have changed anything legally, though it might have slowed the process.

For another thing he must have trustees & I don't know who you want & they'd have to be asked. For another, if he is to inherit in childhood it's important that his trustees should be able to use his money during his minority so that he may have as good an education as possible. We must get all this straightened out properly when you come home but I thought I must cover the possibility that you might be killed within the next few days & I might die on the table on Thursday. If you're killed after I die that'll be just too bad but still my little testament will indicate what I wanted done. Gwen's results in childrearing have not been encouraging so far but after the war she will have a proper house in the country containing both the children & herself, she loves Richard & Laurie adores him. And all the retainers love him dearly.

To broach now, the question of his family – or avoiding them.

I'm sure he would be happier in that household than with Marjorie though I think Marjorie would take him on. Avril I think & hope would not take him on anyway. That I couldn't bear. Norah & Quartus would have him & bring him up beautifully but you've never seen either of them.

It's hard to believe, really – that they have never met, in all this time. She herself has only seen Norah a few times in the whole of her married life. She must write to her too. Though Norah will probably agree with the London doctors and try to stop this operation. So perhaps that letter can wait.

Quartus is in India & I can't arrange it. So in all the circumstances I thought you would agree that this would be the best emergency measure.

Enough! It's done. She changes tone, as if distracting a child from something unpleasant with something shiny and appealing. In this case a baby, and life itself.

RICHARD HAS SIX TEETH. He's pulling himself up in the playpen . . . but not really, so don't expect too much. Yesterday Nurse & I took all three to the doctor for whooping cough injections. He lives about 2½–3 miles away, partly across fields. We got lost & had to cross ploughland. The pram wouldn't perambulate & neither would Mary. She sat in a furrow & bellowed until carried. Laurence cried to be carried too . . . Richard was done last. He played with a matchbox on my knee, looked at the doctor in some surprise when his arm was gripped & then turned to me in astonishment as though to say 'Why is this apparently nice man sticking needles into me? Can it be right?' On being told it was he looked up at the doctor again rather gravely—& then smiled . . .

She turns to publishing business. She's expecting proofs of an article of his to work on, and has conveyed correspondence to Warburg, who's agreed to publish *Animal Farm.* Then:

I suppose I'd better go to sleep.

This may be the last letter. There might be big things to say, if she could think of them. But it's late, and she turns, instead, back to Richard.

By the way the six teeth are 3 top & 3 bottom which gives rather an odd appearance, but I hope the fourth top one will be through soon.

All my love & Richard's

E.

On Wednesday morning she stands in a slip in front of the looking-glass. It is full-length, adjustable on a wooden stand. She remembers suddenly a face – Lydia's – appearing behind her in this mirror, when they'd shared a bedroom at Laurence and Gwen's. Back when she was someone else. She should write to her too.

Her case lies open on the bed: four nighties, a dressing gown and slippers, changes of underwear, clothes, toothbrush, rouge, suspender belt. She has been bleeding for as long as she can remember. If it could stop she will wake up in another life altogether.

She cradles her abdomen with her hands, thumbs to navel. There will never be a blue-eyed girl in the world who is hers. She's never thought deeply about her, but

she realises, now, that she assumed her. Well. She steps
into a maroon tweed skirt, pulls on the jacket. Buttons
stiff under shaky fingers. The hollow feeling in her
sternum. She takes a deep breath and puts on the
yellow hat. She looks, if anything, like a liquorice allsort.
Then she turns, snaps the case closed and walks to the
nursery.

At the bus stop, when the rain meets the black
bitumen the drops dance straight back upwards, a leap
of delight. A surge of freedom – there is a book she loves,
a baby boy, a man she has the measure of. A life to
come.

She sits at the back of the bus, her case beside her. The
ride from Stockton-on-Tees to Newcastle is an hour and
three-quarters.

The next day there is time for another letter, just.

In the hospital bed, waiting to be taken into the operating
theatre, her handwriting starts off rounded and confident as usual,
but as the morphine takes her the lines slip crookedly down the page.
First the words and then the letters themselves stretch out as she
slides under. She has adopted a baby and made a will, she has sent off
a manuscript and dealt with a contract, and now, she conjures him up
for company.

Fernwood House
Clayton Road
Newcastle-on-Tyne

Today she knows what day it is! This is the date by which
everything had to be done:

29.iii.45

Dearest

I'm just going to have the operation, already enema'd, injected (with morphia in the right arm which is a nuisance), cleaned & packed up like a precious image in cotton wool & bandages. When it's over I'll add a note to this & it can get off quickly. Judging by my fellow patients it will be a short note. They've all had their operation. Annoying—I shall never have a chance to feel superior.

She's not uncomfortable. It's more a feeling of monumental surrender, of nothing further to do. For some reason her mind flashes to the washing line at the villa in Morocco, white clothes flapping like live things in a golden world. But fear squats, a toad under her ribs.

The nurse enters. Wimple. Double chin. Watch on a pin chain. She retrieves the clipboard at the end of the bed, then asks her what she is in for.

Eileen smiles. 'It doesn't say?'

'Not here, no. It's blank.' The nurse starts writing on it, as if to remedy that.

'Perhaps I can choose then?'

Not a flicker. 'No, ma'am. Mr Evers will do what *he* thinks best. He will be by soon.'

'Yes, of course,' she says. 'I do have one more question, Sister. Does it say anything about a blood transfusion?'

'Not here it doesn't.' The nurse looks at her properly for the first time and her face changes. Then she taps the blanket briskly at the foot of the bed, hangs the clipboard back. 'Good lass,' she says. As she leaves she pulls the door closed, softly.

With some effort, she uncaps her pen.

I haven't seen Harvey Evers since arrival & apparently

Gwen didn't communicate with him & no one knows what operation I am having!

She pulls herself up a little straighter, balancing the clipboard she's using as a rest for the letter. Her lap keeps sort of collapsing.

They don't believe that Harvey Evers really left it to me to decide—he always 'does what he thinks best.' He will of course. But I must say I feel irritated though I am being a model patient. They think I'm wonderful, so placid & happy they say. As indeed I am once I can hand myself over to someone else to deal with.

Still, she wishes the surgeon would come to see her before she goes under. She would like to be a person to him, not just a case out cold. The shadows are long on the lawn.

She can't think of anything else. What more is there to say, when all is said and done? She'll just share this place with him, this moment.

This is a nice room—ground floor so one can see the garden. Not much in it except daffodils & I think arabis but a nice little lawn. My bed isn't next the window but it faces the right way. I also see the fire & the clock.

Afterwards, the letter was found by her bedside, and packed up with her things.

Box 13

Fernwood House
Clayton Road
Newcastle-n- Tyne.

29. III. 45.

Dearest I'm just going to have the
operation, already enema'd, injected
(with morphia & the right arm which is
a nuisance), cleaned & packed
up like a precious image — cotton
wool & bandages. When 'it's' over
I'll add a note to this so it can
get off quickly. Judging by my
fellow patients it will be a short
note. They've all had their operations.
Annoying — I shall never have a
chance to feel superior.
          I haven't seen Harvey Evans since u

G 21202

Orwell A/1/15/1   14/2

arrival — apparently Gwen didn't communicate with him & no one knows what operation I am having! They don't believe that Harvey Evers really left it to me to decide — he always "does what he thinks best". He will of course. But I must say I feel irritated that I am being a "model patient". They think I'm wonderful, so placid & happy they say. As indeed I am now I can haul myself off to someone else to tea with.

This is a nice room — quiet though so one can see the garden — not much in it except daffodils & little evergreen bushes but a nice little lawn. My bed isn't next the window but it faces the right way. I also see the fire & the clock.

Premonition

Catherine O'Shaughnessy is Gwen's daughter. She was the toddler, then known as Mary, who wound the typewriter ribbon around every chair in the house. In a discussion with her cousin Quentin Kopp and Sylvia Topp in 2021 there's still pain in her voice when she says, 'I never understood why Mummy sanctioned Eileen going up to Newcastle because she knew how sick she was and she also had a premonition that she wasn't going to make it, so . . .' Her voice trails off.

Gwen must have been frightened at this second premonition, when the first, about Laurence, had been tragically accurate. Most likely no one will ever know why Gwen didn't, or couldn't, dissuade Eileen from having the operation on the cheap, when the London surgeons were against it. Or why Eileen went to the hospital alone on the bus.

Quentin, Georges and Doreen Kopp's son, tries to comfort Catherine. 'Most unlike Gwen, wasn't it?' he says.

V

AFTERLIFE

What Orwell did after Eileen's death is easy enough to find in the biographies. Less easy is to see how he must have grieved. But now that I've trained myself to read under the passive voice and omissions, I can see what he is really doing. For the rest of his life he is looking, more or less desperately, for someone – even a team of people – to replace her.

Now that we have seen her, the question is, does he?

Telegram

The fun in Europe is over. He is in a military hospital in Cologne when Gwen's telegram comes. They want to keep him here – his lungs are terrible, and though he insists it's bronchitis no one believes him. He doesn't tell them why he needs to leave. To a friend he says only, 'Oh, I have got things to do at home. I shall be away for a fortnight. See you then.' Later, the friend is shocked when he finds out what has happened, what was left unsaid. Orwell takes eight painkillers, discharges himself, and manages to get on a military plane to London.

He goes first to Inez's, who wrote in her diary of 5 April:

> The bell rang and George Orwell was outside. I did not recognize him at first. He wore a long Guardsman-like coat. He was in the uniform of a war correspondent. A Captain. He had taken eight M and B tablets and left the hospital and flown over. At first I thought that perhaps he did not know. But he had received a telegram. He thought that it was especially sad for Eileen because things were getting better, the war ending, Richard adopted and she believed that her health would be all right after this operation. George was terribly sad.

He stays with Inez, who takes him to the station to get the train north to Stockton-on-Tees.

Gwen gives him the letter retrieved from the hospital bedside table. He reads it sitting on the bed in Eileen's room.

His hands shake. Ash falls on the floor.

Dearest . . .

His vision blurs.

. . . no one knows what operation I am having! . . . I must say I feel irritated . . .

Can't believe it. Doesn't believe it.

They think I'm wonderful, so placid & happy they say. As indeed I am once I can hand myself over to someone else to deal with.

The Olympian elegance of it. His mouth opens, no sound comes out.

In her last letters, the part that most disturbs him, that he cannot get out of his mind, is this:

. . . what worries me is that I really don't think I'm worth the money.

If you don't care for someone, will they care less for themselves? He remembers his shock when the vicar left the word 'obey' out of her marriage vows. 'I couldn't very well have asked your permission not to "obey"!' she'd laughed.

What has he done?

The funeral is a few days later. There's no record of who was there. Lydia and Lettice never refer to it – perhaps they couldn't go, or they went but couldn't find words for it. I imagine Orwell and Gwen are there, possibly the 'household retainers' – Mr and Mrs Blackburn, and Joyce Pollard the nurse. Georges Kopp – devastated and angry.

337

I'd like to imagine that the friends Eileen had written to were there, the ones she'd asked to send her letters before she went under and who didn't, deciding, as one said, that Eileen 'would rather have letters and telegrams [after] she had had the operation'. But she'd written that she wanted letters for company *beforehand*; she wanted to know people were bearing her in mind. I'd like to imagine Norah was there too, but there is no way of knowing.

Orwell is stoic, tight-lipped about his loss. He talks about her so little to so few people that it seems, even in those wartime days of 'brave faces' and 'soldiering on', a failure to feel. When the poet Stephen Spender says how sorry he is, Orwell replies, 'Yes, she was a good old stick.' Spender is shocked at this bizarre faux working-class patois. It's a distancing manoeuvre – from her, from his feelings for her.

Though he must be mourning deeply. The woman who holds his world together is gone.

He confides in his aunt. (Now in her sixties, eccentric, generous Nellie is flowering into her true socialist self, locked in arguments with her landlord in which she's insisting on paying *more* rent.) She writes to his sister Marjorie – ill herself with a kidney disease – that 'Eric wrote to me at some length of Eileen's death and appeared to me to be very grieved about it', a statement that tells us not only that he grieved, but that in this family, such a thing needs to be said. Orwell confides in the poet Paul Potts, who is now reduced to selling handwritten poems in Soho pubs for drinks, 'hawking his words like stolen meat'. He tells Potts that 'the last time he saw her he wanted to tell her that he loved her much more now since they'd had Richard, and he didn't tell her, and he regretted it immensely'.

Eileen's friends are devastated. Lettice is struck with guilt. She hadn't received Eileen's letter before the operation. 'If I had known about the serious operation and that she was going into Newcastle alone, by bus, to have it, with no one there, I should have gone up to her, but I heard too late.' Some of them blame Orwell for not caring adequately for her. Edna Bussey, the bright office girl Eileen had wanted to tutor for admission to university, was as blunt as her love was sharp. 'I didn't like the idea of him. I may be very wrong but I have always had the feeling that he didn't take enough care of her. She should never have died from just a simple operation, nor so young.' Orwell, she said, 'owed a tremendous amount to Eileen for his success as a writer ... It was not until after he had met her that he became famous ... it seems such a pity that she should just be known to the world as his "first wife". She was such a wonderful person and I am sure gave all she had to him to help him to success.' Lettice also thought he hadn't looked after her, but then, 'He couldn't even look after himself.'

Fifteen years later, in 1961, Lydia wrote:

She had watched over his health with all the skill and intelligence at her command – and she had plenty of both. Her conscious, undeviating purpose was to help him to fulfil his destiny – that is, to do his writing, to say what he had to say in the way he wanted ... His illness made her fix her gaze on him as the most imminently threatened, but it was she who succumbed first. 'Greater love hath no man than this.' Eileen, who loved to dramatize for fun life's most ordinary happenings, never dramatized herself. If this had been said of her, she would have dismissed it with a smile, but it was true all the same.

Later on, in an interview, Lydia abandoned the trope of the self-sacrificing wife, and went back to thinking of things from Eileen's point of view. She let fly, saying 'I was always very sorry that Eileen married George. Very doubtful that she was so to speak in love with

him. I think it must have been his outspokenness. He thought in a way
that intrigued her. Interested her. Because he was an unusual person.'
She doesn't comment further on what seems, from my vantage
point, to have been their arms race to mutual self-destruction: she by
selflessness, and he by disappearing into the greedy double life that is
the artist's, of self + work.

There is no apparent way forward.
He can't go to Wallington.
Her clothes hang like questions in the wardrobe at
Canonbury Square.

Everyone assumes he'll give the child up. How can a single man
manage with a twelve-month-old baby? But Orwell loves Richard. He
has Eileen's letter and her will, expressing a preference for Richard to
remain in Gwen's household with his cousins, his nanny, and the other
staff who love him. She'd said he could go to Norah and her husband,
but please not his sisters, and especially not Avril.

As soon as the funeral is over Orwell does a bizarre thing. He takes
Richard back to London on the train and places him with Georges
and Doreen Kopp, who have a baby of their own to look after. And
then he returns to Europe for two months. People do odd things in
grief, but this seems to me beyond strange; to remove your baby from
his home, and then abandon him. It's as if Orwell wants to plant the
seed of a life in London to come back to, even if he is not the one who's
making it.

He travels a day behind the French army as it advances
into devastated Germany. The dead are piled in the streets,

there are fields of Wehrmacht soldiers taken prisoner. He visits a concentration camp in Austria not long after its liberation. If a world is destroyed when one person dies, what is it he is seeing here? He walks through scenes of carnage that make no sense, except to fit with the griefscape inside him.

The reporting he does from Europe is unimportant, and he doesn't need to go back there for *The Observer*. But there are two things he does need. The first is time. Eileen's death, he wrote to a friend, *has upset me so that I cannot settle to anything for the time being . . . I want to go back and do some more reporting, and perhaps after a few weeks of bumping about in jeeps etc. I shall feel better.* The second thing he needs is to avoid the inquest.

In the days at Stockton-on-Tees before the funeral Orwell didn't go to see the surgeon, Harvey Evers, to find out what went wrong, nor how Eileen was before she died, nor how, exactly, she died. Outrageously, Evers doesn't show at the inquest. And afterwards Orwell can't even bring himself to read the coroner's report. Why not?

While he was in Europe he was, consciously or unconsciously, devising a narrative he could live with. In this story Eileen had not been frightened, and he had not abandoned her knowing – or not caring – how ill she was. He told Inez 'things were getting better . . . and she believed that her health would be all right after this operation'. Three days before the funeral he wrote to Lydia: *The only consolation is that I don't think she suffered, because she went to the operation, apparently, not expecting anything to go wrong, and never recovered consciousness.* It was a minor operation, he is telling himself and others, but he knew she had several rapidly growing tumours, and was preparing for the possibility that she might die by making her will and sorting out, so far as she could, his life and Richard's if that were to happen. He'd witnessed one bloody collapse just before he left, and knew how weak and thin she was.

This is how he puts it to Anthony Powell three weeks after her death:

Eileen is dead. She died very suddenly and unexpectedly on March 29th during an operation which was not supposed to be very serious. I was over here and had no expectation of anything going wrong, which indeed nobody seems to have had. I didn't see the final findings of the inquest and indeed don't want to because it doesn't bring her back, but I think the anaesthetic was responsible . . . The only good thing is that I don't think she can have suffered or had any apprehensions. She was actually looking forward to the operation to cure her trouble, and I found among her papers a letter she must have written only about an hour before she died and which she expected to finish when she came round.

Although he recognises that she had had five really miserable years of bad health and overwork he's saying it can't be his fault for not taking the operation seriously. He's making himself innocent of the obligation to care. He'd like to think the anaesthetic was responsible, when reading the inquest report would have told him that was not true.

It is true, as he says, that reading it won't bring her back, but the purpose of an inquest is not to resurrect the dead. It is to do them some kind of justice – the kind that can be done with the truth.

I am trying hard to understand Orwell's reluctance to know how Eileen died. My experience when people close to me have spent a long time dying – my mother, a child in the family while I have been writing this – is that at each step of the medical process, we accompany them in every painful symptom; every hopeful, futile test, scan, result, prognosis. These are stopping points on an inexorable *Via Dolorosa*; we would never leave them alone – although they are at their most alone. We grab on to blood counts, cell numbers and survival statistics like drowning people clinging to lifebuoys, though it is not our time.

While I can see that it would be extremely distressing to read in a coroner's report the minute-by-minute account of what happened to a loved one, it is hard to imagine not wanting to stay with them on this last, posthumous step. Yet Orwell can't, perhaps aware that the coroner's report would detail the neglected state of Eileen's health going into the operation. 'Totalitarianism demands,' he wrote, 'the continuous alteration of the past, and in the long run probably demands a disbelief in the very existence of objective truth.' If he doesn't read the inquest report, he can alter the past with a story.

Although Harvey Evers did not turn up to the inquest, the anaesthetist, Dorothy Hopkinson, did. Dr Hopkinson stated that she had applied a mixture of 'about two ounces of ether, one and a half drachms of chloroform, and also oxygen . . . in drops by the open method' – that is, through a cloth placed over Eileen's mouth and nose – 'as she monitored her pulse and respiration'.

Eileen did not die immediately. Her 'abdomen was opened and the uterus had been lifted out to be prepared for removal', but just before the cut her 'colour changed and her respiration became very shallow'. A minute later her heart stopped beating. For forty minutes, her biographer Sylvia Topp writes, 'Eileen's heart was massaged and artificial respiration was attempted, during which time injections of Coramine (a circulatory stimulant, now banned) and Lobeline (a respiratory stimulant) were administered, all to no avail.' The careful wording of the coroner's report was that Eileen had died of 'cardiac failure whilst under an anaesthetic of ether and chloroform skilfully and properly administered for operation for removal of the uterus'. No one was found guilty of any wrongdoing.

At the bottom of the report someone added, in handwriting: 'The deceased was in a very anaemic condition.'

As she had feared, Eileen was too weak to have surgery. The medical advice from Harvey Evers to go ahead – without blood transfusions, without her weighing more – was wrong, possibly negligently so.

Orwell doesn't seek any kind of justice. Instead, he sticks with comforting fictions. His fear was perhaps not that he would find fault with the surgeon, but that he would find it with himself.

Position Vacant: Bluebeard

⌐

He comes back from Europe in May. He still can't bear
to go to Wallington, so he stays in the London flat. There's
a strange smell, nothing to eat, he can't bring himself to
open her wardrobe.

He has put her last letters in his bedside table
drawer.

Alone, his fear of being the target of a communist
assassination plot increases. A friend sells him a German
Luger, which he keeps about the place. His paranoia
places him at the centre of the malevolent universe, which
is better than being abandoned by it.

⌐

Richard has been taken back to Gwen's up north because it was too
hard for Doreen and Georges Kopp to manage two babies in their
flat. I imagine Georges took him on the train, grieving and ever more
furious with Orwell. But Orwell wants to bring Richard back and to
keep working. For that he needs a woman to care for them both and
run the house.

Susan Watson is twenty-seven, divorced from a Cambridge
philosopher and mathematician, with a six-year-old daughter at

boarding school. She hears he might have a job going, so she arranges to meet him. He doesn't tell her that the entrance to the flat is at the back, so she calls him from a phone box in Canonbury Square. He is watching from the window, then he goes down to get her.

When Susan sees the skinny, chain-smoking widower with his 'hideous haircut', she 'liked him immediately, and he looked so lonely.' He takes her around the decrepit flat. She sees the lathe in his workshop. Maybe she sees the Luger, or maybe he thought to put it away. She's surprised that Orwell doesn't ask her a thing about herself – only if she can cook. She tells him, 'Not very much,' because when she was married they had a cook. 'Never mind,' he says cheerily, 'we can live on fish and chips.' Susan's mother is a publisher, so she is used to writers. She thinks that the more talented they are, the likely more eccentric. They go to Greenwich to meet the bonny, dark-eyed baby. When Orwell shows her how he bathes Richard he says, 'You will let him play with his thingummy, won't you?', a remark which seems to be less about handling a fourteen-month-old than a test of Susan's reactions to sexual comments from him. She passes. 'Yes,' she says calmly, 'of course.'

And then he takes her out to dinner to a 'plush restaurant in Baker Street with gilded marble pillars and middle-aged waiters.' After they're seated he says he has to leave her for a minute and asks her to order two drinks. 'Then,' she remembered, 'he went to stand behind a pillar.' As soon as the waiter brings the drinks, he emerges. Later, he tells her 'he considered waiters to be very good judges of character, so because I had been served quickly I had earned the waiter's seal of approval. It seemed to me,' she said, 'an unusual way to engage a nurse.'

Susan moves in and starts work for board and £7 per week. She learns how to satisfy Orwell's domestic needs, which are organised around his work routine. A cooked breakfast with kippers, after which he goes to his study. He works all morning before going out to lunch, then comes back to work more before the highlight of his day – a high tea, which she learns to prepare: toast with anchovy paste or Oxford Marmalade, chocolate cake, and very strong tea. He then returns to his room and pounds the typewriter till one or two in the morning.

Susan shops, fetches his tobacco, runs out to buy him whatever else he needs. One time it's 'working man's braces', which he wants, provocatively, for a dinner at the Ritz. At his request she dyes his military greatcoat black, to demilitarise it (it doesn't work). She accidentally shrinks his wool beret from the Home Guard when she's dyeing that too – he doesn't care; puts it on his head like a burnt pancake, grabs a Burmese sword from the wall and does 'a kind of waltz'. Once, when she goes to tell him tea is ready, she finds him in his room trying to make gunpowder with charcoal and saltpetre – presumably ammunition for the enemy's Luger was hard to come by in London. He does not seem to have pounced on her, and he does her the kindness of never remarking on the lameness she suffered due to cerebral palsy, except to offer to carry Richard up the six flights of stairs to the flat if she wants him to.

There are unspoken intimacies in this stopgap arrangement. He has nightmares. She teaches Richard to tickle his feet to wake him, as his manservant in Burma had done. One day, he leaves his typewriter on the dining-room table, knowing she must move it to set the places for tea. She feels 'wicked' but her eye can't help falling on what he's typing: 'I have a *dear* little housekeeper' are the words he's left there for her to find, something he wants her to know but can't say.

'Maybe I was unobservant,' Susan said years afterwards, 'but I didn't notice any grief in him whatsoever. Absolutely not. But later I sometimes thought he was feeling extremely lonely.' Scraps of conversation peter out into awkward silences. As he tells her what he wants and needs, he thinks of Eileen, who did it all, and more, before.

'He said once about Eileen, "It wasn't an ideal marriage. I don't think I treated her very well sometimes." I just said I was sorry.'

Susan opens the wardrobe and sees Eileen's clothes hanging there. She asks gently if she should pack them away, or give them to a charity. 'No Susan, you can have them,' he says. He is so sad, so generous, just holding it together. In these raw days he was heard to call several women 'Eileen'.

Susan loves Richard, but if there are differences of opinion about his care she defers to Orwell. He has given Richard a hammer from his workshop as a comfort toy to sleep with – when she offers to buy the child a teddy bear Orwell can't see the point. When it gets really cold she sees him burning some of Richard's wooden toys in the grate, which she thinks 'slightly sadistic'. He doesn't tell her he has TB.

⌒

He has slept in. Susan brings a tray with tea, and a parcel tied with string that came by messenger. After she leaves he opens it in bed. Here it is, finally, after so many rejections, in its elegant grey and green dust jacket: *Animal Farm: A Fairy Story*. Eileen loved fairy stories, understood their deep fable structure, the lightness of their language, the darkness of the fears they corralled. He opens it at random:

> . . . the pigs had to expend enormous labours every day upon mysterious things called "files", "reports", "minutes" and "memoranda". These were large sheets of paper which had to be closely covered with writing, and as soon as they were so covered, they were burnt in the furnace.

Her spirit stuns. She had laughed, head thrown back, white neck so bare. Her job at the Ministry of Information was just this: filing things away from view, altering the public record. He sits up. Bangs his head against the wooden bedstead. This bed they'd worked in.

He reaches to open the drawer of the bedside table. She should be here for this moment. He has taken to reading her last letters according to need. Today:

I think it's quite essential that you should write some book again . . .

He shuffles through them. The final one obsesses him. He reads it over and over again, to the end.

I also see the fire & the clock.

He hears Susan and Richard leaving for the park. It's a bright cold day. After the door shuts he dresses quickly and goes to his study. Pulls aside the green cloth she'd rigged up there as a curtain and types the first line: 'It was a bright cold day in April, and the clocks were striking thirteen.'

He sits in greenish light. They are now beyond time.

They've been – had been – talking about this book for years. There was her poem, '1984', written before they met, in which she'd projected a dystopian future. But the idea became much clearer in her Ministry days, when she had sat in Senate House deleting the news.

I am writing *some book* again! he tells her, in the wordless way they now communicate.

⁓

At the end of summer he has twelve pages. He visits her grave at Newcastle upon Tyne and plants a polyantha rose on it. But about her he finds he can write nothing. Not a word in any personal notebook or letter or diary. 'Unfortunately,' as he puts it in an essay in November, 'there is often a need of some concrete incident before one can discover the real state of one's feelings.' And by then, of course, it's too late.

Love, Work

At present we know only that the imagination, like certain wild animals, will not breed in captivity.

George Orwell, 'The Prevention of Literature', 1946

Orwell's friend, Cyril Connolly, is famed for the quip, 'There is no more sombre enemy of good art than the pram in the hall.' This is one of those apparently universal pronouncements that are, in fact, addressed solely to male readers. Connolly is not warning women artists not to have babies, or sympathising with us for being torn between our work and our children. Nor is he saying, to the male artist he's addressing, that *he* might be torn between his work and caring for his children, turning up sleep-deprived to the blank page or canvas in the morning. Connolly is saying that domesticity curtails a man's freedom to roam sexually and in every other way, and so it deadens his creativity.

Part of the deadening effect of domesticity is that a man must earn money, the 'logic' goes, to keep a wife. But outside of marriage the services she provides – sex, mothering, cleaning, cooking, editing, psychology, management – would be unaffordable, not to mention hard to arrange. Orwell finally has money now from *Animal Farm*, which has sold into America. He is looking for another wife to create the conditions necessary for his productivity. Without that, he can't work.

Susan provides the domestic part of what he needs. Now, the other roles of wifedom must be filled. Over the next few months of 1945–46 Orwell pounces on and proposes to at least four women. He barely knows them but there is a book to write and so, a position vacant. As his attempts are rejected he finds he must describe that position – its duties, its rewards, its start date and likely end date – in more and more intimate detail. It's hard, because in listing what he needs he finds himself describing what Eileen did for him, things he had not acknowledged. Her name pops up abruptly in his proposals to these women, sometimes in letters which are among the most personal he ever wrote. He must at the same time face – or efface – not one, but two devastating truths: the previous incumbent died of overwork and neglect, and he, too, may not have long.

Sonia Brownell, now in her mid-twenties, is seventeen years younger than Orwell. She has effectively taken over the running of *Horizon* while its editor, Cyril Connolly, unencumbered either by the pram in the hall or, apparently, by his day job, 'idled elsewhere'. Sonia is a brilliant judge of talent and a gifted editor, insightful and decisive. She is also a Francophile, sophisticated, 'smart and hard drinking, and amusing and dangerous'. Sonia chooses interesting lovers, among them the painter William Coldstream and the young artist Lucian Freud.

A couple of men mention to her that Orwell is depressed. They ask her if she might go along and cheer him up. She knows him from when he used to hang about the *Horizon* office, and remembers him at a dinner at Connolly's during the war, holding forth about never writing anything the working classes don't understand, nor using adjectives, and complaining about 'foreign stuff in the food'. She'd been underwhelmed. But she agrees to go and visit him.

Orwell is excited. There's no alcohol in the house so he sends Susan out for a bottle of sherry. One biographer writes: 'strong tea did not have quite the effect he was hoping for. Sonia, who was of

Sonia Brownell, at the *Horizon* office on her last day, October 1949.

a generous disposition and inclined to plunge into affairs, took pity on him and surrendered to his advances, although she reported to friends that, "It was not much."' Actually, she tells Lucian Freud that she was 'appalled', when he 'started making advances', and tells another friend it was a 'disaster' as he was 'clumsy' and 'had made love to her quickly and without any great show of passion'. "He seemed pleased," she said, "but I don't think he was aware that there was not any pleasure in it for me."'

And then, duty done, he proposes to her. It's so premature, lacking in feeling, that the nature of wifedom is suddenly laid bare: it's a job vacancy. Sonia turns him down. Why would she move into this forlorn flat fuggy with cigarette smoke, with its swords and its lathe and its Luger, its ancestors glowering from the walls, to service

the needs of this coughing widower and his child? How she refuses
him no one knows, but it must have been gently because occasionally
she returns, on Susan's day off, to mind Richard so Orwell can work.
'Oh, oh, the smell of cabbage and unwashed nappies,' she says.
Sonia shudders, relieved that this is not her life. Not long afterwards
she leaves for France, and a passionate affair with the philosopher
Maurice Merleau-Ponty.

After this Orwell seems to realise that he must try to offer something more than bad sex in return for the work he is asking a wife
to do.

At the end of the year, he takes Richard to Wales to spend
Christmas with the writer Arthur Koestler and his wife Mamaine.
On the train platform he meets Mamaine's twin, Celia Kirwan,
who's joining them. Celia is another young editorial assistant, on
the magazine *Polemic*. Like Susan, she is twenty-seven and recently
divorced. Celia is curious about this 'tall, slightly shaggy figure',
'with his upright brushlike hair, carrying this baby on one arm and
his suitcase in another'. 'George didn't have the sort of obvious sex
appeal,' she remembered. 'But he had this terrific quality which one
just spotted.' She loves small children; Orwell watches her play with
Richard, now twenty-one months old, on the train seat.

When they arrive, Koestler sees that Orwell is sad, and is keen
for Celia to 'pep him up a bit'. So she has sex with Orwell. She relates
that, 'He makes love Burma-Sergeant fashion, afterwards saying
"Ah, that's better," before he turned over.' Orwell is oblivious to how
she feels, and he's in a hurry. 'He would like her to marry him, he
explained, but if not, perhaps they could have an affair?' Like Sonia,
Celia sees things clearly. 'He wanted someone to look after Richard
because he didn't have a wife, you see.'

Celia is ambivalent. When they are back in London she goes to
his flat for high tea, after which Orwell dismisses Susan and Richard
to the kitchen. He starts his couch negotiations with disclosures

and evasions. He tells Celia he has 'bronchiectasis'. 'Sometimes,' she reports him saying, 'he has bad haemorrhages and he easily runs a temperature, which he can only keep down when he is ill by not eating anything but bread . . . He says the doctor says that his haemorrhages are not dangerous really.' It looks as though he is making full and self-deprecating revelations. 'For instance,' Celia says, '[h]e says, "I am 15 years older than you, and if I die in 10 years time you will be 37 which is not too good a time to be left a widow," and all that sort of thing.' Orwell is conducting two negotiations here. One with a woman for services. And the other with fate for time: he wants another ten years.

Five days later she invites him for lunch in return. 'He . . . asked me again whether I would consider marrying him, or at any rate having an affair with him. I am awfully worried about this last,' she tells her sister, 'as he makes it somehow awfully difficult to refuse.' Orwell then writes her a letter so sexually explicit 'she could not bear either to show it to anyone or even to talk about it'. But she really doesn't want to marry him. 'So I wrote back to George some rather ambiguous letter. Anyway, it got sorted out.' She too manages to turn him down and stay friends.

Anne Olivier Popham lives in the same block of flats as Orwell. She is twenty-nine and home on leave from her job in Europe, the only woman working among the three hundred 'Monuments Men' – British conservators, art historians and others retrieving art treasures plundered by the Nazis.

In 2016, on the eve of her one hundredth birthday, Anne remembered her encounter with Orwell.

'I used to see him going down the path with his little boy,' she recalls. One day there came a note from Orwell, inviting her to tea. 'In his flat . . . there was a table, the baby, and its nurse. We had strong Indian tea, with brown bread and treacle.

After tea, he told the nurse to take the baby away, and then he said, "Come and sit on the bed". So I went and sat on the bed in the corner, and he came and sat beside me.'

She laughs in disbelief at the memory. 'In no time at all, his arms were round me, and he was kissing me.'

"'You're very attractive," he said. "Do you think you could care for me?"'

'I was shocked. I said, "What are you up to?" and I pushed him away. I found it all very embarrassing because it was all so precipitate, so calculated. I disengaged myself . . . Later on, I decided this must be how Old Etonians got on with girls, as if no one could resist them. He said, "I'm sorry" and asked about my work, and I said, "I'm governing Germany".'

∽

His novel is going incredibly slowly. He doesn't need to take out her letters any more; he knows them almost by heart. *I think it's quite essential that you should write some book again* . . . Yes, well. Easy for *you* to say.

He flicks through the twenty or so pages that are all he's managed to write. He is giving his character, Winston, feelings he doesn't let himself have. Winston muses:

> For whom, it suddenly occurred to him to wonder, was he writing this diary? For the future, for the unborn. His mind hovered round the doubtful date on the page, and then fetched up with a bump against the Newspeak word doublethink. For the first time the magnitude of what he had undertaken came home to him.

He puts a fresh page in the typewriter. Poor Winston is taking part in the Three Minutes Hate, the frenzy of compulsory political resentment in front of a telescreen, designed to unite the people against an enemy, real or imagined. Winston needs to think of something else, to get his mind off it. Orwell needs to think of something else, to get his mind off her, and off his own foreshortened, wifeless future.

He starts to type:

Winston succeeded in transferring his hatred from the face on the screen to the dark-haired girl behind him. Vivid, beautiful hallucinations flashed through his mind. He would flog her to death with a rubber truncheon. He would tie her naked to a stake and shoot her full of arrows like Saint Sebastian. He would ravish her and cut her throat at the moment of climax. Better than before, moreover, he realized why it was that he hated her. He hated her because she was young and pretty and sexless, because he wanted to go to bed with her and would never do so, because round her sweet supple waist, which seemed to ask you to encircle it with your arm, there was only the odious scarlet sash, aggressive symbol of chastity.

The Hate rose to its climax.

He sits back and lights a cigarette. What emendation would you scrawl on the back of *that*, dear?

He sits back and lights a cigarette. What emendation would you scrawl on the back of *that*, dear?

It happens not long after Anne came to tea.

Susan hears a commotion in the passage outside her room. Orwell is banging along, trying not to spew blood all over the floor.

'Can I help?' she asks.

'Yes, you can. Get a jug of iced water, a block of ice, and wrap it and put it on my head.'

'You go back to bed, *immediately*, at once!' she cries.

'Thank you.'

So she 'got the ice from the ice-chest, wrapped it and put it on his head, sat by him and held his hand until the haemorrhage had disappeared'.

He won't let her call a doctor but she does anyway, from the phone in the hall, pretending it's for Richard. When the man arrives she sends him in to Orwell, but his responses are so terse and evasive the doctor diagnoses 'gastritis'. Susan doesn't feel it's her place to correct her boss's lies.

She isn't angry that he hadn't revealed his illness, though it might have endangered her. '[Y]ou know,' she said later, 'the strange thing about this was, he never told me he was tubercular ... He was very private and very concealing.'

Susan is an acute observer of his suffering. 'After that haemorrhage I think he felt his life span was shortening. I think he was worried. And he just started proposing to girls without any real confidence of being accepted. He proposed to them because he felt desperately lonely and disoriented. His working life was very successful and the baby was extremely fine, but as a person his needs were not being replenished. I think he would have loved a wife.'

As soon as he's well enough he contacts Anne again, who's back in Germany. Now, it is urgent.

He would have written earlier, he says, *but I have been ill all this week with something called gastritis.* He adds detail, as if to make the lie more credible. *I think a word like that tells you a lot about the medical profession. If you have a pain in your belly it is called gastritis, if it is in your head I suppose it would be called cephalitis and so on. Any way it is quite an unpleasant thing to have ...* He spends a long paragraph describing his writing commitments. And then he comes to the kind of apology which also isn't one, in which he concedes to her a right to be angry.

> I wonder if you were angry or surprised when I sort of made advances to you that night before you went away. You don't have to respond – what I mean is, I wouldn't be angry if you didn't respond . . . I thought you looked lonely and unhappy, and I thought it just conceivable you might come to take an interest in me . . . It is only that I feel so desperately alone sometimes. I have hundreds of friends, but no woman who takes an interest in me and can encourage me . . . Of course it's absurd a person like me wanting to make love to someone of your age. I do want to, but, if you understand, I wouldn't be offended or even hurt if you simply say no.

Then he offers to send her some novels which have been banned for sexual obscenity, but which he has managed to get illegally.

Anne writes back asking what attracted him to her in the first place. He responds, *You are very beautiful, as no doubt you well know, but that wasn't quite all.* Her question, though, isn't about whether she is attractive. It is a test to see whether he can apprehend her as a person. He can't. He only sees her as someone to satisfy his needs. *I do so want someone who will share what is left of my life, and my work. It isn't so much a question of someone to sleep with, though of course I want that too, sometimes.*

You say you wouldn't be likely to love me, he writes to her. She wants to know how important love is to him. His response? It's optional. But now, he must face what he really needs. It's so hard.

> What I am really asking you is whether you would like to be the widow of a literary man. If things remain more or less as they are there is a certain amount of fun in this, as you would probably

get royalties coming in and you might find it interesting to edit unpublished stuff etc. Of course there is no knowing how long I shall live, but I am supposed to be a 'bad life'. I have a disease called bronchiectasis which is always liable to develop into pneumonia, and also an old 'non-progressive' tuberculous lesion in one lung, and several times in the past I have been supposed to be about to die, but I always lived on just to spite them . . .

He has disguised the tubercular haemorrhage he's just suffered as gastritis, and relegated his present condition to the past as an old, non-progressive lesion. For him, the work comes first. He had one wife to make it with. Now he wants another, to look after it when he's gone.

I am also sterile I think – at any rate I have never had a child, though I have never undergone the examination because it is too disgusting. On the other hand if you wanted children of your own by someone else it wouldn't bother me, because I have very little physical jealousy.

This he knows to be a lie, because when he and Eileen faced the possibility of her getting pregnant by someone else he'd dismissed it out of hand, horrified. Which brings him to thinking of her.

I don't much care who sleeps with whom, it seems to me what matters is being faithful in an emotional and intellectual sense. I was sometimes unfaithful to Eileen, and I also treated her very badly, and I think she treated me badly too at times, but it was a real marriage in the sense that we had been through awful struggles together and she understood all about my work, etc.

In what way he thought Eileen treated him badly is impossible to know – perhaps by making a 'fiendish row' about some of his infidelities? When we read her last letters to him, and see her kindness and diplomacy as she puts her urgent needs always in terms of the pleasures that might be available to him – fishing, landscape, guns, avoiding hospital, avoiding children who are not his – it's hard to imagine what he's referring to. It would doubtless have been clear to Anne that he did not have the gift of understanding other people's points of view. His letter continues:

> *You are young and healthy, and deserve somebody better than me: on the other hand if you don't find such a person, and if you think of yourself as essentially a widow, then you might do worse – i.e. supposing I am not actually disgusting to you. If I can live another ten years I think I have another three worth-while books in me, besides a lot of odds and ends, but I want peace and quiet and someone to be fond of me. There is also Richard. I don't know what your feelings are about him. You might think all this over . . .*

Then he invites her to Jura, the remote island off the Scottish coast where he wants to be this summer: *I am not asking you to come and be my mistress, just to come and stay.* He signs off: *Don't think I'll make love to you against your will. You know I am civilized. With love, George.*

Anne must have written back turning him down more firmly, not keen on being the wife of an ill man who wants her to 'share' his work, and then handle his literary estate when he's dead. Someone who has to put it in writing that he won't rape her. In his third and final letter to her, he's got the message. *I thought over your letter a lot*, he writes, *and I expect you're right. You're young and you'll probably find someone who suits you. Anyway let's say no more about it.* He signs it, *Yours George.*

Anne did find someone who suited her – Virginia Woolf's nephew Quentin Bell – and lived a long life in which one of her many achievements was as the editor of Woolf's diaries.

There was at least one other proposition, again arising out of a boozy Hampstead party at the Empsons', when Orwell tried his 'wife catching tactics' on a woman called Audrey Jones. At their second meeting he asked her to marry him, 'but she thought it a bit of a joke and laughed off both him and his proposal'.

It's hard for a biographer to watch his hero being laughed at and rejected. One of them hits back straight away on Orwell's behalf with a bit of second-hand, pseudo-scientific misogyny: 'This relentless pursuit of pretty, young women reflected the view he shared with Gissing, "that intelligent women are very rare animals and if one wants to marry a woman who is intelligent *and* pretty, then the choice is still further restricted, according to a well-known arithmetical rule"'.

It is more than a year since she died. He goes back to Wallington for the first time. Lydia and a friend have been living there, but the cottage is all Eileen. The chair Marx mauled. The canisters on the shelf. The jars are still stacked behind the door, though of course they're empty now. It is unbearable. In the bottom drawer of his desk he finds her letters from right back at the beginning, open-hearted and full of a different future.

Lydia sees him burning letters in the garden. She feels a pang of anxiety – they are not his to burn! – but of course they are.

Who will tell this story?

He can't stay at Wallington. But once he's back at Canonbury Square he doesn't want to be there either. He needs to get out of the rubble of London. He's been telling women he has three books in him, so ten years. If you reverse it you get the same answer, so it must be true, like maths: ten years = three books. On the Isle of Jura he will be able to stay away from doctors, from X-rays and chest tapping and sputum tests, so he can maintain this fiction. The end might be coming, but wife or no wife he can outrun it, and he can outwrite it.

⌒

The bombs have stopped now but a roof could fall in at any time, a pipe could burst, so he has removed her last letters from the bedside table and taken to carrying them in the inside section of his satchel. He wonders about the properties of paper as thin as this. He sits at the dining table and takes out the long one. He used to think about her licking the envelope, but he stops himself doing that now.

Eileen would have liked to leave London too.

I don't think you understand what a nightmare London life is to me. I know it is to you, but you often talk as though I liked it . . . I can't stand having people all over the place, every meal makes me feel sick because every food has been handled by twenty dirty hands, and I practically can't bear to eat anything that hasn't been boiled to clean it. I can't breathe the air . . . and I can't read poetry. I never could. When I lived in London before I was married I used to go away certainly once a month with a suitcase full of poetry and that consoled me until the next time—or I used to go up to Oxford and read in the Bodleian and take a punt up the Cher if it was summer or walk in Port Meadow or to Godstow if it was winter. But all these years I have felt as though I were in a mild kind of concentration camp . . .

Does she mean, with that last line – since she was married? His hand, still holding the letter, falls to his lap.

His mind shies away from it, but he realises it is true. She didn't get away much.

He starts to cough; it goes on and on. It hurts, but then it stops, thank Christ.

He keeps reading. She would like him to leave London so as to stop the frittering of his talent and time on reviews and columns and write another novel. Presumably because that is what she would like to do with him. Or possibly on her own.

Where does she say that? He takes the other letters from the satchel and then out of their envelopes. He brushes the crumbs off the table, and spreads the letters over it. Oh, yes, here, about money.

I do hope too that I can make some money when I am well—I could of course do a job but I mean really make some money from home as it were.

Of course she could have written. Maybe she would have. But she was always so busy. Once, in the garden at Wallington, she read out a few lines from a lecture Virginia Woolf had given. Something about measuring the effect of discouragement on the mind of the artist, as a milk company measured the effect of ordinary milk and Grade A milk on the body of a rat.

'I hate rats,' he'd said.

'I know,' she'd laughed.

What he would give to see that nicotine-stained smile now.

His eyes roam over the pages open on the table.

. . . the indications are urgent enough to offset the disadvantages of operating on a bloodless patient . . . So I suppose they'll just do a blood transfusion and operate more or less at once.

They must have done a blood transfusion?

Or not – *to save money?* He pushes the thought away.

His eyes flit from one letter to another, some handwritten, some typed. He reads her words again and again as if new meanings might be disclosed, fresh messages from her.

Here it is. She *did* want to go to the country. For Richard as well.

Whether he can keep his certainties over the difficult second year I don't know of course but he's much more likely to if he has the country and you have the kind of life that satisfies you— and me.

Well, let's go to the country then.

Still Life, with Knife

He can't find a wife. But his younger sister, Avril, has been released from conscripted factory work and agrees to come and keep house for him on Jura. A few weeks later Susan will bring Richard; she will live up there and look after the boy. They will have to do for now.

Before he leaves, Orwell visits Anthony Powell, who also has an infant son. In the nursery they admire the little boy, lying 'quiet but not asleep, in a cot by the window.' Then Powell slips out to get a book they've been talking about. When he returns Orwell is across the other side of the room, 'assiduously studying a picture.' The baby stirs. When Powell reaches into the cot to adjust the blanket his hand knocks something hard. He pulls back the covers to find 'an enormous clasp knife', of the sort used for disembowelling deer. He is shocked.

'Oh, I gave it him to play with,' Orwell says. 'I forgot I'd left it there.' It's a mystery why Orwell carries such a knife, and where on earth he hides it – in a sock?

No one mentions whether the knife was open or closed. One of the biographers thinks this frightening scene is about Orwell merely 'playing with a child' and not wanting to be discovered doing so even though, as Powell said, he 'had to be discovered for the incident to achieve graphic significance' – whatever that means. The biographer thinks it makes Orwell seem 'less rather than more odd, more driven by inner psychological force', and ends his paragraph nonsensically, talking about the qualities of 'decency and kindliness' that Orwell sought in others, as if to blur the unspeakably bizarre provocation to violence that has happened here.

I don't know how to explain putting a knife in a baby's cot. To be armed or be harmed, are these the choices as Orwell sees them? But it was not a single incident. As Orwell lives now with the breath of death on his neck, strange events pile up in which others are endangered, as if he is sharing the precariousness of life, especially with those for whom most of it is still to come: children.

Island, Life

To work is to live without dying.

Rainer Maria Rilke

Jura is a treeless island on the far western edge of Britain, where the land fans into islets like frayed lace. It had then, and has now, about two hundred people on it and some six thousand deer. It takes me a day to get there from London: a train to Glasgow, then a drive through the mountains and along glorious silver lochs to the coast, a car ferry to the island of Islay, then a passenger ferry to Jura. In Orwell's time it took forty-eight hours to get to Barnhill, the house he rented, the last eight miles of the journey on foot. He once invited Sonia and sent instructions that ran to nineteen lines, involving trains, buses, boats and a plane, and asking her to bring flour and tea. If it was a test of practical masochism, she passed – by never going.

On the ferry the sky is a soft, woolly grey. I think of Orwell crossing this dark water, ill and alone 'with barely more than a suitcase, a kettle, a saucepan, and a typewriter'. He wants the peace, the fresh air, the mild microclimate. When the ferry docks I walk past blue-corded lobster traps tossed along the quay to the only town, Craighouse. It's a smattering of white, slate-roofed buildings, the pure essentials: pub, general store, post office. And behind them, where ordinarily a church might be, towers a whisky distillery.

When Orwell arrives it's early summer 1946. He hitches a ride in the postal van from Craighouse for the seventeen-mile trip to the manor house at Ardlussa. He is renting Barnhill from Margaret Fletcher, who owns both. Her husband, Robin, the 'laird'*, is an old Etonian a few years older than Orwell. Barnhill is eight miles further north, along a dirt track so boggy and fissured that neither the postal van nor the sole taxi on the island will venture there.

Margaret Fletcher has small children and a war veteran husband in her care. When she meets Orwell she is immediately struck by 'the very sad face he had ... He was tall and dark and very haggard ... a very sick-looking man'. She puts him up for the night. The next morning she drives him the last eight miles, 'along this bumpy track', in her truck. She later recalled 'coming to the top of this last hill and looking down on Barnhill. It's just open moorland, really, open hill moorland with very few trees. Very few. There's ... a few deer and a few wild goats ...'

She is frightened for him. 'People talk about isolation, but they don't realize until they get there what it's like.' Margaret has been preparing the house – mending the roof, whitewashing walls, fixing the dodgy generator. Everything is touch-and-go. This is a place for hardy crofters, not for an intellectual, sick and alone. 'I remember being extremely anxious about letting him be in Barnhill on his own ... miles from a telephone,' she said. She's slightly hurt when he pushes away her offers of help. Avril will come in a week or two.

Margaret Fletcher's daughter, Kate, drives me the same potholed, eight-mile route in her old SUV. Kate must be six feet tall, a magnificent middle-aged woman long past small talk. She is doing me, a stranger, a kindness. The vehicle lists and heaves and chews up the track and

---

*   'Laird' is a Scottish term for the owner of a large landholding.

then stops for no reason on a hill, looking out across open moorland to where Barnhill must be. She pulls up the handbrake.

'Just a minute.' She gets out, taking the keys. That's when I see, over the bonnet, a metal chain hung between two posts, with a large, medieval-looking lock hanging off it. The posts are attached to no fence. This is a locked path in an open landscape, like a warning in a dream. Kate opens it with an iron key and climbs back in. It doesn't, apparently, need explaining.

I can't help myself. 'Why didn't we just drive around it?'

'We don't,' she says, and that's that.

We have entered some place – the past? the end? – through an unnecessary old gate. Later, I learn that the padlocked chain in the middle of the moor is an island quirk, respected out of traditions no one can remember. No matter: I am with the woman who has the key. I look out to sea; it's dark grey, the colour of a newborn's eye.

Barnhill is a large white farmhouse with a slate roof, nestled in a cleft in hills that roll down to the sea. Orwell's bedroom is on the top floor at one end, above the kitchen. A bed faces a dormer window, which frames a view of lawn sloping gently to water. At some point Margaret Fletcher gave him a bright yellow azalea bush, which he planted right out front so he could see it. It's about to flower.

Barnhill, with the azalea bush in flower, 2017.

When Orwell arrives the house has no electricity, no hot water and the only means of communication with the outside world is a battery radio. There's a gas stove and paraffin lanterns for light. The generator in the utility room off the kitchen is greasy-black and has a mind of its own. There are no trees so there is no firewood, and the peat-cutting season is over. The nearest doctor is thirty-five miles away, the first eight of them back over that track to Ardlussa, then a lift or maybe the cab to Craighouse, and a boat to the next island. Georges Kopp, who is now farming outside Glasgow, sells him a truck that might do those eight miles, but when it arrives on the dock it falls apart like a practical joke, like revenge. So Orwell buys a van. That dies too. Then he buys an old motorbike. The locals are startled at first but they get used to the dark figure in oilskins emerging over the hills with a scythe silhouetted behind him (he said he might need it to cut weeds). But the motorbike, too, 'was constantly breaking down', Margaret remembered. 'He'd be sitting on the roadside with bits of motorbicycle around him. He'd sit there in the sun and fiddle for about an hour; then he'd find the sparking plug or whatever still wasn't working, so he'd abandon the bicycle and walk to our house at Ardlussa to see if he could find someone who'd come and help ... He wasn't very good with engines,' she added, 'although I think he probably thought he was.'

Orwell is at the edge of the known world, fleeing doctors, book reviewing, grief and time. Over this summer and the next two he tries to cobble together a domestic world that will support his life and his novel. And he staves off drowning in his own lungs.

⁓

He has put his desk under the dormer window so he can look out to sea. He winds the roller knob and takes out a finished page, puts it on the small pile to his right. For a paperweight he is using a piece of glinting silver

shale he has collected. This is the slowest writing he's
ever done.

~~~~

In early July Susan arrives with Richard. Orwell hasn't told Susan that
his sister will be there, because she wouldn't have come if he had. But
he knows he needs both a housekeeper and a nanny – and that's before
thinking about who will do the farm work, or editing and typing.
Susan, usually so kind, finds Avril 'very sour', and, as she once told an
interviewer quietly, 'stupid'. She said, 'He might have told me she was
there. After all, it was a forty-eight-hour journey up to Jura.'

Paul Potts, by now semi-vagrant, comes up. Potts had his charms,
among them self-knowledge: 'The difference between me and a great
poet,' he once said, 'is that I am not one.' But he was also, apparently,
a 'self-centred acerbic sot' and his presence seems to have put off
everyone else. As well as Sonia, Orwell invites Brenda, Inez and Sally –
but none of them come.

Avril is appalling to Susan, territorial and vicious. She scolds
her for not slapping Richard when the little boy makes a fuss about
putting his jumper on. She berates her for calling her brother 'George'
when his proper name, she says, is 'Eric'. And she taunts Susan for her
disability because cerebral palsy makes her hand shake. 'Call yourself a
nurse and you can't even darn socks!' she spits. Avril is not much nicer
to Potts, who stutters and blinks and is generally useless. She refers to
him as someone she needs to tame.

Orwell stays upstairs, smoking and typing. Below, the ménage
seethes. Potts ventures out to find wood and chops down the only
tree on the place – a fine nut tree. Susan, rattled, mistakenly kindles
a fire with one of Pott's mangy manuscripts. He departs that night in
a 'moonlit flit', walking the eight miles back to Ardlussa in darkness.

Susan's boyfriend, 23-year-old Cambridge graduate David
Holbrook, comes to visit. He's excited; he's a big fan of Orwell.

His first glimpse of his literary idol is of Orwell shooting a goose at pointblank range in the yard – a creature that next appears incinerated by Avril and served up at the table. David had looked forward to meeting this 'lively and entertaining mind', but finds instead a 'miserable, hostile old bugger'.

At dinner Orwell and Avril, 'a very dismal woman', ignore him. The siblings have long conversations, 'with a lot of space between the sentences, of a very gloomy kind ... I mean, I just sat in a corner, and there would be this slow, miserable conversation about when he would go over to try and rescue the motorcycle, how Donald or somebody would be brought over to mend the boat. It was as if in the interstices they were thinking how miserably they could form the next sentence.'

Perhaps Orwell is hostile towards David because he doesn't want Susan to have a sexual life, or it could be because David is a member of the Communist Party. Orwell is still, even here and even now, paranoid about being on an assassination list. He takes to leaving his Luger loaded and lying about the place.

Sometimes the young couple sneak into Orwell's room and read his manuscript pages on the desk. David thinks it's 'pretty depressing stuff' with 'dismal sexual episodes'. The pair have sexual episodes of their own in the room – curiously like Winston and Julia's lovemaking-as-rebellion in the regime which is coming to life in those pages.

When Robin Fletcher the laird drops in for tea during a shoot, Orwell suddenly becomes 'very "Burma Police", very snobbish'. Susan and David are 'banished below stairs' – to have tea with the retinue of beaters. David finds this amusing – but also very odd.

Eventually, Susan and David flee too. They walk the eight miles to Ardlussa, which is hard for her with cerebral palsy, and for both of them dragging luggage. Richard, now three, is distraught, and Susan is upset at leaving him. Margaret Fletcher puts them up for the night. No record remains of what Margaret thought as she received more refugees from the dysfunctional domestic regime over the hill.

Orwell mentions no fighting or fleeing in his diary. His lungs are hardening. He is just smoking and typing. When he wants a break he goes into the vegetable garden he's planting with Avril, or does some work on the chicken coop he's building, or goes fishing in the dinghy. Sometimes the exertion brings on a temperature, and then, in the shuddering, sweating cold of it, he goes up to bed.

Paradise wouldn't be complete without snakes. There are adders everywhere. They have to look out for them, especially around Richard. Once, when Orwell sees one, he traps it under his foot. But instead of quickly smashing its head as the others expect him to, he takes his flick knife and eviscerates it alive, from throat to tail. Then he 'degutted it, filleted it'. They look on, shocked.

By the end of September he has fifty pages.

It is still going much slower than usual.

He tries to conjure her face but it won't come. He can see her hands on a typewriter. Or around a wineglass, the joints in her fingers. He can see her body, small and white, the points of her hips, breasts, the lines of collarbones and the shadows under them. But her face stays blank. He panics and stands up. At the top of the stairs he pauses. Something is thumping. It's Avril in the kitchen, bashing pastry till it's good and dead. He makes it down without coughing to the dining room, slips the photograph from the mantelpiece and brings it back up. Steadies himself with one hand on the desk, wheezing hard. Then he pulls out the little stand on the back of the frame and sets it aright. A cat's face. A soft face. She's not smiling in it, though she was so funny, laughing inside all the time.

Suddenly, he's angry.

He sits and types, as his character Winston:

It was as though they were intentionally stepping nearer to their graves. As he sat waiting on the edge of the bed he thought again of the cellars of the Ministry of Love. It was curious how that predestined horror moved in and out of one's consciousness. There it lay, fixed in future times, preceding death as surely as 99 precedes 100. One could not avoid it, but one could perhaps postpone it: and yet instead, every now and again, by a conscious, wilful act, one chose to shorten the interval before it happened.

When he coughs hard he checks the handkerchief for blood. He can't risk staying here for the winter.

Eileen, 1941.

He goes back to Canonbury Square. That winter of 1946–47 is so cold he feeds their bedstead into the fire.

Susan had left Jura after Avril asked Orwell to get rid of her. Orwell had given Susan £60 as a kind of severance pay, along with a 'test': 'You can either work it out . . . ,' he said, leaving the rest of the sentence blank, implying that if she took the money she didn't deserve it. '[H]e did do pretty unpleasant tests on people,' Susan said. She simply told him she needed to leave by the next boat. She did not want Avril to 'crow over' her, because she'd got the outcome she wanted.

In London he invites Susan for lunch, and so she can pick up a suitcase of her belongings. He comes to the door holding Richard. Orwell looks 'worse than before, much worse'. Richard is 'delighted, giggling', reaching out to her. Then Avril appears behind them.

'Oh,' she says, referring to the child, 'he's forgotten you.'

Susan comes in and plays with Richard, who remembers their peekaboo game. Then she goes into the bedroom to collect her case. Orwell follows her in, stands there.

'I am so ill, Susan,' he says. Something he doesn't seem to have said to anyone else, ever. Susan 'looked at him and his face looked drained and rather blue and I thought what *can* I do now?'

'I'm very sorry, George,' she says. 'But I don't think I'll stay to lunch.'

Then she goes to see Mrs Harrison, the cleaning woman, to let her know Orwell will need extra care.

Oars

Life is Bad but Death is Worse

George Orwell, last notebook

The next summer, he goes back to Jura. This time the wifeless domestic arrangements are settling differently. Bill Dunn, a returned serviceman with a wooden leg and a drinking problem, has arrived on the island and is keen to work. Richard Rees comes up too, like the ministering bachelor angel he has always been. Rees has decided that Orwell will be – this book will be – his next project. Rees invests £1000 in equipment for Bill to use farming. A makeshift household is cobbling itself together around Orwell: housekeeper, farmhand, financier, editor-encourager.

Still, they are eight miles past the end of the world. A gale blows the henhouse off its foundations. Lightning incinerates a neat patch of garden. The world is fierce and fragile.

Avril dislocates her shoulder and Orwell flutters about, unable to help. He cries out to Rees, 'You've done first aid, haven't you? . . . You'll be able to get it back? You just have to jerk it sharply upwards, isn't that it?' Rees can't 'summon up enough sharpness'; though, as he said, 'Orwell made no attempt to summon up any.' So they make the 35-mile journey over land and water to the doctor. They make the trip again when Richard gashes his head and needs stitches. And again when the child gets measles. Looked at one way, things are holding together. Looked at another, they can come apart any time.

By the end of May, he's one-third of the way through what will become *Nineteen Eighty-Four*.

He buys an outboard motor, which he affixes to the dinghy himself.

Orwell and Avril's elder sister, Marjorie, has died recently, at forty-eight, of the kidney disease she'd long suffered. Her bereaved children come: Henry, who is on leave from the army; Jane, who has been discharged after six years in the Women's Land Army; and their teenage sister, Lucy. Orwell 'looked hellish,' according to Lucy, 'but then he always looked hellish'. Things are easier among family, and Avril relaxes. She, Orwell, Richard and the three young people pack the dinghy to go camping on the other side of the island. To get there they have to pass the Corryvreckan, one of the most treacherous whirlpools in the world. Bill quizzes Orwell again and again about his reading of the tide tables. 'Very dangerous, Corryvreckan,' he tells him, 'very dangerous.' Orwell replies, 'airily' according to Lucy, 'Oh yes, yes, I've looked it all up.'

After two blissful days camping the party prepares to go home. Avril and Jane decide to walk back across the island. Orwell, Richard, Henry and Lucy will come around in the boat. Of course Orwell has misjudged the tides, or misread the tide table, or misread the time of day. The waves there are huge. The dinghy is small, they cling to its edges, they cling to the child. It's not one whirlpool, it's a series of them, each one sucking them into the monster at the centre with waves as high as a building.

Orwell is at the tiller when '[t]here was a cracking noise, and the engine came straight off its mountings and disappeared into the sea,'

Henry remembered. 'And Eric said, "I think you'd better get the oars out, Henry." And he patted his chest and sort of said, "I can't help you, Hen, of course."' Henry thinks they're done for; he sees that Orwell knows this too. They are a teenage girl, a three-year-old boy, an invalid and a young man in a violent sea. Henry takes the oars and pulls frantically but 'nothing happened'. As they are tossed up cliff-faces of water and thrown down again, a seal pops its head out. 'Curious thing about seals,' Orwell says, 'very inquisitive creatures.' Lucy thinks, 'I honestly don't think this is the sort of time to be talking about seals.'

With enormous effort, Henry steers them towards an outcrop of rock. As he jumps off to pull the dinghy in, the force of the waves turns it over, trapping the others underneath.

Lucy surfaces first. Then Orwell, spluttering and holding Richard.

On land Orwell is calm. The others are shivering, terrified. He must know their chances of being rescued are minute. Hardly any boats come over here because it's too dangerous. Orwell takes his Spanish lighter out of his pocket – it's still there and, miraculously, it still works, so they gather kindling and light a fire. They feed Richard the only food they have, a single potato. Then Orwell sets off looking for something to kill and eat. He comes back empty-handed, but with more nature observations. 'Extraordinary birds, puffins,' he says. 'They make their nests in burrows.' He'd found some baby seagulls but hadn't the heart to kill them. When Lucy and Richard are out of earshot he tells Henry 'he thought we'd had it' in the boat. Orwell is dying, and it's as if somewhere inside him he wants everyone to go down with him.

It was an almost freakishly rare thing that happened: a lobster boat carrying tourists came past. The fisherman saw the fire, then the bedraggled group waving, and picked them up.

Richard Blair has been marked by the event in deep ways. As an older man, he has said that when he dies he would like his coffin to be put on his boat and set alight, then sent out on the flood tide in the setting sun into the Corryvreckan. A return on his own terms to the force that didn't take him.

By early December 1947 the first draft of the book is finally done, so Orwell will let himself be examined. The chest specialist comes, presumably at Rees's insistence and cost, from Glasgow to Jura. The doctor agrees to travel to the big house at Ardlussa, but not the last eight miles on the boggy track. Rees drives Orwell over in the farm truck.

Ardlussa House

The doctor finds him 'seriously ill' with TB. On no account, he says, can Orwell be driven back over the track to Barnhill because any pothole could trigger a haemorrhage. But Orwell doesn't want to stay at Ardlussa; he says he doesn't want to infect everyone there, including the Fletcher children. Margaret Fletcher insists, telling him they are boiling all his cutlery, they will destroy his bedding. In the night Robin Fletcher goes to speak with him. When he comes out he tells Margaret, 'he *knows*', by which he means Orwell knows he's dying.

Nevertheless he will not stay. He doesn't want to be an invalid in someone else's house. A house is a life you make, and if he is in his own house he'll still be in his own life. Rees is stiff with fear as he drives him back over the terrible track.

What would she say now? He looks at his notebook, in which he's listed alphabetically ideas to include in the novel. At point 'f' he writes: 'loneliness of the writer. His feeling of being the last man.' He underlines it. He's thinking of calling the book 'The Last Man in Europe'.

Two weeks later he's in a hospital near Glasgow. They disable one lung with a pincer; they pump his diaphragm full of air with a horrible thing like a bicycle pump. Then they treat him with the antibiotic Streptomycin, which is so new no one knows the correct dose – his hair starts to fall out, his nails deaden and drop off, his lips bleed. It's horrendous but he doesn't care. None of it matters, he just wants more time for the book. He needs someone to read the draft, but she's gone.

The healthiest of writers can feel terror racing to finish a book. The idea that it must go off into the world is like watching your inner life continue without you. It will emerge leaving you husked like a cicada skin, to be blown away.

After six months in hospital, he's a little better. Astonishingly, he decides to go back to Jura. More astonishingly, no one stops him.

The domestic situation seems finally resolved now. Avril and Bill have started a relationship. She is looking after Richard, the house and the catering. Richard Rees and Bill are running the farmlet side of things. Rees is here permanently now, as interlocutor, editor, reader, driver, funder, carer and friend. Orwell may be beyond sex, even if anyone would have him as a husband, but there is one other thing Eileen did that has not been replaced: typing. When he finishes this draft he'll write his own emendations all over it. Then it will need to be completely retyped, with him present to decipher his scrawl. It is, he says, 'an unbelievably bad MS'. Both his agent and publisher are trying to find a woman who'll go to Jura to do the work.

There are lots of visitors this year – so many that they set up tents for them to stay in. His old friend Brenda comes, handsome and sexless in a grey suit. Celia comes too. Inez stays for months, bringing her cat – which incenses Avril for no good reason. Avril decides to stop salting the food.

⁓

He watches from his window as they set up the canvas tents on the lawn. There will be a party this evening, though this far north it's light until after 10.00, so a daylight evening party. There is a card table with a cake on it. Richard, unsupervised, is walking towards it. For him the party starts now.

As far as happiness goes, he would say he has been happy here. To say goodbye feels like saying goodbye to what he has loved – the land, the sea, lobsters, chickens, boats. The Corryvreckan that tried to kill him. Even the fucking generator, which he sees now, in its filthy, hulking, greasy-wet menace, never wished him ill. The clouds shift fast over the slope to the water; a gap in them allows, for a moment, a shaft of sun to reach the yellow azalea

Margaret Fletcher gave him, and though it is beautiful he feels its melodrama and shudders. He's not dead yet.

He's changed the title. It will be *Nineteen Eighty-Four* now, like her poem.

⌒

By September 1948 he is getting a temperature if he pulls up a weed, collects an egg.

By October he has corrected the manuscript for another draft, but no woman will come to type a fair copy. So in November he starts the 'grisly job' of retyping it himself. He can no longer sit comfortably for any length of time so he works in bed, bashing out five thousand words a day with the typewriter balanced across his bony legs. The room is a fug of paraffin fumes, cigarette smoke, the ashtray is overflowing by his bed. He gets up only to go down the corridor to the bathroom. Avril brings him tea, toast.

He sends it off on 7 December, by which time he's very weak. He can accept, finally, that he needs a spell in a sanatorium – he'll go to one Gwen has arranged for him in the Cotswolds.

Bill and Avril drive him with Richard, now five and a half, to the big house at Ardlussa. They are in Bill's Austin 12 and on the way they get bogged. Bill and Avril walk back four miles to get the farm truck to haul them out.

Richard remembers sitting in the car with his father, waiting. 'We just sat there together, talking. It was raining. It was cold, and I do remember my father giving me boiled sweets. He was a very sick man, but he was quite cheerful with me, trying to pretend that nothing was wrong. It was getting dark by the time Avril and Bill got back with the lorry.'

Love is what Richard remembers. But it is so close to harm, as he sits in the closed cabin with his father, breathing his disease.

Pluck It

Before I leave Jura I walk all over it. The hills are magical in their bareness, the paths over them scattered with shining silver shale like scales. Down one end of the island are three higher mounts called paps, for the breasts they resemble. The earth, warmed in her sleep, might at any moment stir beneath you. On one of my walks a long-legged hound emerges from nowhere, followed by a tall man. Hugh Carswell, a musician, tells me that in 2013 his wife, Jane, interviewed people on Jura, some of whom had known Orwell.

Jane Carswell shared her recordings with me. One is of a conversation with two old women, Flora McDonald and her friend Nancy MacLean. As a teenager Flora had worked in the Craighouse pub. One time, Orwell turned up holding out a dead bird.

'I remember him coming down to the hotel when I were there working,' Flora says. 'He come in with a hen.' She starts to chuckle. 'And he says, "Would ya like to pluck that for me?"' Both women laugh uproariously. It seems absurd to them, now, the idea of a man coming in and asking the first female he finds to pluck his chicken. But even though as a girl she could see it, there was no escaping the absurdity of the times. Much as you might like to tell him to go pluck it himself, it wasn't possible.

'I had to do what I was told, I suppose . . .' Flora says. The oddness of the world is there, but it has replaced reality with itself. There is no outside of it. All she can do is repeat the funny fact. 'I always remember him coming in and saying to me, "Would ya like to pluck this hen for me?" Why, I don't know.' Her laugh trails off.

Jura, view to the Paps.

Cotswold Sanatorium
Cranham, 1949

In the sanatorium Orwell keeps bottles of rum under his bed and pulls them out for visitors. Now that his book is done, he is making new bargains with the universe. He tells Warburg, his publisher, 'I suppose everyone will be horrified, but apart from other considerations I really think I should stay alive longer if I were married.' Warburg is already horrified – by the manuscript – which he considers among the most terrifying books he has ever read. He is shocked that Orwell has 'given full reign to his sadism and its attendant masochism', which reaches its climax in Winston's plea to throw the woman he loves to the rats, instead of himself. 'I pray I may be spared from reading another like it for years to come,' Warburg thinks. On the upside, he's sure it will be a bestseller.

Sonia is back from France, reeling from the end of her relationship with the philosopher. When she visits Orwell they drink rum and smoke in his room. Her hair is golden, her skin glows like a girl in a Renoir painting. She is so beautiful it is hard to think straight; she is smart, reckless, driven, generous.

At some point here in Cranham Orwell pens his horrified and self-disgusted tirade about the incorrigible dirtiness of women, and the terrible, devouring sexuality of a wife which leads her to despise her husband's lack of virility. He doesn't note the date, so it's impossible to tell whether he writes this in anger at women in general (for not having one) or in trepidation at having to render the 'service owed by the man to the woman' in a new marriage, in order to get the other services he really wants.

Orwell proposes to Sonia a second time, from his bed, or perhaps on a walk in the woods, if he was well enough. When she accepts, the next thing he says is, 'You'll have to learn to make dumplings.' She reports this to a friend, laughing. A woman less likely to be making dumplings is hard to imagine.

Sonia understands the arrangement as a new job. Cyril Connolly is about to wind up the magazine she's been running. 'When *Horizon* folds up,' she tells a friend, 'I'll marry George.' There are terms to be negotiated. Orwell had enumerated for Celia and Anne what he wanted in a wife, and presumably he does again for Sonia. There is sex (or possibly not, as he's so ill). There is comfort, and 'someone to encourage me'. There is an understanding of his work. Perhaps he repeats what he said to Anne, as heartbreaking as it was practical: what he is really asking is if Sonia would handle his literary estate as his widow. Though perhaps he doesn't, because he also needs her to share in the fantasy that he is not dying. All of these things Sonia will do, because they are interesting to her. And then there is Richard. Sonia doesn't see herself taking on that part of wifedom, and she excises it from the deal.

So Richard stays with Avril. He grew up happily with her, and, as Eileen had just about predicted, had a career with tractors, as an agricultural engineer.

During these months in the sanatorium, Jacintha, the love of Orwell's adolescence, writes to him. They have not been in touch since, as he put it, *you abandoned me to Burma all hope denied*, or, as she put it, he 'attempted to go all the way before I was ready'. It's been

more than twenty years since she came in from their 'walk' with
torn clothes and stayed in her room for three days. Jacintha has
just discovered that George Orwell, whose *Animal Farm* she loved,
is her old friend Eric. In February 1949 he writes back two letters,
one formal, the next warmer. *Ever since I got your letter I can't stop
remembering . . . I am so wanting to see you. We must meet when I get out
of this place.*

Jacintha is so agitated she doesn't eat and for several nights in
a row barely sleeps. Her life since their seven-year friendship has
involved an illegitimate pregnancy, abandonment, and the primal
grief of relinquishing a child. Orwell's attempted rape seems small
compared with those things, and small when put against the feelings
she finds she still has for him. Something like love, or like coming back
to who she was before all of that happened to her. But what he wants
from her is not her, but wife-work. He's said it in phone calls from the
hospital, and written it in letters. Years later Jacintha read out one of
these letters to an interviewer. 'His last paragraph, you see, begins, "Are
you fond of children?" Well, that rather unnerved me because if he'd
got a motherless child that he wanted to find a new mother for, well,
I didn't feel it was up to me. I didn't want to encourage him in any
ideas of that sort.'

So Jacintha stays away, to her lifelong regret. She just doesn't know
how to excise the desirable from the undesirable parts of the job of
being a wife. She feels wretched about it, as if she's done something
unpardonable by letting her self-interest interfere with something that
might have been nice (for him). 'I never did seem to treat Eric perhaps
as I might have,' she says, her voice cracking.

Sonia visits often, and starts taking on Orwell's correspondence
and typing, and finding books for him. He sits in bed with 'that
particular soft, purring cough; that almost mystical transparency
of the skin – like a thin sheet of fibre-glass with a furious furnace
[on] the other side'. As a teen Sonia had been in a horrific boating

accident on a Swiss lake. A boy had clung to her but she had saved herself and swum away, leaving him to drown. This one she won't leave.

One day Sonia finds Orwell reading a biography of Joseph Conrad written by his wife. He is incandescent with rage, throws the book across the room.

'*Never* do that to me,' he hisses.

Sonia is mystified.

He forbids any biography to be written.

Metal

In the autumn he's moved to University College Hospital in London, a 'tiny room, like a small cubicle'. He sits in bed in a camel-coloured cardigan. His friend David Astor, editor of *The Observer*, often calls by on his way home from work.

'He was always talking of the things he was going to do,' Astor remembered. 'He said to me casually, "Do you think one can die if one has a book in one's mind one wants to write?" I was taken aback. I couldn't imagine the answer. He answered it for me by saying, "I've asked the doctor here, who has looked after other writing people, and he says, 'Yes, you can have a book in your mind and still die,' but I don't think that's so."' Astor said, 'He was trying to give himself hope.'

The doctors are divided: senior specialist Morland wants to lift Orwell's spirits by sending him to a Swiss sanatorium for fresh air. The younger ones think it's a fantasy plan, a way of shipping him off to 'die comfortably, in a place where they were really used to dealing with that sort of thing'.

Sonia makes the arrangements. A plane is chartered. Lucian Freud, her young artist friend, will come to help lift and carry and care.

The plan is to marry and then fly to Switzerland to fish and get better. Orwell has started to keep a fishing rod in his room as if he might pop out at any moment. In his dreams he sees rivers full of fish;

he dangles in a line. The dreams are comforting, though he knows they are 'sex dreams and death dreams at the same time'. The rod stands ready in the corner. Sometimes visitors notice it laid across the foot of his bed.

The hospital chaplain will officiate; the doctor will be there too, as a guest. As with his first marriage, Orwell can't believe his luck. *I am much encouraged,* he tells Astor, *that none of my friends or relatives seems to disapprove of my remarrying, in spite of this disease. I had had a nasty feeling that 'they' would converge from all directions and stop me, but it hasn't happened.* He is getting away with something, again.

He won't be able to leave the bed, but he can't very well marry in his cardigan. Orwell asks Anthony Powell to buy him a suitable jacket. Powell remembered it as crimson corduroy, Malcolm Muggeridge as mauve velvet. Possibly they were vague because in the end it was Sonia who bought it. Either way, he loves it.

On the day, Sonia's friend Janetta is crying. Orwell is so thin he jokes that the nurses are having a hard time finding enough flesh to put injections into. Everyone thinks of Death and the Maiden, everyone is being asked to participate in a hopeless act of hope. But Orwell is joyful. You can try to tell the truth your whole life and finish up needing serried fictions to sustain it. And other people to share them. Possibly, there is no happy end without fiction. Or, it depends where you stop the story: early for happy, or keep going for the inevitable other. He looks at the fishing rod in the corner. There will be a plane, a mountain, a stream, and he'll dip his rod for all the fish.

After the ceremony they drink a glass of champagne. No one takes a photograph. Sonia kisses his forehead. Then the others leave for a wedding lunch at the Ritz. He lies back.

Orwell is happy. His health rallies briefly. He has what he wanted; he has married a dream. He makes Sonia his literary executor. But over New Year he gets worse.

Stafford Cottman, the boy who'd fled Stalin with Orwell and Eileen in the train, telephones. When would be convenient to visit?

'I'm frightful,' Orwell says. 'I look just like a skeleton.'

Cottman thinks his voice is strong – he'll see him later.

Towards the end of January Orwell tells Paul Potts he's worried they won't have the Ceylonese tea he likes in Switzerland, only 'that filthy Chinese stuff'. Tea is still rationed and Potts broke as usual, but he goes out to find some.

Orwell's old flame and friend Celia calls, asking when she can come in. 'Well, I'm going off next Wednesday with Sonia to Switzerland,' he says.

'Oh, that's wonderful news, George,' she says. 'They must think you're going to get better.'

'Either that or they don't want a corpse on their hands.'

Later that day Potts arrives with the tea. 'There was a window in the door and you could look in, and I saw he was asleep, and I knew he had a great deal of difficulty in getting to sleep, so I didn't wake him up, and I left the tea at the door.'

What would she have said? He sees a wodge of dark hair in the small window in his door. Perhaps she's coming. Or the nurse. He closes his eyes. For some reason, he thinks of tea.

The fishing rod is in the corner of the room, and though he's going along with it he knows it's a lure, a glittering promise that will taste of metal.

Sonia spends the Friday at his bedside. Her friends Anne Dunn and Lucian Freud take her to dinner nearby. Just after midnight she calls the hospital to check on him and they tell her he's dead. A massive haemorrhage. She rushes in. His bed is unmade, the sheets soaked with blood. She is distraught beyond measure.

Celia gets the call the next morning.

Others hear it announced on the BBC.

Later, Potts said, 'I often wonder who got the tea.'

CODA

Back to Life

Writing a book is a horrible, exhausting struggle, like a long bout of some painful illness. One would never undertake such a thing if one were not driven on by some demon whom one can neither resist nor understand.

George Orwell, 'Why I Write', 1946

Around me there are piles of papers, photocopies, books engorged with sticky notes, books doing the splits, notebooks, printed drafts. My studio has been ransacked – by someone killing an angel and looking for an answer. Near my right foot I see material on Aunt Nellie, still on the cutting-room floor. Poor, broke Nellie – in the months after Orwell died, she tried to take her own life.

I look outside. A man from a building site, in a helmet and hi-vis vest, shelters near my bay window, his hands around a takeaway cup. Above him, the wasps are long gone, their house now black coral in my eave. The tradesman stirs something dormant in my mind. There are loops and gaps and glitches in the code we are written by, room for real lives and loves and moments of inherited strength.

My husband, an architect, recently told dinner guests a story dating from the beginning of our relationship. Until he started talking, I had no memory of it. We were visiting a colleague's construction site – a steep beach block with workmen in hi-vis and their trucks all around. The others stayed on the hill while I went down through the bush to the building, which was covered in scaffolding. When I reached the flat I heard shouts. I turned. A dark blur of fur and fangs was flying down. Rottweiler. I stood rooted to the spot. As the dog reached me I raised one hand and commanded in a huge voice both mine and not mine, '*SIT DOWN*.' It did. It seemed as surprised as I was.

In this story, Craig likes what he sees as my presence of mind, or my strength, though I felt neither of those things at the time. He tells it as if something both admirable and frightening were revealed to him that day. He has held on to it for thirty years as a moment in his private story of love, and it is linked to ferocity. As I listened to him the scene came back to me. The voice I'd used was my mother's.

To write this book I have used another voice for parts of it – Eileen's – because I lost the one I had. I retrieved Eileen from behind the Cerberus, from under the ignoring, minimising and passive-voicing. I retrieved her from under her own self-erasure, her attentive listening. When I found her I could see what such forces – and I, as co-conspirator – had done to me.

Orwell's work was essential in this task. It was a joy even, revisiting his writing on the systems of tyranny 'with theft as their aim', and the 'vast system of mental cheating' that is doublethink. It was his insight – and Baldwin's – that allowed me to see how men can imagine themselves innocent in a system that benefits them, at others' cost. I can see Orwell's valiant effort – and Eileen's. I can hold in my mind both sides of things – the blind tyrant and his seeing words, the wife and her husband, my own work and my life and everyone in it.

Craig calls me in for dinner. I look around at my floor and shelves, and decide to leave things where I can see them. In the kitchen my younger daughter is writing an essay. In a strange synchronicity, it's on Lot's wife, who was turned into a pillar of salt when she dared look back at Sodom. My daughter has noticed that the wife, who has no name, is blamed for her own death because she looked, dis-obediently. This is how, my daughter says, the wife is imagined to have deserved what she got, and no man, no system, no god is responsible. It gives me a sense of awe that someone at seventeen can understand instinctively what it seems to be my life's work to unravel. Where will she get to, this young woman? She is starting out in a place I've only just reached.

Norah
Bristol, July 1961

〜

Yesterday she had lunch in town with Mary, their friend
from Oxford. Mary has supported herself for much of
her life on the stock exchange, something Eileen called
'*superlatively clever*', by which Norah knew she meant,
somehow, cheating. Pig could be sharp.

Then as she was walking home there it was – Richard
Rees's book in the window of Stanford's. *George Orwell:
Fugitive from the Camp of Victory*. There are still days when
Eileen is everywhere.

After she married Orwell, Norah had barely seen her.
Their intimacy was transmuted to letters, so it is easy to fall
back into imagining that her absence is due not to death,
just to distance.

And Norah has seen her sometimes. In someone's
stoop-shouldered walk. A head of stray dark curls – though
of course they'd be grey by now. A laugh overheard on a
train. What to do with love that has lost its object? It lives
on, lost and looking.

Now, it's late afternoon. Norah sits in the garden. The
day is coming to an end. The book is coming to an end. She
is interested in Orwell, has enjoyed his work, especially
Animal Farm. But as she takes stock of her mounting

anxiety she realises that she has been reading Rees's book to see Eileen. She has two pages to go.

There was one mention – she flicks back to find it. Here it is, Rees visiting her in Spain at her workplace. Eileen is 'talking about the risk, to me', he writes, when she was suffering 'political terror'. Norah feels a flush of something – cold or hot she couldn't say; no, hot, though the heat has gone out of the day. She should be past the climacteric, Quartus says. She looks up, sees him moving, a comforting blur behind the kitchen window.

She turns to the last page.

Rees is ending with Orwell's 'exaggerated sense of honor'. This, he says, 'explains his ruthlessness toward himself and perhaps also his occasional inconsiderateness toward others. And yet it would not be easy to think of many victims of his inconsiderateness, apart from his wife . . .'

She catches her breath. Will this be it?

'. . . and anyone else who was concerned to counteract his disregard of his own health and safety . . .'

No, Eileen's not there.

Then, finally, this: 'But everything in life has to be paid for and sometimes . . . the price of associating with a man of exceptional disinterestedness and courage is a high one . . . it is to be expected that the progress through life of a man of superior character will leave behind it a more disturbing backwash than the sluggish progress of the average man.'

She turns the page. There are only blank endpapers.

Death, of course, will make us all disappear, which is why it seems to those of us who are left to be such a nasty trick. She sees she was hoping for words to reverse it.

Then she remembers she has some. They are inside, in the top compartment of a desk. She goes in, opens it with a key.

> *I wrote the address quite a long time ago & have since played with three cats, made a cigarette (I make them now but not with the naked hand), poked the fire & driven Eric (i.e. George) nearly mad—all because I didn't really know what to say. I lost my habit of punctual correspondence during the first few weeks of marriage because we quarrelled so continuously & really bitterly that I thought I'd save time & just write one letter to everyone when the murder or separation had been accomplished . . .*

No, Norah thinks, her hand with the letter in it falling into her lap. No. It was life itself she accomplished instead.

Now what?

Notes

Preliminary pages

vii   **'Love, ... sexual or non-sexual, is hard work'**: George Orwell, 'Reflections on Gandhi', *Partisan Review*, 1949.

vii   **'We all make up the people we love'**: Phyllis Rose, *Parallel Lives: Five Victorian Marriages*, Penguin Books, 1985, p. 136.

vii   **'[M]en and women read'**: Vivian Gornick, 'Why Do These Men Hate Women?', in *Taking a Long Look: Essays on Culture, Literature, and Feminism in Our Time*, Verso, 2022, p. 256.

Suffolk, November 1936

4   **'I wrote the address'**: In Peter Davison (ed.), *George Orwell: A Life in Letters*, Liveright Publishing Corporation, 2013 (hereafter *A Life in Letters*), pp. 66–7. All of Eileen's letters quoted are from this source. A note on names. George Orwell's birth name was Eric Blair. Eileen called him George. I call him Orwell, to distinguish him from other Georges in this story – Kopp and Tioli. And I call Eileen's brother by his first name, Laurence, rather than Eric, as he was sometimes known, so as not to confuse him with Eric Blair. When other names in the text have doubles, I use surnames or first names to distinguish people – e.g. Rees from Richard Blair, Charles from Lois Orr, Wickes and Crook (who were both 'David').

5   **'gummed his food'**: Jane Morgan (Orwell's niece) to Gordon Bowker, in Bowker, *George Orwell*, Abacus, 2004, p. 39.

5   **'those brutes'**: Henry Dakin, Ida's grandson, in Stephen Wadhams, *Remembering Orwell*, Penguin Books, 1984, p. 30. Henry's sister Jane had fond memories of visiting her grandparents' 'small, but rather exotic' house, filled with 'rainbow silky curtains, masses of embroidered stools, bags, cushions, pincushions done by my grandmother, interesting mahogany or ivory boxes full of sequins, beads, miniatures ... most of the work of the house was done by my grandmother, with the able assistance of a tiny Suffolk woman. Grandmother and Aunt Avril took breakfast in bed, one at the head, one at the foot. Earl Grey tea, toast and Patum Peperium

[anchovy paste]. The dachshunds usually sat on the bed, which delighted and scandalised us.' Jane Morgan (née Dakin) in Audrey Coppard and Bernard Crick (eds), *Orwell Remembered*, Ariel Books, 1984, p. 85.

Present, Tense

9   **'In Moulmein, in Lower Burma'**: 'Shooting an Elephant', *The Collected Essays, Journalism and Letters of George Orwell*, Sonia Orwell and Ian Angus (eds), Secker & Warburg, 1968 [1970] (hereafter *Collected Essays, Journalism and Letters*), vol. 1, p. 265. Moulmein, as it was then known, is present-day Mawlamyine, and Burma is Myanmar.

11   **'smelly little orthodoxies'**: George Orwell, 'Charles Dickens', in *Collected Essays, Journalism and Letters*, vol. 1, p. 504. See also *The Complete Works of George Orwell*, 20 vols, Peter Davison (ed.), Secker & Warburg, 1998 (hereafter *CW*), vol. 12, p. 56 [597].

11   **'six major biographies of Orwell'**: The biographies are: Peter Stansky and William Abrahams, *The Unknown Orwell* (1972) and *Orwell: The Transformation* (1979), published in one volume in 1994 by Stanford University Press; Bernard Crick, *George Orwell: A Life*, Secker & Warburg, 1980; Michael Shelden, *Orwell: The Authorized Biography*, HarperCollins, 1991; Jeffrey Meyers, *Orwell: Wintry Conscience of a Generation*, W. W. Norton, 2001; D. J. Taylor, *Orwell: The Life*, Vintage, 2003; and Gordon Bowker, *George Orwell*, Abacus, 2004. I am enormously indebted to them.

11   **'one of the greatest'**: Bowker, p. xi.

11   **'a moral force'**: Taylor, p. 2.

12   **'muffle or suppress'**: Bowker, p. 194.

12   **'a type of woman who is sexually over-demanding'**: Crick, p. 400.

12   **'a means of controlling their husbands'**: Meyers, p. 127.

Black Box

20   **'a superior person'**: Charles Orr, in Lois Orr, *Letters from Barcelona: An American Woman in Revolution and Civil War*, Gerd-Rainer Horn (ed.), Palgrave Macmillan, 2009, p. 179.

20   **'diffident and unassuming', 'a quiet integrity', 'deeply, but with a tender amusement'**: Lettice Cooper, 'Eileen Blair', *The PEN: Broadsheet of the English Centre of International PEN*, no. 16, Spring 1984, p. 19.

20   **'extraordinary political simplicity'**: Eileen to Marjorie Dakin, 27 September 1938, in Davison (ed.), *A Life in Letters*, p. 121.

20   **'extraordinary political sympathy'**: Crick, p. 251.

20   **'one or two teeth missing'**: Eileen's friend Lydia Jackson to Bernard Crick, 27 November, 1974, Crick Archive, cited in Sylvia Topp, *Eileen: The Making of George Orwell*, Unbound, 2020, p. 364.

21   **'Six letters from Eileen'**: The letters, discovered by Norah's nephew Jim Durant, were all published in Davison (ed.), *A Life in Letters*.

22   **'a very affectionate nature'**: Davison (ed.), *A Life in Letters*, p. xv.

22 **'liveliest girls'**: Esther Power quoted in Topp, p. 42.

23 **'differing portraits of Eileen'**: Sylvia Topp's *Eileen: The Making of George Orwell*
has been an important source of information about Eileen. Topp's point of view is
clear in her dedication of the book to 'the many others like Eileen in the world, all
the wives, husbands and partners of celebrated people who have devoted their lives
joyfully to assisting their talented partners in all their various needs, knowing all along
that they would be underappreciated and often ignored, and yet never faltering in
their dedication, or in their willingness to submerge their own personal talents into
their partners' success' (p. 455). It is perhaps this imagined joyful acceptance of being
ignored, or submerged, that leads Topp to interpret Orwell's, Eileen's and Lydia's
accounts differently from me. By way of example, Topp characterises Eileen's 'murder
or separation' letter as 'cheerful bantering'. When Eileen tells Norah that Orwell gets
a haemorrhage or 'something' every time she tries to leave, Topp writes, 'Perhaps she
was flattered that Orwell sometimes used his illnesses as a way to keep her at home
with him' (p. 151). Of the passage in Orwell's last notebook about the sexual insatiability
and 'incorrigible dirtiness & untidiness' of women, Topp writes, 'He does not explicitly
mention Eileen, but he did indeed marry a messy woman' (p. 117). As well as Eileen's
messiness, Topp also finds her sexual desire responsible for Orwell's strange rant: 'Orwell
apparently was conventional enough to think that making love happened when the
man was in the mood, and the woman shouldn't initiate it or expect it at random
times' (p. 156). Topp writes that 'Eileen understood that Orwell hadn't promised to be
faithful', although there's no evidence to support this before it started to happen. And
she is scathing about their close friend, the writer and psychologist Lydia Jackson's own
account of her relationship with Orwell. Topp's view of Eileen is nuanced and detailed.
She concludes, as I do, that Eileen saved Orwell's life. She writes of Eileen essentially
as a helpmeet to genius who 'shared with Orwell a more traditional understanding of
marriage' (p. 117) that involved 'transforming herself into part of his dream' (p. 123). My
interest is in examining what it took, perhaps, to be in that marriage and that dream.

Falling in Love

25 **'a quiet presence'**: Meyers, p. 120, citing Gwen's daughter, Catherine Moncure.

26 **'almost complete lack of self-confidence'**: Elisaveta Fen, *A Russian's England:
Reminiscences of Years 1926–1940*, Paul Gordon Books, 1976, p. 340 (hereafter
A Russian's England). Lydia's birth name was Lidiia Vitalievna Zhiburtovich, and
her married name was Jackson. She wrote under the name Elisaveta Fen.

26 **'knee was bleeding'; 'moth-eaten'**: Ibid. p. 345.

27 **'jolly, smiling, warmhearted'**: Crick, p. 168.

27 **'gay and lively and interesting'**: Kay Ekevall quoted in Wadhams, *Remembering Orwell*,
Penguin Books, 1984. p. 58.

27 **'Eileen O'Shaughnessy is the girl I want to marry'**: Stansky and Abrahams, *Orwell:
The Transformation* (hereafter *The Transformation*), p. 108. Rosalind put it another
way in a letter to Bernard Crick: *Now* that *is the kind of girl I would like to marry!*,
quoted in Crick, p. 172.

27 **'I was rather drunk'**: Cooper, 'Eileen Blair', p. 19.

27 **'a copy of ... Burmese Days under her arm'**: Rosalind to Bernard Crick, in Crick, p. 172.

28 **'I did not like it at all'**: Fen, *A Russian's England*, p. 345.

30 **'In the 1960s she wrote'**: The essay is Elisaveta Fen, 'George Orwell's First Wife', *The Twentieth Century*, August 1961, pp. 115–26 (hereafter *George Orwell's First Wife*).

30 **'In the 1980s she spoke about'**: Stephen Wadhams (presenter), 'The Orwell Tapes', part 2 [radio program], *Ideas*, 23 August 2017 (originally aired on 11 April 2016), Canadian Broadcasting Corporation (hereafter 'The Orwell Tapes'). Edited excerpts of these interviews can be found in Wadhams, *Remembering Orwell*.

Who is he?

31 **'a rather pale dry skin'**: Taylor, p. 152.

31 **'deplorable cigarettes'**: Malcolm Muggeridge in Miriam Gross (ed.), *The World of George Orwell*, Weidenfeld & Nicolson, 1971, p. 170.

31 **'he really smiled'**: Susan Watson in Wadhams, *Remembering Orwell*, p. 157.

31 **'the jolly rich girls quiver'**: Cyril Connolly: the 'nice, jolly girls with lots of money ... all wanted to meet him and started talking to him and their fur coats shook with pleasure'. In Bowker, p. 194, quoting from Melvyn Bragg (director), *George Orwell: The Road to the Left* [documentary film], BBC Bristol, 1971.

32 **'something charming and winning', 'original in himself'**: Muggeridge, 'A Knight of the Woeful Countenance', in Gross (ed.), p. 169.

32 **'All tobacconists are fascists'**: Adrien Fierz (Mabel's son) in Wadhams, *Remembering Orwell*, p. 47.

32 **'a gangling, physically badly co-ordinated young man'**: Geoffrey Gorer, in Bowker, p. 173, quoting from Bragg.

32 **'FAMOUS WRITER'**: Jacintha Buddicom, *Eric & Us: The First-Hand Account of George Orwell's Formative Years*, Finlay Publisher, 2006 [1974], p. 38. Jacintha writes: 'Of course, Eric was always going to write; not merely as an author, always as a FAMOUS AUTHOR in capitals.'

33 **'deep-seated grudge', 'very intelligent'**: Ruth Pitter quoted in Coppard and Crick (eds), p. 71.

33 **'a slacker'**: Orwell's tutor Andrew Gow quoted in Crick, p. 51.

33 **'the school wouldn't recommend him anyway'**: Andrew Gow, despite being fond of Orwell, said that to recommend Orwell for university would bring 'disgrace on [the] College', Crick, p. 73.

33 **'It is a stifling, stultifying world in which to live ...'**: George Orwell, *Burmese Days*, Oxford University Press, 2021 [1934], p. 56.

34 **'I wouldn't care to have your job'**: Orwell, *The Road to Wigan Pier* [1937], (hereafter *Wigan*) in *The Penguin Complete Longer Non-Fiction of George Orwell*, Penguin Books, 1983, p. 245.

34 **'no cunt no oil'**: An unnamed 'old Burma hand' recounted this story to Bernard Crick quoting 'coarse' American oil men who wrote the unsigned letter to Government House. Crick, p. 89.

34 'with three of her sixth form': Crick, p. 91.

35 'vast system of mental cheating': *Nineteen Eighty-Four*, Penguin Books, 1984 [1949], p. 184.

35 'It is not permissible that the authors of devastation...': James Baldwin, 'My Dungeon Shook: Letter to My Nephew on the One Hundredth Anniversary of the Emancipation', in Toni Morrison (ed.), *James Baldwin: Collected Essays*, Library of America edition, 1998, p. 292.

35 'he'd been buying girls': Some biographers like to render doubtful Orwell's visits to the waterfront brothels of Moulmein. Stansky and Abrahams, for instance, refer to his accounts of them to others as 'hearsay', or fabulation 'out of pride and for effect', *The Unknown Orwell*, p. 190. But the visits were real, (Shelden, p. 63) and immortalised in poems, such as Orwell's 'Ironic Poem About Prostitution':

> When I was young and had no sense
> In far-off Mandalay
> I lost my heart to a Burmese girl
> As lovely as the day.
> Her skin was gold, her hair was jet,
> Her teeth were ivory;
> I said, 'for twenty silver pieces,
> Maiden, sleep with me'.
> She looked at me, so pure, so sad,
> The loveliest thing alive,
> And in her lisping, virgin voice,
> Stood out for twenty-five.

Crick thinks the poem was composed either shortly before or after Orwell left Burma in July 1927, as it was written 'improperly' on Burmese Government paper (Crick, p. 93). On Orwell's visits to prostitutes in Burma, Paris and London, see also Bowker, p. xiv. Sometimes though, Orwell's blindness to the work of women lifted. There is one beautiful moment in *Wigan* where Orwell notices a woman of about thirty, ground down by domestic work, with her hand up a filthy drainpipe.

> She had a round pale face, the usual exhausted face of the slum girl who is twenty-five and looks forty, thanks to miscarriages and drudgery; and it wore, for the second in which I saw it, the most desolate, hopeless expression I have ever seen. It struck me then that we are mistaken when we say that 'It isn't the same for them as it would be for us,' and that people bred in the slums can imagine nothing but the slums. For what I saw in her face was not the ignorant suffering of an animal. She knew well enough what was happening to her – understood as well as I did how dreadful a destiny it was to be kneeling there in the bitter cold, on the slimy stones of a slum backyard, poking a stick up a foul drain-pipe. (*Wigan*, p. 165)

This insight, however, did not change the way he lived with Eileen, who did all the domestic work.

36 'too cynical or too sardonic': According to her daughter. Taylor, p. 125.

36 'had to be shooed away': Taylor, pp. 136–7.

36 'forthright, intelligent and independent-minded': Stansky and Abrahams, *The Unknown Orwell*, p. 280.

36 'Never write about people': Stansky and Abrahams, *The Transformation*, p. 38.

37 'Burn it, and keep the clips': Stansky and Abrahams, *The Unknown Orwell*, p. 299.

37 'badgered': Mabel Fierz in Coppard and Crick, p. 94.

37 'unbeknown to him, she paid part of his rent': Kay told this to Bowker, Bowker, p. 164.

37 'confided secrets to her that he seems to have told no one else': For example, Orwell confided to Mabel that his piece of reportage, 'A Hanging', was fiction – he'd not been to one. See also below, note for p. 59, 'She was beautiful'.

37 'Mabel gave interviews to Canadian broadcasters': Stephen Wadhams, 'The Orwell Tapes', parts 1 and 2. Mabel, born in 1890, was forty when she met Orwell, who was twenty-seven. She was ninety-three when speaking with the CBC producers.

37 'a vivacious and opinionated middle-aged woman': Gordon Bowker, 'Orwell's London', The Orwell Foundation, 2008 [2006].

37 'a wee bit of a crank': Crick, p. 131.

38 'attributes it to a kindly providence': Richard Rees, *A Theory of My Time: An Essay in Didactic Reminiscence*, Secker & Warburg, 1963, p. 31 (hereafter *A Theory*).

38 'no more than a symptom': Richard Rees, *George Orwell: Fugitive from the Camp of Victory*, Southern Illinois University Press, 1961 (hereafter *Fugitive*).

39 'never really looked at another human being': Rees, *Fugitive*, p. 65.

. . . and who is she?

40 'faces and manners were glass', 'What she sees are their feelings': Lettice Cooper, *Black Bethlehem*, Cedric Chivers Ltd, 1971 [1947], p. 180. Cooper, a novelist and close friend of Eileen, based the character Ann in her 1947 novel *Black Bethlehem* on Eileen. 'Ann' was 'her best attempt at portraying her friend Eileen, a person she truly admired'. Topp, p. 357, citing Lettice Cooper, Crick Archive.

40 'Sophisticated, fastidious, highly intelligent', 'Physically, she was very attractive': Fen, 'George Orwell's First Wife', p. 115.

40 'proletarian fancy dress': Muggeridge in Gross (ed.), p. 168. 'He was dressed in a sort of proletarian fancy dress; an ancient battered sports jacket and corduroy trousers, not actually tied up with string as in old comic drawings, but of the kind that could still be bought in those days in working-class districts and in seaside towns where fishermen live.'

40 'shabby and unbrushed clothes': Lettice Cooper in Coppard and Crick, p. 163.

40 'rather unkempt': Henry Dakin in Wadhams, *Remembering Orwell*, p. 129.

40 'a body beautifully poised': Lettice Cooper in Coppard and Crick, p. 163.

40 'very thoughtful': Cooper, 'Eileen Blair', p. 19.

40–1 'because her sense of life': Cooper, *Black Bethlehem*, p. 154.

41 **'when she told you something amusing', 'Her stories were often told against
herself'**: Fen, *A Russian's England*, pp. 343–4.

41 **'mad gay'**: Edna Bussey quoted in Topp, p. 80.

41 **'lash'**: Crick Archive.

42 **'vagaries of chance'**: Fen, 'George Orwell's First Wife', p. 115.

42 **'no effort was worth making'**: Fen, *A Russian's England*, p. 346.

42 **'Women had only been allowed'**: Topp, p. 69.

42 **'as she did later in her psychology class'**: Fellow student John Cohen, who
partnered with Eileen in experiments, recalled her as 'bright, rather tough, could be
argumentative and "provocative"', Stansky and Abrahams, *The Transformation*, p. 118.
Eileen, however, found Cohen entertaining. Lydia remembered him 'showing off'
by 'involving lecturers in hair-splitting arguments about minor points of theory', but
Eileen being 'amused by his cleverness and persistence'. *A Russian's England*, p. 341.

42 **'Career paths for women in the 1920s**: Approximately 40 per cent of British
women were employed in domestic service at this time. T. J. Hatton and R. E. Bailey,
Oxford Economic Papers, 40(4), 1988, pp. 695–718.

42–3 **'own and staff such schools'**: Fen, 'George Orwell's First Wife', p. 115.

43 **'presumably social work among prostitutes'**: Stansky and Abrahams, *The
Transformation*, p. 115. Topp suggests rather that she worked as a shorthand taker
at this board, which was set up to investigate 'the important subject of Sex and its
bearing on all human relationships'. Topp, p. 76.

43 **'walking out in triumph'**: Fen, 'George Orwell's First Wife', p. 115.

43 **'Edna's jealous mother wouldn't allow it'**: Topp, p. 81.

44 **'short, brisk, eloquent'**: Ibid., p. 87.

44 **'more than ordinary aptitude'**: Stansky and Abrahams, *The Transformation*, p. 117.
Lydia describes Eileen as a 'brilliant student' whom Burt 'greatly encouraged' to go
on with her work, 'George Orwell's First Wife', p. 118.

44 **'word association', 'reliability of eye-witnesses', 'psychopathology'**: Topp,
p. 93. Lydia observed that 'He was on the defensive against her psychological
knowledge . . .' Fen, 'George Orwell's First Wife', p. 119.

45 **'poem she'd written'**: Eileen wrote this poem in 1934 for the fiftieth-anniversary
commemorations of her alma mater, Sunderland High School for Girls. It is
possible that Orwell's title for his last novel, *Nineteen Eighty-Four*, is a homage to it.

End of the Century, 1984

Death

Synthetic winds have blown away
Material dust, but this one room
Rebukes the constant violet ray
And dustless sheds a dusty gloom.
Wrecked on the outmoded past

Lie North and Hillard, Virgil, Horace,
Shakespeare's bones are quiet at last,
Dead as Yeats or William Morris.
Have not the inmates earned their rest?
A hundred circles traversed they
Complaining of the classic quest
And, each inevitable day,
Illogically trying to place
A ball within an empty space.

Birth

Every loss is now a gain
For every chance must follow reason.
A crystal palace meets the rain
That falls at its appointed season.
No book disturbs the lucid line
For sun-bronzed scholars tune their thought
To Telepathic Station 9
From which they know just what they ought:
The useful sciences; the arts
Of telesalesmanship and Spanish
As registered in Western parts;
Mental cremation that shall banish
Relics, philosophies and colds –
Manana-minded ten-year-olds.

The Phoenix

Worlds have died that they may live,
May plume again their fairest feathers
And in their clearest songs may give
Welcome to all spontaneous weathers.
Bacon's colleague is called Einstein,
Huxley shares Platonic food,
Violet rays are only sunshine
Christened in the modern mood,
In this house if in no other
Past and future may agree,
Each herself, but each the other
In a curious harmony,
Finding both a proper place
In the silken gown's embrace.

45   '**with a suitcase full of poetry**': Eileen to Orwell, 21 March 1945, in Davison (ed.), *A Life in Letters*, p. 251.

45   '**kissing the bums of verminous little lions**': *Wigan*, p. 157.

Southwold

46   '**marmalade**': Lettice Cooper in Coppard and Crick, p. 162;

46   '**dress for dinner**': Jock Branthwaite in Wadhams, *Remembering Orwell*, p. 99.

47   '**he'd never "go Dutch" in a restaurant**': Kay Ekevall tells this story in Wadhams, *Remembering Orwell*, pp. 56–7.

47   '**houseboy in Burma**': See his account in *Wigan*, p. 243: 'The essential point was that the "natives", at any rate the Burmese, were not felt to be physically repulsive. One looked down on them as "natives", but one was quite ready to be physically intimate with them; . . . I habitually allowed myself, for instance, to be dressed and undressed by my Burmese boy . . . I felt towards a Burman almost as I felt towards a woman.'

Free

49   '**high judicial office**': Brett Kavanaugh was appointed to the Supreme Court of the United States, despite the evidence of Christine Blasey Ford.

50   '**Patriarchy**': In *The Creation of Patriarchy*, Oxford University Press, 1986, historian Gerda Lerner tracks its development in Mesopotamia to between 3500 and 600 BCE; others have it earlier.

50   '**it is not in giving life**': Simone de Beauvoir, *The Second Sex*, Random House, 2011 [1949], p. 76; '**The world has always belonged to males**': Ibid., p. 73.

51   '**The overthrow of mother-right**': Frederick (Friedrich) Engels, *The Origin of the Family, Private Property and the State*, ed. Eleanor Leacock, International Publishers Co., 1972 [1884], pp. 220–1.

51   '**women were the first slaves**': Lerner. See, in particular, the chapter 'The Woman Slave', in which she describes how 'Biological and cultural factors predisposed men to enslave women before they had learned how to enslave men.' In her analysis, the 'subordination of women by men provided the conceptual model for the creation of slavery as an institution, so the patriarchal family provided the structural model' (p. 89). Lerner makes a historically comprehensive and racially aware account of slavery, noting, for example, that 'The sexual use of black women by any white male was also characteristic of eighteenth- and nineteenth-century race relations in the United States, but it survived the abolition of slavery and became, well into the twentieth century, one of the features of race and class oppression' (p. 88).

51   '**Behind us lies the patriarchal system**': Virginia Woolf, *A Room of One's Own and Three Guineas*, Penguin Books, 2019. Searchable at gutenberg.net.au/ebooks02/0200931h.html.

52   'mid-century misogynists': See, for example, the discussion with Emily Gould and others in *The Cut*, 3 December 2013, 'Reading While Female: How to Deal with Misogynists and Male Masturbation'.

55   '**Statistically, there is an irrefutable, globally intransigent heterosexual norm**': There are reams of evidence on this. See, for example, Jacques Charmes, 'The Unpaid Care Work and the Labour Market: An Analysis of Time Use Data Based on the Latest World Compilation of Time-use Surveys', Gender, Equality and Diversity & ILOAIDS Branch, International Labour Organization, Geneva, 2019, available at ilo.org/wcmsp5/groups/public/---dgreports/---gender/documents/publication/ wcms_732791.pdf. This ILO report found that:

> Across the world, without exception, women carry out three-quarters of unpaid care work, or more than 75 per cent of the total hours provided. Women dedicate on average 3.2 times more time than men to unpaid care work. There is no country where women and men perform an equal share of unpaid care work. As a result, women are constantly time poor, which constrains their participation in the labour market.

See also, for example, Gaëlle Ferrant, Luca Maria Pesando and Keiko Nowacka, 'Unpaid Care Work: The Missing Link in the Analysis of Gender Gaps in Labour Outcomes', OECD Development Centre, December 2014, available at atoecd.org/dev/development-gender/Unpaid_care_work.pdf. This OECD report found that:

> Around the world, women spend two to ten times more time on unpaid care work than men ... Unpaid care work is both an important aspect of economic activity and an indispensable factor contributing to the well-being of individuals, their families and societies ... Every day individuals spend time cooking, cleaning and caring for children, the ill and the elderly. Despite this importance for well-being, unpaid care work is commonly left out of policy agendas ... neglecting unpaid care work leads to incorrect inferences about levels and changes in individuals' well-being and the value of time, which in turn limit policy effectiveness across a range of socio-economic areas, notably gender inequalities in employment and other empowerment areas.
> Women typically spend disproportionately more time on unpaid care work than men. On account of gendered social norms that view unpaid care work as a female prerogative, women across different regions, socio-economic classes and cultures spend an important part of their day on meeting the expectations of their domestic and reproductive roles. This is in addition to their paid activities, thus creating the 'double burden' of work for women ... The unequal distribution of unpaid care work between women and men represents an infringement of women's rights ... and also a brake on their economic empowerment.

55   '**if it had to be paid for**': UN Women reports that 'Women's unpaid work subsidises the cost of care that sustains families, supports economies and often fills in for

the lack of social services. Yet, it is rarely recognized as "work". Unpaid care and domestic work is valued to be [between] 10 and 39 per cent of the Gross Domestic Product and can contribute more to the economy than the manufacturing, commerce or transportation sectors. With the onslaught of climate change, women's unpaid work in farming, gathering water and fuel is growing even more.' See 'Redistribute Unpaid Work', UN Women website, citing *Women's economic empowerment in the changing world of work: Report of the Secretary-General*, E/CN. 6/2017/3, December 2016. For the global value of women's work estimated at US$10.8 trillion see, for example, Gus Wezerek and Kristen R. Ghodsee, 'Women's Unpaid Labor is Worth $10,900,000,000,000', *New York Times*, 5 March 2020 and Kadie Ward, 'Time to Care: Recognising the Truth Behind the Economy of Unpaid Care', OECD Forum Network, 10 September 2022.

Passive, Tense

58 **'demonstrated for women's suffrage'**: On Nellie's life see Darcy Moore, 'Orwell's Aunt Nellie', *George Orwell Studies*, vol. 4, no. 2, 2020, pp. 30–44 and 'Orwell in Paris: Aunt Nellie', Darcy Moore website, 21 January 2020, darcymoore.net/2020/ 01/21/orwell-paris-aunt-nellie/.

58 **'Nellie was connected'**: Taylor has this as Aunt Nellie 'using one of her husband's Esperanto connections', p. 142. But they were Nellie's own ILP connections – the bookshop owners, the Westropes, were her close friends and fellow party members.

58–9 **'abandoned him to Burma'**: Orwell to Jacintha Buddicom, 15 February 1949, in Davison (ed.), *A Life in Letters*, p. 445.

59 **'a torn skirt and a tear-stained face like thunder', 'badly bruised a shoulder and her left hip'**: Dione Venables, 'Postscript' to Buddicom, p. 182. Jacintha didn't write of this sexual assault in her reminiscences of Orwell, published in 1974. It only became widely known when her niece, Dione Venables, revealed it in a 2006 postscript to Jacintha's book. A note on his height: Venables has Orwell as 6 foot 4 inches, though Orwell said he was 6 foot 2½.

59 **'loved best', 'She was beautiful'**: Mabel Fierz in Coppard and Crick, p. 95. Taylor (pp. 97–8) tries to throw doubt on Mabel's account and to make the 'fracas' between Orwell and Suzanne's boyfriend (or possibly pimp), rather than have Orwell defrauded by a woman. 'According to Mabel Fierz, whom Orwell *had not yet met* but to whom he later confided *various semi-intimate details*, the culprit was a "little trollop" named Suzanne, picked up in a café, with whom he was *currently infatuated*. Suzanne, *in the Fierz version*, had an Arab boyfriend with whom Orwell was involved in some kind of fracas. *Whatever the truth of this explanation*, as with the Burmese girls and other later episodes, there is a sense that one never quite knows with Orwell, that vast areas of his personal life stretch out in to impenetrable blackness.' Italics mine, to show the creation of doubt and trivialisation, leading ultimately to the 'impenetrable blackness' where the accounts of women would be.

59 **'fictional backstory'**: *Down and Out in Paris and London* [1933] hinges on Orwell's descent into poverty in Paris, which he fictionalises as follows, in order to conceal what happened with Suzanne:

> One day there turned up at the hotel a young Italian who called himself a compositor. He was rather an ambiguous person, for he wore side whiskers, which are the mark either of an apache or an intellectual, and nobody was quite certain in which class to put him. Madame F. did not like the look of him, and made him pay a week's rent in advance. The Italian paid the rent and stayed six nights at the hotel. During this time he managed to prepare some duplicate keys, and on the last night he robbed a dozen rooms, including mine. Luckily, he did not find the money that was in my pockets, so I was not left penniless. I was left with just forty-seven francs – that is, seven and tenpence.

In *The Penguin Complete Longer Non-Fiction of George Orwell*, Penguin Books, 1983, pp. 16–17.

59 **'Aunt Nellie again'**: The meals Nellie was giving Orwell might have been like one Ruth Pitter remembered her preparing in London, 'some fearsome dish such as one would have in Paris if one was a native Parisian and dreadfully hard up'. Coppard and Crick, p. 70.

60 **'footnotes in 8-point font'**: See, for example, Stansky and Abrahams' discussion of Orwell's account of 'Moroccan girls' in *The Unknown Orwell*, pp. 190–1.

60 **'fictitious "*ménage à trois*"'**: Bowker, p. 266.

61 **'make what he does to a woman disappear'**: Behind the closed door of the marital black box what a man does to a woman has been, historically, his own business. Not even the law would protect her. Until the 1980s and 1990s in Australia, the UK and the US, once she was married a woman could lawfully be raped because according to law she had consented once and for all time to access to her body. She belonged to her husband and the law existed to protect his property rights, rather than to give (human) rights to that property (see, for example, in the UK: Regina Respondent and R. Appellant [House of Lords] [1992] 1 AC 599. In Australia rape in marriage was not outlawed by statute until the *Sexual Offences Act* 2003. In the US it was not until 1993 that all fifty states penalised marital rape.) The law has been changed, but women are still less entitled to protection from rape (prosecutions are low, convictions risibly so). And from murder. Today in Australia, for instance, one woman a week is killed by her male partner and these murders are trivialised as 'domestic', as if there were tamer ways to be dead. In a rape trial, a male accused's innocence is presumed, despite any record of prior assaults, and he can remain silent, while a woman's account and her integrity are called into question on the stand.

Engagement

62 **'family of mice'**: Stansky and Abrahams, *The Transformation*, p. 96. Though the biographers concede that Janet had to listen to the mice rustling about at night in his room, when she calls this 'filthy' her criticism is made into a character defect –

of hers. 'As a former Head Girl, Janet tended to be censorious where cleanliness and neatness were concerned ...'

62–3 **'resolutely working class'**: Taylor, p. 160.

63 **'fellow-student as a landlady'**: Crick, pp. 176–7. Also Stansky and Abrahams, *The Transformation*, p. 73.

Running

67 **'rather despised marriage', 'liked women well enough', 'very secondary'**: Wadhams, 'The Orwell Tapes', part 1. See also Taylor, p. 153.

Deleting Obscenities and Drawing a Blank

70 **'I am getting married very shortly'**: *Collected Essays, Journalism and Letters*, 1968, vol. 1, p. 222.

71 **'Dear King-Farlow'**: Ibid. p. 224.

Idyll

73 **'Eileen cheered him up'**: Taylor, p. 159.

73 **'that first year with Eileen'**: Geoffrey Gorer in Stansky and Abrahams, *The Transformation*, p. 176.

73 **'In any study of Orwell's life'**: Stansky and Abrahams, *The Transformation*, pp. 203–4.

74 **'all my writing life'**: Orwell's last literary notebook, in *Collected Essays, Journalism and Letters*, vol. 4, p. 573.

75 **'cleaning out the whole privy'**: Jeffrey Meyers, *Orwell: Wintry Conscience of a Generation*, p. 124. Meyers is the only biographer to address directly who did the work: 'Orwell enjoyed this hair-shirt existence, but Eileen, who did most of the work, suffered terribly' (p. 124).

75 **'hazardous'**: Lettice Cooper in Wadhams, p. 116.

75 **'battalions of mice'**: Eileen said this to Patricia Donoghue, as reported in Wadhams, *Remembering Orwell*, p. 118. See also Stansky and Abrahams, *The Transformation*, p. 205.

75 **'completely broke'**: Eileen's letter to Norah, November 1936 in Davison (ed.) *A Life in Letters*, p. 66.

76 **'If we were at opposite ends of the world'**: Fen, 'George Orwell's First Wife', p. 122. See also Wadhams, *Remembering Orwell*, p. 68.

Confessions of a Gendered Soul

78 **'must charm', 'what you think to be the truth', 'Had I not killed her'**: Virginia Woolf, 'Professions for Women', a paper read to the Women's Service League in 1931. See wheelersburg.net/Downloads/Woolf.pdf.

Mint Humbugs

79 **'I came in a mood'**: Fen, *A Russian's England*, 1976, p. 349. Subsequent notes in this section are also from here.

81 **'an enormous change'**: Rees, in Coppard and Crick, p. 124.

81 **'did not have the grace and charm and humor'**: Rees, *Fugitive*, p. 37.

81 'There was such an extraordinary change': Rees, in Coppard and Crick, p. 124.

82 'it is not just coincidence': Stansky and Abrahams, *The Transformation*, p. 184. Bowker puts it this way: 'It is likely that the transformation in Orwell's work from *Wigan* onwards owes a great deal to the intellectual stimulus his marriage brought him.' Crick writes, 'Whether by coincidence or influence, [Orwell's] writing improved greatly after meeting Eileen, becoming a settled, simplified and consistent style . . .'

82 'My impression was': Fen, *A Russian's England*, 1976, p. 377.

82 'a children's book with a cast of hens in leading roles': Stansky and Abrahams, *The Transformation*, p. 208; 'barely twenty-five minutes': Ibid., p. 207.

82–3 'not strong enough': Fen, *A Russian's England*, p. 378.

82 'They soon discovered': Ibid.

83 'doubtless considerable': Bowker, p. 193.

83 'I want passionately': Davidson (ed.), *A Life in Letters*, pp. 66–7.

Too Much Sex

84 'He was as secretive about his private life': Fredric Warburg, *All Authors Are Equal: The Publishing Life of Fredric Warburg 1936–1971*, Plunkett Lake Press, 2015 [1973], p. 97.

84 'his experience of women thus far': Stansky and Abrahams, *The Transformation*, p. 76. This is an instance of ignoring Orwell's sexual experiences in Burma and Paris, as if, somehow, prostitutes and Burmese women do not count as 'women' with whom he had sex.

84 'The couple's physical intimacy': Bowker, p. 193.

84 'jaded and unresponsive': Meyers, p. 127.

85 'passionate dedication to truth': Malcom Muggeridge, in Gross (ed.), p. 167.

86 '*femme libre*': Crick, p. 14. Crick describes Ida as having 'the up-and-away over-practicality of the woman on her own who might have quite liked to have been almost a *femme libre*.' Whether he means a politically or sexually free woman remains obscure.

86 'The conversations he overheard': Ibid, p. 13.

86 'a refutation of the generally accepted ideas': Moore, 'Orwell's Aunt Nellie', p. 40; Adrienne Sahuqué, *Les Dogmes Sexuels*, Félix Alcan, Paris, 1932.

87 'so permanent and universal an error', 'a rationalisation of masculine supremacy': from Robert Marjolin's review of *Les Dogmes Sexuels*, *American Journal of Sociology*, vol. 39, no. 4, 1934, p. 537.

87 'as if to a life-belt': Review of *The Rock Pool* by Cyril Connolly and *Almayer's Folly* by Joseph Conrad, in *Collected Essays, Journalism and Letters*, vol. 1, p. 256. The italics are Orwell's.

87 'Misogynistic he was not': Stansky and Abrahams, *The Transformation*, p. 37.

88 'deep internal revulsions' and other quotes in this paragraph: Empson in Gross (ed.), p. 97.

88 'call-boy arrangements': Malcolm Muggeridge recounts Connolly telling him this in Gross (ed.), p. 169.

88 'slipped Connolly a note': Part of this letter, in which the teenage Orwell writes *I'm afraid I'm gone on Eastwood (naughty Eric)*, is reproduced in Bowker, p. 65.

88   '**I think it's disappointed homosexuality**': Bowker, p. 177.

88   '**homoerotic**': Ibid., p. 175. Stansky and Abrahams minimise Mabel's insight and power ('exaggeration never bothered Mabel', p. 133) and write that she 'in an enthusiastic flurry of invention revealed a surprising secret; that Eric had a suppressed homosexual passion for him (Heppenstall), or so she deduced from his having mentioned that he admired Rayner's hair. Whatever the particulars, and it is not unlikely that time has distorted them . . .' (p. 136). In the recordings made by Wadhams, Mabel comes across as a serious, intelligent woman. She knew Orwell very well, and her comment about 'disappointed homosexuality' was not in reference to hair, but to Orwell's violence against Heppenstall, when he bashed him with a shooting stick for coming home drunk. Orwell had come in from a day spent with Eileen, walking.

88   '**was not a true one**', '**seemed somehow wrong**': Topp, p. 145, referencing the Crick Archive. Topp interpolates, in brackets within Jack Common's words, '(this not meant in a sex sense)', though how she would know this is not clear. She speculates that 'Perhaps, as a more conventional couple, the Commons didn't approve of Eileen and Orwell's somewhat open marriage in later years.' But 'not a true' marriage and 'wrong' might be a veiled reference to Orwell's homosexuality. Jack Common, who worked as Richard Rees's assistant at *The Adelphi*, was a writer who chose his words carefully. He described himself as 'a poorly-educated, hard up, working-class dialect-speaker', and Orwell as 'an *enfant terrible* in decay'. Coppard and Crick, p. 140. Darcy Moore tells of another gay friend of Orwell, the 'well-educated, multi-lingual American poet and playwright' Édouard Roditi, who Orwell met through Jack Common. Roditi was also connected to Rees, and *The Adelphi*. Although gay, Moore writes, he was 'not attracted to "outright homosexuals" and most of his relationships were "with bisexual or otherwise normal men" in whose love life he was an exception.' Moore is the only scholar to note Orwell's year-long close relationship with Roditi, writing that, 'Roditi and Blair were constant companions during 1931, roaming London, talking with people on the streets, eating inexpensive Chinese food in the East End before walking to Ebury Street in Pimlico, where Roditi lived. They were habitués of the notorious all-night Café Bleu in Soho. . .' Darcy Moore, 'The True Artist: Poverty, Networking and Literary Artifice', *George Orwell Studies* (2021) vol. 6, no. 1, pp. 7–31. See also darcymoore.net/2021/12/12/the-beat-of-the-tambour/.

89   '**revolted by homosexuality**': Bowker, p. 83, citing Orwell's last literary notebook, in *CW*, vol. 20, p. 206 [3725].

89   '**a man in a gallery**': 'I wondered whether the Jew was getting any real kick out of this new-found power that he was exercising. I concluded that he wasn't really enjoying it, and that he was merely – like a man in a brothel, or a boy smoking his first cigar, or a tourist traipsing round a picture gallery – TELLING himself that he was enjoying it, and behaving as he had planned to behave in the days he was helpless.' 'Revenge is Sour', *Tribune*, 9 November 1945, in *Collected Essays, Journalism and Letters*, vol. 4, pp. 19–22.

90   '**virility**': Crick Archive.

Mistletoe

91   'My first reaction': Fen, *A Russian's England*, p. 417. All quotes in this page are from here.

92   'pawned all the Blair spoons and forks': Anthony Powell, *Infants of the Spring*, Heinemann, 1976, p. 136.

92   'could not be arranged': Fen, *A Russian's England*, p. 417.

A Plague of Initials

97   'kill fascists', 'common decency': *Homage to Catalonia*, Penguin Books, 2000 [1938] (hereafter *Homage*), p. 197. All references to *Homage* are to this edition. The text of 2000 incorporates changes Orwell wanted to make that are not reflected in earlier editions published in his lifetime, primarily that chapters 5 and 11 have been turned into appendices. The full text can also be found at gutenberg.net.au/ebooks02/0201111.txt; the Project Gutenberg text is based on the original editions.

97   'a tough-looking youth', 'in my bad Spanish', 'in utter intimacy': *Homage*, pp. 1–2, 4.

98   'like a cow with a musket': The poet Ruth Pitter's view, Coppard and Crick, p. 69. Bowker notes that Ruth and her friend Kate considered his work 'hilarious', and that Ruth was amused because it was laced with obscene words incorrectly spelled – 'a fault in his Eton education she thought'. Bowker (p. 101) lashes out, calling this 'the unappreciative response to his work of two potters' (Ruth and Kate worked at a pottery company) though Ruth was already a published poet, and later a distinguished one.

98   'The Italian soldier shook my hand': George Orwell, 'Looking Back on the Spanish War', *Collected Essays, Journalism and Letters*, vol. 2, pp. 286–306, at p. 306. While several biographers reproduce parts of this poem, none includes this anti-woman stanza.

99   'no more than a centralized swindling machine': *Homage*, p. 200.

99   'The Spanish POUM': In Catalan, 'Partit Obrer d'Unificació Marxista'. The POUM was an anti-Stalinist communist party.

100 'In Catalonia the elimination of Trotskyites': *Pravda*, 16 December 1936, as cited in Crick, p. 219.

101 'launch a campaign among the masses and in the press': Bowker, p. 213, n. 46, PRO/HW 17/127 Public Record Office, Kew. There are strange echoes, as I write this, of Putin, a successor to Stalin, accusing those he wants to kill in Ukraine of 'fascism'. This is less the repetition of history than the lack of imagination of the tyrant who would rewrite it.

101 'stout Belgian commandante': *Homage*, p. 17.

102 'Alas! I ducked': Ibid., p. 22; 'a comic opera with an occasional death': Ibid., p. 34; 'a disgusting thing': Ibid., p. 32.

103 'It was a very costly shot at a rat': Wadhams, *Remembering Orwell*, p. 79. Orwell, however, did tell Eileen about constructing a shelter in the dugout that fell down, as she later expresssed it, 'not under any kind of bombardment but just from the force of gravity'. Though that story didn't make it into *Homage* either. *CW*, vol. 1, p. 205.

104 'your whole body a most unpleasant sensitiveness': *Homage*, p. 44.

Miracle, Manicure

106 **'Her common-law husband'**: 'L'Anti', meaning 'he who is against the system', was the pseudonym of Eugène Adam (1879–1947), an Esperantist and radical socialist with whom Nellie Limouzin lived for many years, eventually marrying him in her sixties, before he disappeared on a 'world tour' in 1936 never to return to her. L'Anti committed suicide in Mexico in 1947. See Moore, 'Orwell in Paris: Aunt Nellie'.

107 **'have the family crest engraved'**: Powell, *Infants of the Spring*, p. 36.

108 **'I am leaving for Spain'**: Davison (ed.), *A Life in Letters*, pp. 69–70.

Backwater

111 **'By this time my wife was in Barcelona'**: *Homage*, p. 76.

111 **'a volunteer's post'**: Taylor, p. 210.

111 **'her husband's interests'**: Ibid., p. 213.

111–12 **'she decided that she would go out to Spain too'**: Stansky and Abrahams, *The Transformation*, p. 247.

Spies and Lies

116 **'Living is very cheap here'**: Davison (ed.), *A Life in Letters*, p. 72. The 'ps' are pesetas; 500 ps in 1937 is equivalent to about €1000 today.

116 **'running the supply, communications and banking operation'**: Bowker refers to Eileen as 'helping' or 'even spending her own money' as if her work were not work, but acts of personal kindness.

117 **'nice but very vaguish'**: Orr, p. 139. Lois told her story as an old woman, in her 'long southern drawl', the tinkle of ice in a highball glass audible on the tape. Orr, p. 202.

118 **'Everyone liked her', 'not too proud'**: Charles Orr, in Orr, p. 179.

118 **'very much a figure in ILP quarters'**: John Kimche, who'd worked with Orwell in the Westropes' bookshop in Hampstead. This material is used by none of Orwell's biographers. Crick Archive, as cited by Topp, p. 170, n. 26. Kimche spelt it 'Continentale'; it is corrected here.

119 **'a trained communist spy'**: Bowker, p. 220.

119 **'It was my privilege'**: Charles Orr, in Orr, p. 180.

119 **'tall, lean and gangling', 'outreach to the world'**: Orr describes an instance of this. When the celebrated American writer John Dos Passos comes to Barcelona, it falls to Eileen to organise his visit. Orwell is a huge fan, desperate to meet him. 'He could have asked me directly,' Charles remembered, as 'he dropped by our office every day. But, no, Eileen brought me his request. "Could I find some excuse or some way for Eric to meet JDP?"' Charles agrees and Eileen engineers it so that Orwell happens to be in the corridor before Dos Passos goes into his meeting with Republican leader Nin. Orwell gets to chat for a few minutes. He is bowled over by his brush with the great man. But he doesn't do his own thanking either. A few days later, Charles writes, 'Eileen brought me a message: "Eric wants me to thank you from the bottom of his heart."' And then, in a subtle apology for Orwell's social awkwardness, she adds, '"He asked me to thank you for him, because he knows he can't talk."'

120 **'a good man'**: Charles Orr, in Orr, pp. 179–81.

The Go-Between

121   'a big, heavy, ruddy, blond Belgian': Topp, p. 175, n. 41, citing Charles Orr, 'Homage to Orwell, as I Knew Him in Catalonia', unpublished pamphlet, 1984, p. 5.

121   'gross', 'pot-bellied': Orr, p. 195.

122   '90% certain', 'intimate terms': Bowker, p. 219 and n. 68, citing KGB File, David Crook Report, Alba Collection.

122   'nondescript hangers-on with nominal jobs': Rees, *A Theory of My Time*, p. 106.

122   'swell dinners at all the fine places': Lois Orr, in Orr, p. 151; 'elegant, spare, Italian gentleman': Ibid., p. 199.

123   'Tuesday we had the only bombardment': Eileen to her mother, 22 March 1937, in Davison (ed.), *A Life in Letters*, p. 71.

124   'I was allowed to stay': Letter to Leonard Moore, Orwell's agent, 12 April 1937, in *CW*, vol. 11, p. 17.

124   'motherly interest': Bowker, p. 211.

125   'We went to bed at 10 or so': Davison (ed.), *A Life in Letters*, p. 72.

127   'two perfectly innocent British citizens': John McNair, *Spanish Diary*, pamphlet produced by the Greater Manchester ILP branch, n.d., p. 18. Available at independentlabour.org.uk/publications/.

128   'I *thoroughly* enjoyed being at the front': Eileen to her mother, 22 March 1937, in Davison (ed.), *A Life in Letters*, pp. 71–3.

Terror

130   'in a mixed state of exaltation and despair': Rees, *A Theory of My Time*, p. 95.

130–1   'I called on Orwell's wife, Eileen, at the POUM office', 'the risk, to me, of being seen in the street with her', 'I realized afterward': Rees, *Fugitive*, p. 139.

131   'an amorous Kopp': Bowker, p. 214.

131   'the practice of tipping was coming back': *Homage*, p. 99.

132   'major ILP figures': Bowker, p. 216. Bowker writes that it was 'the Blairs' who were the focus of the spying. British Communist spies had reported that Eric Blair 'has little political understanding' and 'is not interested in party politics'. And as he was mostly away in the trenches, it seems reasonable to assume that Eileen, working at the headquarters of the ILP, was the better informed, and therefore more valuable target.

132   'not proud of his role': Bowker, p. 213; '90% certain': Ibid., p. 219, as cited above at page 122.

133   'all the truth': Eileen to her brother, 1 May 1937, in Davison (ed.), *A Life in Letters*, pp. 76–7.

Looking for a Fight, 3 May 1937

135   'get back to the hotel at once': *Homage*, p. 106; 'was likely to be attacked at any moment': Ibid., p. 108.

In the Fight, 3 May 1937

139 **'Measures for Liquidating Trotskyists and Other Double Dealers'**: This is as Orwell gave the pamphlet's title. It is officially known as 'Defects in Party Work and Measures for Liquidating Trotskyite and Other Double-Dealers', from a speech Stalin delivered on 3 March 1937.

141 **'filled to the brim with a most extraordinary collection'**: This is from *Homage*, p. 121. Orwell's account was most probably informed by Eileen who was there in the hotel. The OGPU was the Soviet secret police organisation, precursor to the NKVD and KGB.

143 **'a wedge of goat's-milk cheese'**: *Homage*, p. 113.

144 **'comparable to the din of a battle'**: Ibid., p. 114.

144 **'as though playing skittles'**: The quotes in this section are from *Homage*, pp. 114–16.

146 **'a horrible atmosphere'**: Ibid., p. 135.

148 **'his exploits in the brothels of Paris'**: Crick, p. 223, quoting eyewitness Frank Frankford.

148 **'under his neck there was a puddle of blood'**: Harry Milton, *Fighting Back*, radio program, cited in Topp, p. 180.

149 **'As soon as I knew that the bullet had gone clean through my neck'**: *Homage*, p. 145.

149 **'Please tell Eileen that I love her'**: Bowker, p. 221.

149 **'having helped to carry a wounded man down a day or two earlier'**: *Homage*, p. 146. Orwell doesn't tell this story, perhaps because they had taken the wounded man to a fascist-held village by mistake, and had to turn away. See McNair's account of this, p. 250, also Stansky and Abrahams, *The Transformation*, pp. 249–50.

150 **'She was with him "every minute"'**: Crick, p. 224.

151 **'lifted by Moscow's own man'**: Bowker, p. 221.

152 **'a letter resting on the typewriter ... It's from David Wickes'**: I'm grateful to Masha Karp for sending me a copy of a letter from David Wickes to Eileen of 5 June 1937. In that letter, translated into German by the Comintern, Wickes, who has fled the 'May Days' in Barcelona to the communist HQ at Albacete, opens by saying that he's 'taken aback' that Eileen is on first-name terms with 'the American gent' (possibly Charles Orr) and not with Wickes himself, and that 'the lack of any rejection of my clumsy attempts at closer friendship' with her had left him 'in the dark about what you think of me, indeed if you think of me positively in any way at all. And I wish you would – because I like and admire you so much.' He says he can't report on his activities, but has fulfilled his plans and 'has no illusions of being a tender youth'. Then he complains about the conversation of his companions consisting of about 50 per cent swearing, and signs off 'devotedly' to her. (Translation mine.)

153 **'*incriminating* maps in his possession, he tells her'**: Charles Orr writes, 'The most intriguing of the communist agents was George Tioli, a refugee from fascist Italy.' Tioli was 'caught up in the Stalinist apparatus' but 'was indeed human and could

not accept the brutality required' of him. 'He pretended to be a journalist. He was friendly and helped us in many ways . . . Orwell speculates as to why his wife was not arrested along with the rest of us [Orwell assumes she's left there to lure him into a trap], but he does not question why GT was not arrested. I believe that by June 1937 Tioli had been assigned either to survey Orwell and Eileen or, more likely, just to gather information from the talkative, but non-political, Eileen. In June 1937 following my release after ten days in a communist prison, I met Eileen, together with George Tioli, in the streets of Barcelona. They told me this strange story: In the hotel the two of them happened to live in adjacent rooms. Eileen had permitted George to store a roll of supposedly incriminating maps on her balcony. When George noticed that the police were searching Eileen's room, he reached across from his balcony and took the maps. When the police left her room on their way to search his, he handed the maps back to Eileen's balcony. Were these maps intended to incriminate Eileen and the POUM? Did George, then, try to protect Eileen? Or was this just . . . another play – an episode contrived to cover George's role as an inter-party spy? But George was different from the other communist agents. At times he gave me enigmatic tips which – if I had understood them – would have saved me and others much trouble.' As far as Charles can tell, Tioli disappeared in Spain. Charles suspects he might have been killed by 'his communist masters', 'in order to forestall their defectors or cover their trail'. Charles Orr, in Orr, pp. 181–2.

157 'I was "declared useless"': *Homage*, p. 163.

157 'Orlov instructs the Spanish police to carry it out': Orlov passed on the command to Colonel Ortega, the director-general of security in Barcelona. See Boris Volodarsky, *Stalin's Agent: The Life and Death of Alexander Orlov*, Oxford University Press, 2014, pp. 280–2.

158 'It might be a joke': See, for Lois's account of this conversation, 'The May Days and My Arrest' in Orr, p. 189.

Five Days – Five Nights

161 'there are warrants out for our arrests': McNair, p. 24.

163 'bring us blankets when we too would be in prison': Orr, p. 182.

164 'incriminating documents', 'I tried with the tracing paper': McNair, p. 25.

165 'things that we had lost and could not find ourselves': Orr, p. 184.

165 'because my life story was so short': Ibid., p. 193.

166 'You will never be able to escape from your crimes': Ibid., p. 190.

166 'a classic GPU frame-up': The GPU was the Soviet secret police organisation, precursor to the OGPU, NKVD and KGB.

166 'working overtime': Orr, p. 195.

In Plain Sight

172–3 'Trotskyist documents under the pillow', 'generosity, a species of nobility': *Homage*, pp. 187–8. Italics in original.

173 'It was late when I got back to Barcelona': Ibid., pp. 165–6.

175 'she was being used as a decoy duck': Ibid., p. 172.

176 'The Chief of Police was the danger, of course': Ibid., p. 174.

176 'Had Orwell and Eileen remained in Spain': Taylor, p. 231. Another biographer leaves out Eileen going to the Police Prefecture altogether, and passive-voices away her going to the consulate, all the while implying they did it separately for themselves, 'Each of them had obtained proper travel documents from the British consulate . . .' Shelden, p. 275.

177 'I suppose we shall all be shot', 'a massacre': *Homage*, pp. 181–2.

Seen

180 'my wife slipped out of the hotel successfully': *Homage*, p. 191.

180 'I was reading Wordsworth': McNair, p. 26.

181 'So we slipped through': *Homage*, p. 192; 'the spirit of the Gestapo, but not much of its competence': Ibid., p. 174.

181 'somehow got the visas to save them all': Topp's view is also that Eileen saved his life in Spain, along with McNair's and Cottman's. 'There is no doubt that Eileen was responsible for saving all of their lives.' (p. 288).

182 'Tribunal of Espionage & High Treason': Bowker, p. 227.

Wallington, New Years Day, 1938

188 'You see I have no pen, no ink, no glasses': Davison (ed.), *A Life in Letters*, pp. 94–7.

194 'So much blood': Eileen to Jack Common, 14–15 March 1938, in Davison (ed.), *A Life in Letters*, pp. 103–4.

195 'fearful letters to write to relations': Ibid.

Tongue Kiss

197 'I was to take George': Quotes by Lydia in this section are from Fen, *A Russian's England*, pp. 418–19.

198 'typing to keep them afloat': This included a novel in which, Eileen told a friend, 'The grammar is as original as the plot & the punctuation perhaps unique.' Topp, pp. 218–19.

199 'I don't remember the last few weeks in England': Eileen to Geoffrey Gorer, 4 October 1938, in Davison (ed.), *A Life in Letters*, p. 128.

Morocco

203 'may have been quite good once': Eileen to Ida Blair, in Davison (ed.), *A Life in Letters*, pp. 117–19.

204 'unable to think of any more lies about the disease': This letter is in Davison (ed.), *A Life in Letters*, pp. 146–8. Eileen writes that *(they'd kept him in Preston Hall on a firm and constantly repeated diagnosis of phthisis [TB] for two months after they knew he hadn't got it & I discovered in the end that on the very first X-rays the best opinions were against even a provisional diagnosis of phthisis)* (p. 146). Orwell suffered from lung complaints all his life, and at some point contracted tuberculosis. TB is caused by a bacteria, and is transmitted by coughing, sneezing or spitting. It can be latent or symptomatic, and a massive haemorrhage is one of the more severe

symptoms of active TB. Others include coughing, chest pain, weight loss, weakness, fever and night sweats. Drugs to treat TB came into widespread use only in the late 1950s. Many people still die of it in the developing world, though (unless it is an antibiotic-resistant strain) it is treatable by a six-month course of multiple antibiotics. Eileen appears not to have contracted the disease in her lungs. TB can infect the womb, but it can't be known if this was a cause of her bleeding and pain.

204 'The Arabs favour bright green [shrouds]': Eileen to Geoffrey Gorer, in Davison (ed.), *A Life in Letters*, pp. 128–9.

205 'mutual observations and discussion with the poetic Eileen': Bowker, p. 244.

205 'doubtless dominate them for the rest of their lives': Eileen to Orwell's sister Marjorie, 27 September 1938, in Davison (ed.), *A Life in Letters*, pp. 120–2, at p. 121.

206 'Mahjroub's anxiety was unbearable to her': Eileen to Mary Common, ibid., p. 143.

207 'Georges Kopp proposes to come & stay with us': Eileen wrote 'George' instead of 'Georges' Kopp in this letter. It has been standardised here for clarity.

208 'Marx is being perfectly good': Letter from Marjorie Dakin, 3 October 1938, copy in Orwell Archive, University College London; see Crick, p. 252.

Break

212 'True or imagined? It did not matter': T. R. Fyvel, *George Orwell: A Personal Memoir*, Weidenfeld & Nicolson, 1982, p. 109.

212 'I prompted him to reminisce': Stansky and Abrahams, *The Unknown Orwell*, footnote on p. 190. This footnote extends over two pages. See also Harold Acton, *More Memoirs of an Aesthete*, Hamish Hamilton, 1986 [1970].

212 'This evidence is very hard to handle': Crick, p. 91.

213 'Masculine pride, of which Orwell had his share': Stansky and Abrahams, *The Unknown Orwell*, pp. 190–1.

213 'In the end Eileen had allowed', 'lent an odd gloss': Taylor, p. 279.

214 'So looking forward to seeing you': Fen, *A Russian's England*, pp. 430–1.

216 'needing comforting . . .': Ibid., p. 431. Ellipsis in original.

217–18 'My main memories of [Orwell]': Topp, p. 273.

Mind the Gap

221 'DOUBLETHINK': *Nineteen Eighty-Four*, p. 183.

222 'dirty little scoundrel': 'Benefit of Clergy: Some Notes on Salvador Dalí' [1944], in *Collected Essays, Journalism and Letters*, vol. 3, pp. 185–95. Accessible at orwell.ru/library/reviews/dali/english/e_dali. Dalí writes with self-conscious humour and exaggeration, but Orwell was not amused.

222 'a merely personal attack': 'Charles Dickens' [1940], in *Collected Essays, Journalism and Letters*, vol. 1, pp. 454–504. Orwell is discussing Carl Eric Bechhofer Roberts' novel *This Side Idolatry*, Bobbs-Merrill, 1928.

224 **'somebody who has no real being'**: Virginia Woolf, *A Room of One's Own*, Penguin Books, 2000 [1929], p. 6.

224 **'harassed and distracted with hates and grievances'**: Ibid., p. 60.

Editing, in Real Time

227 **'Dalí grew up in the corrupt world'**: Orwell, 'Benefit of Clergy: Some Notes on Salvador Dalí', *Collected Essays, Journalism and Letters*, vol. 3, pp. 185–95, at p. 194.

Strawberries

230 **'remarkable political simplicity'**: Eileen wrote to Orwell's sister Marjorie in 1939: *Eric, who retains an extraordinary political simplicity in spite of everything, wants to hear what he calls the voice of the people. He thinks this might stop a war, but I'm sure the voice would only say that it didn't want a war but of course would have to fight it if the government declared war.* Davison (ed.), *A Life in Letters*, pp. 120–1.

231 **'that field of light'**: William Wordsworth, *The Prelude*, Book 1 (1805), ll. 608–9.

233 **'fix the wavering balance of her mind'**: Wordsworth, *The Prelude*. 'Meanwhile my hope has been that I might fetch / Invigorating thoughts from former years, / Might fix the wavering balance of my mind . . .' Book 1 (1805), ll. 648–50.

233 **'Ah, that's better'**: Crick, p. 325, n. 54 from Paul Potts, *And Dante Called You Beatrice*, p. 82.

234 **'She had a flat chest, an Eton bob'**: Mabel said that Orwell 'once said that of all the girls he'd known before he met his wife, the one he loved best was a little trollop he picked up in a café in Paris. She was beautiful, and had a figure like a boy, an Eton crop and was in every way desirable.' Coppard and Crick, p. 95.

235 **'too disgusting'**: Orwell told Anne Popham that he'd not undergone an examination for sterility as it was 'so disgusting'; see below p. 359. Orwell also told Kay that he was sterile. 'We did discuss children once or twice. I said did he ever want any – not that I wanted any by him but' – here she laughs – 'just a general conversation you know, and he said, "Well I don't think I can have any" and I said, "Why do you say that?" and he thought a moment and then he said, "Well I've never had any you know," so I felt like – I didn't say it at the time – but I felt like well how do you know? You might have and they'd never told you.' Wadhams, 'The Orwell Tapes', part 1. Bowker refers to rumours Orwell fathered a child in Burma, but these are unsubstantiated (p.xiv). If he did, and if he was later sterile as he thought, this may have been due to contracting a sexually-transmitted disease.

235 **'Her doctor has said that . . . the problem is not with her'**: Lettice remembered Eileen telling her that the problem was not her, as 'I am anatomically perfect'. 'The Orwell Tapes', part 3.

236 **'it might even be good for you'**: Orwell to Richard Rees, in Bowker, p. 249.

236–7 **'not to worry about coughing up blood'**, **'silk top hat'**: Ibid.

237 **'living a hand-to-mouth existence'**, Orwell to Dorothy Plowman, 20 June 1941, in Davison, *A Life in Letters*, p. 192.

237 **'completely unbearable'**: Crick, p. 266, quoting a diary entry from 9 August 1940.

237 **'war is "almost certain"'**: Topp, p. 277, n. 66, from *CW*, vol. 11, p. 399.

239 **'She tells no one but the nurse'**: Gwen told Joyce Pollard; in Topp, p. 290.

Propaganda

240 **'somebody who knew somebody, etc., etc.'**: Orwell to Geoffrey Gorer, 10 January 1940, in Davison (ed.), *A Life in Letters*, p. 174.

241 **'a vast barrage balloon floats in the sky'**: Taylor, p. 275.

241 **'it would be wrong for her to stay in a safe place'**: Fen, 'George Orwell's First Wife', p. 121.

241 **'a new, dramatic experience'**: Fen, *A Russian's England*, p. 449.

241 **'an unconscious *wish* to risk her own life'**: Fen, 'George Orwell's First Wife', p. 121. Emphasis in original.

241–2 **'inconceivable dullness', 'almost as frightened of me as he is of taking any decision on his own'**: Eileen to Norah, in Davison (ed.), *A Life in Letters*, pp. 187–8, at p. 188.

242 **'a masochist of the extreme type in his sexual life'**: Topp, p. 280, citing *CW*, vol. 11, p. 402.

242 **'more likely to betray Britain than defend her'**: Bowker, p. 270; Crick, p. 263.

242 **'flocks of hares, sometimes about 20 together'**: Topp, p. 285, citing *CW*, vol. 11, p. 320.

242–3 **'Jack Common . . . is shocked'**: Meyers, p. 194.

243 **'the most miserable two-room fourth-floor flat'**: Crick, p. 263.

243 **'and a portrait of an ancestor, "Lady Mary"'**: Bowker, p. 265.

243 **'from the point of view of safety in air-raids'**: Fen, 'George Orwell's First Wife', pp. 121–2.

243 **'"unruffled" by their "gypsy lifestyle"'**: Cooper, 'Eileen Blair', p. 19.

243–4 **'half the men in this country would give their balls'**: Empson in Gross (ed.), p. 94.

244 **'he was offered steady work'**: Bowker, pp. 264–5.

244 **'her salary was . . . their main support'**: Taylor, p. 283.

244 **'I had to nip in and do it for him'**: Cooper, 'Eileen Blair'.

244 **'He found occasional work for the Ministry of Information'**: Bowker, p. 269.

245 **'fresh-faced blonde woman'**: All quotes in this paragraph are from Taylor, p. 277.

245 **'Nobody listens to it'**: Topp, pp. 307–8, quoting *CW*, vol. 12, p. 479.

246 **'Eileen paced up and down'**: Fen, 'George Orwell's First Wife', p. 122.

Shock

248 **'making no attempt to take cover', 'repeatedly refused'**: I am particularly indebted to Topp for this description, p. 291.

250 **'professor Saarbuck'**: This is as in the original; his name was spelled Sauerbruch.

Summer, 1940

252 'Eileen's own grip on life': Fen, 'George Orwell's First Wife', p. 122.

252 'Everything is disintegrating': Taylor, p. 273.

252 'highly civilized human beings are flying overhead, trying to kill me':
'The Lion and the Unicorn: Socialism and the English Genius', in *Why I Write*
(Penguin Great Ideas), Penguin Books, 2005 [1946], pp. 11–94.

252–3 'sunk in unmoving silence while we talked', 'Since both Orwell and Eileen were
reticent': Fyvel, *George Orwell: A Personal Memoir,* p. 105. 'Lawrence' is misspelled in
the source.

253 'severely depressed' and other quotes in this paragraph: Margaret Branch in ibid.,
pp. 135–6.

Treat

255 'openly hankering after Brenda': Some biographers omit this episode altogether,
but Bowker sets it out here with a combination of good grace and shock, p. 266.

256 'rather clumsy attempt to establish a *ménage à trois*': For example, Bowker,
p. 266. Bowker creatively also uses this letter Orwell wrote to Brenda in 1940
relating Eileen's 'permission', to retrospectively justify Orwell's sexual advances to
Brenda in 1939: 'He tried to broach the subject of an affair, intimating that he and
Eileen enjoyed an open marriage and neither was at all jealous and possessive of
the other.'

257 'He didn't really like women', 'He was a sadist': Coppard and Crick, p. 68.

Self-Arming

258 'The Nazis have prepared lists of the names': Bowker, p. 269.

258 'shoot all the artists': Taylor, p. 315.

258 'inevitable move towards Fascism': Bowker, p. 268.

258 'represented a greater danger': Warburg told this to Muggeridge; see his account
in Gross (ed.), p. 170. Warburg's affection for Orwell, however, is clear. He described
him as the 'pessimistic genius . . . I came to know and admire, the man whose work
obsessed me, the man I tried to help and cherish, the man I could not succeed in
keeping alive.' Warburg, p. 11.

259 'knocking out one man's teeth': Bowker, p. 268. Bowker doesn't mention that
the man was hospitalised: 'He attempted to master the intricacies of the Spigot
mortar, but, using the wrong ammunition, almost decapitated a fellow soldier.'
Crick puts it in the passive voice, so as to blur what he did: 'The wrong training-
charge was put into a trench mortar . . .' (p. 272). Warburg, who was there, reported
that as the Spigot mortar which had launched the (wrong) bomb recoiled, 'Private
Smith lost virtually all his front teeth top and bottom, while Private Jones was
unconscious for at least 24 hours.' Orwell told Warburg he'd had to appear at a
Court of Inquiry, and the cost (paid for by the authorities) of a new set of dentures

for Private Smith was over £100, 'a sum which appeared to Orwell altogether excessive'. Warburg, p. 38.

259 **'I can put up with bombs on the mantelpiece'**: Bowker, p. 268, n. 57.

259 **'the shadow of the dark horse'**: Taylor, p. 286.

259 **'calling Mabel an 'Egeria''**: Stansky and Abrahams, p. 208, and using *'femme libre'* with regard to Ida; Crick, p. 14.

259 **'How _you_ must have suffered during this war Eileen dear'**: Kopp to Eileen, 8 September 1940, in Orwell Archive, University College London.

Blitz

261 **'her heart beats faster'**: Cooper, 'Eileen Blair', p. 19.

261 **'Eileen no longer cares if she lives or not'**: Fen, *A Russian's England*, p. 346. Also Lettice Cooper in Wadhams, *Remembering Orwell*, p. 130.

261 **'I do not think she ever used an air-raid shelter herself'**: Fen, 'George Orwell's First Wife', p. 122.

262 **'insanities'**: Taylor, p. 288.

263 **'bodies brought up in pails'**: Ibid; **'eleven evacuees'**: Ibid., p. 289.

263 **'It's never an assassin'**, **'very nice apple meringue pie'**: Patricia Donoghue, a journalist and friend of Lydia, tells this story of them arriving at the cottage in Wadhams, 'The Orwell Tapes', part 3, extracted in Wadhams, *Remembering Orwell*, pp. 117–19. 'George immediately picked up his gun, stood behind the door at the ready, tense', then asked [Eileen] to open it. His plan? 'If it was an unwelcome visitor he could be shot forthwith!' Donoghue also noted that 'He made bombs, you know. Probably Molotov cocktails.'

263 **'children playing in a vault full of corpses'**: Taylor, p. 296.

263 **'boiled eels for a cat'**: Crick, p. 295.

263 **'Only the windows falling in'**: Meyers, p. 19, quoting Orwell's War Diary from 20 March 1941, *CW*, vol. 12, p. 452.

265 **'This is to accompany'**: Davison (ed.), *A Life in Letters*, p. 183. The letter is undated, and as usual contains no salutation. Davison suggests it is from 5 December 1940.

266 **'nephrolithiasis'**: Kidney stones.

266 **'Malta fever'**: Brucellosis, a bacterial infection often suffered by goats, which can be transmitted to humans. Symptoms include fever, joint pain and weight loss.

266 **'I couldn't possibly guess what they were testing for'**: Eileen was 'constantly' being tested for TB, according to Lettice, but miraculously was always negative. Coppard and Crick, pp. 164–5.

268 **'He has no idea of the size of rations'**: Topp, p. 364, n. 51, citing Lydia to Crick, 27 November 1974, Crick Archive.

270 **'Please write a letter'**: Davison (ed.), *A Life in Letters*, pp. 187–8.

270 **'Eileen did not expect to live'**: Fen, *A Russian's England*, p. 346.

Dissociating

271 **'entertaining'**, **'fragility of feature'**, **'consumptive charm'**: Anthony Powell, in Bowker, p. 277.

271 **'intensity and urgency'**: Bowker, p. 278.

271 **'at least Orwell thought they had'**: Ibid., p. 266.

272 **'as if to disassociate himself'**: Ibid., p. 278.

272 **'Inez saw him . . . for at least some of that period, for sex:** 'Orwell,' Bowker writes, 'began meeting her regularly in early 1941, taking her to lunch and back to the flat while Eileen was at work' (p. 278). Another biographer omits this altogether, saying only of Inez Holden that they 'became close friends' (Crick, footnote on p. 264).

272 **'never hinted at knowing or even caring'**: Bowker, p. 278.

272 **'making assignations with fans'**: Shortly after the couple's return from Spain Orwell flirted in letters with a fan, Amy Charlesworth, who wrote to him and suggested they meet (Bowker, p. 230). Eileen is apparently 'gleeful' when she finds out the woman is thirty-three and a single mother of two 'who had left her husband because he struck her too often' (Topp, p. 203). These characteristics make the woman unattractive to Orwell. Bowker glosses that from now, the marriage, 'in his mind at least', 'seems to have been declared open and he was at liberty to cast his eyes elsewhere whenever the mood took him'. This is another example of a biographer being keen to give him permission – by imagining Eileen's consent – because that way he's not a betraying husband.

272 **'the luscious, Rubenesque Sonia'**: Bowker, p. 277.

273 **'at least once she told him she would leave him'**: Bowker, p. 316.

Prey

274 **'grabbed up a few things and went out'**: Orwell's War Diary in *CW*, vol. 12, pp. 495–6. See also Topp, p. 310.

274 **'kneeling on the floor by her'**: Wadhams, *Remembering Orwell*, p. 132;

274 **'compassionate, though more so to strangers'**, **'What do you think your own is like?'**: Topp, p. 310, citing Lettice Cooper, letter held in Crick Archive.

274 **'bread-winner'**: Fen, *A Russian's England*, p. 449.

275 **'he decided that Eileen was overworking'**: Bowker, p. 278.

275 **'I have induced her'**: Letter to Dorothy Plowman, 20 June 1941, Davison (ed.), *A Life in Letters*, p. 192. Topp, puts it this way (p. 311–12): '"For more than a year Eileen was working in the Censorship Department, but I have induced her to drop it for a while," Orwell told a friend at that point, somehow underestimating her almost two years at the hated job.' He underestimates her work by shortening its period to almost half, not saying that she was supporting them, and painting him as saving her from it by 'inducing' her to stop – though the real reason she could was that he had found paid employment.

275 **'mixture of whoreshop and a lunatic asylum'**: Bowker, p. 299; Taylor, p. 324.

275 'his voice is too thin and flat for him to read much on air': Crick, p. 284.
No audio recording of Orwell's voice survives.

275 'Eileen must have helped': Desmond Avery, an expert on Orwell's time at the BBC,
'was often puzzled by how academically thorough [Orwell] seemed to be' in his
writings at this time. He noticed 'how much deeper [Orwell's] critical intelligence
and wider his knowledge became after their marriage', and 'felt sure Eileen must
have helped with at least some of them'. Topp, p. 313.

275 'unworldly', 'of a rare moral dignity': Bowker, p. 301.

275 'generally bored with what he was doing': Crick, p. 284.

275 'all seemed young enough': Bowker, p. 283.

275 'a normal part of office life': Crick, p. 287

276 'a dear creature': Bowker, p. 284; 'he refused to attend the wedding': Ibid., p. 283;
'hinted at "a fling"': Ibid., p. 284.

276 'masculine lunch à trois'; 'Nowhere else to go': Crick, p. 289.

277 'persistently linked with this tale': Ibid.

277 'murderous [and] mad': Bowker, p. 284; 'working in filthy hotel kitchens': Ibid.,
p. 285; 'keenly perceptive but put-upon women': Ibid.

Eat

278 'She walked into my room': Cooper, 'Eileen Blair', p. 191.

278 'like *Yes Minister*, but with a more intelligent minister': She was referring to the
1980s hit BBC TV series *Yes Minister*.

279 'the British people, apparently, have never been healthier': BBC 100, 'Under
Siege: The Kitchen Front', BBC website, bbc.com/historyofthebbc/research/
kitchen-front/

279 'we had a sort of continuous conversation going on all the time': Topp, p. 318.
See also Wadhams, *Remembering Orwell*, p. 130.

280 'munitions of war': Topp, p. 318.

280 'She liked meat, eggs, cheese, wine': Coppard and Crick, p. 163.

280 'Eileen as the model for the character Ann in her 1947 novel *Black Bethlehem*':
Lettice wrote, 'I tried to do her portrait in *Black Bethlehem . . .*', Crick Archive.

280 'drifts': Cooper, *Black Bethlehem*, p. 177; 'like a leaf': Ibid., p. 181; 'hardly looks at
hers': Ibid., p. 176; 'When you speak to her': Ibid., p. 154.

281 'immense charm': Coppard and Crick, p. 163.

281 'almost stupid': Crick Archive, Birkbeck Library Archives and Special Collections,
University of London. See also Topp, p. 349.

281–2 'you wanted rather to laugh at him': Wadhams, *Remembering Orwell*, p. 132.

282 '"Why?" George asked': Coppard and Crick, p. 164.

282 'In a sort of way', 'Stevie Smith and Inez Holden both fell in love with [Orwell]',
'an affectionate, amused, somewhat sceptical love of [Orwell]': Crick Archive.

282 'jealousy or rancour': Cooper, in Coppard and Crick, p. 163.

282 'No, no – not *again!*': Crick, p. 295.

282 'all the time': Wadhams, 'The Orwell Tapes', part 3.

283 'I felt her spirit near me': Cooper, *Black Bethlehem*, p. 247; 'people like Ann': Ibid. p. 209.

Fun

284 'a date to invade Britain: 25 May 1942': Taylor, p. 313.

284 'even to want to write about': Review of *The Rock Pool* by Cyril Connolly and *Almayer's Folly* by Joseph Conrad, in *Collected Essays, Journalism and Letters*, vol. 1, p. 255.

284 'What can you expect?': Bowker, p. 276.

285 'squandered his talents', 'shallow, inadequate thinker': *The Listener*, 'Wells, Hitler and the World State', in *Collected Essays, Journalism and Letters* 1970, vol. 2 [originally published in *Horizon*, August 1941], pp. 172, 171.

285 'I've heard what you've been saying': Wadhams, *Remembering Orwell*, p. 135.

285 'in a nonchalant way': Jane Morgan, in Coppard and Crick, p. 87.

285 'dazzling': Topp, p. 328; 'Uncle Eric would appear in full regalia': Ibid., p. 309.

285 'Eileen none too well either': Bowker, p. 296.

285 '"anxious" to core the apples properly': Ruth Pitter in Coppard and Crick, pp. 74–5.

285–6 'It's ludicrous you shouldn't be on good terms with H. G.': Michael Meyer's account, in Wadhams, *Remembering Orwell*, p. 135.

286 'I shall be delighted to come to dinner': Ibid, p. 136.

286–7 'full of amiability', '"Oh dear," said Eileen . . . never did see each other again': Michael Meyer in Gross (ed.), pp. 128–9. Meyer became a noted translator of Ibsen and Strindberg.

287 'Read my early works you shit': Taylor, p. 305. Topp (p. 333) reports that this comes from a story Eileen told Inez.

Friendly Memories

288 'a psychical or even physical inability to answer letters': Bowker, p. 305, citing Orwell's column 'As I Pleased' [sic] of 31 January 1947, in *Collected Essays, Journalism and Letters*, vol. 4, p. 278.

288 'I just didn't have the courage to send them back': Tosco Fyvel in Wadhams, *Remembering Orwell*, p. 149.

288 'sadly eyeing a pile of new books for review': Tosco Fyvel, 'The Years at *Tribune*', in Gross (ed.), p. 112; 'a whole mass of unrejected literary rejects': Ibid., p. 115.

289 'I have friendly memories of my cramped little office': Bowker, p. 305, citing Orwell's column 'As I Pleased' [sic], 31 January 1947. See *Collected Essays, Journalism and Letters*, vol. 4, p. 322.

289 'embarked on yet another affair': Bowker, p. 316.

289 'fiendish row': Shelden, p. 383, citing an interview with Celia Paget Goodman, June 1989.

289 'after a row with [Eileen] in London': Topp, p. 349. None of the biographies of Orwell includes this.

Other Animals

290 'Despite the incredibly strenuous life': Fen, 'George Orwell's First Wife', p. 123.

290 'at once that it was a winner': Cooper, in Coppard and Crick, p. 165.

290 'Eileen suggests it be a novel': Topp, p. 368. Topp relates that Quentin Kopp's mother Doreen told him that Eileen had suggested rewriting the work as an allegory when the issue of Stalin made it difficult for his publisher in the original format.

290 '[S]he would quote bits out of it': Cooper, in Wadhams, *Remembering Orwell*, p. 131.

291 'a new vein of fantasy, humor and tenderness': Rees, *Fugitive*, p. 84.

291 'this writer of rather grey novels', 'There was, after all': Warburg, p. 56. Warburg 'never doubted that it was a masterpiece' (p. 48) and, like most commentators, considered *Animal Farm* to be Orwell's 'greatest work' (p. 56). Orwell thought it was his best work too. 'None of his books except *Animal Farm*,' Crick writes, 'measured up to his great expectations' (note on p. 384).

292 'It has so often been remarked', 'with his wife': Fyvel, *George Orwell: A Personal Memoir*, pp. 137–8.

292 'even helped in the planning of': Orwell to Dorothy Plowman, 19 February 1946, in Davison (ed.), *A Life in Letters*, pp. 289–90. Orwell, though, develops a different origin story. He writes that the idea for the book had come to him 'one day (I was then living in a small village) [when] I saw a little boy, perhaps ten years old, driving a huge cart-horse along a narrow path, whipping it whenever it tried to turn. It struck me that if only such animals became aware of their strength we should have no power over them, and that men exploit animals in much the same way as the rich exploit the proletariat. I proceeded to analyse Marx's theory from the animals' point of view. . .' But 'Marx's theory from the animals' point of view' is not the question to which *Animal Farm* is the answer. (Marx's theory, after all, is *already* from the animals' – the working classes' – point of view.) It's possible that Orwell saw such a scene, but it sounds like too neat a metaphor, like the detail of the condemned man sidestepping the puddle that Orwell admitted inventing in his essay 'A Hanging' (Mabel Fierz's account, in Wadhams, *Remembering Orwell*, p. 45; see also Stansky and Abrahams, *The Unknown Orwell*, p. 269), or the invention of the 'Italian compositor with side-whiskers' to replace the 'trollop' who fleeced him in Paris. It's also possible that, as he first gave this account in the introduction to the 1947 Ukrainian edition of the book, he needed a story of its origins that avoided mentioning Stalin, who controlled Ukraine.

292 **'One biographer deletes the "even"'**: Bowker, p. 308.

292 **'Some people who knew Eileen'**: Wadhams, *Remembering Orwell*, p. 131.

292 **'I could recognize touches of Eileen's humour'**: Fen, 'George Orwell's First Wife', p. 123.

293 **'icily-cold first-floor bedroom'**: Ibid.

Bud

297 **'love and empathy'**: Cooper, 'Eileen Blair', p. 19.

297 **'I am anatomically perfect'**: Wadhams, 'The Orwell Tapes', part 3.

297 **'Orwell had blanched'**: Shelden, p. 263.

297 **'collect the three-week-old baby from the hospital alone'**: I have Topp to thank for these details: 'Eileen arrived at the hospital with a little suitcase containing a nightgown and shawl to dress the baby in, after which she somehow got him back to Mortimer Crescent, apparently without Orwell's assistance' (p. 377).

297 **'took possession of'**: Bowker, p. 316.

297–8 **'The paperwork covering his adoption'**: Taylor, p. 338.

299 **'perambulator', 'Eton'**: Cooper, 'Eileen Blair', p. 19.

299 **'cigarette'**: Bowker, p. 318.

300 **'covers him with her body'**: Lettice Cooper, Crick Archive, in Topp, p. 379, n. 25. Also Wadhams, 'The Orwell Tapes', part 3.

300 **'She had bathed the baby'**: Fen, 'George Orwell's First Wife', p. 124.

300 **'Eileen stops saying'**: Topp, p. 386.

Fight or Flight or F‑‑‑

301 **'a woman in a park'**: This is euphemised by Bowker, as a 'penchant for pastoral seductions', p. 316.

302 **'"blitzed" condition'** Orwell to T. S. Eliot, 28 June 1944, in Crick, p. 314. Eliot seemed not to understand *Animal Farm*'s commentary on the corrupting nature of power, telling Orwell that what was needed was 'more public-spirited pigs'. T. S. Eliot to Orwell, 13 July 1944, in Crick, p. 315.

302 **'leprous', 'in drifts', 'dark and dingy'**: Bowker, p. 317.

302 **'the doors must have been sawn off deliberately to create draughts'**: Mary Fyvel in Wadhams, 'The Orwell Tapes', part 3.

302–3 **'We have a flat in Canonbury Square'**: Davison (ed.), *A Life in Letters*, p. 239.

303–4 **'in the back garden trying to bring the pram', 'at last agreed to do something about her health', 'where she could have complete rest'**: Fen, 'George Orwell's First Wife', p. 125.

304 **'I've been dressed every day'**: Eileen to Orwell, 21 March 1945, in Davison (ed.), *A Life in Letters*, pp. 247–54, at p. 254. Eileen seems to have spent more time with Laurence, Richard and Mary than the customary hour of the 'social'.

305 **'Perhaps, as he wrote in a column at the time'**: Orwell opened his 'As I Please' column that month with: 'Every time I wash up a batch of crockery I marvel at the unimaginativeness of human beings who can travel under the sea and fly through the clouds, and yet have not known how to eliminate this sordid time-wasting drudgery from their daily lives.' He says it's 'of its nature an uncreative and life-wasting job', which must be outsourced and done like laundry unless one is 'to assume, as our ancestors did, that life on earth is inherently miserable, and that it is entirely natural for the average woman to be a broken-down drudge at the age of thirty . . .', *Tribune*, 9 February 1945, in *Collected Essays, Journalism and Letters*, vol. 3, p. 375.

305 **'That autumn, six months after'**: Bowker, pp. 320 and 326. See also Crick: 'The baby had been born on 14 May and they named him Richard Horatio Blair when they adopted him in June' (p. 319).

305 **'she had bought a yellow felt hat'; 'She came round to the Ministry with Richard'**: Cooper, 'Eileen Blair', p. 19.

306 **'She seemed much better'**: Fen, 'George Orwell's First Wife', p. 125.

306 **'George didn't tell her he was disappearing either'**: Topp, p. 395, citing Inez Holden's private diary, 30 March 1945, Crick Archive.

Money

308 **'Dearest your letter came this morning'** and quotes from this letter on pages 309–18: Davison (ed.), *A Life in Letters*, pp. 247–54.

312 **'She seems to have frozen with things she is not saying'**: Meyers writes that 'Gwen O'Shaughnessy had a premonition that Eileen would not make it and asked her pharmacist to let her know immediately when the call came through. It did in the middle of a crowded surgery' (p. 237).

314 **'Ivor Brown'**: Editor of *The Observer*.

316 **'It is cancer, but it's operable'**: 'Eileen, and several of her friends, suspected it was cancer.' Meyers, p. 235.

317 **'Mary and Laurence'**: 'Mary' is Gwen's adopted daughter, now known as Catherine.

318 **'This is the most terrifying letter'**: Though some biographers do not find it so. Shelden, for instance, glosses that Eileen 'Was (rather perversely) more worried about the "outrageous" expense of surgery than about her own health and survival . . .' and that she had a '"hysterical" desire to please him'. Meyers, p. 235.

319–20 **'23 March 1945 or thereabouts . . . Emily'**: Davidson (ed.), *A Life in Letters*, pp. 256–8. Eileen used the name Emily at the Ministry of Food, possibly adopted from one of the radio sketch characters she wrote and perhaps voiced: 'Emily Buggins'.

321 **'she played the whole thing down'**: Bowker, p. 326.

Amusing Himself

322 'Have a drink': Crick, p. 325, n. 54 from Paul Potts, *And Dante Called You Beatrice*, p. 82.

323 'he was quite safe': Bowker, p. 325, n. 9. Ernest Hemingway to Harvey Breit, 16 April–1 May 1952, University of Tulsa Special Collections.

323–6 'I'm trying to get forward with my correspondence': This letter, though undated, is from 25 March 1945. *CW*, vol. 17, pp. 107–9.

Premonition

332 'I never understood', 'Most unlike Gwen, wasn't it?': Orwell Society, 'George Talks' Sylvia Topp 21 March 2021', YouTube.

Telegram

336 'Later, the friend is shocked': A. J. Ayer, interview with Stephen Wadhams, Canadian Broadcasting Corporation (1983), in Bowker, p. 327.

336 'The bell rang and George Orwell was outside': Inez Holden diary, 5 April 1945, in Bowker, pp. 327–8.

338 '[after] she had had the operation': Inez Holden, quoted in Topp, p. 402, n. 116; Inez Holden diary, Crick Archive.

338 'Yes, she was a good old stick': Spender quoted in Wadhams, *Remembering Orwell*, p. 145.

338 'hawking his words like stolen meat': Jason Crimp, 'A Man of Much Voice and No Song', *Orwell Society Journal*, no. 14, Spring 2019, pp. 15–18, at p. 15.

338 'he regretted it immensely': Potts in Wadhams, *Remembering Orwell*, p. 145.

338–9 'If I had known about the serious operation': Topp, p. 402, n. 118 citing Lettice Cooper, Crick Archive.

339 'He couldn't even look after himself': Wadhams, 'The Orwell Tapes', part 3.

339 'She had watched over his health': Fen, 'George Orwell's First Wife', p. 125.

339–40 'I was always very sorry that Eileen married George': Wadhams, 'The Orwell Tapes', part 2.

340 'He takes Richard back to London': It is such a strange thing to do that one biographer makes sense of it by writing that Eileen had wanted Georges and Doreen Kopp to bring up Richard, though there is no evidence for this. Bowker, p. 329.

341 'has upset me so that I cannot settle to anything': Orwell to Dwight Macdonald, in Shelden, p. 384, n. 19.

341 'things were getting better': Shelden, p. 382.

341 'The only consolation': Orwell to Lydia, 1 April 1945, in Davison (ed.), *A Life in Letters*, p. 261. Eileen knew that it was *quite a big job*, as she wrote to Orwell's agent, Leonard Moore, three days before her death; Eileen to Moore, 22 March 1945,

in *CW*, vol. 17, p. 104 [2639]. Fyvel, for instance, remained under the impression that Eileen 'had died under a minor operation': Gross (ed.), p. 114.

342 **'Eileen is dead'**: Orwell to Powell, 13 April 1945, in *Collected Essays, Journalism and Letters*, vol. 3, p. 408.

343 **'Totalitarianism demands'**: Orwell, 'The Prevention of Literature', *Polemic*, January 1946.

343 **'about two ounces of ether'**: I am grateful to Sylvia Topp for this account of the inquest, at pp. 403–4.

Position Vacant: Bluebeard

346 **'hideous haircut', 'liked him immediately'**: Wadhams, *Remembering Orwell*, p. 157; '[H]e looked so lonely': Ibid., p. 156; 'we can live on fish and chips': Ibid., p. 157. Susan wasn't keen on this, so she bought a cookbook and taught herself to cook.

346 **'You will let him play with his thingummy, won't you?'**: Coppard and Crick, p. 217.

346 **'plush restaurant in Baker Street with gilded marble pillars'**: Ibid., p. 218. No biographer uses this anecdote.

346 **'£7 per week'**: Taylor p. 349. Susan considered this quite generous.

347 **'a kind of waltz'**: Susan Watson in Taylor, p. 360.

347 **'ammunition for the enemy's Luger'**: Shelden puts a more paranoid cast on Orwell making ammunition, writing that he was 'presumably practising his skills for the day when bullets would be scarce or illegal' (p. 387).

347 **'I have a *dear* little housekeeper'**: Taylor, p. 360. Taylor glosses that Orwell had left it 'absent-mindedly' in his study, but Susan's own account is that it was on the table they used to eat on, and she understood it as his way of sending a message to her without speaking. Wadhams, *Remembering Orwell*, p. 158.

347 **'Maybe I was unobservant'**: Wadhams, *Remembering Orwell*, p. 157.

348 **'he was heard to call several women "Eileen"'**: Orwell said this to Paul Potts, who told Wadhams, ibid., p. 145.

348 **'sadistic'**: Crick Archive.

349 **'Unfortunately'**: 'Revenge Is Sour,' *Tribune*, November 1945.

Love, Work

350 **'There is no more sombre enemy of good art'**: Cyril Connolly, *Enemies of Promise*, University of Chicago Press, 2008 [1938], pp. 115–16.

350 **'Orwell finally has money now'**: *Animal Farm* was written between November 1943 and February 1944, and published in the UK in August 1945. The first print run of 4500 sold out in six weeks, and further print runs followed, as well as sales of translation rights. The first significant money came to Orwell upon the American publication in August 1946. During his life his earnings from the book came to about £12,000 (equivalent to almost £600,000 at the time of writing).

351 'idled elsewhere': Taylor, p. 364.

351 'smart and hard drinking, and amusing and dangerous': Michael Meyer, in Wadhams, *Remembering Orwell*, p. 133.

351 'cheer him up': At this point two men want to take credit for 'sending Sonia': Michael Sayers and Arthur Koestler. When Orwell's former flatmate Sayers (from the all-male flat in Kentish Town) meets him for a long lunch he finds Orwell 'very ill and deeply depressed' and speaking 'touchingly about the death of Eileen'. When Sayers meets Sonia Brownell at a *Horizon* party he relates this, and suggests she go along and, in the biographer's words, 'try to cheer him up'. Sonia had slept with Koestler previously (and apparently had to have an abortion as a result). Bowker relates a sexual slur of Koestler's against her, at the same time as he implies Koestler is suggesting she sleep with Orwell. Bowker, p. 340. See also Taylor, p. 364.

351 'foreign stuff in the food': Taylor, p. 364.

352 'It was not much': Bowker, p. 340. Bowker then immediately throws doubt on whether they had sex or not: 'Whether he pounced or simply propositioned her is not known.' But two pages later he addresses the reader assuming that they did: 'Seemingly, Sonia's readiness to sleep with him . . .' (p. 342). This is another instance of separating cause and effect, or events, in the biographer's narrative, so as not to have to link them in a way that attributes responsibility.

352 'started making advances': Taylor, p. 365.

352 'there was not any pleasure in it for me': Shelden, p. 409.

353 'the smell of cabbage': Bowker, p. 341.

353 'tall, slightly shaggy figure', 'upright brushlike hair', 'George didn't have the sort of obvious sex appeal': Wadhams, *Remembering Orwell*, p. 163.

353 'pep him up a bit': Taylor, p. 362.

353 'He makes love Burma-Sergeant fashion': Arthur Koestler – Ian Angus interview, 30 April 1965 in Bowker, p. 82.

353 'He would like her to marry him': Taylor, p. 362.

353 'He wanted someone to look after Richard': Wadhams, *Remembering Orwell*, p. 163.

354 'He tells Celia he has "bronchiectasis"' and other quotes in this paragraph: Bowker, p. 342.

354 'He . . . asked me again whether I would consider marrying him': Bowker, p. 343, n. 72; Wadhams, *Remembering Orwell*, p. 174.

354–5 'I used to see him going down the path with his little boy', 'You're very attractive . . . for me?': Wadhams, *Remembering Orwell*, p. 167. The rest is from Robert McCrum, 'HG Wells, Keynes, Orwell . . . My Years at the Heart of the Bloomsbury Set', *The Guardian*, 12 June 2016.

357 'got the ice from the ice-chest': Wadhams, p. 161; 'He was very private and very concealing': Ibid; 'After that haemorrhage': Ibid., p. 102.

358 'I wonder if you were angry or surprised': Orwell to Anne Popham, 15 March 1946, in Davison (ed.), *A Life in Letters*, p. 293. Bowker reverses the embarrassment of this scene, writing, 'Having clearly embarrassed her, he wrote to smooth things over. In his somewhat insensitive fashion, he seems to have been taken aback at being rebuffed . . .' (p. 346)

358 'You are very beautiful', 'I do so want someone': Orwell to Anne Popham, 18 April 1946, in Davison (ed.), *A Life in Letters*, p. 307. Anne can be heard reading this letter in Wadhams, 'The Orwell Tapes', part 3.

360 'I thought over your letter a lot': Orwell to Anne Popham, 7 August 1946, in Davison (ed.), *A Life in Letters*, p. 321.

361 'wife catching tactics', 'she thought it a bit of a joke': Bowker, p. 346.

361 'This relentless pursuit': Ibid. George Gissing (1857–1903) was an English novelist Orwell admired. This quote comes from Orwell's essay 'George Gissing', in [1948], *Collected Essays, Journalism and Letters*, vol. 4, p. 488. Orwell writes:

> Doubtless Gissing is right in implying all through his books that intelligent women are very rare animals, and if one wants to marry a woman who is intelligent *and* pretty, then the choice is still further restricted, according to a well-known arithmetical rule. It is like being allowed to choose only among albinos, and left-handed albinos at that. But what comes out in Gissing's treatment of his odious heroine, and of certain others among his women, is that at that date the idea of delicacy, refinement, even intelligence, in the case of a woman, was hardly separable from the idea of superior social status and expensive physical surroundings. The sort of woman whom a writer would want to marry was also the sort of woman who would shrink from living in an attic. When Gissing wrote *New Grub Street* that was probably true, and it could, I think, be justly claimed that it is not true today.

361 'unbearable': Bowker, p. 342, has this as Orwell to Dorothy Plowman, 18 February 1946. Davison has this letter dated 19 February 1946, in which Orwell writes that he must go to the cottage some time 'to sort out the furniture and books, but I have been putting it off because last time I was there it was with Eileen and it upsets me to go there.' Davison (ed.) *A Life in Letters*, p. 290. Orwell was seen burning letters at Wallington. It's impossible to know exactly which they were – from Eileen? Or to her, from Norah, or Kopp? Eileen didn't keep many letters anyway, but the sight of this, coming on his first visit after her death, disturbed Lydia.

363 'a few lines from a lecture Virginia Woolf had given': 'For surely it is time that the effect of discouragement upon the mind of the artist should be measured, as I have seen a dairy company measure the effect of ordinary milk and Grade A milk upon the body of the rat. They set two rats in cages side by side, and of the two one was furtive, timid and small, and the other was glossy, bold and big.' Virginia Woolf, *A Room of One's Own*, Penguin Books, 2000 [1929], p. 55.

Still Life, with Knife

365 'quiet but not asleep', 'assiduously studying a picture', 'enormous clasp knife', 'Oh, I gave it him': Powell, *Infants of the Spring*, p. 140.

365–6 'less rather than more odd', 'decency and kindliness': Taylor, p. 366.

Island, Life

367 'To work is to live without dying': Rainer Maria Rilke, *Letters of Rainer Maria Rilke, 1892–1910*, (trans. Jane B. Greene and M. D. Herter Norton), W. W. Norton, 1969, p. 77.

367 'He once invited Sonia and sent instructions': Orwell to Sonia, 12 April 1947, in Davison (ed.), *A Life in Letters*, p. 351.

367 'a suitcase, a kettle, a saucepan, and a typewriter': Bowker, p. 353. For Mrs Fletcher's account as quoted in these paragraphs see Wadhams, 'The Orwell Tapes', part 3 and Wadhams, *Remembering Orwell*, pp. 170–4.

370 'He'd be sitting on the roadside': Wadhams, *Remembering Orwell*, p. 173.

371 'very sour': Ibid., p. 160; 'He might have told me she was there': Ibid., p. 176.

371 'self-centred acerbic sot': Crimp, p. 15.

371 'She scolds her for not slapping', 'She berates her for calling her brother "George"': Coppard and Crick, p. 223.

371 'Call yourself a nurse': Wadhams, *Remembering Orwell*, p. 177.

371 'She refers to him as someone she needs to tame': Avril wrote to her brother-in-law, Humphrey Dakin, 'Paul Potts takes all my shafts of scintillating wit quite seriously & suffers from fits of temperament, but I think I am welding him into a more human shape.' Avril Blair to Humphrey Dakin, 1 July 1946, in Davison, (ed.) *A Life in Letters*, p. 315.

371 'moonlit flit': Taylor, p. 375.

372 'miserable, hostile old bugger', 'a very dismal woman': Wadhams, *Remembering Orwell*, p. 180; 'with a lot of space between the sentences': Ibid. pp. 179–80.

372 'He takes to leaving his Luger loaded': Bowker, p. 356.

372 'pretty depressing stuff', 'dismal sexual episodes', 'very "Burma Police"': Wadhams, *Remembering Orwell*, p. 180.

373 'degutted it, filleted it': Bill Dunn, ibid., p. 184.

374 'It was as though they were intentionally stepping nearer to their graves': *Nineteen Eighty-Four*, p. 115.

375 'he feeds their bedstead into the fire': Shelden, p. 418.

375 'You can either work it out', 'pretty unpleasant tests on people', 'I don't think I'll stay to lunch': Susan Watson, Crick Archive at Birkbeck Library Archives and Special Collections, University of London, GB1832 CRK6/1/52.

Oars

376 'LIFE IS BAD BUT DEATH IS WORSE': Orwell Archive, University College London Folio 15. Capital letters in original.

376 **'You've done first aid, haven't you?'**: Rees, *Fugitive*, p. 144.

377 **'Orwell "looked hellish"', 'Very dangerous, Corryvreckan'**: Wadhams, *Remembering Orwell*, p. 189.

377–8 **'[t]here was a cracking noise', 'time to be talking about seals'**: Ibid., pp. 190–1.

378 **'I can't help you, Hen'**: The biographer here uses the passive voice to obscure that it is Henry, not Orwell, who must row. 'However, taking to the oars produced no visible effect,' Taylor writes (p. 387). And then later, 'Oar power brought them to a rocky outcrop a mile from the Jura coast.' This is a rare example in the biographies of the passive voice being used to obscure the actions of a man (rather than a woman), in order not to diminish the main character.

378 **'extraordinary birds, puffins', 'he thought we'd had it'**: Wadhams, *Remembering Orwell*, p. 192.

378–9 **'his coffin to be put on his boat and set alight'**: In Jane Carswell's recordings, *Jura Lives*, which are part of the Jura Development Trust Project funded by Argyll and the Islands Leader. More information at isleofjura.scot/jura-lives-project/ and discovery.nationalarchives.gov.uk/details/a/A14084701.

379 **'seriously ill'**: Taylor, p. 389.

379 **'he *knows*'**: Wadhams, *Remembering Orwell*, p. 195.

380 **'loneliness of the writer'**: See Crick, Appendix A, p. 408.

381 **'an unbelievably bad MS'**: Orwell, letter to Warburg, 22 October 1948, in Warburg, p. 102.

381 **'Avril decides to stop salting the food'**: Crick, p. 356.

382 **'grisly job'**: Orwell, letter to David Astor from Barnhill, 19 November 1948, in Davison (ed.), *A Life in Letters*, p. 422.

382 **'We just sat there together, talking'**: Wadhams, *Remembering Orwell*, p. 202.

Pluck It

383–4 **'I remember him coming down to the hotel'** and other quotes in this section: Jane Carswell interview in *Jura Lives*. Nancy MacLean was born in 1927, Flora McDonald in 1931.

Cotswolds Sanatorium, Cranham, 1949

385 **'I suppose everyone will be horrified'**: Warburg, p. 119. **'among the most terrifying'**: Ibid., p. 103; **'I pray I may be spared'**: Ibid., p. 106. Stansky and Abrahams think Eileen would have ameliorated the 'vehement bitterness' of *Nineteen Eighty-Four*. *The Transformation*, p. 184. When Brenda visited she recognised there was 'this sadistic side to him, even in the little things … he told me he wasn't supposed to have face contact with any visitors, but then said now kiss me, and I said no, I'm not going to, but he tried to make me drink out of the same glass as him, but I refused.' Crick Archive.

385 **'Sonia is back from France, reeling'**: Sonia's lover Maurice Merleau-Ponty had said to her, 'I love you, I think,' a statement that gives perhaps some indication of both philosophical and romantic stumbling blocks in the relationship; Shelden, p. 348.

385 **'her skin glows like a girl in a Renoir painting'**: Diana Witherby in Wadhams, *Remembering Orwell*, p. 212.

386 **'You'll have to learn to make dumplings.'**: Taylor, p. 413. Also see Hilary Spurling, *The Girl from the Fiction Department: A Portrait of Sonia Orwell*, Hamish Hamilton, 2002, p. 96.

386 **'"When *Horizon* folds up, I'll marry George."'**: Sonia to Diana Witherby, in Wadhams, *Remembering Orwell*, p. 212.

386–7 *'you abandoned me to Burma all hope denied'*, *'Ever since I got your letter I can't stop remembering'*: Orwell to Jacintha Buddicom, 15 February 1949, in Davison (ed.), *A Life in Letters*, pp. 444–5.

387 **'Are you fond of children?'**: Wadhams, *Remembering Orwell*, p. 205;

387 **'I never did seem to treat Eric perhaps as I might have'**: Wadhams, 'The Orwell Tapes', part 1.

387 **'that particular soft, purring cough'**: Muggeridge, 'A Knight of the Woeful Countenance', in Gross (ed.), p. 173.

388 **'*Never* do that to me'**: Spurling, pp. 149–50. Sonia took him at his word and prevented any biographies being written for many years, as well as editing and promoting his works with great skill and care, including by working with the Information Research Department (a propaganda section of the British Foreign Office) to have *Animal Farm* translated into many languages, and with the CIA for a film of it (which she ultimately considered a travesty and refused to have shown in schools). With Ian Angus she edited the magisterial *Collected Essays, Journalism and Letters of George Orwell*, published by Penguin Books in 1968. Sonia looked after the estate in Richard's interests, but was swindled by an accountant and died in poverty, after helping many other writers.

Metal

389 **'tiny room, like a small cubicle'**: Wadhams, *Remembering Orwell*, p. 10; **'He was always talking of the things he was going to do'**: Ibid., pp. 209–10.

389 **'die comfortably'**: Dr James Nicholson, in Wadhams, 'The Orwell Tapes', Part 3.

390 **'sex dreams and death dreams'**: Last literary notebook, 1949, University College London Folios 5 and 6.

390 **'I am much encouraged'**: Orwell to David Astor, 5 September 1949; Crick, pp. 399–400.

390 **'it was Sonia who bought it'**: Crick, p. 403.

391 **'I look just like a skeleton'**: Wadhams, *Remembering Orwell*, p. 215.

391 **'that filthy Chinese stuff'**: Crick, p. 404.

391 'Either that or they don't want a corpse on their hands': Taylor, p. 418.

391 'There was a window in the door': Wadhams, *Remembering Orwell*, p. 216.

392 'His bed is unmade, the sheets soaked with blood': Bowker, p. 414.

392 'I often wonder who got the tea': Wadhams, *Remembering Orwell*, p. 216. For Anthony Powell, it was the crimson corduroy jacket he thought of, writing, 'I have often wondered whether he was buried in that coat.' Coppard and Crick, p. 247.

Back to Life

395 'Material on Aunt Nellie': Nellie had trouble obtaining the pension to which she felt entitled, and suffered a nervous breakdown in the months after Orwell died. She was admitted to the psychiatric hospital at Springfield in the summer of 1950, where she 'attempted suicide by opening the veins in her wrists', and died on June 22 from a brain haemorrhage. See Darcy Moore, 'Orwell's Aunt Nellie,' *George Orwell Studies*, vol. 4, No. 2 (2020), pp. 30–44, at p. 42.

Norah

398 'superlatively clever': Eileen to Norah, New Year's Day, 1938; Davison (ed.), *A Life in Letters*, p. 97.

399 'political terror': Rees, *Fugitive*, p. 139.

399 'exaggerated sense of honor', 'more disturbing backwash than the sluggish progress of the average man': Rees, *Fugitive*, p. 146.

Image Credits

Images that appear in this book are reproduced with the kind permission of the associated copyright holders. The publisher welcomes hearing from anyone not correctly acknowledged.

ix Eileen O'Shaughnessy's notebook from Oxford, c. 1924; Orwell Archive, and the estate of the late Sonia Brownell Orwell.

19 Hat; © Noun Project.

21 Cerberus; © Noun Project.

23 Norah Symes Myles; © Margaret Durant.

26 Laurence and Gwen's home at Greenwich; © Quentin Kopp.

29 Lydia Jackson; Special Collections, Leeds University Library, Leeds Russian Archive LRA 1394/11988.

38 Richard Rees; Orwell Archive.

50 Eileen's notebook from Oxford, c. 1924; Orwell Archive, and the estate of the late Sonia Brownell Orwell.

72 Wedding certificate, June 1936; the publishers acknowledge Crown copyright of the layout of this form and understands the Crown does not assert any rights of ownership of the contents of the forms.

77 Office whiteboard © Anna Funder.

89 Orwell in the churchyard at Wallington, possibly on his wedding day; Orwell Archive.

100 Lenin Barracks, Barcelona, 1936; World History Archive / Alamy Stock Photo.

103 Georges Kopp, Catalonia, 1937; Orwell Archive.

104 Sierra d'Alcubierre. Reconstructed trenches at Orwell's first posting, looking across to the fascist position outside Huesca; © Quentin Kopp.

106 Goat; © Noun Project.

113 Memorial to those shot in Huesca, between 1936 and 1945; © Anna Funder.

117 Lois Orr, in Barcelona; courtesy of Elizabeth Cusick.

124 The British 'Tom Mann' Centuria; Australian National University Archives, N171.

125   Eileen at the battlefront; Orwell Archive.

133   David Crook, Spain, 1937; David Crook © 1990; Crook family © 2004.

137   Café Moka, Barcelona, 1930s; Spain, Ministry of Culture and Sports, Documentary Centre of Historical Memory, Centelles Archive, photo.2911.

143   Inside the Café Moka, May 1937; Unknown author. National Archive of Catalonia. Generalitat of Catalonia (Second Republic). ANC1-1-N-3996, May 3rd and May 7th 1937.

151   Eileen's telegram to the Blairs; Orwell Archive, and the estate of the late Sonia Brownell Orwell.

155   'Tear off the mask!' Communist propaganda poster, Barcelona, 1937; originally published by the Spanish communist party POUM, found at the Modern Records Centre, Warwick University.

193   Marx; Catherine Moncure.

209   Eileen in Morocco; Orwell Archive.

232   The Wallington cottage from the end of the garden; Catherine Moncure.

238   Laurence at Greenwich; Orwell Archive.

240   Senate House; Paul Riddle-VIEW / Alamy Stock Photo.

250   Laurence, photographing Gwen holding baby Laurence; Orwell Archive.

262   Contrails in the sky over London, 1940; PA Images / Alamy Stock Photo.

264   Barrage balloons over London; Niday Picture Library / Alamy Stock Photo.

279   Lettice Cooper; Persephone Books.

300   Eileen and Richard, 1944; Orwell Archive.

329   Arabis; Frank Hecker / Alamy Stock Photo.

330-1   Eileen's final letter to Orwell; Orwell Archive, and the estate of the late Sonia Brownell Orwell.

345   German Luger pistol; Carl Miller / Alamy Stock Photo.

352   Sonia Brownell, at the *Horizon* office on her last day, October 1949; Orwell Archive.

369   Barnhill, with the azalea bush in flower, 2017; © Anna Funder.

374   Eileen, 1941; Orwell Archive.

379   Ardlussa House; © Andrew & Claire Fletcher.

384   Jura, view to the Paps; © Anna Funder

Bibliography

Works by George Orwell referenced in *Wifedom*

Animal Farm, Penguin Books, Harmondsworth, 1980 [originally published in 1945].

Burmese Days, Oxford University Press, Oxford, 2021 [1934].

The Collected Essays, Journalism and Letters of George Orwell, vols 1–4, Sonia Orwell & Ian Angus (eds), Penguin Books, Harmondsworth, 1970.

The Complete Works of George Orwell, Peter Davison (ed.), Secker & Warburg, London, 1998.

Down and Out in Paris and London [1933], in *The Penguin Complete Longer Non-Fiction of George Orwell*, Penguin Books, Harmondsworth, 1983, pp. 7–153.

Essays, Penguin Modern Classics, Penguin Books, London, 2000.

Homage to Catalonia, Penguin Books, London, 2000 [1938].

Nineteen Eighty-Four, Penguin Books, Harmondsworth, 1984 [1949].

Politics and the English Language and Other Essays, Benediction Classics, Oxford, 2010.

The Road to Wigan Pier [1937], in *The Penguin Complete Longer Non-Fiction of George Orwell*, Penguin Books, Harmondsworth, 1983, pp. 155–299.

Books

Acton, Harold, *More Memoirs of an Aesthete*, Hamish Hamilton, London, 1986 [1970].

Baldwin, James, 'My Dungeon Shook: Letter to My Nephew on the One Hundredth Anniversary of the Emancipation' [1963], in Toni Morrison (ed.), *James Baldwin: Collected Essays*, Library of America edition, New York, 1998.

Bowker, Gordon, *George Orwell*, Abacus, London, 2004.

Buddicom Jacintha, *Eric & Us*, Finlay Publisher, Chichester, 2006 [1974].

Connolly, Cyril, *Enemies of Promise*, University of Chicago Press, Chicago, 2008 [1938].

Cooper, Lettice, *Black Bethlehem*, Cedric Chivers Ltd, London, 1971 [1947].

Coppard, Audrey & Bernard Crick (eds), *Orwell Remembered*, Ariel Books, London, 1984.

Crick, Bernard, *George Orwell: A Life*, Secker & Warburg, London, 1980.

Davison, Peter (ed.), *George Orwell: A Life in Letters*, Liveright Publishing Corporation, New York, 2013 [2010].

—— *The Lost Orwell*, Timewell Press, London, 2006.

De Beauvoir, Simone, *The Second Sex*, Penguin Random House, New York, 2011 [1949].

Engels, Friedrich, *The Origin of the Family, Private Property and the State*, Penguin Books, London, 2010 [1884].

Fen, Elisaveta, *A Russian's England: Reminiscences of Years 1926–1940*, Paul Gordon Books, Warwick, UK, 1976.

Fyvel, T. R., *George Orwell: A Personal Memoir*, Weidenfeld & Nicolson, London, 1982.

Gross, Miriam (ed.), *The World of George Orwell*, Weidenfeld & Nicolson, London, 1971.

Lerner, Gerda, *The Creation of Patriarchy*, Oxford University Press, New York, 1987.

Meyers, Jeffrey, *Orwell: Wintry Conscience of a Generation*, W. W. Norton, New York, 2000.

Orr, Lois, *Letters from Barcelona: An American Woman in Revolution and Civil War*, Gerd-Rainer Horn (ed.), Palgrave Macmillan, London, 2009.

Powell, Anthony, *Infants of the Spring*, Heinemann, London, 1976.

Rees, Richard, *George Orwell: Fugitive from the Camp of Victory*, Southern Illinois University Press, Carbondale, 1961.

—— *A Theory of My Time: An Essay in Didactic Reminiscence*, Secker & Warburg, London, 1963.

Rilke, Rainer Maria, *Letters of Rainer Maria Rilke, 1892–1910* (trans. Jane B. Greene and M. D. Herter Norton), W. W. Norton, New York, 1969.

Rose, Phyllis, *Parallel Lives: Five Victorian Marriages*, Penguin Books, Harmondsworth, 1983.

Shelden, Michael, *Orwell: The Authorized Biography*, HarperCollins, New York, 1991.

Spurling, Hilary, *The Girl from the Fiction Department: A Portrait of Sonia Orwell*, Hamish Hamilton, London, 2002.

Stansky, Peter & William Abrahams, *The Unknown Orwell* (1972) and *Orwell: The Transformation* (1979), published in one volume by Stanford University Press, Stanford, 1994.

Taylor, D. J., *Orwell: The Life*, Vintage, London, 2003.

Topp, Sylvia, *Eileen: The Making of George Orwell*, Unbound, London, 2020.

Volodarsky, Boris, *Stalin's Agent: The Life and Death of Alexander Orlov*, Oxford University Press, Oxford, 2014.

Wadhams, Stephen, *Remembering Orwell*, Penguin Books, Ontario, 1984.

Warburg, Fredric, *All Authors Are Equal: The Publishing Life of Fredric Warburg 1936–1971*, Plunkett Lake Press, Lexington, 2019 [1973].

Wildemeersch, Marc, *George Orwell's Commander in Spain: The Enigma of Georges Kopp*, Thames River Press, London, 2013.

Woolf, Virginia, *A Room of One's Own*, Penguin Books, London, 2000 [1929].

—— *A Room of One's Own* [1929] and *Three Guineas* [1938], Penguin Books, London, 2019.

Wordsworth, William, *The Prelude*, Penguin Books, London, 1996 [1798, 1799, 1805, 1850].

Journals

Cooper, Lettice, 'Eileen Blair', *The PEN: Broadsheet of the English Centre of International PEN*, no. 16, Spring 1984, pp. 19–20.

Crimp, Jason, 'A Man of Much Voice and No Song', *Orwell Society Journal*, no. 14, Spring 2019, pp. 15–18.

Fen, Elisaveta, 'George Orwell's First Wife', *The Twentieth Century*, vol. 168, August 1960, pp. 115–26.

Hatton, T. J. & R. E. Bailey, 'Female Labour Force Participation in Interwar Britain', *Oxford Economic Papers*, vol. 40, no. 4, December 1988, pp. 695–718.

Orwell, George, 'As I Please', *Tribune*, 9 February 1945. *Collected Essays, Journalism and Letters*, vol. 3, pp. 375–78. Accessible at telelib.com/authors/O/OrwellGeorge/essay/tribune/AsIPlease19450209.html.

—— 'Benefit of Clergy: Some Notes on Salvador Dalí' [1944], in *The Collected Essays, Journalism and Letters of George Orwell*, Sonia Orwell & Ian Angus (eds), Secker & Warburg, London, 1970, [1968], vol. 3, pp. 156–65. Accessible at orwell.ru/library/reviews/dali/english/e_dali.

—— 'Charles Dickens' [1940], in *Essays*, Penguin Books, London, 2000.

—— 'The Lion and the Unicorn: Socialism and the English Genius' [1941], in *Why I Write* (Penguin Great Ideas), Penguin Books, New York, 2005, pp. 11–94.

—— 'The Prevention of Literature', *Polemic*, no. 2, January 1946, in Sonia Orwell & Ian Angus (eds), *The Collected Essays, Journalism and Letters of George Orwell*, Secker & Warburg, London, 1970, [1968], vol. 4, pp. 59–72. Accessible at orwellfoundation.com/the-orwell-foundation/orwell/essays-and-other-works/the-prevention-of-literature/.

—— 'Reflections on Gandhi', *Partisan Review*, January 1949, in *The Collected Essays, Journalism and Letters of George Orwell*, Sonia Orwell & Ian Angus (eds), Secker & Warburg, London, 1970 [1968], vol. 4, pp. 463–70. Accessible at orwell.ru/library/reviews/gandhi/english/e_gandhi.

—— 'Revenge is Sour', *Tribune*, 9 November 1945, in *The Collected Essays, Journalism and Letters of George Orwell*, Sonia Orwell & Ian Angus (eds), Secker & Warburg, London, 1968, vol. 4, pp. 3–6. Accessible at orwell.ru/library/articles/revenge/english/e_revso.

—— 'Why I Write' [1946] (Penguin Great Ideas), Penguin Books, New York, 2005, pp. 1–10.

Stradling, Rob, 'The Spies Who Loved Them: The Blairs in Barcelona, 1937', *Intelligence and National Security*, vol. 25, no. 5, pp. 638–55.

Woolf, Virginia, 'Professions for Women', a paper read to the National Society for Women's Service, London branch, 21 January 1931.

Online

Bowker, Gordon, 'Orwell's London', The Orwell Foundation, 2008 [2006], orwellfoundation.com/the-orwell-foundation/orwell/articles/gordon-bowker-orwells-london/.

McCrum, Robert, 'H. G. Wells, Keynes, Orwell . . . my years at the heart of the Bloomsbury Set', *The Guardian*, 12 June 2016, theguardian.com/books/2016/jun/11/anne-olivier-bell-last-survivor-bloomsbury-set.

McNair, John, 'Spanish Diary', pamphlet produced by the Greater Manchester Independent Labour Publications, 1979, independentlabour.org.uk/wp-content/uploads/2015/11/John-McNair-Spanish-Diary.pdf.

Moore, Darcy, 'Orwell in Paris: Aunt Nellie', 21 January 2020, darcymoore.net/2020/01/21/orwell-paris-aunt-nellie/.

The Orwell Archive, University College London, ucl.ac.uk/library/digital-collections/collections/orwell.

'Richard Rees', Spartacus Educational website, September 1997 (updated January 2020), spartacus-educational.com/SPreesR.htm.

Topp, Sylvia, 'George Talks', The Orwell Society, interview with Sylvia Topp, 21 March 2021, orwellsociety.com/about-the-society/george-talks/page/3/.

Tortorici, Dayna (ed.), 'Reading While Female: How to Deal with Misogynists and Male Masturbation', *No Regrets: Three Discussions*, n+1 Small Book Series #5, *The Cut*, 3 December 2013, thecut.com/2013/12/reading-while-female-misogynists-masturbation.html.

UN Women, 'Equal Pay for Work of Equal Value', n.d., unwomen.org/en/news/in-focus/csw61/equal-pay#:~:text=This%20stubborn%20inequality%20in%20the,in%20different%20jobs%20than%20omen.

'Under Siege: The Kitchen Front', website about *The Kitchen Front* radio program produced by Ministry of Food & BBC Radio, 2023, bbc.com/historyofthebbc/research/kitchen-front/.

Audio

Carswell, Jane, *Jura Lives* [audio interviews], Jura Development Trust Project. More information at isleofjura.scot/jura-lives-project/ and https://discovery.nationalarchives.gov.uk/details/a/A14084701.

Wadhams, Stephen (presenter), 'The Orwell Tapes', parts 1–3, Canadian Broadcasting Corporation, originally aired April 2016, cbc.ca/radio/ideas/the-orwell-tapes-part-1-1.3513191.

Acknowledgements

I thank Bill Hamilton at AM Heath Literary Agency for allowing me to use Eileen's letters, and the Orwell Archive at University College London, especially Dan Mitchell, for helping with other important source material. I also thank the Crick Archive at Birkbeck Library, University of London, and the literary executors of the estate of Professor Sir Bernard Crick, for the kind permission to use material from the collection, and Sarah Hall for her assistance.

As is clear from my text, I'm deeply indebted to the work of the biographers of Orwell: Peter Stansky and William Abrahams, Bernard Crick, Michael Shelden, Jeffrey Meyers, Gordon Bowker and D.J. Taylor. It is my sincere hope they embrace this work in the spirit in which it is intended: we are all caught in this gendered fiction, not of our own making. I also learned a great deal from Sylvia Topp's work *Eileen: The Making of George Orwell*, which I wouldn't have found elsewhere.

I am grateful to Quentin Kopp who has been extremely generous with his time and stories about his family, provided crucial help sourcing photographs and materials, and organised the glorious trip in Orwell's footsteps through Catalonia. I'm also indebted to the Orwell Society, and its patron, Richard Blair, especially for letting me quote him about being with his father in the lorry and his own Corryvreckan plans. My warm thanks to Catherine Moncure, for the wonderful pictures of Marx and the garden at Wallington.

I thank Masha Karp for sharing with me the letter David Wickes wrote to Eileen in Spain, and Darcy Moore for fascinating conversations, especially about Aunt Nellie.

On Jura I thank Kate Johnson and Rob and Sofie Fletcher, and, for the photograph of Ardlussa House, Andrew and Claire Fletcher. Jane and Hugh Carswell were very helpful, and I thank Jane for her excellent interviews with Jura residents who remembered Orwell. In London I am grateful to my dear friends Jane Johnson and Brian Murphy, Megan Davis and Tom Grayson, and Michael Blakemore for their hospitality while I began exploring the UCL Archive, and Claire Tomalin and Michael Frayn – in particular for a vital explanation of some early twentieth-century slang ('side').

I thank the Oxford Centre for Life-Writing at Wolfson College, especially Professor Dame Hermione Lee and Charles Pidgeon, for hosting me as I roamed around Eileen's Oxford haunts. I'm deeply indebted to the University of Technology Sydney for its generosity and wonderful research facilities, to vice-chancellors Attila Brungs and Andrew Parfitt, and to my friends and colleagues there for invaluable conversations over many years, especially Delia Falconer, Anna Clark and Roy Green.

My deepest and most heartfelt thanks go to my agent Sarah Chalfant, extraordinary reader and friend, who coaxed this book into being. Sarah's astonishing mind and her kindness undergird my working life.

Wifedom has been a publishing feat conducted on three continents. I am more grateful than I can really say to Nikki Christer at Penguin Random House Australia, whose editorial brilliance, publishing wisdom and personal generosity have been phenomenal. Editing is an art that leaves no trace, but Rachel Scully is a dazzling practitioner of it, and her intellectual insight and meticulous care have made *Wifedom* a better book. I thank Catherine Hill, too, for an important early read, Katie Purvis for invaluable editorial work, Angela Meyer for proofreading, Adam Laszczuk in design, Benjamin Fairclough in production, and Rebekah Chereshsky and Jessica Malpass in marketing and publicity. At Viking in the UK I am indebted to the terrific team of Isabel Wall, Mary Mount, Venetia Butterfield, Mary Chamberlain, Chloe Davies, Julia Murday, Annie Mount and to Karishma Jobanputra, for her efforts tracking down images across the world. At Knopf in the US I thank Reagan Arthur, Lexy Bloom and Morgan Hamilton for their enthusiasm, important editorial conversations and publishing nous, and Erinn Hartman and Amy Hagedorn for publicity and marketing.

I'm enormously grateful to my friends Sara Holloway and Mary Spongberg, who read the manuscript and gave generous and hugely valuable critical feedback. At a crucial stage I was extremely fortunate to work with Meredith Rose, an exceptional and gifted editor, and I'm very grateful to her. I thank Kris Olsson too, for her expert read, and Jessica Bullock at the Wylie Agency for so much, including Spanish translations. And I thank my COVID walking friends and creative partners Drusilla Modjeska, Suzie Miller, Lenore Taylor, Stephanie Smee and Diana Leach, and, for important conversations, Nick Drake, John Collee, Sally Murray and Anne Marie Swan. The friendship and generosity of Susan Rawling, Hélène Devynck, Fleur Wood and Nick Bryant, Alex Bune and John Chalmers, Hilary Charlesworth and Charles Guest, and Sam Mostyn and Simeon Beckett have been sustaining, and I thank Hugh Funder and John Funder for all their support over these years of writing this book.

I'm grateful to my children for living with *Wifedom* for so long, and for letting me write about them. Most of all I'm grateful to my husband, Craig Allchin, who jokes that without him this book would never have been written. But he's right. It is his creative insight and open heart that have made this venture, like so many others in our lives, possible.

Anna Funder is UTS Luminary, and acknowledges the support of the School of Communication, University of Technology Sydney, Faculty of Arts and Social Sciences, Ultimo NSW 2007, Australia.